D1267349

From Liberty to Democracy

Economics, Cognition, and Society

This series provides a forum for theoretical and empirical investigations of social phenomena. It promotes works that focus on the interactions among cognitive processes, individual behavior, and social outcomes. It is especially open to interdisciplinary books that are genuinely integrative.

Editor: Timur Kuran

Editorial Board: Tyler Cowen   Advisory Board: James M. Buchanan
Diego Gambetta   Albert O. Hirschman
Avner Greif   Thomas C. Schelling
Viktor Vanberg

Titles in the Series

Ulrich Witt, Editor. *Explaining Process and Change: Approaches to Evolutionary Economics*
Young Back Choi. *Paradigms and Conventions: Uncertainty, Decision Making, and Entrepreneurship*
Geoffrey M. Hodgson. *Economics and Evolution: Bringing Life Back into Economics*
Richard W. England, Editor. *Evolutionary Concepts in Contemporary Economics*
W. Brian Arthur. *Increasing Returns and Path Dependence in the Economy*
Janet Tai Landa. *Trust, Ethnicity, and Identity: Beyond the New Institutional Economics of Ethnic Trading Networks, Contract Law, and Gift-Exchange*
Mark Irving Lichbach. *The Rebel's Dilemma*
Karl-Dieter Opp, Peter Voss, and Christiane Gern. *Origins of a Spontaneous Revolution: East Germany, 1989*
Mark Irving Lichbach. *The Cooperator's Dilemma*
Richard A. Easterlin. *Growth Triumphant: The Twenty-first Century in Historical Perspective*
Daniel B. Klein, Editor. *Reputation: Studies in the Voluntary Elicitation of Good Conduct*
Eirik G. Furubotn and Rudolf Richter. *Institutions and Economic Theory: The Contribution of the New Institutional Economics*
Lee J. Alston, Gary D. Libecap, and Bernardo Mueller. *Titles, Conflict, and Land Use: The Development of Property Rights and Land Reform on the Brazilian Amazon Frontier*
Rosemary L. Hopcroft. *Regions, Institutions, and Agrarian Change in European History*
E. L. Jones. *Growth Recurring: Economic Change in World History*
Julian L. Simon. *The Great Breakthrough and Its Cause*
David George. *Preference Pollution: How Markets Create the Desires We Dislike*
Alexander J. Field. *Altruistically Inclined? The Behavioral Sciences, Evolutionary Theory, and the Origins of Reciprocity*
David T. Beito, Peter Gordon, and Alexander Tabarrok, Editors. *The Voluntary City: Choice, Community, and Civil Society*
Randall G. Holcombe. *From Liberty to Democracy: The Transformation of American Government*
Omar Azfar and Charles A. Cadwell, Editors. *Market-Augmenting Government: The Institutional Foundations for Prosperity*
Stephen Knack, Editor. *Democracy, Governance, and Growth*

From Liberty to Democracy

The Transformation of American Government

Randall G. Holcombe

The University of Michigan Press
Ann Arbor

2005   2004   2003   2002   4   3   2   1

A CIP catalog record for this book is available from the British Library.

Library of Congress Cataloging-in-Publication Data

Holcombe, Randall G.
    From liberty to democracy : the transformation of American
government / Randall G. Holcombe.
        p.   cm. — (Economics, cognition, and society)
    Includes bibliographical references and index.
    ISBN 0-472-11290-2 (Cloth : alk. paper)
    1. Democracy—United States.   2. United States—Politics and
government.   I. Title.   II. Series.

JK1726 .H65   2002
320.973—dc21   2002007127

For Lora, Ross, Mark, and Connor

Contents

Tables

Figures

Preface

Describing the changes in American government during its first two centuries as a transformation suggests dramatic change rather than gradual evolution. The facts support this terminology. Yet while government grew steadily throughout the twentieth century, there was relatively little growth in the nineteenth century; the great transformation occurred at the end of the nineteenth century and the beginning of the twentieth century. By many measures, however, the government did grow in the nineteenth century, and the roots of twentieth-century government growth go back to the earliest days of the nation. But that early growth was checked by a constitutional government that had as its overriding goal the protection of individual rights. By the beginning of the twentieth century the overriding principle behind American government was transformed from the protection of individual rights to the principle of democracy.

The tendency of democracy to lead to government growth is not a new idea, and indeed the intellectual foundations of this book can be traced back to Alexis de Tocqueville's *Democracy in America*, first published in 1835.[1] Since that time, many accounts of government growth have been written, and while many of them offer a great deal of insight into the phenomenon of government growth, there has not been a good explanation of the transformation of American government from protector of individual rights to promoter of majority opinion and along with it the tremendous growth of government in the twentieth century.

Describing the change in American government as a transformation does not seem overly dramatic, considering the facts. Indeed, Karl Polanyi uses the same term to describe more general historical events covering the same time frame, focusing on the emergence of the market economy, as does Raoul Berger, who describes the impact of the 14th Amendment on the Constitution; Morton Horwitz, who describes the impact of Progressive thought on the American legal system; and Paul

Starr, who more narrowly describes the evolution of the practice of medicine.² The common thread linking all of these transformations is the transformation of government. Evolutionary changes in government had been taking place since the birth of the United States, and under different political institutions the change in American government might be described as an evolution rather than a transformation. A big part of the story is how a gradual evolution, filtered through American political institutions, created a major transformation in American government. A government originally motivated by the principle of liberty was transformed into a government motivated by the concept of democracy. Originally, the government's overriding goal was to protect the rights of its citizens, whereas now the government's actions are determined by the will of the majority.

It took more than 10 years to finish this book, partly because I undertook other projects, which slowed this one, but also because the nature of the book continued to evolve from the way I initially envisioned it. This surely would have been a different book if I had completed it rapidly. I originally conceived of the subject more narrowly, in two dimensions. First, I intended to focus on the growth of government in the twentieth century, where most of the development in government regulation and expenditures was concentrated; second, I conceived of the subject matter as growth in the government's economic activities of taxing, spending, and regulating rather than as the broader subject of the increasing scope of democracy, which led to these other things. The book's scope broadened as I realized, first, that the big changes that occurred in the twentieth century were enabled by earlier changes in the nineteenth century and, second, that the substantial changes in the nature of the government's economic activities were propelled by changes in the underlying political structure, as a government with a constitutionally limited scope gave way to one that was limited only by the will of the majority.

From the beginning I envisioned writing a book on this subject, but along the way I took some of my work in progress and published it as articles. Several parts of the book draw upon work I have previously published, and I am grateful to those publishers for allowing me to use those works here. Parts of chapter 3 were adapted with permission of the publisher from the article "Constitutional Theory and the Constitutional History of Colonial America," *Independent Review: A Journal of Political Economy* 3, no. 1 (summer 1998): 21–36, © Copyright 1998, The Independent Institute, 100 Swan Way, Oakland, CA, 94621–1428,

<http://www.independent.org>; chapter 4 was drawn from "Constitutions as Constraints: A Case Study of Three American Constitutions," *Constitutional Political Economy* 2, no. 3 (fall 1991): 303–28; portions of chapter 6 come from "The Distributive Model of Government: Evidence from the Confederate Constitution," *Southern Economic Journal* 58, no. 3 (January 1992): 762–69; chapter 7 is based on "Veterans Interests and the Transition to Government Growth: 1870–1915," *Public Choice* 99, nos. 3–4 (June 1999): 311–26; and chapter 9 is based on "The Growth of the Federal Government in the 1920s," *Cato Journal* 16, no. 2 (fall 1996): 175–99.

Because this book has taken shape over a long period, any attempt to try to acknowledge those who have assisted my efforts is sure to leave many people out. Nevertheless, I do want to acknowledge the helpful comments of Ben Baack, Keith Dougherty, Jeffrey Lipkes, and several anonymous reviewers who read the manuscript. Ellen McCarthy at the University of Michigan Press was helpful throughout the review process. Many more people read parts of the manuscript or papers that provided the raw material for the book, and I am greatly indebted to them. Some of those who deserve mention are James Buchanan, Robert Higgs, Lawrence Kenny, Russell Sobel, Michael Stroup, and Gordon Tullock. I am also grateful for financial support for some of this work from the Earhart Foundation and the Institute for Humane Studies. My greatest debt is to my family—my wife, Lora, and my three sons, Ross, Mark, and Connor—who allowed me the time to complete this project. Lora, who is also an economist, offered many suggestions, and I appreciate not only her professional contribution but also her support throughout this project.

CHAPTER 1

Liberty: The Revolutionary Cause

When the Founding Fathers joined the thirteen American colonies together to form the United States of America, they intended to create a government that would protect the rights of its citizens, ensure their freedom, and do little else. The U.S. government was carefully and deliberately designed to be constitutionally limited in scope. The limits of the federal government's functions and powers are enumerated in the Constitution, but because some of the Founding Fathers felt that the principle of limited government was not clearly enough spelled out in the Constitution, they added the 10th Amendment, which was ratified shortly after the Constitution. It explicitly states that "The powers not delegated to the United States by the Constitution, nor prohibited by it to the States, are reserved to the States respectively, or to the people." The founders did not intend for government policy to be democratic. Rather, the role of democracy was very limited and was intended to be a means to an end. Democratic decision making was a mechanism by which Congress could make collective decisions, and democracy provided a mechanism by which the nation's citizens could replace the leaders of government as a check on their exercise of power. But the role of the government itself was to undertake those activities explicitly enumerated in the Constitution, not to further the will of the majority.

At the end of the twentieth century, Americans viewed their government very differently from the way it was viewed at the beginning of the nineteenth century. When the nation was founded, the federal government was viewed as a protector of individual rights, but by the end of the twentieth century, the federal government was viewed as a collective decision-making institution to implement the will of the majority and to protect and further the economic interests of its citizens. The idea of limits on the government's power has been completely eroded. Even the fundamental idea of equal protection under the law has been subordinated to the will of the majority.[1] The founders viewed government as a necessary evil. It was necessary, they believed, to protect the rights of its citizens, but a government powerful enough to protect people's rights might also have the power to violate them. The revolution that established the new government of the United States was fought to free the colonies from the abuses of the government of Britain. By the end of the twentieth century, however, government was no longer viewed as a necessary evil but as a potential power for good.[2] At that time the criterion that determined the activities the government should undertake was not the protection of liberty, as the founders had intended, but the will of the majority. Democracy had replaced liberty as the fundamental principle of American government.

This transformation of American government occurred slowly but steadily. The notion of gradual but steady evolution of government stands in contrast to common perceptions that changes in American government have been associated primarily with major events that have ratcheted up the government's power and presence. It is quite true that major events such as the War between the States,[3] the two world wars, and the Great Depression were associated with substantial changes in the scope and role of American government. It is also true that even without these events there has been a steady move toward increasing democracy, away from the protection of individual liberties, and as a result toward more government power, more government programs, and more government expenditures.

The influence of major events over the scope of American government has been well documented and is undeniable.[4] Yet focusing on the role of major events in transforming government overlooks the fact that the transformation began at the nation's founding and would have continued without any crisis to push it along. Similarly, although Lincoln, the two Roosevelts, and other leaders were major players in the evolution of American government, the process would have continued without them, and these major figures often get more of the credit (or blame) for changing the course of history than they deserve.[5] Because the effects of major events on the transformation of American government have been emphasized in other accounts, this volume focuses on the continuing process by which the American government has been transformed, discussing the many small events along the way that led the nation's priorities to evolve from liberty to democracy, and deliberately devotes relatively little discussion to major historical events. These events are de-emphasized not because they were unimportant but because they have been so thoroughly discussed elsewhere, to such an extent that the gradual transformation of American government has been overlooked in favor of analyses of the effects of major events.[6]

The most dramatic changes have come in the twentieth century, but even as early as 1835 Alexis de Tocqueville was able to foresee the path over which American government would evolve.[7] The constitutional limits placed on American government by the Founding Fathers have been gradually eroded by the democratic institutions embodied in the Constitution itself. "Democracy" means "accountability" to the voting public, and this accountability gives voters the ability to demand that public policies be responsive to their interests. Citizens always want to see the general public interest advanced, but often their vision of the general public interest is colored by their own specific interests. This leads to natural disagreements, and when those on the losing end of a political struggle view the outcome as favoring some interests over their own, there is a tendency for them to attempt to use the political process for their benefit, in the same way they view that it has been used against them by their opponents. The constitutional challenge, the Founding Fathers clearly realized, was to limit the scope of government so that it could not be used to further the interests of particular groups over the general public interest.

The tremendous growth of government in the twentieth century has made this challenge even more formidable. When government is small and the scope of its activities is limited, there is little incentive for special interests to try to use the government to advance their interests rather than to rely on their own productive activities in the marketplace. When the government is large and when its limits are less sharply defined, there are potentially large gains to be had if government policies can be steered in a particular way. Thus, the growth of government makes the government act more for the benefit of narrow interests and less for the benefit of the general public interest.

People are inevitably biased in favor of the status quo, if only because they are familiar with it, and at the beginning of the twenty-first century it may be difficult to understand the nature and implications of the way in which American government has been transformed. Unthinkingly, the typical American accepts democracy as the underlying principle of American government rather than liberty. Liberty, to those in the eighteenth century, meant freedom from government oppression. They were willing to fight for liberty; their writers, intellectuals, and political leaders made eloquent pleas for liberty; and they designed the Constitution with the intention of preserving liberty. The eighteenth-century conception of liberty is completely at odds with twentieth-century American government, despite the apparent reverence the Constitution is accorded.[8] In large part, that is because most of the voting public accepts the political status quo as an extension of the original constitutional ideas to modern times. The status quo is easy to accept because it is familiar, and as the American economy has prospered citizens have had little incentive to reflect on two centuries of change in their government.

There are at least two good reasons why citizens have little reason to question the idea that America's political status quo is merely an extension of the constitutional principles of the eighteenth century. First, they are propagandized to believe that it is so. Everyone from politicians to civics teachers instills patriotic messages to all willing (and some unwilling) listeners. There are dissenters, to be sure, but they do not have the visibility and status of those who sell the principles of democratic government. Second, citizens have little incentive to consider political issues, because as individuals they do not make policy decisions. Voters face a very limited set of political choices, and when they do cast their ballots they know that their one individual vote will not affect the final tally. Voters are interested in election outcomes, certainly, but they have little incentive to cast an informed ballot.

Rational Ignorance in Politics

One problem that plagues political systems in general, but especially democratic political systems, is the absence of incentives for the general public to be informed about political matters. Most voters have little idea about the types of activities being undertaken in their legislatures and are poorly informed about the choices they make at the ballot box.[9] This is because the opinion of an individual voter will have no perceptible effect on the outcome of a political decision. Despite the frequently heard claim that every vote counts, and that one of the duties of citizens in a democratic nation is to vote—and even the admonition that if you do not vote you have no right to complain— voters realize that their one vote will not determine an election's outcome. This may not be as true in local elections, where there are fewer voters, or for votes on issues in Congress, where again there are fewer voters. Even then, however, outcomes that are determined by a vote or two are rare. But these elections with a small number of voters are not relevant to the transformation of the U.S. government. In national elections, where there are many voters, the probability of an individual voter casting a decisive vote is minuscule. Dennis Mueller has noted that in presidential elections one is more likely to be killed in an accident driving to the polls than to cast a decisive vote.[10]

Counterarguments to the idea that one's vote does not count typically rely on the fallacy of composition, noting that all votes together determine the outcome of the election, such that each individual vote must count. "What if everybody thought that, and didn't vote? Then your vote would determine the outcome of the election." But many people do vote, and when they do, no one vote affects an election's outcome. Despite the statistical reality that one vote will not change an election's outcome, many voters insist that their votes are important. Individually they are not important, but collectively they are. Without a substantial voter turnout democracy loses some of its moral legitimacy, so supporters of democracy rightfully argue about the importance of voting, which is not only a right but a patriotic duty. But even those who vote must realize that the outcome of any national election will be the same regardless of how they vote or regardless of whether they vote.[11]

The result is that voters have little incentive to become informed about the issues. When asked, a surprisingly large percentage of people cannot even name the candidates, let alone tell you anything about their positions. Once elected, representatives put in full days passing legislation, yet most people do not know anything about most of it. This does not mean that all voters are ignorant about everything. Some people are interested in politics and become informed for their own enjoyment, in the same way that some people are interested in sports and gather information, go to games, and cheer for teams, even knowing that their activities will have no effect on who wins. Readers of this book are likely to be more informed than most people. Ask yourself this: Is Congress in session this week? If so, what issues are they considering? What are the positions of your representatives on these issues?

The reason why voters tend to be uninformed is because it is rational to be ignorant about political matters because one voter's opinion is not going to change the outcome of the democratic decision-making process. People have an incentive to be informed about their market choices because those choices have a big impact on their lives. People collect information about automobiles when they are considering buying a new one because they care about what type of car they drive.

People collect information about even seemingly minor things such as the differences between hamburgers at fast-food restaurants because the information can affect the quality of their lunches. People also care about who their representatives are and what decisions those representatives make, but because the choices of individual voters do not affect who represents them or what those representatives do, they have little incentive to collect information about the choices they can make. Why collect information about the different candidates in an election when the winner will win regardless of how you vote? Consumers are better off collecting information about restaurants because they get to eat at the restaurant they choose. But the politicians who represent them will do so regardless of how they cast their one vote.

The Constitution of the United States was designed to insulate the federal government from the negative effects of the rational ignorance of voters. The government was divided into legislative, executive, and judicial branches, which were designed so that each branch would check the powers of the others. The Founding Fathers did not want to rely on the nation's citizens to check the government's power. Originally, citizens had a very limited power over the selection of federal officials. The judicial branch is run by justices appointed by the president and confirmed by Congress. The president, as head of the executive branch, is still chosen by an electoral college rather than by voters directly, although this system has become more democratic over time.[12] In the legislative branch, members of the Senate were originally chosen by their state legislatures, and that was not changed until 1913, when the 17th Amendment created the system of direct election. Only the members of the House of Representatives were originally elected directly by the citizens.

One must be struck by this lack of democratic representation in the early United States. In a nation with checks and balances for three branches of government, the Constitution provided for direct election only for one house of the bicameral legislature. The Constitution did not provide for citizen voting to select senators, Supreme Court justices, or the president. That is but one of the things that has changed in the transformation of American government from liberty to democracy. Despite the changes, Americans at the end of the twentieth century hold their Constitution in reverence, rarely considering how it has changed in the course of two centuries. Democratic political institutions are also held in reverence, as citizens are told that it is their patriotic duty to vote and are propagandized through the institutions of public education about the virtues of their political system and the importance of being a good citizen. When the Berlin Wall fell in 1989 and the communist nations of Eastern Europe overthrew their dictators, Americans were quick to urge the adoption of democratic political institutions as the path toward freedom and prosperity.

These urgings are in contrast to the view of the American revolutionaries two centuries earlier, who championed liberty, not democracy, and who wanted to escape the oppression of government by placing constitutional limits on government power. The founders designed a government with very limited democratic input. The U.S. Constitution was drawn up in this manner, but the Articles of Confederation, the first American constitution, drawn up in 1776, were even less democratic. Citizens were not able to vote for any federal officials during the years when the Articles of Confederation were in effect. This naturally raises the question about why there is such widespread support for democratic government at the beginning of the twenty-first century. The propaganda suggests that America was always democratic, but the facts show that this is not so.

Democracy and Ideology

The idea that democratic government thrives in part because of propaganda deserves additional consideration. Indeed, propaganda helps support any government. Americans have often been critical of propaganda in other nations. The communist bloc nations during the cold war and Nazi Germany stand out, but post–World War II Japan has been criticized for whitewashing its record during the war, and almost any nondemocratic nation is subject to criticism that propaganda supports the nondemocratic regime.[13] In more open and democratic societies, there is more dissent from the official government positions, but dissent is checked through both formal and informal means. The U.S. government controls the flow of much information, citing national security purposes, but dissent is often stifled for patriotic reasons. Citizens tend to support their governments and identify with its policies because of institutions that give them ideological support.

Citizens accept the government's actions when they view those actions as legitimate. A major function of propaganda is to convince citizens that the government is acting in their interests and that its actions are widely supported by the citizenry. The role of propaganda is clear in a dictatorship, but political institutions serve similar effects in a democracy. An important function of democratic elections in a democracy is to convey legitimacy upon those who make the government's decisions. One agrees with the democratic process, so even though one may disagree with some specific decisions made by the president or by Congress, one still agrees that they are our legitimately elected representatives and therefore legitimately have the right to make those decisions for us. Thus, democratic governments can generate citizen support more easily than can dictatorships, because the collective decision-making process appears more representative and more legitimate.[14]

The democratic ideology that creates this view of legitimacy helps explain why politicians always urge citizens to vote, despite the fact that most voters are very uninformed. If arriving at a good collective decision were the goal, one would hope that those voting would be limited to people who had the knowledge and motivation to best understand the choices; yet there has been a consistent push throughout American history to extend the franchise to everybody, even those who show little desire to even want to register to vote. As Tocqueville noted in 1835, "When a nation begins to modify the elective qualification, it may easily be foreseen that, sooner or later, that qualification will be entirely abolished. There is no more invariable rule in the history of society. . . . no stop can be made short of universal suffrage."[15] If everybody has the right to vote, and if everybody votes, then one can hardly object to the decisions that are made by popularly elected representatives. After all, those representatives were chosen by the citizens to make those decisions. If turnout is low, however, elected officials will have a more difficult time claiming to be the legitimate representatives of the population.

The ideology of democracy conveys substantial powers to government, so it is easy to see why governments have an incentive to nurture it.[16] Any government has an incentive to win its citizens over to its ideology, of course, but within the context of the American experience it is worth emphasizing the advantages to political leaders of the ideology of democracy over the ideology of liberty. Liberty means freedom from the powers of government, and there is no doubt that the attempt to escape from government oppression was the motivation behind the American Revolution. An ideology of liberty naturally creates a population that is suspicious of government power, that wants the government to act within strict limits, and that will be intolerant of a government that tries to expand beyond those limits. Indeed, that is descriptive of the popular sentiment through the first hundred years of U.S. history. In contrast, the advantages of a democratic ideology for those in power should be clear. If the popular ideology changes from one that advocates constraints on government power to one that advocates furthering the will of the majority through the actions of popularly elected representatives, then the most severe constraints placed on those in power will have been removed.

The Founding Fathers were inherently suspicious of those with political power and undoubtedly would have supported any attempts to show ways in which political power could be used against the public interest. The public choice analysis done in the last half of the twentieth century has attempted to understand the incentive structure of the public sector and has revealed that in many cases government institutions can work against the public interest. Some critics have attacked this analysis, not because it is incorrect but because it might serve to elicit behavior that is not public spirited and could help to undermine public sector institutions.[17] Thus, supporters of democratic political institutions are willing to make the argument that those institutions rely so much on the acceptance of democratic ideology for their successful operation that a critical academic analysis of the institutions could cause them substantial harm. Indeed, one can see that, were the American public to adopt the ideology of liberty as espoused at the time of the Revolution, this would undermine to a substantial degree the democratic ideology upon which twentieth-century American government has been built. What is less clear is whether democracy makes a better ideology for its citizens than liberty.

The story of the transformation of the fundamental principle of American government from liberty to democracy is compelling, partly because the powers embodied in America's twenty-first-century democratic government are those that eighteenth-century Americans revolted against to escape.

The Political Philosophy of the American Revolution

At the time of the American Revolution, the concept of liberty was relatively new. With hindsight any generally recognized idea might be traced back for centuries, but for practical purposes the idea of liberty, as it applies to the American Revolution, goes back to John Locke, who first published his treatises on government in 1690, less than a century prior to the Revolution.[18] The intellectual fathers of the Revolution were familiar with classical Greek and Roman writers but found little in their works on which to build their political philosophy.[19] Rather, the secular writers of the European Enlightenment, including Locke, Montesquieu, Voltaire, and others, were the sources most often referenced by the revolutionaries. The literature of the Revolution did not come in the form of abstract philosophical treatises but rather pamphlets that circulated extensively throughout the colonies. The pamphlets did make reference to classical sources, but these references were often mere embellishments that did not accurately represent the classical writers' ideas.[20] The true inspiration behind the colonial pamphleteers came from the European Enlightenment writers, of which Locke was the most important.

Locke's ideas of property, individual rights, and social contract provided substantial intellectual support for the American revolutionaries, and Cato's letters, first published in the 1720s and extensively reprinted, generated popular support for liberty as the revolutionary cause. By 1775 American newspapers were filled with arguments for and against the Revolution, and printers were turning out large numbers of pamphlets in support of the cause of liberty. Throughout history citizens had been viewed as servants of their governments, but the new idea that government should be the servant of its citizens took hold and sparked the American Revolution.

Hobbes and Locke

A good contrast for examining the ideas of the American Revolution is found in the works of Thomas Hobbes and John Locke. Both are known for their support of the concept of a social contract, but the different rationales of the two writers give some insight into the newness of the revolutionary idea of liberty. Hobbes's famous treatise, *Leviathan,* was published in 1651, only about forty years before Locke's *Two Treatises of Government,* but the substantial differences in the ways they supported their ideas of the social contract show how new the idea of liberty really was at the time of the American Revolution. Both Hobbes and Locke viewed the government as the result of a social contract that citizens were bound to obey for the common good. Despite the superficial similarities, there was a fundamental difference between the thinkers: Hobbes argued that citizens were obligated to serve the government because of the social contract, while Locke viewed government as the protector of individual liberty.

Hobbes's analysis began with a vision of life in anarchy, without the protections of government. In Hobbes's view, life in anarchy would be solitary, poor, nasty, brutish, and short. Anarchy, Hobbes argued, would be a war of all against all. Would life in anarchy really be this bad? It is worth remarking that not everyone thinks so; there is a group of anarchists that believes that market arrangements and voluntary transactions by themselves could substitute for government and even make individuals better off than being protected by government.[21] This orderly alternative to the chaotic Hobbesian vision of anarchy is relevant because it takes to the logical extreme the concept of liberty that provided the foundation for the American Revolution. If freedom from government oppression is desirable, then the complete elimination of government is the way to provide citizens with the maximum amount of liberty. The minimal state envisioned by the American founders was not far from this vision but, especially philosophically, it was very different from what Hobbes envisioned. Not everybody thinks that life in anarchy would be nasty, brutish, and short, but Hobbes did, so this type of unpleasant anarchy is often referred to as Hobbesian anarchy to clearly identify the concept.

Hobbes believed that the only way to prevent this war of all against all was to form a government and to have all citizens submit to the power of that government. Hobbes argues, "The only way to erect such a Common Power, as may be able to defend them from the invasion of Forraingers, and the injuries of one another, and . . . that . . . they may nourish themselves and live contentedly; is, to conferre all their power and strength upon one Man, or upon one Assembly of men, . . . and therin submit their Wills, every one to his Will, and their Judgments, to his Judgment."[22] Under this social contract, as envisioned by Hobbes, every person would promise to all others, "*I Authorise and give up my right of Governing my selfe, to this Man, or to this Assembly of men, on this condition, that thou give up thy Right to him, and Authorise all his Actions in like manner*" (original emphasis).[23] Hobbes makes it perfectly clear that to produce an orderly society citizens must give up to the government all of their rights and that any rights they might be able to exercise would be only those rights that the government would allow to its citizens.

In Hobbes's state, everybody would agree to be subject to the rules of the government. But what about those dissenters who did not want to agree to the state's social contract? Hobbes argued that "because the major part hath by consenting voices declared a Soveraigne; he that dissented must now consent with the rest; that is, be contented to avow all the actions he shall do, or else justly be destroyed by the rest."[24] Thus, Hobbes's government has absolute power over its citizens. Citizens have only those rights that the government allows, and those who do not agree with the government's rules can justly be destroyed. This line of reasoning would be consistent with the monarchies that ruled Europe at the time Hobbes wrote, but the novel part of his argument is that there is some type of social contract that obligates citizens to obey the sovereign's rules.[25]

The key point for the purpose of comparing Hobbes with Locke is that Hobbes believed everyone had to give up their rights to the state. This stands in stark contrast to the Declaration of Independence, written a mere 125 years after *Leviathan,* which states that "Governments are instituted among Men, deriving their just powers from the consent of the governed," and goes on to grant the citizens of government "the Right of the People to alter or abolish it." With Hobbes, ultimate power rests with the sovereign, whereas the Declaration of Independence grants citizens the ultimate power over their government.

As Hobbes saw it, by necessity the sovereign had more power than a government's citizens and citizen rights came as granted by the sovereign. Locke saw things differently. He believed that people were born into a state of nature, "A *State* also *of equality,* wherein all the Power and Jurisdiction is reciprocal, no one having more power than another, . . . without Subordination of Subjection."[26] People have natural rights, he argued, "And that all Men may be restrained from invading others Rights, and from doing hurt to one another, and that the Law of Nature be observed . . . [and] . . . every one has a right to punish the transgressors of that Law to such a Degree, as may hinder its Violation."[27] Locke believed that these natural rights implied that nobody had more rights than anyone else. The natural rights that Locke envisioned also implied the right to property. "Whatsoever then he removes out of the State that Nature hath provided, and left it in, he hath mixed his *Labour* with, and joyned to it something that is his own, and thereby makes it his *Property.*"[28]

Locke's vision of the social contract begins with the concept of liberty. "Many being born, as has been proved, with a Title to perfect Freedom . . . hath by Nature a Power, not only to preserve his Property, that is, his Life, Liberty, and Estate, . . . but to judge of, and punish the breaches of that Law." But in a political society "the Community comes to be Umpire, by settled standing Rules, indifferent, and the same to all Parties."[29] "Hence it is evident, that *Absolute Monarchy,* which by some Men is counted the only Government in the World, is indeed *Inconsistent with Civil Society,* and so can be no Form of Civil Government at all."[30] "The only way whereby any one divests himself of his Natural Liberty, and *puts on the bonds of Civil Society* is by agreeing with other Men to Joyn and Unite into a Community, for their comfortable, safe, and peaceable living amongst one another."[31] Locke refers to this agreement as an original compact.

Whereas Hobbes envisions people subjecting themselves to the rules dictated by a sovereign to create an orderly society, Locke envisions people agreeing with each other to produce a government for the purpose of protecting their natural liberties. Locke believes that citizens have the power to form and to dissolve governments and, in stark contrast to Hobbes, that government is subservient to its citizens. He argues that the sole purpose of government is to protect the rights of its citizens. Philosophically, Locke provided the foundation for liberty, property, and equality upon which the American Revolution was born. Locke's ideas, being part of the American ideology today, are easy to take for granted, but when contrasted with Hobbes's vision of only a few decades before, the idea of liberty is startling. Locke is saying that, in contrast to even recent philosophical writings and to the idea of monarchy, where rights are granted by government, people have natural rights and that a just government is one that protects those rights and preserves the liberty of its citizens.

Cato's Letters

While the Founding Fathers were familiar with the classical and Enlightenment writings on liberty that built the intellectual foundations of the revolutionary movement, the typical citizen became familiar with the ideas of liberty through pamphleteers and newspapers. Among the most influential of these sources were Cato's letters, which originally were published in the *London Journal* in the 1720s but were collected and widely reprinted. The letters were signed using the name Cato, after Cato the Younger (95–46 B.C.), who was a defender of liberty in the Roman republic and opposed Julius Caesar's rise to power. Pursued by Caesar's forces, he killed himself rather than fleeing or allowing himself to be captured, making himself an ideal role model for eighteenth-century defenders of liberty. Cato's letters were authored by John Trenchard, who was a lawyer by training and had been a pamphleteer prior to writing Cato's letters, and by Thomas Gordon, who also had studied law and was employed as a language tutor.

The *London Journal* published 93 of Cato's letters, 45 were published in the *British Journal,* and six more were added to the series later. The publication of the letters greatly increased the influence of the *London Journal* and popularized the ideas of liberty that had been espoused by Locke. "All men are born free; liberty is a gift which they receive from God himself; nor can they alienate the same by consent, though possibly they may forfeit it by crimes. No man has power over his own life, or to dispose of his own religion; and cannot consequently transfer the power of either to anybody else."[32] In contrast with the Hobbesian vision of the social contract, whereby people give up their rights to the government, Trenchard and Gordon make clear that no such transfer of rights is even possible in their view. As did Locke, they believed that people have a natural right to liberty—a natural right that they cannot give up even with their own consent.

The ideas of natural rights and equality were clearly at odds with a society of royalty and monarchy, and the newspapers that published Cato's letters were created as opposition newspapers to counter the official government sources.[33] This in itself may have increased their interest, but they also were collected and published in book form very shortly after they appeared in the newspapers, making them readily available and a popular source for the ideology of liberty in America. Though they wrote the letters for a British audience, Trenchard and Gordon consider the issue of colonies and argue that only by preserving their liberty can a successful colonial operation continue.[34] If a nation must resort to violence to preserve its colonies, they argue, then the value of the colonies will fall to such a degree that they will not be worth keeping.

The idea of liberty was a bold challenge to the governance structure of the world's most advanced nations. In the monarchies of the day, people accepted the idea that they received their rights from government and were obligated to obey whatever laws the sovereign imposed. The Hobbesian vision of the social contract provides the philosophical foundations that support this view of government. Locke's idea that people have natural rights, independent of government, and that the role of the government is to protect the natural rights of its citizens was literally a revolutionary notion. This new idea of liberty inspired a host of popular writers and ultimately provided the intellectual underpinnings for the American Revolution. The result was a new nation, conceived in liberty and dedicated to the proposition that all men are created equal.

This Lockean ideology, spread through the colonies by Cato's letters and other pamphleteers, was strong enough not only to create a revolutionary fervor in the colonies but also to inspire the American founders to write a constitution that embodied these principles. They believed that governments do not give people rights but rather that people have rights and the role of the government is to protect them. The Constitution of the United States explicitly recognized this by limiting the powers of the new government only to those enumerated in the Constitution. This ideology of liberty, so strong when the nation was founded, has been replaced by an ideology of democracy, where the legitimate bounds of government are defined by the will of the majority.

Ideology and Constitutional Design

Any government requires the ideological support of its citizens to keep it in power. The spread of the ideology of liberty throughout the American colonies during the 1700s laid the foundation for the American Revolution both by undermining the legitimacy of British rule and by suggesting the principles by which a new government for the colonies could be formed. The ideology for a limited government, dedicated to the protection of the liberty of its citizens, was promoted not only by the abstract intellectuals of the European Enlightenment but also by the popular pamphleteers and newspaper writers throughout the colonies. The ideas were there, and they clearly had an impact on the government that was created when the colonies declared their independence.[35] But while the ideology of liberty goes a long way toward indicating the freedoms that government ought to protect, it does not go very far toward explaining how governmental institutions can be designed to protect those liberties.

The American Revolution was fought to secure the liberty of Americans from the rule of British government; that is, the war was fought to free Americans from government power. To ensure that one oppressive government was not replaced by another, the states were united under a constitution that was designed to limit the powers of government and to guarantee the rights of citizens. The ideology of liberty that prompted the Revolution, however, provided no specific guidance as to how such a constitution should be constructed, leaving the Founding Fathers to design their own constitution. History shows that they were dissatisfied with their first attempt. The Articles of Confederation were replaced by the Constitution of the United States in 1789. Even then, the Constitution's authors envisioned a process of continual amendment and revision.

The principles of liberty provided a revolutionary cause but not a blueprint for designing a government that could preserve liberty. Thus began the transformation of American government from one based on liberty to one based on democracy. To understand the transformation, one must understand the history of American constitutional design and the evolution of collective decision making, but one must also understand theories and principles that explain the workings of government. In a democratic nation, one might wonder what alternatives there are for designing a government to preserve liberty. Chapter 2 considers the concepts of liberty and democracy in more detail, and chapter 3 examines the political institutions in eighteenth-century America to see how the ideas of liberty influenced the design of American government.

CHAPTER 2

Liberty and Democracy as
Economic Systems

In the nineteenth century economics and politics were studied jointly under the heading of political economy, until increasing specialization in academia split them into the two distinct disciplines of economics and political science at the end of that century. At least some of the subject matter of political science can be understood without any economic content. Institutional processes such as how bills become law, how representatives are elected, and other procedural topics need no economic analysis, although if one wants to understand why particular bills are proposed in the first place, how likely they are to pass, and what types of candidates are likely to run and be elected as representatives, an economic foundation is helpful. However, none of the subject matter of economics can be understood without an understanding of the political framework within which economic activity takes place. Economics was able to separate itself from political science only because economic analysis was undertaken with the (often tacit) assumption that economic activity takes place within a particular set of political institutions, which makes the political system relatively transparent to economic decision makers.

The dominant paradigm in twentieth-century economics is referred to by economists as neoclassical economics. In the neoclassical setting, economic activity (with some exceptions) is undertaken completely by voluntary exchange, and all property rights are clearly defined and never violated. Economic agents are perfectly informed, and economic transactions are never tainted by fraud or contract violation. There is no theft, so goods are acquired only by the voluntary consent of their owners. There are exceptions, and the exceptions are often what makes the study of economics interesting. What if, within this setting, some property rights are not clearly defined? What if, within this setting, one party to a transaction has information that the other party lacks? Even when specific exceptions are studied within the neoclassical framework, they are done so with the assumption that the rest of the economy fits the neoclassical model.[1] Despite that economists analyze government policy alternatives within the neoclassical framework, the framework itself is exceedingly laissez-faire in its orientation. The political foundation of neoclassical economics is rarely analyzed explicitly, but neoclassical economics rests on the same structure of liberty that guided the political thought of the American founders.

One way of viewing the concepts of liberty and democracy is as principles that define the relationship of individuals to their political systems. The principle of liberty suggests that, first and foremost, the government's role is to protect the rights of the individual. The principle of democracy suggests that collective decisions are made according to the will of the majority. The founders recognized that in order to preserve liberty the scope of collective decision making—that is, the degree to which democracy could be used as a guide to public policy— would have to be constitutionally limited. The greater the allowable scope of democracy in government, the greater the threat to liberty. Another way of viewing the concepts of liberty and democracy is that they are methods of determining the way in which the allocation of economic resources will be determined. Liberty implies private ownership of resources, with the owners determining how resources will be allocated, as is assumed in neoclassical economics. Democracy implies collective ownership of resources, with the will of the majority determining the allocation of resources.

The idea that liberty and democracy are economic systems seems out of place at the beginning of the twenty-first century, because they are primarily political concepts, and economics and political science were separated as academic disciplines for the entire twentieth century. In the nineteenth century, however, when the study of economics and politics was undertaken together under the heading of political economy, it would have been more natural to examine the economic implications of these political concepts. Indeed, all economic activity takes place within some political environment that defines the relevant property rights, and without saying so, most of twentieth-century economics assumed that markets operate under a system of extreme liberty, where property rights are clearly defined and all resource allocation decisions are made by the resource owners. Even when exceptions are studied, such as poorly defined property rights in air that lead to problems of air pollution, the unstated assumption holds that the remainder of the economy operates under a system of pure liberty.

By examining the political structure explicitly it is possible to relate the political environment to the performance of the economy in a manner similar to the aims of nineteenth-century political economy. In fact, the economic system is not independent of the political system, as the separation of economics from political science might make it appear. Twentieth-century analysis of economic and political systems augmented this impression by dividing economic systems into capitalist economies, socialist economies, and the mixed economies that fall in between, while political systems were ranked from democracy to dictatorship in the same way. Thus, a fascist system could combine a capitalist economy with dictatorship, while the Swedish model combined socialism with democracy. Within this framework, political systems and economic systems could be mixed and matched in any combination. Following this taxonomy, Francis Fukuyama has declared "the end of history," arguing that the liberal democracy has established itself as the "final form of human government" and that the free market has established itself as the ultimate destination in the evolution of the economic system.[2]

The analysis developed in this chapter questions Fukuyama's conclusions, first by arguing that political systems inescapably lay the foundation for economic systems, so that both liberal democracy and the free market are simultaneously political and economic systems, and ultimately that the economic and political aspects of those systems cannot be separated. The second problem with this end of history is that there are inherent tensions between democracy and a free market economy that make it difficult to maintain a stable system. In particular, the ascendancy of the concept of democracy threatens the survival of the free market economy, which itself is an extension of the founders' views of liberty. The idea that the direction of an economic system is determined by its political institutions has been discussed by many others, but the notion that liberty and democracy are economic systems as much as they are political systems has never been fully developed.[3] This chapter argues that there are important reasons to do so.

The Concepts of Liberty and Democracy

The inherent tensions between liberty and democracy may not at first be apparent. In one sense, they deal with different aspects of the political system. The notion that they are in fundamental conflict was expressed well by José Ortega y Gasset. Using the term "liberalism" to refer to the ideas of liberty described earlier, Ortega writes,

Liberalism and democracy happen to be two things which begin by having nothing to do with each other, and end by having, so far as tendencies are concerned, meanings that are mutually antagonistic. Democracy and liberalism are two answers to two completely different questions.

Democracy answers this question—"who ought to exercise the public power?" The answer it gives is—"the exercise of public power belongs to the citizens as a body.". . . .

Liberalism, on the other hand, answers this other question— "regardless of who exercises the public power, what should its limits be?" The answer it gives is—"whether the public power is exercised by an autocrat or by the people, it cannot be absolute; the individual has rights which are over and above any interference by the state."[4]

The Founding Fathers attempted to create a government that was both liberal and democratic, following Ortega's meanings of the terms. The underlying philosophy of the American Revolution was liberty, and the founders explicitly wanted to avoid creating a democracy, in the sense of a government that was directed by the preferences of its citizens.[5] But once the new government was created, somebody had to run it. The founders wanted those in charge of the government's operations to be selected by a democratic process because they believed that was the best way to keep the nation from falling under the control of a ruling elite. But the founders also wanted to insulate those who ran the government from direct influence by its citizens, which is why the Constitution originally specified that only members of the House of Representatives would be elected by the people. Senators were to be chosen by the state legislatures, the president was to be chosen by the electoral college, and Supreme Court justices were to be appointed by the president. By insulating political decision makers from direct accountability to citizens, the government would be in a better position to adhere to its constitutionally mandated limits and would be relatively free from political pressures from the electorate. Only the House of Representatives was there to give citizens some direct check on the activities of their government. Thus, the Constitution created a limited government designed to protect liberty, not to foster democracy.

A theme that develops throughout the following chapters is that the federal government has become increasingly more accountable to the pressures of citizens, which has led to an erosion of liberty, replaced by public policy created in response to democratic pressures. At the surface, liberty and democracy deal with two different aspects of government, but below the surface there is a closer relationship, and the promotion of the principle of democracy has come at the expense of liberty.

Liberty as an Economic System

The idea that liberty is an economic system finds its origins in the idea of political liberty. As discussed in chapter 1, John Locke's ideas of rights provided the intellectual foundation for the American Revolution. Prior to Locke, people accepted the notion that they obtained their rights from government. The rights people had were the rights their governments gave them. Locke's revolutionary idea was that people were endowed with natural rights, and it was the role of government to protect them. Locke also revolutionized thinking about property. In a state of nature, Locke reasoned, property was unowned and people came to own property by combining their labor with it. In Locke's words, "every man has a property in his own person. This nobody has any right to but himself. The labour of his body, and the work of his hands, we may say, are properly his."[6] Once property is owned, Locke argued, the only way that an individual can legitimately obtain that property is to engage in a mutually agreeable exchange with the property's owner. Property rights are a part of people's overall rights, as Locke viewed it.

One could not expect Locke, writing almost a century before Adam Smith, to develop a sophisticated and modern economic treatise. At the same time, one must recognize that the political philosophy espoused by Locke did more than just imply an economic system based on liberty. By describing the origin of property and arguing that property rights were an integral part of the rights protected by the social contract, Locke was arguing for the institutions of laissez-faire capitalism.[7] The means of production were property, just like any other property, which provided an argument for capitalism and against socialism more than 150 years before Karl Marx began an intellectual movement that argued the other way. When considering democracy as an alternative to liberty, Locke's argument clearly supports a property owner's right to determine the use of property rather than reliance on any type of democratic decision-making process.[8]

Locke's reasoning that defined the liberty the colonies were fighting to gain simultaneously identified an economic and a political system. Indeed, the characteristics of the Lockean economic system of liberty were even clearer than the characteristics of the Lockean political system. Locke's vision of economic liberty rested on the notion of private ownership of property. In a state of nature, property was unowned, but individuals could come to own property by combining their labor with nature. From that point on, ownership is clearly established, and the only legitimate way that one person could acquire the property of another was through voluntary exchange. The free market economy, with complete private ownership of property, was quite clearly a part of the concept of liberty that guided the Founding Fathers, and liberty was as much an economic system as a political system in the minds of eighteenth-century Americans.

The Politics of Economic Man

One outgrowth of economics from political economy was the development of the caricature called "economic man." Economic man has the goal of maximizing income or wealth. As C. E. Ferguson, one of the most prominent promoters of neoclassical economics, said, "In short, a consumer arranges his purchases so as to maximize satisfaction subject to his limited money income."[9] The neoclassical framework then assumes (with some exceptions in specific cases) that satisfaction, or utility, is simply a function of the quantities of goods and services the consumer consumes. In mathematical form, the consumer has a level of utility, U, that is a function of goods that can be symbolically notated x_1, x_2, and so forth. Utility can then be represented in a general functional form, f, as $U = f(x_1, x_2, x_3, \ldots x_n)$, for the n goods the consumer consumes. The assumption is made that more is preferred to less, so the single goal of economic man is to maximize his satisfaction from the consumption of goods and services.

This caricature of economic man has met with a substantial amount of criticism by noneconomists because it implies that the only thing people care about is their own consumption. Economic man is materialistic, does not care about the well-being of others, gets no satisfaction from the beauty of a sunset or a flower, and, more significant, places his own materialistic goals above those of the community. Economists often take this caricature seriously, as, for example, in public goods theory, which assumes people will free ride by consuming goods without paying for them whenever they have the chance, causing a "market failure" that requires the intervention of the government to correct.[10] Are people really as selfish as economists assume?

The description of economic man given by his critics, including many economists, falls well off the mark of the actual economic man who populates the models of neoclassical economics, but economists (let alone others) rarely recognize the fact because they do not recognize the political institutions that have been tacitly assumed to form the foundation of the neoclassical framework. Economic man forms the foundation of producer and consumer behavior, which means that in his market activities he always tries to get the most satisfaction possible from each of his purchases and sales. However, in the neoclassical economic framework, market opportunities are the only opportunities available to economic man. Would economic man turn his back on his best friend to make a buck? The model does not allow it, because people in the neoclassical model interact with each other only by buying and selling. Is it worth nothing to economic man to view a beautiful sunset? The neoclassical model does not say, because all economic man can do in the model is buy, sell, consume, and combine inputs in a production process to get more output. The point is that this model of economic man applies only to production and consumption activities, not to interpersonal relationships, aesthetic matters, or even politics.

The neoclassical model does give some indication about the *assumed* political behavior of economic man, however. As already noted, any economic theory or model must have an implied political foundation, and the implied political foundation in the neoclassical model is an extreme version of political liberty. Everyone is fully informed of all of their opportunities. Full information rules out fraud or other types of misrepresentation. All property rights are clearly defined and never violated.[11] There is no theft or other types of violence. Nobody violates laws or engages in any type of criminal behavior.[12] The only way one economic man ever acquires the property of another is to buy it at a mutually agreed upon price. In its basic form, the model has no government, no police, and no courts. It does not need them, because all rights are clearly defined and everybody always respects the rights of others.[13]

The neoclassical model does, indeed, assume that economic man's only goal is to maximize his satisfaction from the consumption of goods and services, but it also assumes that he does so in a completely honest way. Economic man never cheats, engages in fraudulent behavior, or steals, even when the opportunity presents itself, and in the neoclassical model there must be many opportunities for this, because the neoclassical market economy is unregulated and unpoliced. The political foundation of neoclassical economics is one of extreme liberty, and within this setting economic man is an individual of extreme principle. Surely if this type of behavior is extrapolated into the public sector, economic man would be just as principled. There would be no bribes, no sacrificing the general public interest to favor special interests, and no political scandals. Just as economic man respects the property of others, surely he also would accept his civic responsibilities.

From a strictly economic standpoint, one might argue that the neoclassical economic framework has no political institutions, but that cannot be true. Property rights must somehow be defined, and somebody must have the right (or responsibility) to determine how resources will be allocated. In the neoclassical framework, there is the strong assumption of clearly defined and strongly protected private property rights and the strong assumption that the only way people acquire goods and services is by purchasing them from someone else at mutually agreeable terms. Thus, the neoclassical economic framework is built solidly on the political foundation of liberty. Because it is the indispensable foundation for the standard neoclassical model, liberty is as much an economic concept as a political one.

The point of this section is not to describe actual human behavior but rather to attack the myth that the assumed economic man is entirely selfish in his motivations. He does try to get the most satisfaction out of his purchases, by assumption, but also by assumption he does so only in the most honest and principled way, through mutually agreed upon market exchanges. That is the way the economic model works, and if people actually behaved in the public sector the way the neoclassical model assumes economic man behaves, politics would be much more civil. Economic man operates within the framework of economic and political liberty and always respects the rights of others, although the political aspects of most economic models remain implied rather than explicitly developed. The neoclassical economic model depends on this type of principled behavior for its results. Twentieth-century neoclassical economics describes an economic system based on the same principle of liberty that was promoted by Locke.

Democracy as an Economic System

The idea that democracy is an economic system is more abstract, because many different types of democratic institutions could be designed through which democracy can guide the economy. Nevertheless, the dangers of democracy as an economic foundation were clearly evident to the founders, who wanted to design a government that could keep the forces of democracy in check to preserve liberty. One of the motivations for replacing the Articles of Confederation with the Constitution of the United States was to strengthen the powers of government to protect against the democratic impulses of those who would want to redistribute land, forgive debts, and otherwise violate the Lockean vision of rights. The most prominent example of such impulses was Daniel Shays, leader of Shays' Rebellion, who wanted debts to be forgiven and property redistributed for the benefit of the common man.[14] The Constitutional Convention was called for partly by those who supported the creation of a stronger federal government that could guarantee the rights of individuals and aid the states in cases where there was a danger of rights being violated.

What is the alternative to liberty as an economic system? If liberty implies private ownership of property and allows the property owner the right to determine how that property will be used, then the alternative must mean that private owners do not have the right to determine how property is to be used. Within the twentieth-century framework, capitalism, the embodiment of economic liberty, has been contrasted with socialism, in which there is not private ownership of property, so the use of property is determined by the society as a whole rather than by individuals. This concept of socialism leaves too many ambiguities, however. One can easily understand how an individual might make a decision, but how would a society decide? In twentieth-century socialism, the actual answer was dictatorship. The dictator would determine the allocation of resources, perhaps by assigning various other individuals the responsibility or by creating a central planning bureaucracy to undertake it. Nevertheless, the collective decision-making process was to vest the decision-making authority in the dictator and then, in hierarchical fashion, have those below the dictator implement the dictator's plans.

Conceptually, such a system is closer to capitalism than to socialism, although it is a type of capitalism where ownership of resources is vested in a single individual. Experience throughout the twentieth century has shown that economies that have called themselves socialist for the most part did not have any type of collective ownership. Most people owned little if anything beyond their personal possessions, while the political leaders had the right to determine how resources would be allocated. The economic system of liberty allows individual property owners to determine how resources will be allocated. Dictatorial socialism allows the dictator to make those decisions. Closer to the spirit of socialism would be a system where the people, collectively, had the right to decide how resources will be allocated. That idea points toward the economic system of democracy.

Democracy as a political system implies that the government's leaders are chosen by a democratic decision-making process, and as many analysts have noted, political democracy can coexist with economic liberty if there are strict limits on the powers of the majority.[15] However, democracy can also be extended to the economic system to allow democratic decision making to determine the allocation of resources in addition to the selection of political leaders. Indeed, there are good reasons to believe that political democracy has a natural tendency to evolve into economic democracy. As Karl Polanyi remarked, "Socialism is, essentially, the tendency inherent in an industrial civilization to transcend the self-regulating market by consciously subordinating it to a democratic society."[16]

Liberty, as an economic system, implies that all exchanges are made voluntarily and that property rights are respected and secure. However, not everybody has the same principles as the economic man described earlier, and as a result there is a demand for some government to enforce economic liberty. U.S. history provides a good example, as the threats to liberty by Daniel Shays and his supporters led to the demand for a stronger government to suppress those who wanted to overturn the economic system of liberty. Government, even one that works to protect liberty, does so by force. If disputes among individuals cannot be settled peacefully, the government settles those disputes by using its coercive power. In settling disputes and trying to define property rights, the government regulates individual behavior, and to finance its activities, it levies taxes. Both have the potential to reduce liberty.

When political decisions are made democratically, the government ultimately becomes accountable to the majority. It is easy, therefore, to see that decisions made through the political process will be more inclined to further the will of the majority rather than to protect economic liberty. Originally, taxes were collected for the purpose of financing the activities of government, but after two centuries of taxation the tax system has become so explicitly redistributive that no serious questions are raised about its redistributive role. At the end of the twentieth century, even individuals who are widely regarded as defenders of liberty, such as Milton Friedman and Alan Peacock, were arguing in favor of using the tax system for redistribution.[17]

When deciding what rights people have in the use of their property, democratic decision making leads toward determination by the will of the majority rather than by the principles of liberty. Land use has become heavily regulated, and many characteristics of labor contracts are determined by law, including restrictions on how much must be paid to a worker, what types of benefits workers must be offered on the job, work and safety conditions, and the number of hours that can be worked. Characteristics of products sold in the market are controlled by the government, including what sizes are allowed, what information must be displayed on the product, and how products are constructed and even extending to the prohibition of the sale of some goods and services. Economic liberty has been sacrificed to the will of the majority.

The advantages of economic democracy over economic liberty can be debated, but the point of this section is to establish that democracy is an economic system where the allocation of resources is determined by the will of the majority.

Nineteenth-Century Democracy

The Constitution of the United States was designed to create a limited government, and democracy was employed as a means to an end. The founders had no intention of creating a democratic government in the sense that the activities of government would be determined by the will of the majority.[18] As the following chapters indicate, the concept of democracy became more firmly established as a principle of government in its own right, but still, by the end of the nineteenth century, the federal government remained relatively limited in scope and the concept of liberty remained well understood as a principle of government. While democracy made inroads as a political system in the nineteenth century, the economy remained based on the principle of liberty. Thus, the study of the transformation of American government from liberty to democracy in the nineteenth century is primarily an examination of the political foundations of American society rather than its economic system.

If the reach of government is measured by the money it spends, by 1913 the federal government spent only 2.5 percent of the nation's income, and as a percentage of income its expenditures had been declining steadily in the period between the War between the States and World War I. Of course, government controls the economy in other ways, and the end of the nineteenth century had seen more growth in governmental regulatory control than in government expenditures. Nevertheless, democracy in nineteenth-century America was primarily a political phenomenon, because the founders deliberately tried to insulate public policy from democratic impulses.

Twentieth-Century Democracy

The situation changed substantially in the twentieth century, when democracy became much more of an economic phenomenon in addition to a political phenomenon. Early in the twentieth century, two constitutional amendments substantially extended the political reach of democracy, almost to the point where it was at the end of the twentieth century. The 17th Amendment, mandating direct election of senators, ratified in 1913, meant that a larger part of the federal government was directly accountable to the voters. Prior to 1913, the Constitution specified that state legislatures chose the state's senators, insulating them from the voters and making them accountable to the state's political elite. After 1913, senators were accountable to voters in the same way as were members of the House of Representatives. In 1920 the 19th Amendment was ratified, mandating that women had the right to vote, again extending the reach of democracy to a larger fraction of the citizenry. At one time, elections might have been viewed as a method of selecting competent people to undertake a job with constitutionally specified limits. With the extension of democracy, elections increasingly became a referendum on public policy.

The political extension of democracy was well under way early in the twentieth century, but the economic extension of democracy had only begun. The Sherman Act, passed in 1890, was one of the early measures taken to use the political process to redistribute economic power from those who had more of it to those who had less. Antitrust laws, by defining the limits of acceptable business activity, and even in the extreme by allowing the government to dismember companies, began replacing the allocation of economic resources by voluntary contracts, mutually beneficial exchanges, and the market mechanism with a system that allocated resources through democratic decision making and oversight. Regulation of the railroads and food and drug regulation, undertaken in the late nineteenth and early twentieth centuries, were an extension of the same principle. Some economic activities became illegal even if all parties to them were in agreement, and the government mandated the conditions of some exchanges and even ruled that ownership of property was subject to government approval.

Early twentieth-century examples include the regulation of food and drug suppliers, which prevented some mutually agreeable exchanges that would have taken place; the regulation of railroad rates that mandated terms under which certain exchanges had to be made; and the enforcement of the antitrust laws. The breakup of Standard Oil was the most visible example of the application of antitrust, which forced John D. Rockefeller to divest himself of property that he had acquired through market activity. Rockefeller, labeled a "robber baron," was quite unpopular in his day, and one might dispute the conditions under which his Standard Oil was able to amass such a large share of the market. Regardless, he had to divest himself of much of his property not because of the way in which it was acquired but rather because he had such a large share of the market that his business was determined to be a monopoly.

The point is that around the turn of the twentieth century democracy was extended from a political concept and a mechanism for selecting government officials into an economic concept, with the implication that, if public opinion demanded it, the government could intervene in people's economic affairs to direct the allocation of resources. This principle, although never fully articulated, was continually extended throughout the twentieth century, and the government gained more latitude to intervene in people's economic affairs and even to direct the allocation of economic resources itself.

Comparative Economic Systems

Just as political economy divided into economics and political science, economics also subdivided into many areas of specialization in the twentieth century, one of which is comparative economic systems. Following world political divisions, comparative economic systems primarily has dealt with the differences between capitalist and socialist economies in the twentieth century, with political structures being left aside for the most part. Capitalist economies were characterized as those with private ownership of the means of production and market allocation of resources. Socialist economies were those that did not have private ownership of the means of production.

While the concept of capitalism has always been relatively easy to understand and conforms with the idea of the Lockean liberal economy discussed earlier, the concept of socialism has never been entirely clear. In a capitalist system, that somebody owns something implies that the owner has the power to determine how the resource will be used, whether it is a consumption item, such as clothing, or a capital good, such as a factory, or a natural resource, such as a coal mine. In a socialist system, where there are no private owners of the means of production, the way in which resource allocation will be directed is left unspecified. Socialism, seen in this way, is not an economic system at all. An economic system must provide a mechanism for defining the way in which economic resources will be allocated.

Marx's influential book, *Capital,* was highly critical of the capitalist system (it was Marx who gave capitalism its name) and advocated abolishing the private ownership of the means of production but did not provide a blueprint for how the resulting socialist economy would allocate resources. Thus, when the Soviet Union was established in 1917, its founders knew what economic institutions they wanted to abolish but did not have a clear concept of what they would create to replace them. Within a few years of the Soviet Union's creation, Austrian economist Ludwig von Mises challenged the supporters of socialism by claiming that a socialist economy could not work. In a paper delivered to the Economic Society in Vienna, Mises argued that market prices are a requirement for successful economic calculation and allocation of resources, dooming a centrally planned economy to failure.[19]

The challenge that Mises raised motivated economic theorists to try to understand how a centrally planned economy could work. Socialist writing before the creation of the Soviet Union was critical of the operation of capitalist economies but did not explain how the socialist replacement would work or even how a socialist economy would be organized. Economists who supported the idea of socialism answered Mises's challenge by developing a theory of market socialism, where the means of production would not be privately owned but where central planners would create a system that would mimic market pricing and market allocation of resources.[20] Thus, they asserted that Mises's assertion had been refuted. If so, they would have demonstrated how markets could coexist with socialist ownership of the means of production in an economy, but Mises and his student Friedrich Hayek argued that the supporters of market socialism misunderstood their critique of socialism and that rational resource allocation through central planning was not possible even in theory.

The most articulate critic of the market socialists, and indeed of socialists of all types, was Hayek.[21] He argued that markets operated by making efficient use of the specific knowledge of time and place, which everyone in an economy had but which would be impossible to effectively communicate to a central planning authority. The market was able to make use of this information by allowing people to use resources at their disposal to improve efficiency, to offer new or improved goods or services, or to undertake other innovations. Profits and losses play the crucial role of rewarding efficient allocations of resources and punishing inefficient allocations. The system works because the market economy rewards those who make efficiency-enhancing decisions and penalizes those who squander resources, but that system depends crucially on private ownership of economic resources.

Public ownership hinders resource allocation in several ways. For one thing, bureaucratic decision makers do not have the same stake in the outcome as does a private resource owner. Typically, the penalties for bad decisions are not as great, nor are the rewards for good decisions. More crucially, however, government decision makers are more likely to be called to task for making bad decisions than they are to be rewarded for making good decisions, which, after all, is what they are supposed to be doing anyway. Thus, government decision making will be systematically less efficient than private sector decision making. While this idea was generally accepted by the end of the twentieth century, it was not accepted at midcentury, when Mises and Hayek were defending markets in the socialist calculation debate.[22] Indeed, in 1973, the year Mises died, Paul Samuelson, a Nobel laureate in economics, argued that although the Soviet Union had a per capita income about half that of the United States, the superiority of central planning over market allocation of resources gave them a higher growth rate, and he projected that the Soviet Union would catch up to the United States in per capita income perhaps as soon as 1990 but almost surely by the year 2010.[23]

This notion of market socialism and of comparative economic systems as promoted by market socialists viewed political and economic systems as completely separate and even viewed the issue of markets versus central planning as independent of private versus collective ownership of resources. Mises and Hayek, in contrast, took a more Lockean view of the market system, arguing that its operation rested critically on private ownership, the protection of property rights, and freedom of exchange. A market economy required liberty, as Locke described it, and a movement away from liberty was a movement toward socialism. Political systems and economic systems are inextricably linked.[24]

Political and Economic Systems

This chapter breaks with twentieth-century tradition by treating liberty and democracy as economic systems as well as political systems. The standard taxonomy would place economic systems on a continuum from capitalist economies to socialist economies, with mixed economies lying somewhere in between, and would place political systems on a separate continuum ranging from democracy to dictatorship. Figure 1 represents the traditional taxonomy within a two-dimensional diagram, with the horizontal axis representing the economic continuum from capitalism to socialism and the vertical axis representing the political continuum from dictatorship to democracy.

Following this traditional taxonomy, political and economic systems can exist independently of each other, so particular nations can locate anywhere from one extreme to the other in either dimension. Fascism has been characterized as a system of capitalist dictatorship, located in the lower left corner of the figure.[25] The twentieth-century communist countries were socialist dictatorships, located in the bottom right corner of the figure. Nations like Sweden have been held as examples of democratic socialism, in the top right. Fukuyama's history ends at the upper left corner of the figure, with capitalist democracies. Mixed systems might fall anywhere within the boundaries of the figure.

One problem with this taxonomy is that the extreme case of capitalism—the type represented by twentieth-century neoclassical economic theory—has very little government of any type. The government protects the rights of its citizens and prevents citizens from using force against each other. Resources are allocated through markets as a result of voluntary exchange. In this setting, there is a minimal role for either democracy or dictatorship. Perhaps there will be room for a minimal state to overcome the conflicts inherent in Hobbesian anarchy, but this minimal state has almost no control over the allocation of resources.

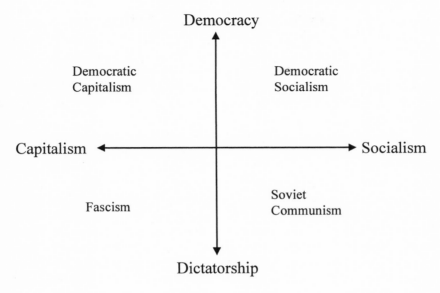

Fig. 1.   Traditional taxonomy

Figure 2 provides a better depiction of the relationship between political and economic systems.

The system of pure capitalism conforms to the economic system of liberty advocated by Locke. Thus, liberty can be substituted for capitalism on the horizontal axis. If anarcho-capitalism were feasible, figure 2 would come to a point at the liberty end of the economic axis, showing that pure capitalism would be characterized by no government at all: no democracy, no dictatorship. The feasibility of anarcho-capitalism is not an issue here, because the American founders intended to create a minimal government to protect the rights of its citizens and to guarantee their liberty. This minimal state is represented by the short side of the quadrangle, at the liberty end of the liberty-socialism axis. The idea behind diagramming it this way is that, if an economic system of liberty exists, there will be little room for either democracy or dictatorship. Most decisions in a liberal society will be made as a result of voluntary exchange rather than of any type of collective decision making.

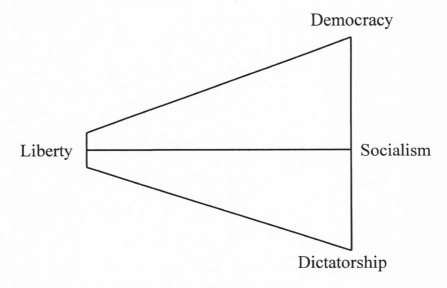

Fig. 2.   Economic and political systems

As one moves away from liberty toward socialism, there becomes an increasingly broad range for government allocation of resources. Collective decision making increasingly replaces individual decision making as a society moves from the left portion to the right portion of figure 2. Thus, the potential range for both democracy and dictatorship increases, as reflected in the broadening of the figure. As noted in the previous section, socialism refers to the collective ownership of the means of production, but it does not define the type of decision making that will be used to allocate resources. The alternatives shown in figure 2 are dictatorship and democracy. In extreme socialism, represented by the line at the right of the figure, pure democracy is represented at the top. As a society moves down from democracy, the degree of democracy declines and the degree of dictatorship increases, until at the bottom the society arrives at pure dictatorship. The figure visually indicates that as one moves from socialism to liberty the potential role for both democracy and dictatorship declines.

The twentieth-century ideological divide between the Western and Eastern blocs has been visualized as taking place along the very bottom axis of figure 2—the continuum from liberty to dictatorship. The Western capitalist democracies were not at the extreme liberty end of the continuum but argued the virtues of free markets and the protection of individual rights. The Eastern bloc communist countries were not pure socialist economies either, because they contained elements of private property and freedom of exchange both in some areas of the legal economy and in a substantial underground economy. Nevertheless, the ideological debate fit well on the bottom axis of the diagram.

The alternatives were more complex than just defining a system on the bottom axis of the diagram, to be sure, but the ideological debate never has taken full account of the nature of the political and economic choices available to nations. Partly this is because political and economic systems were viewed as independent choices rather than the interdependent choices they really are. Meanwhile, as the ideological debate took place over where nations should locate along the bottom axis, from liberty to dictatorship, the United States was continually moving along the top axis, from liberty to democracy. As this movement has taken place, the majority has gained increasing claim over the right to determine how resources are allocated, eroding the property rights that are protected under a system of liberty. While resisting socialist dictatorship, as depicted at the bottom right of the diagram, the United States has unwittingly moved toward democratic socialism, at the top right. Within a simple analytical framework, this depicts the movement from liberty to democracy that will be described throughout this book and is contrasted with the intellectual paradigm of economics and political science that has dominated twentieth-century academic discussion on the subject.

Conclusion

Fukuyama declared that the evolution of political and economic systems has come to an end with the ascendancy of liberal democracy as a political system and the free market economy as an economic system. The analysis that follows questions the ultimate compatibility of democracy with a free market economy. The fact is that, as the United States has become more democratic, it has narrowed the scope of the market economy, and if democracy is viewed as an economic system in addition to a political system there is reason to think that the decline in economic liberty and the rise in political democracy are not independent events. The United States has consciously moved toward increasing democracy, and the unintended side effect has been a reduction in liberty.[26] Political and economic systems are interdependent, and the move from liberty to democracy has substantial economic as well as political implications. Rather than draw conclusions at this point, however, this chapter can serve as a framework for understanding the evolution of American political ideology from liberty to democracy.

CHAPTER 3

Consensus versus Democracy: Politics in Eighteenth-Century America

At the beginning of the twentieth-first century, democracy, embodied in the principle of majority rule, is so universally viewed as the most desirable form of government that alternatives to the principle of majority rule are not often considered with any seriousness. Yet, at least in theory, decision making by consensus is a compelling alternative to majoritarian democracy. In a political environment where democracy is unquestioningly accepted, the idea that political decisions can be made by consensus is novel, but when the American constitution was evolving in the eighteenth century, political decision making by consensus was accepted as desirable and even preferred to democracy by those who were promoting the cause of liberty in America. By the end of the eighteenth century, however, majoritarian democratic principles had largely supplanted consensus in political decision making. Decision making by consensus offers some clear advantages to majority rule but has some drawbacks too. Consensus decision making played an important role in colonial American government, so it is of historical interest, and also offers some theoretical principles that can help understand contemporary constitutional democracy.

Collective decision making can be undertaken with greater or lesser degrees of consensus. Even today, when the most common collective decision rule used in the public sector is simple majority rule, Congress still must muster a two-thirds majority to override a presidential veto, and in criminal cases juries must reach unanimous agreement—complete consensus—to render a verdict. Would it be possible to replace majority rule voting with consensus decision making in the United States today? Focusing on the word *possible,* the answer clearly is yes, but it would require some changes in political institutions and would also alter the scope and character of government. The best way to see how the nature of government would be affected is to compare majority rule and consensus decision making from a theoretical perspective, but the best way to understand what institutional changes would be required is to examine the actual use of consensus decision making in colonial America.

This chapter offers two main theoretical points. First, the optimal scope of collective action declines as the level of consensus required in collective decision making increases. This happens because when a higher level of consensus is required, such as moving from simple majority rule to two-thirds majority, collective decision making costs rise. Collective decision-making costs refer to the costs involved in having a group arrive at a group decision. Higher decision-making costs mean that some collective activities that would have produced net benefits in the absence of decision-making costs, and that would have been undertaken with a less inclusive decision rule, will no longer be worthwhile because they are too costly. Second, a requirement of more consensus in collective decision making entails not only more agreement but institutional changes designed to facilitate the reaching of agreement. Political institutions that efficiently produce majority rule decisions will be different from political institutions that efficiently produce collective decisions with a more inclusive decision rule. These theoretical concepts will be explored in more detail and then will be applied to the constitutional history of colonial America.

Agreement and Social Welfare

One of the fundamental ideas of economics is that a competitive market economy allocates resources in a manner that maximizes the well-being of those in the economy. The idea goes back at least to Adam Smith's monumental treatise, *The Wealth of Nations,*[1] where Smith argues that individuals pursuing their own self-interest are led by an invisible hand to further the best interest of the whole society. Smith's point does not address the conditions under which government intervention might be welfare enhancing but rather emphasizes that market exchange is welfare enhancing. Perhaps the government can help the process by enforcing property rights, or by preventing transactions that harm third parties, or by other means. Nevertheless, when clearly defined property rights prevent people from engaging in activities that harm nonconsenting third parties, the market process works to enhance social welfare.

The mechanism by which Smith's invisible hand operates begins in a setting where property rights are clearly defined and enforced so that people cannot harm others without their consent. How is such an environment produced? That is the role the Founding Fathers envisioned for their constitutionally limited government, so that issue will be analyzed in detail after some groundwork is laid. Within that environment, the market process works by encouraging individuals to engage in market exchange whenever it is mutually advantageous to do so. Parties to exchanges must be made better off according to their own evaluations, or they would not engage in the exchanges. The ability to participate in such exchanges encourages individuals to be productive, because the more they produce, and the greater the value of their production, the more they will be able to obtain in exchange for what they produce. This is how market activity enhances social welfare.

Looked at from a political vantage point, the key to welfare enhancement in a market economy is that whenever any decision is made it is made with the unanimous consent of those who participate. Thus, with voluntary market exchange, everybody is made better off, according to their own evaluations of their welfare. If the same criterion for social welfare enhancement that was used to evaluate the market was applied to political decision making, one could be sure that political decisions enhanced social welfare if everyone were required to agree.[2] Under simple majority rule, for example, some people agree with the decision but others do not. Because there is no good way to compare the gains to the gainers against the losses to the losers in such a situation, even when a majority agrees to something there is no way to be confident that what they agreed to is in the public interest. In other words, under majority rule, there is no guarantee that the gains to the majority are greater than the losses to the minority.

James Buchanan and Gordon Tullock, in their pioneering work, *The Calculus of Consent,*[3] discuss at length the individualistic postulates that underlie this view of social welfare, so a brief summary can suffice here. The most fundamental idea is that social welfare can be nothing more than the aggregate of the welfare of each member of the society. It makes no sense to talk about the well-being of a group of people independently of the well-being of the group's members. A group is better off when its members are better off; it is worse off when its members are worse off. This leaves some ambiguous situations in which changes might improve the well-being of some group members while harming others, but in those cases, if one wants to say something about the group's welfare, any conclusions must be based on a comparison of the value of the gains to some people against the losses imposed on others. If the gains to the gainers can, in some sense, be judged to outweigh the losses to the losers, then the group would be better off.

A conceptual problem that arises here is that there is no foolproof way to weigh the gains of one person against the losses of another to see if the gainers gain more than the losers lose. Various mechanisms have been devised to try to weigh these gains and losses, but every mechanism leaves some uncertainty, because there is no way for an external observer to measure the harm that befalls those who are made worse off as a result of a group decision. In practice, democratic politics, which assigns each voter an equal weight, is most often used as an approximation, but using democratic decision making as a measure of social welfare has the obvious drawback that often each loser in the collective decision-making process loses more than each gainer gains. It is easy to see why group decisions made by majority rule could end up leaving the group worse off, but even more sophisticated measures of trying to weigh the gains against the losses from collective action suffer from the same basic problem.

The argument in favor of collective decision making by consensus is thus relatively straightforward. When there is a consensus of opinion, everyone is in agreement, so the collective decision is in the best interest of the group because it is in the best interest of every member of the group. One could hardly object to decisions that are made by consensus. The drawback is that often it is difficult to get everyone in a group to agree to anything, so a requirement for consensus can prevent groups from undertaking collective action that would, on net, be beneficial. A trade-off exists, and a group is able to undertake more extensive collective action if it requires less of a consensus to act.

Some Constitutional Principles

In *The Calculus of Consent,* Buchanan and Tullock build on their discussion of individualism to discuss the desirable properties of unanimity in collective decision making.[4] They make the insightful point that people might unanimously agree to make certain decisions under majority rule, or under other rules besides unanimity, so a less than unanimous decision rule could be optimal if everyone would agree to it. That is, there should be a consensus approval at a constitutional level for any deviations from the requirement of a consensus in post-constitutional collective decision making. What, exactly, might be required to signify a consensus in favor of a less than unanimous collective decision rule has been the subject of debate in an extensive academic literature.[5] Nevertheless, the principle remains that, with a requirement of unanimous agreement, collective decisions will be welfare enhancing, though there can be no guarantees when the unanimity requirement is dropped.

When one thinks of consensus in collective decision making, one tends to think in terms of modern majoritarian democracy and to extend that political setting toward the requirement of unanimous, rather than majority, consent. If one thinks more broadly about consensus, better examples can be found. In medieval towns formed in the period from 1050 to 1150, it was common to have meetings where all of the residents would gather in the center of the town to verbally affirm their allegiance to the town's rules. This may be the historical antecedent to the theory of the social contract developed by Hobbes, Locke, and later writers.[6] For contemporary examples, unanimous agreement in a contractual setting is more common, even when many parties are involved. For example, the agreement to restrictive covenants when a home is purchased means that there is unanimous agreement among all homeowners in a subdivision. Often, subdivisions have requirements such as how far houses must be from lot lines, size and other architectural restrictions, and even restrictions on the kinds of vehicles that can be parked in driveways. These requirements, if they are in restrictive covenants, are contractual and not a part of local government law, but all homeowners signify their agreement when they buy a house.[7] Thus, the requirement for unanimous agreement, while rare in contemporary political settings, is not beyond the realm of possibility and even happens with some regularity. But as the example of restrictive covenants shows, political institutions may have to be structured differently if one hopes to garner unanimous agreement.

With less than unanimous agreement, one problem is that some people can impose costs on others through the political process.[8] The greater the degree of consensus required by a decision-making rule, the lower would be the expected costs that are imposed on nonconsenting individuals who are party to the decision-making process. For example, if 90 percent agreement were required of the group, then individuals in the group would be less likely to bear costs associated with being outvoted than if 51 percent of the group were required to agree. Unanimous agreement completely eliminates the possibility of costs being imposed on some members of the group by a group decision, because the group cannot do anything without the approval of everyone. One benefit of a unanimous decision rule is that all collective decisions will benefit some people but nobody is made worse off, and thus they will be efficient in the sense that they produce a net improvement in the welfare of the decision-making group.[9]

One problem with requiring unanimous agreement is that it is very difficult to get everyone to agree on anything. Thus, with a unanimity requirement, government would not be able to get much done. Individuals might unanimously agree to a less than unanimous decision rule, such as majority rule, for some decisions if they could be assured that they would not have to bear excessive costs for doing so. For many routine government decisions, citizens may believe that sometimes they gain and sometimes they lose, but on net they are beneficiaries from government action.[10] Thus, they could agree to majority rule decision making and believe they are better off than if unanimity was required and the government could do almost nothing. However, under such a circumstance, citizens should demand strong constitutional constraints on the scope of government to assure that some do not pay disproportionately for benefits that go to others.

One can be assured that a group decision enhances the welfare of the group only if there is the requirement of unanimous approval by everyone in the group. However, because it is difficult to actually reach unanimous agreement, a group may be better off deciding some issues with less than unanimous approval (simple majority, for example), accepting the risk that some of the group's decisions may lead to a reduction in welfare.

Decision Rules and the Scope of Collective Action

As the degree of consensus required increases, it becomes more difficult and more costly to arrive at a collective decision. Some projects that would be cost-effective under simple majority rule will not be when more consensus is required, because the additional decision-making costs offset the benefits of collective action. Thus, the more inclusive the decision rule, the more limited will be the optimal scope of collective action. For this reason, a government requiring a high degree of consensus before undertaking action will have a more limited scope than will a government that makes decisions by simple majority rule. Thus, an increased demand for collective action would cause people to be willing to accept higher costs imposed on them from the collective action. In political terms, when there is an increased demand for collective action, one would expect that the group would be willing to undertake collective action with less of a consensus.

Examples include wars and depressions, where citizens believe that nations can deal with their problems more effectively though collective action. In the United States in the twentieth century, both world wars and the Great Depression brought with them an increased demand for collective action and an increasing willingness for people to bear costs in exchange for lower decision-making costs to promote government action. The willingness to bear increased costs in such situations comes from the perception of increased benefits from a broader scope of collective action.

Robert Higgs, in his discussion of the growth of twentieth-century American government,[11] clearly documents the costs imposed on citizens as a result of increasing government power during the world wars and the Great Depression. In times of crisis, the government imposes more costs on its citizens, which they are willing to accept in exchange for a larger scope of collective action to further some collectively held goals. During the world wars, industries were nationalized, prices and wages were frozen, and government bureaucrats gained more power to act at their discretion, without being subject to some type of consensus approval for their actions. Furthermore, people volunteered to bear a disproportionate part of the costs by engaging in activities such as purchasing war bonds and volunteering for military service. Less consensus was required for collective action, so more collective action was possible.

Because there are costs incurred in making collective decisions, some collective activities that would be optimal without decision-making costs will not be undertaken because the decision-making costs outweigh the benefits of collective action. Just as transaction costs in private markets can prevent exchanges from being made that would occur if transactions could be undertaken costlessly, decision-making costs in collective decisions can prevent collective action in instances where such action would be efficient in the absence of decision-making costs.[12] The higher the degree of consensus that is required to undertake collective action, the higher will be the decision-making costs, which will cause fewer collective activities to be undertaken when more consensus is required than when less is required.

The acceptance of the threat of greater costs due to collective action does allow lower decision-making costs, but the real reason for accepting the possibility of bearing greater costs of collective action is not to have lower decision-making costs per se but rather to have a broader scope of collective action, which can be undertaken more efficiently because of reduced decision-making costs. The primary dimension in which the trade-off is being made, then, is the dimension between the degree of consensus in collective decision making and the scope of collective action.

There may be differences among nations regarding their perceptions of the net benefits from accepting higher external costs to expand the scope of their governments, and there may be differences in the same nation at different times, as the wartime example suggests. The more consensus a group demands in its collective decision-making procedures, the more limited will be the group's ability to engage in collective action. Conversely, the more the citizens of a state want to further national goals through collective action, the less consensus it will be able to demand in its collective decision-making process.

The Meaning of Consensus

In the framework of contemporary democracy, consensus might be viewed narrowly as the number of people required to agree when making specific types of collective decision rules. Sometimes simple majority rule is used, other times a two-thirds majority is required, and in other cases group action can only proceed if there is unanimous agreement. This depicts only the end of what may be a lengthy political bargaining process. Group decisions can also be made by logrolling, or political exchange, where agreement can be forged by trading off various aspects of a collective decision to reach agreement. Under a simple majority rule, logrolling is prevalent, but there is no reason for supporters of particular measures to continue logrolling for additional support after they have the support of a majority. The requirement that only a majority needs to agree may lead to an inefficient allocation of resources, even if everybody does agree,[13] but it lowers decision-making costs and enables the group to undertake more collective action.

If a two-thirds majority rather than a simple majority were required, logrolling would have to continue until two-thirds supported the proposal in question. This would eliminate some inefficient proposals that would impose substantial costs on the minority but also would eliminate some proposals that would produce net benefits for the group in the absence of decision-making costs, because the decision-making costs involved in putting together a coalition composed of two-thirds of the group would be too high. If unanimity were required, logrolling would have to extend even further until everyone agreed. This would guarantee the efficiency of all proposals that were passed by eliminating external costs, but because of higher decision-making costs, unanimity rule would reduce the scope of collective action even further.

In the collective decision-making setting, consensus might be viewed as a unanimous decision-making rule, but to capture all of the institutional detail the analysis must also take into account the logrolling and bargaining that lead up to the production of a proposal that can be accepted by everybody in the group. Achieving consensus is not just unanimous approval in a vote but rather is a negotiating process that leads up to a consensus among group members. The process entails more than just adjusting the voting rule; it entails an institutional process that can produce a proposal that will meet with everyone's approval. Majority rule encourages the formation of coalitions in which the majority creates benefits for itself, perhaps at the expense of the minority.[14] Unanimity encourages more inclusive institutions in which everyone must feel, first, that the group's goal really is in the collective interest and, second, that some people are not being exploited to further those collective goals.

As the degree of required agreement changes, the types of institutions that will minimize collective decision-making costs will change also, so many institutional changes will accompany changes in the degree to which consensus is required for collective action. It is not simply a matter of changing the voting rule. If less consensus is required, political institutions designed to build consensus are less necessary. This suggests why, as more consensus is required to undertake collective action, the optimal scope of collective action falls. Furthermore, it shows that changes in the degree of consensus required for collective decisions will be accompanied by other institutional changes, because the institutions that are optimal for producing agreement under one rule will be different from those that would be optimal under a different rule.

This abstract discussion of principles of constitutional theory can help to clarify the changes that took place in the evolution of constitutional rules in colonial America. A good example of the idea of consensus in collective decision making is found in the Iroquois constitution that governed the native population at the time the American colonists arrived from Europe.

The Iroquois Constitution

The Iroquois were a confederation of five native American nations[15] established between 1000 and 1400 A.D.[16] During colonial times they were the dominant power east of the Mississippi and significantly outnumbered the colonial population. The Iroquois were united by a constitution that contains many features familiar to contemporary American government, including a federal system with substantial sovereignty and independence among the five nations, a common military defense, and a collective decision-making process that allowed all of the nations to work together to produce unified policies in foreign affairs that were carried out by the central government. The collective decision-making process of the Iroquois is of particular interest within the context of the evolution of U.S. constitutional history.

The Iroquois constitution was not a written document. Its principles were passed orally from generation to generation. Knowledge of the constitution was preserved on wampum belts and strings, which represented certain laws and regulations. Knowledge of specific provisions was passed along by instructing individuals about the details of the provisions represented by each wampum. While seemingly primitive, there is a similarity between this type of law and modern common law, which is not stated directly but passed along through the particular decisions in each case, allowing the law to evolve.[17] More significant, there is also a similarity to modern constitutional law, to the extent that the actual constitution is not so much what the U.S. Constitution literally says but rather what the Supreme Court has decided in specific cases. The articles and amendments of the Constitution are equivalent to the wampum, in that they provide a reminder about the meanings of various constitutional provisions, but the actual meaning in a particular circumstance might change as the Supreme Court modifies its opinion on issues or as the Iroquois oral tradition slowly changes over time. In either case, this allows the constitution to evolve gradually, while maintaining long-standing constitutional principles.

In the case of the U.S. Constitution, the actual document provides only the vaguest guidance to contemporary constitutional rules. To understand the rights and duties implied by constitutional law, one must look at Supreme Court decisions, not the original document.[18] Just as U.S. constitutional rules have evolved over time yet are constrained by the precedent of previous decisions, the wampum of the Iroquois representing constitutional rules would serve the same function. Each generation might interpret a wampum slightly differently yet always within the context of the well-known constitutional tradition represented by the wampum. The wampum belts anchored the Iroquois constitution in the same way that the Constitution of the United States provides an anchor for contemporary U.S. constitutional rules. Even though the Iroquois constitution was oral, it nevertheless contained clearly defined constitutional rules and a collective decision-making process that in many ways is the epitome of the normative aspects of contemporary constitutional economics.[19]

One of the normative principles implied in modern constitutional economics is that of equality. Using unanimity as a benchmark, all individuals are equally empowered in the ideal political decision-making process, because when unanimity is required every individual has veto power over any decision.[20] Cadwallader Colden, a firsthand observer of the Iroquois, wrote in 1727 that "The Five Nations have such absolute Notions of Liberty that they allow no kind of Superiority of one over another, and banish all Servitude from their Territories."[21] In modern democracy this type of political equality is taken for granted, at least as an ideal, but it is very different from the hierarchical political structure that existed in eighteenth-century Europe. Yet while the European governments from which they came were very hierarchical, the colonists did not have to imagine a political system of equality. They could imitate the example of the Iroquois.[22]

Unanimity: The Iroquois Example

Using modern governments as a frame of reference, the use of unanimity to make collective decisions might seem like an unrealistic abstraction. As the previous discussion suggests, unanimity must be thought of not just as a voting rule in which everyone is required to agree but rather as a political bargaining process that is designed to build a consensus. This section discusses the collective decision-making procedures of the Iroquois nation in the 1700s to give an idea of how unanimity might actually be used to arrive at collective decisions.[23]

The Great Council of the Iroquois Confederacy was the Iroquois legislature and consisted of 50 tribal chiefs.[24] There were two types of chiefs in the Iroquois: civil chiefs (called sachems) and war chiefs. The war chiefs, as leaders in battle, are not considered in this section.[25] The civil chiefs acted not so much as contemporary legislators but rather as spokesmen for the councils of their own tribes. While the legislature might make some decisions on its own, important decisions were always taken back to the tribal councils to be decided. Thus, the collective decision-making process began with individual tribes and their chiefs. The concept of considering some individuals to be chiefs was a projection of the European hierarchical form of government onto the Iroquois. Iroquois chiefs were not rulers in the same sense as European kings but were more like chairmen who facilitated the creation of consensus and acted as spokesmen for their councils. As Daniel Richter notes, "despite differences in status and ceremonial roles among their members, councils functioned as bodies of equals."[26]

Within the individual tribes, collective decision making was a slow process that involved arriving at a consensus. A meeting would be held and issues discussed until it could be agreed among individuals that the group did have a consensus opinion.[27] This consensus opinion would then be taken to the legislature by the chief, who acted as a spokesman for the tribe's views rather than as a legislator with his own views. The chiefs, who were always men, were chosen by the women of the tribe. They served for indefinite terms but could be replaced if there was a consensus that they were not representing the group.[28] Thus, representatives had to carry out the views of those they represented, or they would be replaced.

The general principle at work in Iroquois collective decision making was consensus, not democracy. The group would discuss issues at length until a consensus emerged, which would both foster logrolling to help arrive at an optimal decision and provide the chief with not only a final outcome but a deeper understanding of the issues. Thus, the chief would be prepared to effectively represent his tribe at the legislature. In this collective decision-making process, the chief was not like a head of state who had the power to decide what he thought was best but rather was a spokesman for the group he represented who had the power only to convey to the other members of the Great Council the decisions of the group he represented and to agree to actions that were in accordance with the decisions of his tribe. If an issue or alternative came up that the chief's tribe had not discussed, the chief was not in a position to do what he thought was best for his group; rather, he would have to go back to the group to find out their opinion before taking action.[29] Following the logic of modern constitutional theory, the resulting decisions would be more likely to fairly represent everyone's opinion and would minimize the possibility that a majority could exploit the minority through the collective decision-making process.

The legislature itself was divided into three deliberative bodies based on tribal membership.[30] The three groups discussed issues separately and then compared deliberations to see if a consensus had been reached among the three groups. For any decision to be made, there had to be unanimous approval of the three groups. If there was not unanimity, the groups would meet individually again to try to work out a consensus. Within the process there was no leader. Rather, temporary spokesmen would be appointed to report the groups' conclusions. Within the framework of the constitutional theory discussed earlier in the chapter, requiring consensus like this would seem to place very high importance on potential costs imposed by collective action relative to decision-making costs. That is, the Iroquois were willing to expend great effort to reach a consensus to avoid making a decision that went against the best interests of a part of the group.

One effect of this type of decision-making process is that it would tend to preserve the status quo when compared to a simple majority rule system. When it is more difficult to make collective decisions, it is less likely that the collectivity will decide to do something that will change present conditions. Another effect is that decisions would be made slowly, because, unlike European kings, Iroquois chiefs could not decide matters as individuals but always had to take the issues back to their people. This type of decision making, however, does provide powerful protection to minorities from political exploitation and created an Iroquois society of relative freedom and equality—two goals of interest to the colonists.[31] The colonists were familiar with the Iroquois and their government, and features of the Iroquois constitution found their way into the U.S. Constitution.

Implications of Government by Consensus

The colonists saw the Iroquois government as a slow and cumbersome process for making decisions, and indeed it was when compared to taking a vote and going with majority opinion or to allowing a representative to make a decision on behalf of the group. As noted earlier, when the degree of consensus in collective decision making changes, other institutions must also change to be able to create consensus. In dealing with the colonies, the colonists would complain that the Iroquois chiefs could never come to a decision but rather always had to go back to consult their people. By requiring a consensus, the Iroquois minimized the costs that their collective decisions could impose on the group, but because of high decision-making costs the consensus requirement made collective action more difficult and therefore less likely. The Iroquois requirement of consensus also tended to preserve the status quo when compared to a simple majority rule system and slowed down the collective decision-making process. The Iroquois were willing to expend great effort to reach a consensus to avoid making a decision that went against the best interests of a part of the group.

Seen as an example of an implementation of a unanimous collective decision rule, unanimity in Iroquois society is not just a decision rule but rather an institutional process that fosters agreement. Not only is the level of agreement different in political systems that are based on majority rule compared to those based on consensus, but political institutions must also be different to arrive at a broader degree of agreement. Because decision-making costs are high, decisions are slow to be made and the scope of government is necessarily limited. As a government, the Iroquois did little and had relatively little power when compared to the European governments of the time.

Looked at from the European point of view, the Iroquois government was hampered by its cumbersome collective decision-making process that relied heavily on consensus. Looked at from an Iroquois point of view, the heavy decision-making costs associated with the requirement of consensus limited the scope of government to allow a high degree of political freedom and equality. The Iroquois government provides an example of government designed to run on consensus, minimizing the costs that government can impose on its citizens. In the framework of modern constitutional theory, decision-making costs are high, which necessarily limits the scope of government.

The European Alternative

In the 1700s the colonies, moving toward self-government, had the Iroquois government to use as an example of a federal system of government with limited power that preserved freedom and political equality for its citizens and that limited the costs imposed on citizens by collective action by relying on consensus for approval of collective action. At the same time the colonists, largely of British descent, had Europe to look toward for examples of limited government. European governments were organized very differently from the Iroquois government. They were monarchies, and the chain of decision making tended to be from the top down rather than from the bottom up, as in the case of the Iroquois. Among European governments, Britain clearly provided the best model for limiting the power of government in America, notwithstanding that it was the oppression of the British government against which the colonies revolted.

The most significant political idea to come from the British model of government was the idea of separation of powers and the use of checks and balances in government to control government power. Although Britain was a monarchy, the powers of the crown had been continuously eroding since the signing of the Magna Carta in 1215, and by the 1700s Parliament gave representation to nobility through the House of Lords and to the rest of the population through the House of Commons, creating a balance of power in which the three groups (royalty, nobility, and commoners) each checked the others. The creation of an independent judiciary further assured the freedom of the government's citizens by placing another check on the arbitrary expansion of government power.[32]

Europe was also the origin of the ideas that pushed Americans toward revolution. Chapter 1 described the influence of John Locke as well as a large number of pamphleteers who championed the principles of liberty in the colonies, further justifying an American revolution to free the colonies from British rule. But while writers both in Europe and America persuaded the colonists that they were entitled to be free of British rule, and demonstrated the value of a limited government that would protect and guarantee the rights of its citizens, those writers did not lay out a blueprint for government. They were influential beyond measure in promoting American independence, but their influence stopped short of producing a design for American government. Thus, the British example was more influential over the design of American government than were those European writers who pushed the concepts of liberty.

In matters of constitutional design, then, as opposed to constitutional philosophy, the American founders had two distinct examples from which they could draw. One was the hierarchical system of European government, in which people were divided into classes with differing interests and differing abilities to influence government. Among these hierarchical governments, Britain provided the best model because of its system of checks and balances that limited the powers of the crown and provided substantial representation to the common citizens. The other alternative was the Iroquois system, based on consensus, which led to relative political equality and minimized the external costs of collective decision making. The founders took some elements from each model to create a new constitution.

The Albany Plan of Union

The Constitution of the United States was not produced de novo from the Constitutional Convention in 1787 but rather evolved from earlier constitutional agreements. After declaring independence, the nation was governed by the Articles of Confederation, but prior to that the Albany Plan of Union had been drawn up in 1754. The Albany Plan of Union was a document intended to unite the colonies. It was drawn up and approved by the Albany Congress, which met in Albany, New York, but was never ratified by the colonial legislatures, so it never took effect. It was, nevertheless, an important precursor to the subsequent constitutions that did take effect, and understanding the provisions of the Albany Plan of Union sheds some light on subsequent American constitutional development.

The Albany Plan of Union was affected in at least two important ways by the Iroquois. First, the Iroquois believed that they would benefit from encouraging the colonies to unite. One complaint the Iroquois had voiced strongly in a 1744 treaty was that they had to deal with many separate colonial governments. The Iroquois believed that the colonies could form a confederation, just as the Iroquois had, to facilitate negotiation between the two groups. Because he published the treaty, Benjamin Franklin was well aware of the Iroquois desire for a union among the colonies similar to the Iroquois confederacy. In 1751 Franklin asserted, "It would be a very strange thing if Six Nations of Ignorant Savages should be capable of forming a Scheme for such an Union and be able to execute it in such a manner, as that it has subsisted Ages, and appears indissoluble, and yet a like Union should be impracticable for ten or a dozen English colonies."[33] Franklin further argued that the English colonies should find it in their interest to form an alliance with the Iroquois, partly in the interest of mutual peace but also partly because of the threat of French colonists. In disputes between French and British colonists, both sides felt that it was a major advantage to have the Iroquois on their side.[34]

The Iroquois influenced the Albany Plan of Union, first, because of their encouragement for the union and, second, because their union provided a model for a union among independent states. Franklin undoubtedly was the most influential of the delegates to the Albany Congress. In his role as publisher of documents related to the Iroquois, he was familiar with Iroquois government, and he was also an advocate for the creation of a confederation among the colonies similar to that of the Iroquois. Iroquois influence went deeper than Franklin's presence at the Albany Congress, however. For one thing, several Iroquois were in attendance at the congress. While there, James de Lancy, acting governor of New York, expressed to them that he hoped an agreement could come out of the congress that would make the union of states as powerful and prominent as the Iroquois union.[35] The Iroquois influence at the Albany Congress was substantial.[36]

The Constitutional Structure of the Albany Plan of Union

The resulting Albany Plan of Union was similar to the Iroquois constitution in many ways.[37] The individual colonies would retain their own constitutions and their own individual sovereignty under the plan. Because they were colonial governments, the plan would be administered by a president general appointed by the British crown but would be governed by a Grand Council. The members of the council would choose their own speaker. States were represented in the Grand Council roughly in proportion to their populations, but each state (rather than each representative) had one vote. The Grand Council amounted to a unicameral legislature, but a rule of unanimity would be used to allow any colony to veto any action. Thus, all colonies had to be in agreement before the union could take action.

There was only one branch of government in the Albany Plan of Union, which oversaw all of the government's activities. The power of the union government would be checked by the power of the states to select their delegates and by the Grand Council's unanimity decision rule. The Albany Plan of Union gave the Grand Council the power to raise an army and navy and to build forts, and it gave the president general, with the advice of the Grand Council, the exclusive right to make treaties with the native population and to declare peace and war with them.

The two most notable similarities between the Iroquois government and the government proposed in the Albany Plan of Union are the federal system of government and the reliance on a rule of unanimity in a unicameral legislature. The unanimity requirement in the Albany Plan of Union was weaker than that in the Iroquois constitution, because while the Grand Council would be chosen by the colonial governments it would not be accountable to them to the same degree as the Iroquois chiefs were accountable to their people. If all of the state delegations agreed, then the Grand Council could take action. This would allow the union government more autonomy, so it would not be as hampered by high decision-making costs as would be the Iroquois. By reducing decision-making costs in this way, the union government would be able to broaden its scope and power beyond those of the Iroquois.

The Albany Congress approved the Albany Plan of Union, but when it was sent to the colonial legislatures it failed to win their approval. As a practical matter, the colonies never were governed by the Albany Plan of Union, but it is a significant and underrated part of America's constitutional history because it was the first attempt to form a union among the colonies. As such, it is interesting to note how much the collective decision making of the states united under the Albany Plan of Union would have been based on consensus, as opposed to the majoritarian-democratic decision making that was being used in Britain and that eventually supplanted consensus in the United States.

The Articles of Confederation and the U.S. Constitution

Chapter 4 discusses the Articles of Confederation and the Constitution in more detail, so this section confines its attention to considering the concepts of consent and democracy as American constitutional history moved from the Albany Plan of Union to the Articles of Confederation to the Constitution of the United States. After declaring independence, the United States wrote their first constitution, the Articles of Confederation, which was approved in 1781.[38] There are many similarities between the Articles of Confederation and the Albany Plan of Union, making the Albany Plan of Union an integral part of U.S. constitutional history. There is a clear chain of constitutional evolution from the Albany Plan of Union to the Articles of Confederation to the Constitution of the United States.

Like the Albany Plan of Union, the Articles of Confederation created a unicameral legislature and had no provision for executive or judicial branches of government. Each state had one vote in the legislature under the Articles, as they did under the Albany Plan of Union, and many decisions required a supermajority approval for passage. Amendment of the Articles required unanimous approval by the states. In overall structure, the U.S. government under the Articles was similar to what would have been in effect under the Albany Plan of Union and was very different from the European governments of the time.

A major difference between the Articles and the Albany Plan of Union from the standpoint of constitutional theory was the reduction in the degree of consensus required for collective decision making under the Articles of Confederation. Whereas the Albany Plan of Union always required the consent of all of the state delegations (which, in itself, was weaker than the kind of consensus the Iroquois required), the Articles required unanimous consent only for amendments. As noted earlier, there is a trade-off in which the potential for higher costs imposed by government action might be accepted in exchange for a government with more expansive powers, and the Articles of Confederation were approved by states intent on becoming independent from their colonial master through military means. This kind of national crisis is the type of event that would be likely to convince citizens to accept higher costs from government action in order to give themselves a government that could undertake more substantial collective action.[39]

Under the Articles, representatives to the federal legislature were chosen by the state legislatures and could be recalled at any time by their state legislatures. This ensured that representatives would truly represent the views of their constituents, for if they did not they would be recalled. An additional factor reinforcing the representativeness of the federal legislature was that states each got one vote, even though the state delegation consisted of many legislators. This required some type of agreement among the state's representatives and prevented representatives who wanted to be unrepresentative from being able to do so. These institutions that make representatives more closely represent the views of their constituents create more consensus regardless of the voting rule used in the congress. One way to create more consensus is to have a more inclusive voting rule, but these examples show that the level of consensus in political decision making is affected by more than just the voting rule.

The Articles of Confederation created a government much like the one that would have existed under the Albany Plan of Union. Its reliance on consensus for decision making, its unicameral legislature, and the fundamental federal system itself were derived from the Albany Plan of Union, which in turn was similar to the type of government the Iroquois had. Despite the similarities, each of these constitutions relied less on the principle of consensus than the one before it, creating governments with a greater potential scope of action but with a greater potential to impose costs on their citizens through collective action. The principles behind American government moved away from consensus toward democracy, even in the nation's earliest years.

The Constitution of the United States

The Articles of Confederation did not last long as the U.S. constitution. A convention was called for the purpose of amending the Articles of Confederation in 1787, and the result was the Constitution of the United States, which was ratified in 1788.[40] All of the changes that resulted from adopting the Constitution in place of the Articles were designed to make the U.S. government more autonomous and less accountable to its citizens. The Constitution was purposefully designed to increase the power of the federal government, accepting the trade-off that created more opportunities for the imposition of external costs on its citizens. The basic federal system remained, but even that began eroding early in the nation's history as the federal government enhanced its power over the states. When compared to the Articles of Confederation, the U.S. Constitution gives the federal government more power and subjects it to fewer constraints.

A fundamental normative principle of collective decision making in constitutional theory is consensus, and this principle was carried through the government of the Iroquois, the Albany Plan of Union, and the Articles of Confederation to a substantial degree, although it was weakened at every step. The Constitution of the United States, however, deviates significantly from the principle of consensus to favor the principle of democracy. The decision rule of unanimity, which was a part of the Albany Plan of Union drawn up just 35 years before the Constitution was written, was abandoned and replaced by the majority voting rule. As noted, a unanimity voting rule is only a small part of government by consensus. When consensus is required, political institutions will be designed in such a way as to foster agreement. Other changes in the Constitution also reflect this move away from consensus. The next chapter discusses in more detail the substantial changes that were the result of the adoption of the U.S. Constitution.

Constitutional Theory and the Evolution of Colonial American Government

Modern contractarians such as Buchanan and Rawls[41] place heavy emphasis on consensus in decision making, as opposed to the unrestricted use of majoritarian democracy. The Iroquois constitution, with its heavy reliance on consensus at all levels of decision making, comes close to the constitutional ideal as described in the modern literature on constitutional economics and so provides a historical example to show that unanimity, so desirable in theory, can also be applied in practice. As the American constitution evolved, it moved further from the constitutional principle of consensus in collective decision making. That movement is best understood as a way to reduce decision-making costs in order to expand the scope of government. These changes might have been adopted to make government more effective but might also have been adopted to further the interests of those who were rewriting the rules.[42]

The American Revolution was founded on the concept of freeing citizens from the powers of government. Eighteenth-century Americans clearly recognized that the majority in a democratic government could be just as tyrannical as any dictator and sought to protect themselves from all types of government power. Liberty quite simply meant freedom from the oppression of government. In the Albany Plan of Union, this freedom would have been achieved by collective decision making through consensus, but as the American constitution evolved through the Articles of Confederation to the Constitution of the United States, reliance on consensus was progressively replaced by democratic decision making and protection from government oppression was to be designed by a system of checks and balances within the government itself. But, as the following chapter suggests, this opened the door for increasing government power and increasing erosion of liberty, as it was understood by colonial Americans.

The Iroquois government provides a historical example to show that it was possible to use the principle of unanimity as the standard collective decision-making rule in a real-world government. As the American constitutions evolved, they relied less on consensus and more on majoritarian democracy. Certainly there are differences between modern governments and the colonial American governments of centuries ago, and it may well be true that these constitutional principles of consensus could not be applied effectively to governments with the scope and power of modern governments. To implement these principles, we would have to be willing to accept a government that is smaller in scope, that has less power over its citizens, that takes greater account of the views of minorities, that distributes political power more equally, and that would be less able to undertake initiatives without a genuine consensus of its citizens. If we were able to tolerate these things, then the colonial period of American constitutional history could be viewed as relevant to the evolution of current political institutions rather than as just an interesting episode in history.

CHAPTER 4

Constitutions as Constraints: The Articles of Confederation and the Constitution of the United States

The American colonies united in 1776 to escape the oppression of the British government, and its founders were keenly aware of the potential for the newly formed U.S. government to oppress them in the same way as the British government had. Their solution was to try to design a constitution that would protect the rights of citizens but would constrain the government's power. The requirement of a consensus of opinion in collective decision making can provide a substantial constraint on government, but as argued in chapter 3, a requirement of consensus also severely limits the scope of government action because the collective decision-making costs are so high. To allow a broader scope of action, the new government was designed to be able to undertake certain actions without the direct consent of its citizens, but the scope of allowable government action was limited by constitutional constraints. The concept of constitutionally limited government, now familiar, was an innovation in the eighteenth century. The powers of government were limited only to those enumerated in the Constitution, and to act the government had to follow those procedures the Constitution prescribed. Embodying the new American philosophy, the role of a constitution was to guarantee the rights of individuals and to limit the powers of government.

The challenge of constitutional design is to construct a constitution that allows those in government enough flexibility and discretion to engage in activities that serve the public interest while at the same time constraining them from engaging in activities that are inefficient or that serve no purpose other than to transfer resources from those outside government to those within. Surely legislation is the most significant area in which government discretion is used, because through legislation the government can change the rules under which it operates. A constitution can constrain the government's discretion over legislation in two ways. First, it can enumerate the types of legislation in which the government can engage or can prohibit certain types of legislation. Second, it can design a system of accountability whereby legislators can be controlled by citizens or by other parts of the government. The Constitution of the United States uses both types of constraints.

A related issue is that constitutional rules must be enforced to be effective. A system of checks and balances within different branches of government has served this role in the United States, but only imperfectly. Over time the interpretation of the Constitution has changed substantially, and indeed that has been an important part of the story of the transformation of American government, especially in the twentieth century.[1] However, the evolution of American democracy was not substantially affected by questions regarding the enforcement of constitutional provisions until the War between the States, so enforcement issues will not be considered in this chapter. Rather, this chapter will focus on the challenge of designing constitutional rules that can effectively constrain the powers of government.

The design of the U.S. government illustrates the challenge of designing effective constraints into a constitution. The Articles of Confederation contained the general types of constraints that would be advocated by the contemporary theory of constitutional economics. They required the unanimous approval of the states (but not of every individual) to be adopted and required the same unanimous approval to be amended. Thus, the importance of consensus was recognized, at least in principle. It enumerated the allowable activities of government and prohibited any activities not specifically enumerated. It limited the federal government's ability to raise revenue and was designed so that the federal government's activities were very accountable to the states. Recognizing the dangers of government power and attempting to preserve the liberty of its citizens, the Articles of Confederation were designed to be an effective constraint on the powers of the federal government.

Within a few years many influential Americans felt that the Articles were too constraining on the new government, and they were replaced by the Constitution of the United States. When viewed in isolation, the Constitution is rightly seen as a document that constrains government. But when compared with the Articles of Confederation, the Constitution is clearly less constraining. The net effect of replacing the Articles with the Constitution was to reduce the constraints on the U.S. government. This chapter compares the Articles of Confederation and the Constitution of the United States to show what types of constraints were built into the Articles, why the Articles were more constraining than the Constitution, and why the Founding Fathers wanted to rewrite the original constitution to allow the federal government to operate in a less constrained environment.

Government under the Articles of Confederation

The Articles of Confederation were submitted to the states for their approval in 1777 and were finally ratified by all 13 states in 1781. Because each state already had its own government, the Articles essentially provided for the common defense of the United States, for the citizens of each state to be accorded free movement of themselves and their property among the states, and for the states to provide the same rights to the citizens of any state. Furthermore, the Articles tried to establish a framework for a peaceful interrelationship among the states and gave most powers for military operations and international affairs to the government of the United States.

By giving most military and diplomatic powers to the federal government, the Articles created a single unified government with which other nations would deal. But the Articles severely limited the power of the new government. The U.S. government had no direct power over its citizens; it interacted with them indirectly through their states. Rather than directly raising an army, Congress directed the states to do so. Congress also had no direct power to levy taxes. Article VIII of the Articles of Confederation gave Congress the ability to requisition funds from the states in proportion to the value of property in the state, but Congress was required to get its funding from the states and could not levy taxes directly.

After the Revolutionary War ended in 1782, the effective power of the U.S. government began to wane. A major motivation for forming the government initially was to fight for independence, but with that matter settled the U.S. government was not as important to its citizens as it had been. Indeed, when a similar attempt to unify the states in 1754 produced the Albany Plan of Union, it was rejected by the states. Once the states had gained their independence after the American Revolution, there is little reason to believe that they would desire unification any more than they had back in 1754.[2] With waning interest in the union, the U.S. government was having trouble raising the revenues to pay off its war debts. Approval of nine states was required to requisition revenues from the states. Getting approval was often difficult, and even if requisitions were approved states were often delinquent in making payment. It was the responsibility of the states to levy taxes and forward revenues to the United States, because the Articles gave Congress no power to levy taxes directly. Under the Articles, the government of the United States did not deal with its citizens but rather interacted with them indirectly through their state legislatures.[3]

The conventional wisdom about the Articles of Confederation is that it was flawed by several weaknesses. It was inadequate in areas of international commerce, and commercial interests were concerned about the possibility of additional taxation or regulation of trade by the states. It provided inadequate means for the United States to raise revenue because its revenue had to come from taxpayers through their state governments.[4] There was also concern about the degree to which the Articles provided for the security of the states, because Congress had little authority to raise an army on its own. This would be particularly true if quarrels erupted between states.[5] Finally, the Articles were difficult to amend because amendment required the approval of all states. Essentially, many believed the Articles were flawed because they constrained the federal government too much and in too many ways. However, another view is that the Articles were drafted to provide a common face in international affairs, to provide for collective defense during times of war, and to serve as a treaty to provide peaceful coexistence among the states as they already existed. In this context, severe limits make sense, much as they do with groups such as the United Nations, the European Union, and the North Atlantic Treaty Organization (NATO).

The context under which the Articles were replaced must make one cautious of the conclusion that the Articles were flawed or that they somehow failed as an acceptable constitution. They were replaced by the Constitution of the United States, but not without considerable debate and controversy; of course those who favored the new document were quick to point out the failures of the old one. Thus, the argument that the Articles were somehow inadequate was the explanation for why the new Constitution was needed. This explanation served as propaganda for supporting the new Constitution, but that the new Constitution won out over the old in the political arena does not necessarily make the propaganda that supported it true.[6] Regardless of how government under the Articles was viewed, surely experience would have exposed defects in the original agreement. In this context, a convention was called to try to amend the Articles in such a way as to secure the unanimous agreement that was required for amendment.

The Constitutional Convention

The Constitutional Convention can only be called such with the benefit of hindsight, because at the time the convention was called, its express purpose was not to write a new constitution but to amend the Articles of Confederation. The act of Congress calling for the convention states, "it is expedient that . . . a Convention of delegates . . . be held . . . for the sole and express purpose of revising the Articles of Confederation."[7] For this reason, some delegates to the convention felt that the group was overstepping its authority by drafting an entirely new document. Furthermore, the convention was shrouded in secrecy, such that nobody but the delegates knew what was taking place, beyond the fact that a convention was meeting to propose revisions to the Articles of Confederation.

The idea of replacing the Articles with a new constitution, brought to the convention by Governor Edmund Randolph of Virginia, was known as the Virginia plan. William Paterson of New Jersey proposed an alternative plan to revise the Articles substantially without completely abandoning them, which became known as the New Jersey plan. Some proponents of the New Jersey plan favored it because they felt that the Virginia plan went beyond the authority of the convention; others opposed the Virginia plan more directly because they were afraid that the Virginia plan would reduce—or even abolish altogether—the independent authority of the states.[8] While this concern is evident from the 10th Amendment to the Constitution, it is important to note that Article II of the Articles of Confederation closely parallels the 10th Amendment by affirming that powers not expressly given to the U.S. government remain with the states.

The New Jersey plan would have given Congress the power to levy taxes on imports directly, to regulate trade and commerce, to establish a U.S. judiciary to which state court decisions could be appealed, to modify the nine-thirteenths rule for requisitioning the states (the replacement rule was not specified), to establish an executive branch of government, as well as other provisions.[9] However, the New Jersey plan's underlying philosophy was to retain a confederation of states, whereas the underlying philosophy of the Virginia plan was to establish a national government.

The New Jersey plan would have retained the unicameral legislature in the Articles, whereas the Virginia plan specified a bicameral legislature. The Virginia plan specified representation in proportion to a state's population in both houses but would have selected one by popular vote while the other would have been chosen by state legislatures. The latter provision was retained in the U.S. Constitution, but a compromise was worked out between the small and large states on the matter of representation. Under the Articles, each state had the same power because each state, as opposed to each representative, was given a vote under the Articles. As a compromise, the Senate, under the Constitution, retained this representation by giving each state the same number of senators, and the House of Representatives was apportioned in proportion to population.[10]

The history of the drafting of the Constitution is well enough documented that there is no need to go into more detail here. This section establishes the points that (1) the Constitutional Convention was not called for the purpose of drafting a new constitution and (2) there was a clear alternative to the new Constitution in the form of the New Jersey plan, which proposed revising the Articles. Thus, there was no reason for the Constitutional Convention to produce a new constitution except that those in attendance preferred the new Constitution to an amended Articles of Confederation.[11] As a matter of underlying philosophy, retaining the Articles would have retained a federal government as a federation of states, whereas adopting the Constitution meant establishing a national government with powers greater than the states. Those who favored the new Constitution did so because they felt that the Articles of Confederation were too constraining on the federal government.

The eventual adoption of the Virginia plan for the new Constitution greatly expanded the powers of the federal government, but it was not intended to create government by democracy. Indeed, Governor Randolph, the chief proponent of the Virginia plan, wanted to avoid government by democracy. At the Constitutional Convention, Randolph said, "Our chief danger arises from the democratic parts of our constitutions. It is a maxim which I hold incontrovertible, that the powers of government exercised by the people swallow up the other branches. None of the constitutions have provided sufficient checks to the democracy."[12] While the authors of the Constitution did deliberately increase the powers of the federal government, they just as deliberately tried to prevent the creation of a democratic government.

One of the most vocal critics of the Constitution on the grounds that it gave too much power to the federal government was George Mason, a delegate to the convention from Virginia and one of those who did not sign the Constitution. Mason is perhaps best known for championing the addition of a Bill of Rights to the Constitution, but his proposals for modifying the Constitution had more to do with limiting the powers and terms of officeholders in the federal government.[13]

The Interests of the Founding Fathers

Beyond a doubt, the Founding Fathers were public-spirited individuals who wanted to draft a constitution that would further the public interest. Just as surely, people tend to see the public interest filtered through their own lives and experiences, so the public interest, as viewed by the founders, would tend to be slanted toward the interests of people who found themselves in circumstances similar to those of the founders. This observation must be tempered by the fact that the document would have to be approved by the state legislatures to be ratified. Under the Articles of Confederation, unanimous approval of the states would have been required, although this requirement was circumvented in two ways by the new Constitution. First, the Constitution was written to take effect when only nine states had agreed to it, and, second, it was to be approved by conventions held in each state rather than by the state legislatures. Nevertheless, the process was designed so that the new document could not favor some states over others. Such favoritism could not receive approval at the convention, because there was a wide representation among the states, and also could not have mustered the approval needed for the document to become effective.

Representation at the Constitutional Convention was not that broad, however; while there was representation from all of the states, those at the convention were not a cross-section of the population. Rather, they were selected by the state legislatures, and most states had requirements of property ownership, wealth, and income to be a legislator.[14] Clearly the convention was manned by individuals chosen from among the wealthier citizens who had business and commercial interests and landholdings. Attendance at the convention meant that the representatives had to leave their work. Individuals who could afford to make this sacrifice had an incentive to see that the document they produced would protect their interests. The convention lasted from May 14 to September 17, 1787. It is difficult to imagine that farmers who worked their own land could give up an entire growing season to attend; property owners who employed others to work their land could more easily afford the time away.

Charles Beard proposed a theory along these lines early in the twentieth century.[15] The Constitution, he argued, was crafted to further the economic interests of those in commerce and banking, of landowners, and of creditors, including those who owned debt issued by the U.S. government. A more recent investigation by Robert McGuire and Robert Ohsfeldt supports Beard's hypothesis.[16] McGuire and Ohsfeldt, like Beard, recognize that the effect of the Constitution can only be analyzed by comparing it to its predecessor, the Articles of Confederation. Beard's thesis was controversial when it was introduced and remains so today, but it fits comfortably within a rational choice framework where people are assumed to act in their own interests.[17]

Beard does not accuse the Founding Fathers of creating a Constitution that furthers their interests at the expense of others[18] but rather of representing those interests they knew best from firsthand experience. Property owners were afraid of losing their property to those who had ideas of a more egalitarian redistribution of property. Commercial interests were concerned about the possibility of trade barriers. Banking interests were worried about the stability of the monetary system, about the ability of the government to raise revenue, and about the ability of the government to pay the debts it already had outstanding. They believed that the public interest would be served by a stronger central government with greater regulatory powers, with the power to independently raise revenue, with greater power to create legislation, with a more fully developed executive branch, and, perhaps most significant, with the power to act independently, without the approval of the states. These changes were embodied in the Constitution of the United States.

James Madison viewed the Constitution as a set of rules that were intended to regulate the economic interests of those governed by it, and there is no doubt that others at the Constitutional Convention saw that the Constitution could be a vehicle to protect their economic interests. In *The Federalist,* no. 10, Madison argued,

> The most common and durable source of factions has been the various and unequal distribution of property. Those who hold and

those who are without property have ever formed distinct interests in society. Those who are creditors, and those who are debtors, fall under like discrimination. A landed interest, a manufacturing interest, a mercantile interest, a moneyed interest, and many lesser interests, grow up of necessity in civilized nations and divide them into different classes, actuated by different sentiments and views. The regulation of these various and interfering interests forms the principal task of modern legislation, and involves the spirit of party and faction in the necessary and ordinary operations of the government.

This passage is significant in light of the political climate, in which there were a significant number of individuals who wanted to redistribute property, who wanted to tax exports, who wanted to abolish the slave trade, who would be content to renege on the U.S. government's debt, and who favored the easy creation of money to make it easier for debtors in general to pay their debts. Quite clearly, there were already factions in the United States, and the founders were in one faction that wanted to protect its status and wealth against another more populous faction. Against such threats, all of these economic interests came to be protected in the Constitution.

The Founding Fathers succeeded in writing a constitution that created a stronger central government with the power to protect their interests. The role of the economic interests of the Founding Fathers is controversial and has been debated extensively, but that the Constitution enhanced the power of the central government—and was intended to do so—is not in dispute. When viewed as a replacement for the Articles of Confederation, the Constitution cannot be seen as a document that limits the power of government but rather as a vehicle for relaxing constraints on the federal government, for creating greater government power, and for creating greater government growth. The following sections examine this issue more carefully by comparing the Articles of Confederation and the Constitution from the perspective of modern constitutional economics.

The Articles of Confederation and the Constitution: A Comparison

The Constitution of the United States is a document that was created out of an attempt to modify the Articles of Confederation. Therefore, the effects of ratifying the Constitution were the changes that the Constitution made over the status quo embodied in the Articles. The next several sections consider these changes with respect to the effects that they had on the scope and power of the federal government.

Five major areas of change will be considered: (1) the role of unanimity as a decision rule; (2) the role of state legislatures in the federal decision-making process; (3) taxation; (4) commerce; and (5) the organization and institutional structure of the federal government. A more extensive analysis might also include changes in military organization and the disposition of western lands.[19] The Constitution did transfer military power from the states to the U.S. government and did open the way for new states to be added to the United States. Furthermore, this list leaves out some of the economic issues that were mentioned earlier. For example, Article I, Section 10 of the Constitution prevents states from issuing money, which was in the interest of creditors rather than debtors. Individuals at the time understood that the issuance of paper money by the states would lower the value of debt. While it is clear that the scope of inquiry could be widened from the five issues listed, these issues were selected because they are directly relevant to the fundamental constitutional changes that paved the way for later changes that led to a more democratic nation.

Unanimity

In chapter 3, the fundamental importance of the principle of consensus in collective decision making was noted. Consensus means that everyone in the decision-making group sees the advantage of the group's actions, and the political decision rule that embodies consensus is the requirement of unanimous agreement. The prominence of the rule of unanimity in the contemporary analysis of constitutional rules is due to James Buchanan and Gordon Tullock, who note, "The individualistic theory of the constitution that we have been able to develop assigns a central role to a single decision-making rule—that of general consensus or unanimity. . . . In political discussion . . . many scholars seem to have overlooked the central place that the unanimity rule must occupy in any normative theory of democratic government."[20] Buchanan and Tullock go on to illustrate how less than unanimous decision rules might unanimously be chosen but stress the significance of unanimous approval of rules at the constitutional stage.[21] One of the main normative conclusions of constitutional economics is the desirability of unanimous approval for constitutional rules.[22]

Also as noted in chapter 3, the concept of consensus in collective decision making was the underlying principle in the government of the Iroquois who populated colonial America, and that principle carried over to a substantial degree in the Albany Plan of Union, which was drawn up in 1754 but never implemented. The requirement of consensus in collective decision making was weakened in the Articles of Confederation, but it was still there, and the Articles more closely conform to this criterion than does the Constitution of the United States. Thus, eighteenth-century constitutional history of the United States is a history of continual moves away from the requirement of consensus in collective decision making. In the Articles, unanimous approval of all state legislatures was required for the Articles to take effect, and amendment of the Articles required the unanimous consent of the states. Unanimous approval of the state legislatures is considerably less constraining than requiring unanimous agreement of all individuals. This is particularly true because, as noted earlier, state legislators were hardly representative of the general population of their states. However, the Constitution required approval of only nine states to become effective, and amendments require two-thirds approval from both houses of Congress and three-quarters approval from the states.

The elimination of the unanimity requirement when the Articles were replaced by the Constitution was no accident. One of the defects of the Articles, as perceived by its critics, was the difficulty with which the Articles could be amended. One might refer to Buchanan and Tullock's *The Calculus of Consent* to justify eliminating the unanimity requirement, noting that the less than unanimous rule for amendments had been agreed upon in the Constitutional Convention but was not agreed upon unanimously. This justification for weakening the unanimity rule falls short on two counts. First, the Articles required unanimous approval of the states to be amended, and because the Constitutional Convention was originally called to amend the Articles one might presume that unanimous agreement of the states would be required under the existing constitution to adopt its replacement. However, as just noted, a nine-thirteenths rule was written into the Constitution, in apparent violation of the existing and unanimously (at least by the states) agreed upon rule.[23] A unanimously agreed upon rule of unanimity was overturned by a nine-thirteenths majority!

A second problem with using the Buchanan and Tullock framework for justifying the approval of a less than unanimous rule is that there was not unanimous approval of the new Constitution in the Constitutional Convention. One state (Rhode Island) had nobody in attendance when the final document was ready for approval, and several individual delegates to the convention declined to sign. Interestingly, the significance of the unanimity rule is clearly recognized in the document, even though the exceptions just mentioned meant that the document did not receive unanimous approval. Because most members of every state delegation present signed, the Constitution reads, "Done in Convention by the Unanimous Consent of the States present." The aura of unanimity is there even though there was not actual unanimous approval, even of those at the convention.

In *The Federalist,* no. 40, Madison states

> In one particular it is admitted that the convention have departed from the tenor of their commission. Instead of reporting a plan requiring the confirmation *of the legislatures of all the States,* they have reported a plan which is to be confirmed by the *people,* and may be carried into effect by *nine States only.* It is worthy of remark that this objection, though the most plausible, has been the least urged in the publications which have swarmed against the convention. The forbearance can only have preceded from an irresistible conviction of the absurdity of subjecting the fate of twelve States to the perverseness or corruption of a thirteenth.

Thus Madison concedes that the most plausible objection to the Constitution has nothing to do with the government that would result from it but comes from the fact that procedurally it calls for an end run against the unanimity requirement in the existing constitution (the Articles) and that it violates the commission of the convention itself. Madison's only argument for violating both the charge given to the convention and the existing constitution is that it would be absurd to abide by those rules.[24] This seems an especially weak argument, because it could plausibly be used against the replacement rules contained in the Constitution.

Madison's argument in *The Federalist,* no. 40, against following the constitutionally mandated unanimity rule is meanwhile couched within a broader argument in support of unanimity. In *The Federalist,* no. 39, Madison stresses that the decision rule for ratification is not majority rule but "the *unanimous* assent of the several states that are parties to it." Article VII of the Constitution states that it will take effect over the states that have ratified it when nine states agree. Quite clearly Madison and the other founders recognized the importance of unanimity, so much so that they were willing to invoke the concept even when the principle of unanimity was clearly violated.[25]

The requirement of consensus is an important element in the preservation of liberty and has been recognized throughout the history of the United States. The principle was recognized prior to the Declaration of Independence and continues to retain an important place in the contemporary theory of constitutional economics. The Articles of Confederation more closely conformed to this criterion than did the Constitution of the United States. This is one way in which the constraints that were placed on the federal government were relaxed when the Constitution was adopted.

The Role of the States

One of the frequently cited virtues of the Constitution is its system of checks and balances. One branch of government always stands ready to check the abuse of power from another. This virtue finds support among contemporary writers in constitutional economics through the recommendation that rules be established to control the arbitrary exercise of power by those in government. Geoffrey Brennan and James Buchanan wrote *The Reason of Rules* to explain the role of such constraints within a framework of the theory of constitutions, building on the foundation of other twentieth-century writers, such as Friedrich Hayek, in his *The Constitution of Liberty,* and Bruno Leoni, in *Freedom and the Law.*[26] By checking one branch of government against another, the checks and balances in the Constitution constrain those in government to follow the constitutional rules rather than to act at their discretion.

The constitutional constraints in the Articles were much more effective as checks and balances because, rather than have the federal government checked by branches of itself, it was checked by the states. One important check, discussed in the next section, was that states controlled the flow of revenue into the U.S. government. Also under the Articles, state legislatures selected their state representatives to Congress rather than representatives being elected directly, which gave state governments direct control over Congress. Furthermore, the Articles gave states the power to recall and replace their delegates at any time. If a state legislature felt that its representatives in Congress were not representing the interests of the state, it could immediately replace them. The Articles attempted to guarantee that representatives in Congress could not act in a way that did not directly represent the wishes of the state legislatures. In promoting the virtues of the new

Constitution, *The Federalist,* no. 51, mentions the role of the states as additional checks on the power of the federal government but does not consider that the Constitution greatly limits the ability of the states to control the federal government when compared to the Articles.

When Congress was not in session, the Articles provided for the Committee of the States to oversee the administrative functions of the federal government. The committee was composed of one representative from each state, and such decisions as engaging in war, borrowing money, coining money, and appropriating money required the approval of nine members of the committee. The method of representation and the supermajority voting rule provided additional constraints on the federal government.

In general, the Articles created a federal government that reported to and was run by the state legislatures, whereas the Constitution replaced that government with a national government that had more power to act on its own.[27] Contemporary constitutional analysis sees virtue in constraining government to act within a well-defined body of rules. The Articles were more constraining than the Constitution that replaced them; indeed, a common argument for the benefits of the new Constitution was that it allowed the national government to be more independent of constraints. The Articles more effectively constrained the government to act through adherence to rules—and, in particular, rules of accountability—while the Constitution of the United States provides greater opportunity for government officials to act at their discretion.

Taxation

One of the big factors pushing the Founding Fathers to amend the Articles was that the U.S. government had no power to raise revenue directly but rather had to get it from the states. Because members of Congress were selected by and represented states rather than representing individuals directly, state legislatures indirectly determined the amount that the federal government would spend and the amount of revenue it would ask states to contribute, and state legislatures directly approved the payment to the federal government. The Articles specifically provided that states pay in proportion to the value of property in the state. One notable feature of this method of public finance is that it forces state governments to take account directly of the opportunity cost of federal government spending. Any money going into the federal treasury is money that is taken directly from state treasuries, which directly reduces the money that state legislatures have to spend themselves.

The modern theory of special interest spending by government relies on the notion of rational ignorance. Each taxpayer pays relatively little for each special interest project and therefore has little incentive to actively oppose it. Rationally ignorant taxpayers will not even be aware of most special interest projects or of how much they cost. Special interests who receive the concentrated benefits are well aware of them, however, so the projects receive much support from those who benefit but little opposition from those who pay.[28] This model of government suggests the possibility that government will overspend on special interest projects because the full opportunity cost of government spending is not considered in the decision to undertake the project. However, when state legislatures must give up funds that they otherwise could use for their own spending projects, states have an incentive to consider the opportunity cost of foregone state spending to finance federal programs.

Individuals have little chance of overturning spending legislation and would have little to gain individually even if they did. Each individual expenditure program takes only a little from each taxpayer, even though in the aggregate all expenditure programs can sum to a substantial amount. States, however, contributed large amounts of money under the Articles, making an obvious and direct trade-off between state spending programs and federal programs. The method of federal revenue collection under the Articles provided a much better method of weighing the opportunity cost of federal spending.[29]

One frequently cited problem with the Articles at the time was that under that method of federal revenue generation the federal government was chronically short of funds and had difficulty collecting from the states. One possible explanation is that state legislatures evaluated the benefits of federal spending and decided that their money would be better spent in their home states rather than on federal activities. Recall that the immediate motivation for forming the United States was to fight a war of independence, and once that war was over the importance of the federal government to the states declined. It is reasonable that states would want to contribute less to an institution that now provided less in collective benefits.

One alternative at that point would have been to modify the Articles in the other direction: to make them more of a treaty among states and dissolve the federal government or at least greatly weaken it. However, as noted earlier, many politically powerful individuals had an economic interest in retaining and strengthening the federal government. One of the most significant ways in which the powers of the federal government were enhanced by the adoption of the Constitution was that the federal government was given the power to directly tax its citizens rather than having to go to the states for revenue. Many of the Founding Fathers had loaned the federal government money to help finance the war and were bondholders concerned that their bonds would never be repaid because of the difficulty the U.S. government had in raising revenue. This difficulty was overcome by granting the federal government the power to tax.

William Riker discusses federalism "as a bargain between prospective national leaders and officials of constituent governments for the purpose of aggregating territory, the better to lay taxes and raise armies."[30] The raising of armies was obviously important to the formation of the nation for the purpose of fighting the Revolutionary War, but once the war was over the raising of taxes became a more significant issue. Allowing the federal government to levy taxes directly lessens revenue constraints on the government, making it easier to raise revenue, as Riker observes. From the perspective of modern constitutional economics, constraining the government's power to tax is an important function of constitutional rules.[31] The government should have the power to raise revenue only insofar as those who are taxed agree. In this area, the Articles were much more constraining than the U.S. Constitution. The Constitution gives the government much more power to raise revenue unilaterally without the direct approval of those who pay. Surely the activities of the U.S. government would be very different at the beginning of the twenty-first century if the current Constitution contained the federal revenue-raising provisions in the Articles.

Commerce

Charles Beard's economic interpretation of the Constitution clearly shows that commercial interests were heavily represented in the decision to replace the Articles with the Constitution. The Constitution's commerce clause gives the U.S. government virtually unlimited latitude to regulate commerce. However, Roger Pilon argues, this was not the founders' original intent. The commerce clause was intended to facilitate the free flow of commerce among the states, not create federal regulation that inhibits commerce.[32] But congressional regulation, supported by Supreme Court decisions, has continued to expand the scope of federal regulation of commerce in response to interest group pressures. In addition to the commerce clause, several other aspects of the Constitution relate to the commercial interests of the nation. Two issues of concern to different factions were the importation of slaves and the taxation of exports. The Constitution specifically prohibits taxes on exports and prohibits states from imposing duties on goods shipped from other states. The Constitution allowed the importation of slaves to continue until 1808.

Another fear of commercial interests was that states would create paper money, which would cause inflation and transfer wealth from creditors to debtors. The Constitution prevents states from doing so. This was clearly a special interest issue that constrained states by giving power to the federal government. Farmers as a group borrowed money to purchase their farms and favored easy money to facilitate repayment of loans. Lenders—the commercial interests represented at the Constitutional Convention—were on the other side. As noted, the Constitution favored the commercial over the farming interests. One can easily argue the merits of restraining the creation of money by the states. However, following the argument made by Beard, incorporating this provision into the Constitution was the result of the self-interests of the commercial interests at the Constitutional Convention as much as of a public interest perspective of the Founding Fathers.[33]

The Articles say little about commerce but, like the Constitution, leave powers not specifically given to the federal government to the states. The commerce clause in the Constitution gives broad powers to the federal government. In yet another area, the Constitution is clearly less constraining than the Articles.

Organization and Institutions

Most of the changes the Constitution makes over the Articles concern the organization of government. An almost unlimited amount could be written under this heading; indeed much of the study of government has involved analyzing how various institutional structures affect the outcomes of collective decision making. This section will mention a few of the most significant changes.

According to conventional wisdom, one of the great achievements of the Constitution was the creation of a system of checks and balances through the establishment of three branches of government. Under the Articles, there were no federal courts, so legal decisions—except when the dispute was between states—were made by state courts. The Articles did provide for a method of dispute resolution between states at the federal level. It must be clear to the contemporary observer that the creation of federal courts enhances the power of the federal government. With regard to the judicial system, the changes brought about by the Constitution enhance rather than limit the power of the federal government.

The Articles did not provide for a separate executive branch of government. All government activities were done under the direction of Congress. When Congress was not in session, the Committee of the States oversaw government business, but the committee was essentially an arm of Congress and had no independent power when Congress was in session. While the committee might be viewed as a sort of executive branch, it was subservient to the legislative branch. Because Congress acted as an agent of the states and had limited power to act in a way of which states did not approve, both the legislative and rudimentary executive branches of government under the Articles had little power to act in a way that would be unpopular with state legislatures. The establishment of an independent executive branch clearly enhanced the power of the federal government and clearly gave the federal government a greater ability to make decisions that could prove unpopular with the population at large. In short, the establishment of an executive branch of government enhanced the discretionary power of the federal government.

Congress under the Articles was unicameral, and each state was entitled to one vote. The bicameral legislature under the Constitution consists of one house in which states are represented equally and one house in which they are represented in proportion to their populations. The Senate is more comparable to the Congress under the Articles. There are, however, significant differences between the Congress as specified in the Articles and the Senate as specified in the Constitution. The original constitution specified that senators be chosen by the state legislatures, just as were the representatives under the Articles. However, under the Articles states could send anywhere from two to seven representatives, but each state had only one vote. The state's vote would be determined by the majority of the state's delegation. Furthermore, state representatives could be recalled and replaced at any time.

Under the Constitution, senators, although they were still chosen by the state legislatures, served six-year terms, and each senator got one vote in the Senate. Thus, senators did not have to agree on a state's position on the issues, as they would under the Articles, and those who voted in a manner not consistent with the desire of the state legislature could not be replaced until the expiration of their six-year term. Thus, senators under the Constitution were able to exercise much more discretion and deviate much more from the desires of state legislatures than was the case under the Articles.[34] Senators under the Constitution were much less accountable to anyone than were representatives under the Articles. This enhanced their discretionary power and increased the power of the federal government. Again, the Constitution, when compared to the Articles, is less constraining on the federal government.

Representatives in the House of Representatives under the Constitution were elected in proportion to a state's population. The debate between whether to have the same number of representatives per state, as is the case in the Articles, or to have states represented in proportion to their populations was really a debate between whether the new government was to be more of a federal government or a national government. A federation of states would imply that each state is represented equally, while a national government would represent each individual equally. The establishment of one house of each type is the result of a compromise, but it clearly shows that the change from the Articles to the Constitution was a movement away from a federal government and toward a national government. The establishment of a national government in place of a federation of state governments is a change that enhances the power of the central government.

The Constitution provides that members of the House of Representatives be elected by popular vote. In the Articles, all representatives were chosen by state legislatures. Thus, the popular election of legislators further increases the national character of the U.S. government. According to the original constitution, senators were chosen by state legislatures and the president was chosen by an electoral college. The method of selecting the electors in the electoral college was left up to the states. Over time the popular election of these officials has made the government even more national and less federal than it was as originally organized by the Constitution.

This overview of the organizational and institutional changes that occurred as a result of replacing the Articles with the Constitution illustrates that the institutional changes in the U.S. government that resulted from adopting the Constitution produced a U.S. government with increased power and less accountability. While the Constitution is correctly viewed as a document that constrains government, it is much less constraining than the Articles of Confederation it replaced. The net effect of replacing the Articles with the Constitution was to increase the power of the federal government and to reduce its accountability for its actions.

The Growth of Government

The changes that came with the adoption of the Constitution had an immediate impact, but the most important effects were not felt right away but rather took place over time. Immediately, the Constitution created a government more powerful and less constrained than the one that existed under the Articles. The Constitution also created an environment within which the U.S. government had a greater ability to grow than would have been the case under the Articles. The underlying argument in this hypothesis is an extension of Beard's hypothesis that the Constitution was designed to further the interests of those who wrote it. By the same logic, once in place, any changes in the rules would be likely to favor those who have the power to change them. Therefore, the less the government is constrained, the more the evolution of rules over time will change to enhance the power of those in government.[35]

A comparison of the Articles with the Constitution shows that there are four important reasons why the replacement of the Articles with the Constitution laid the foundation for the transformation of American government from its limited origins as a defender of liberty into a democratic government designed to further the will of the majority.

1. The Constitution gives those in the legislative and executive branches of the government more discretion than did the Articles. Under the Articles, Congress was directly accountable to the state legislatures, whereas, once elected, Congress could act without direct accountability under the Constitution.

2. The Constitution gives the federal government the power to independently raise revenue, which means that it is not accountable to the states for tax increases.

3. The powers of the federal government were more closely enumerated under the Articles than under the Constitution. The Constitution gives the federal government poorly specified powers, such as to coin money and to regulate commerce, and then gives a procedure for deciding how the government should act rather than clearly stating the bounds of government action, as is done in the Articles. Perhaps most significant, Section 8 of the Constitution gives Congress the power to collect taxes to promote the general welfare of the United States, without specifying at all what activities fall under the heading of promoting the general welfare.

A careful reading of the Constitution's reference to the general welfare suggests that the intention was not to allow Congress to do anything that promotes the general welfare but rather to restrict Congress to those activities that are in the general public interest rather than to further special interests. First, the phrase is clearly linked to the government's new power to levy taxes directly, rather than indirectly, from the states. Second, there would be no reason to enumerate the scope of government in the Constitution if the enumeration was meant to include anything that was in the general welfare. Third, the 10th Amendment explicitly prohibits the government from exercising any powers not given it in the Constitution. Again, there would be no reason for such a restriction if the government were permitted to do anything it decided would promote the general welfare.

The contemporary interpretation is different, however, and gives Congress broad latitude to produce legislation because it promotes the general welfare. The vague wording in this clause has been interpreted more loosely over time as an open-ended permission for the government to promote the general welfare in ways that it sees fit. This open-endedness in the activities allowed by the government paves the way for increased government activity over time.[36]

4. The government created by the Constitution is more of a national government than a federation of states, which gives it more power over the states and provides another vehicle for growth, as power is transferred from the state governments to the central government.

When the impact of replacing the Articles with the Constitution is evaluated in terms not only of the immediate effects but also the longer-term effects, it is clear that the new Constitution opened the door for increasing government growth.[37] The Articles constrained the federal government much more than does the Constitution by more carefully enumerating the powers of government, by constraining representatives to be more accountable to their constituents, by constraining the government's ability to raise revenue, and by making the federal government more explicitly a federation of state governments rather than a national government that exists above the states.

Federal versus State Government Power

Perhaps the argument could be tempered in one way. It is quite clear that the replacement of the Articles with the Constitution of the United States had the effect of enhancing the power of the federal government and laying the foundation for federal government growth. But while the Constitution transferred power from state governments to the federal government, and while the federal government might have had less power under the Articles, the states were in a position to exert more power.[38] John Jay makes a similar point in *The Federalist,* no. 2: "It is well worthy of consideration, therefore, whether it would conduce more to the interest of the people of America, that they should, to all general purposes, be one general nation, under one federal Government, than that they should divide themselves into separate confederacies, and give to the head of each, the same kind of powers which they are advised to place in one national Government."[39]

It may be that, with many states, intergovernmental competition would have the ability to limit the power of the states,[40] but there is at least room for debate as to whether individual liberty would have been better preserved under the Articles or under the Constitution. Perhaps a strong constitutionally limited federal government is a good way to constrain the power of states, but another alternative would have been to constrain the federal government as in the Articles while revising the Articles to limit the power of the states also. The clear conclusion is that the adoption of the Constitution of the United States reduced constraints on the federal government, but when considering both state and federal governments an argument could be made that the federal constraints on state government have resulted in a more constrained government overall.

The Effect of Adopting the Constitution

The ultimate conclusion of this chapter stands somewhat at odds with the conventional wisdom on the U.S. Constitution. The Constitution is often portrayed as a document that limits the powers of the federal government and guarantees the liberty of its citizens. When put in historical perspective, the effect of the Constitution must be evaluated in light of the status quo that it replaced. When compared to the Articles of Confederation, the Constitution placed less constraint on the federal government and allowed those who ran the government more discretion and autonomy and less accountability. The adoption of the Constitution enhanced the powers of the federal government and laid the foundation for two centuries of government growth.

CHAPTER 5

The Growth of Parties and Interests before the War between the States

The American Revolution was fought to secure the liberty of the citizens of the United States, and the nation's citizens viewed the most serious threat to liberty to be the power of government. Thus, the founders sought to produce a government that walked a fine line. They wanted a government that could protect the rights of individuals but that was constitutionally constrained from violating them. One of the most immediate threats the founders viewed to liberty was the threat of interest groups, or factions, within government. The founders were a part of a political elite that governed the fledgling nation, and the first six presidents, also a part of this elite, consistently warned against the rise of parties and factions in American politics. But there was an abrupt change with the election of Andrew Jackson in 1828. Jackson was the first president elected through the support of an organized political party, and after his election Jackson rewarded his supporters with political favors. With the election of Jackson, American government felt an abrupt shift away from political elitism and toward a more democratic representation of political interests.

The creation of the Democratic party to elect Jackson to the presidency changed the political landscape significantly. Jackson amassed a substantial amount of political power because he had an organized party behind him, which prompted those who opposed Jackson to create their own party. Thus, the Whig party was born, and the two-party system that characterizes American politics today came into being. Although the 12th Amendment to the Constitution modified slightly the way in which the president was chosen, the biggest changes came not from modifications in the constitutional rules but rather from two significant modifications in political institutions. The first, which was mostly complete by the time Jackson was elected, was the selection of electors by citizen vote. The second was the creation of the party system.

The Elitist Constitution

The Constitution designed democratic processes for collective decision making, but the founders obviously did not intend to design a government that would respond to the will of the majority. Indeed, citizens had almost no direct input into the federal government as the Constitution was originally designed and implemented. The federal government was designed to have three branches of government, each checking the others, to limit governmental power and was designed to operate within the limited bounds specified by the Constitution. None of the branches of government was designed to implement the will of the majority, and the Constitution gave citizens only a limited amount of input into the selection of some members of one of the branches.

Supreme Court justices (and all federal judges) are appointed by the president and confirmed by Congress, giving citizens no direct oversight or representation in the judicial branch. The president and vice president were chosen by an electoral college, and the Constitution makes no provision for direct voting for electors. The legislative branch of government was the only one in which citizens had a limited say. The founders created a bicameral legislature in which the Senate was composed of members chosen by state legislatures; with two senators for each state, states were represented equally, as was the case under the Articles of Confederation. Representatives were elected by direct vote of the citizens, but even here the Constitution does not provide the unlimited right to vote.

Article I, Section 2 of the Constitution states that when choosing members of the House of Representatives, "Electors in each State shall have the Qualifications requisite for Electors of the most numerous Branch of the State Legislature." Thus, states set their own qualifications for the right to vote, and at the time of independence every state but one had either a requirement of property ownership or some level of wealth or both. Because of the design of the Constitution, it is apparent that the founders did not intend for public opinion to have any influence over federal government policies or operations. In two of the three branches of government the general public had no direct say, and in the third branch a subset of citizens, determined by the states, was able to vote directly for members of only one of the two houses. If the founders had intended for this vote to convey the general public's opinions on public policy, then it would have established uniform voting requirements across states. It is apparent that this direct voting for representatives was designed as a check on the power of the representatives, not as a vehicle for voter input into the congressional decision-making process. The Constitution was originally designed to ensure that only those voters the states determined to be qualified would have a say in electing representatives.

If each branch of the federal government were equally powerful, as it would have to be for a system of checks and balances to be effective, and if each house of the legislature were equally powerful, then, as the Constitution originally designed the federal government, only one-sixth of the government would have any direct democratic oversight. At the beginning of the twenty-first century, with the direct election of presidential electors and senators, two-thirds of the government is democratically overseen. Such measurement is obviously unscientific but probably understates the growing influence of democratic input. Because the Supreme Court justices are appointed by the president and confirmed by Congress, the increased democratic input in the legislative and executive branches also undoubtedly has had a spillover effect on the judicial branch.

The Constitution designed the U.S. government to be run by a political elite and to undertake the very limited function of preserving the liberty of its citizens. It did not take long after the creation of the federal government for it to become more democratic and more broad in its scope of operations.

The Election of Representatives

The place in which the founders designed the government to be most directly accountable to its citizens was the House of Representatives. This was the only place in which the founders provided for citizens to vote directly in the new federal government they had designed. The vote was not intended to give citizens any direct input with regard to public policy but only to elect the members of one of the houses of the bicameral legislature, to provide a check that any legislation would meet the approval of the representatives of the people. Even this very small democratic input was more than was allowed under the Articles of Confederation.

As previously noted, the Constitution originally gave the states the right to determine who has the right to vote in state elections but then made those state qualifications apply to the election of members of the House of Representatives. Amendments to the Constitution have subsequently created a federal right to vote and in the process have expanded the franchise, but originally no restrictions were put on the ability of states to restrict the eligibility to vote, and this was deliberately so. The right of citizens to vote, which became regarded as an axiom of democracy in the twentieth century, was clearly not given in the Constitution of 1789.

By the end of the twentieth century members of the House of Representatives were all elected from single-member districts. Apparently this method of election was envisioned by the founders, but it was not specified in the Constitution, and it was not until 1972 that all members of the House were elected this way.[1] The most common alternative to election from single-member districts was general ticket representation, in which representatives were elected in statewide elections where all voters voted for all of the choices, with the top vote getters being elected. In the first congressional election Connecticut, New Hampshire, New Jersey, and Pennsylvania elected their representatives by general ticket. The practice was common until 1846, when it was discouraged but not totally prohibited by federal law. Hawaii, in 1968, was the last state to elect its representatives by general ticket, but New Mexico continued the practice until 1966 and North Dakota only gave the practice up in 1962.

Typically, states began using general ticket elections as a substitute for redistricting when they had a change in their number of representatives. From 1918 to 1932 there were no general ticket states, but five states used general ticket elections in 1932. By 1934 only New Mexico retained general ticket elections, but in 1942 Arizona and North Dakota also went to general ticket elections. In the twentieth century every general ticket election except one was in a state that elected only two representatives. The exception was Alabama, which elected eight representatives by general ticket in 1962. The disadvantage often cited with general ticket elections is that people who are geographically separated from state population centers will be unable to elect representatives and so will be underrepresented.

If states gain representatives, another alternative to redistricting is to retain the same districts but elect the new representatives at large. At-large representation has also been common throughout American history. In 1852 Mississippi was the first state to elect an at-large representative. Mississippi also had four representatives elected from single-member districts. In 1912, 12 states elected some at-large representatives, including Pennsylvania, which elected four of its representatives at large; Oklahoma, which elected three; and four other states that elected two at-large representatives. Three states elected at-large representatives in 1964, the last year the practice was used. At-large representatives have the same characteristics as general ticket representatives, the distinction being that general ticket elections refer to cases where all of the state's representatives are elected statewide, whereas at-large representatives are elected along with other representatives who are chosen from districts.

Early in the nation's history many states also used plural districts in which more than one representative was elected from a district. Plural districts were last used in 1840, when Pennsylvania elected five of its 28 representatives that way, Maryland elected two of eight, and New York elected 12 of 40 representatives from plural districts. Plural districts were established to maintain the contiguity of high-population geographical areas such as cities. More representatives could be elected from the area without dividing it into smaller political units.

The details are interesting, but the larger point is that the election of representatives from single-member districts, a firmly established political institution by the end of the twentieth century, was not the only way representatives were elected all the way up through the 1970s, and a number of different alternatives to single-member districts were employed. Especially in the first half-century of the Constitution, there was considerable variety in the way that even this, the most democratic of U.S. government institutions, was implemented. Increasingly, however, the states moved toward electing their representatives from single-member districts.

The Logic of Single-Member Districts

Legislative institutions can have a substantial impact on the types of legislation that is produced. Chapter 4 made this case when examining the differences between government under the Articles of Confederation and government under the U.S. Constitution. Similarly, a House of Representatives elected by general ticket would differ from one elected by single-member districts, because the nature of representation and political competition will be different. In general ticket elections, all potential candidates run against each other and all voters are represented by all representatives. With single-member districts, incumbents never compete against each other (except in rare cases when redistricting puts two incumbents in one district), and each constituent is represented by only one representative, giving that representative a degree of monopoly power. Single-member districts create a Congress that is organized like a cartel.

In markets, a cartel is a group of producers in an industry who organize to act like a monopoly. While monopolies wield considerable economic power they are not all-powerful, because the economic law of demand applies to monopolists as much as to any other type of market; therefore, if monopolists raise their prices, the amount they can sell at the higher price declines. The profit-maximizing monopolist sets its price higher than a competitive industry would in order to get more profit but as a result must sell less than a competitive industry would at the lower competitive price. Many readers will recall the Organization of Petroleum Exporting Countries (OPEC) oil cartel that was able to restrict its output and raise the price of oil substantially. Eventually the OPEC cartel broke down, however, because many of its members were selling more oil than the cartel agreement allowed and the greater quantity of oil could only be sold at a lower price.

All cartels are threatened by the type of breakdown experienced by OPEC. To sell at a monopoly price, cartel members must reduce their output; the problem arises because at a higher price each individual member would rather sell more, not less. Thus, members have an incentive to cheat on the cartel agreement, which leads to the destruction of the cartel and the return of competition. How could a cartel enforce its agreement and maintain its monopoly power? In the real world, the most common way is to seek government protection. Throughout most of the twentieth century, the trucking and airline industries were organized through government regulation and electric utilities were allowed to combine into monopoly suppliers, protected from competition by government regulators.[2] If government protection is not available, then any cartel hoping to be successful must find some way to detect cheaters to maintain the cartel agreement.

One method of organizing a cartel is to divide up the market into individual territories and give each firm the right to be a monopolist within a territory. This method has several advantages. First, it is relatively easy to detect cheating, because if any cartel member finds products being sold in its territory it did not sell, the member knows somebody is cheating. Second, if the exclusive territories can be established, the cartel does not need to give any more instructions to its members—they all are free to act like profit-maximizing monopolists in their own territories.

This method of cartelization is exactly the method used by the House of Representatives. States are divided up into exclusive territories, and each representative is the monopoly supplier of legislation within his or her district. Incumbents never compete with each other.[3] The organization within the House of Representatives has another advantage that an economic cartel does not have. If a competitor does arise and displace an existing cartel member, the successful challenger automatically becomes a member of the cartel, thus preserving the monopoly power of all cartel members.[4]

A similar arrangement exists in the Senate: even though two senators are elected from each state their terms are staggered so that incumbent senators never compete against each other. One crucial difference is that both senators represent the entire state, giving citizens two senators whom they can approach. With single-member congressional districts, citizens have two senators but only one representative. These differences were not created by the original constitution, however. Senators were originally chosen by the state legislatures, and the Constitution provided two senators, each with a separate vote, who could be appealed to by state legislatures. Recall that under the Articles of Confederation, each state had only one vote in the Continental Congress. While the Constitution did specify the nature of representation for the Senate, it was silent on the way that the House of Representatives would represent its constituents, and single-member districts evolved over time.

Single-member districts were not specified in the Constitution, and many other systems of representation were used throughout American history, as the previous section documented. However, the discussion in this section makes it apparent that single-member districts provide a clear advantage to the representatives by giving them monopoly power to represent a group of constituents and by insulating them from having to compete with other incumbents. But how did the system of single-member districts evolve?

The Development of Single-Member Districts

While the advantages of single-member districts to the representatives are plain, the arguments given for the creation of single-member districts had more democratic origins. The argument went that statewide representation tended to concentrate representation in populous areas, disenfranchising those further from population centers, and also greatly reduced any diversity of opinion among representatives. Those elected in general ticket elections would tend to have the political opinions similar to the median opinion of the voters, and if political opinion around a state differed from region to region, such differences would not be reflected in the opinions of the state's representatives. Furthermore, election by district meant that each representative had fewer constituents, making it easy for constituents to know and interact with their representatives.

These arguments in favor of single-member districts are quite valid, but none of them overturns the analysis of the previous section showing that single-member districts reduce political competition and give representatives monopoly power. Furthermore, the arguments in favor of single-member districts are all about how the principles of democracy can be furthered by single-member member districts, but democracy was not the goal of the federal government as envisioned by the founders. Indeed, they were wary of democracy and wanted to design a government that would be constitutionally protected from the desires of the majority. In this case, however, the cause of democracy can be furthered by an organization of the House that benefits House members and enhances their political power. One should not be surprised, therefore, to find that single-member districts were created by federal laws passed by Congress that would benefit from such an organization.

As previously noted, with no guidance from the Constitution, representatives have been elected in different ways over the years. Single-member districts have been the most common way, but general ticket elections and plural districts were common early in the nation's history. For example, in 1812 there were 19 states, and six elected their representatives by general ticket while another four had plural districts. In total, 29 representatives were elected from general ticket states and another 34 were elected from plural districts, for a total of 63 out of 182 representatives who were not elected from single-member districts. By 1842 three states still had plural districts, and seven elected their representatives by general ticket, although a growing population and the admission of new states meant that only 50 of 242 representatives were not elected from single-member districts. Still Congress took the first of many steps to try to legally mandate single-member districts.

In 1842 Congress passed legislation mandating geographically contiguous single-member districts. Legislation mandating single-member districts was also passed in 1862, 1872, 1882, 1891, 1901, 1911, and 1967.[5] However, each of these pieces of legislation had some exceptions and had a broader scope than just requiring single-member districts, so states that wanted to use general ticket or other electoral methods continued to do so. For example, if states were unable to redistrict in time for a congressional election, they had the option of electing any additional representatives at large or electing all of their representatives by general ticket until the redistricting could take place. Thus, states could employ these alternatives, despite legislation requiring single-member districts, merely by not getting around to defining districts. Plural representation was eliminated in 1840, at-large representation was eliminated in 1966, and the last general ticket election was held in 1968. Alternatives to single-member districts were quite persistent, especially in light of the fact that Congress had frequently mandated that states had to elect their representatives from single-member districts.

The evidence suggests that, given the choice, many states would have used election methods other than single-member districts, because many states did use other methods despite legislation beginning in 1842 that required single-member districts, and other states likely would have deviated from single-member districts without federal legislation requiring them. The previous section argues that representatives are the beneficiaries of single-member districts, so it is interesting to note that single-member districts were established by congressional mandate. With no specific type of representation specified in the Constitution, Congress mandated the type of representation that furthered its members' own interests.

This type of representation was also more democratic, because it gave greater representation to citizens who lived away from population centers and made each representative accountable to fewer citizens. Yet it is not implausible to believe that the motivating factor behind the actions of Congress was not to further the nation's democratic impulses but rather to solidify the political power of representatives. Indeed, if one motivation for establishing single-member districts was to have each representative be accountable to a smaller number of citizens, the legislation passed in 1929 fixing the House size at 435 had the opposite effect. Nevertheless, in addition to enhancing the political power of the representatives, single-member districts did also have the effect of making representation more democratic, taking yet another step in the transformation of American government from liberty to democracy.

The Logic of Bicameralism

Article I, Section 2 of the Constitution originally specified that "The Senate of the United States shall be composed of two Senators from each State, chosen by the Legislature thereof." As noted, representatives in the House of Representatives were elected by those citizens the state determined were eligible to vote. The logic of such a system is that the two houses of the legislature represent different constituencies with different interests, so it is more difficult to pass legislation through both houses than it would be to get approval of either one.

Recall from chapter 3 the framework that James Buchanan and Gordon Tullock developed in *The Calculus of Consent* for analyzing collective decision-making rules. They noted that, as a group moves away from the requirement of unanimous approval toward majority rule, the likelihood of having the group make collective decisions that would go against the interests of members of the group would increase. The only way to completely eliminate the possibility of these costs in collective decision making is to require unanimous consent for all group decisions. This, however, creates large decision-making costs, and it is likely that groups might pass up many opportunities beneficial to the group because the collective decision-making costs for unanimous decisions are so high. Thus, while a movement away from the unanimity requirement increases the expected costs imposed on citizens by government action, it lowers the expected decision-making costs, and groups often find it worthwhile to accept higher expected costs imposed by government action in exchange for lower decision-making costs by requiring less than unanimous agreement.[6]

A bicameral legislature provides a mechanism for lowering the expected costs of government action without an appreciable increase in decision-making costs.[7] Given a certain number of representatives, it should not affect the collective decision-making cost much whether they are all placed in one legislative body or whether they are divided into two houses. While decision-making costs would be only slightly affected, the expected costs imposed by government action could be reduced significantly if the houses are designed so that they represent heterogeneous groups with different interests. For example, if there was a readily identified minority of significant size, with a unicameral legislature the minority would always be outvoted by the majority, but if a bicameral legislature were created with one house representing the majority group and the other representing the minority, any legislation would have to pass both houses and would have to be approved by both the majority and the minority group to become effective.

This same outcome could be produced by requiring a very inclusive decision-making rule, such as requiring a 90 percent majority to pass any legislation. The drawback to the more inclusive decision rule is that the decision-making costs would be very high. In contrast, a bicameral legislature with houses representing heterogeneous groups could use simple majority rule in both houses yet could be assured that no legislation could pass without the approval of both groups. The ability of the majority to impose costs on the minority is reduced but without much, if any, increase in decision-making costs. Indeed, if it is easier to create political bargains in smaller groups, a bicameral legislature might also reduce decision-making costs.

The bicameral legislature in the United States was not intended to represent different population groups but rather the different interests of citizens and of state governments. Recall that under the Articles of Confederation state governments were able to exert considerable oversight over the federal government, and while most of that oversight disappeared when the Constitution was adopted, some remained, because the state legislatures chose their U.S. senators. Thus, any legislation that garnered the approval of both houses of Congress was approved by both the representatives of the people and the representatives of the state governments. The design of the federal government shows that the founders made a serious attempt to have the interests of state governments represented in federal government decision making as a method of ensuring that the states had some power to check the activities of the federal government.

The founders were inclined to use the British government as the example of where liberty had been most fully developed in Europe, and a part of what they saw was a system of checks and balances in which the aristocracy, represented in the House of Lords, and the general population, represented in the House of Commons, checked the power of each other. Although the Senate was not an aristocracy, its members were chosen by their state governments and therefore represented a political elite, whereas the members of the House of Representatives were chosen by the general population of voters. This parallel is more than just a coincidence. While the founders did not talk in terms of decision-making costs versus costs imposed on citizens by government action, those ideas were clearly what they had in mind when they created a House and Senate chosen by different populations. They would provide a check on each other, reducing the expected costs imposed on citizens by their government while at the same time keeping decision-making costs manageable.

The passage of the 17th Amendment in 1913 mandated that senators be elected by direct vote rather than chosen by the state legislatures. This had two major effects. First, it eliminated any representation of state government interests from the system of checks and balances, and, second, it made the two houses of Congress more homogeneous, which increased the expected costs of congressional decision making by making it easier to pass legislation. The implications of the 17th Amendment will be discussed further in chapter 8. At this point, note the logic of creating a bicameral legislature as an additional barrier against passing legislation that imposed costs on a significant minority of the population. The selection of the House and Senate from different populations was an integral part of the checks and balances the founders originally envisioned and reinforces the idea that the federal government was originally designed not to carry out the will of the majority but rather to preserve liberty by constraining the powers of the federal government.

The Electoral College

The Constitution was designed so that a group of highly qualified experts would be designated to select the president and vice president. Article II, Section 1 states, "Each State shall appoint, in such a Manner as the Legislature thereof may direct, a Number of Electors, equal to the whole Number of senators and representatives to which the State may be entitled in the Congress; but no Senator or Representative, or Person holding an Office of Trust or Profit under the United States, shall be appointed as an Elector." Constitutional amendments have changed some aspects of the process by which the president is elected, but this provision remains unchanged.

It is apparent from the wording of this provision of the Constitution that the founders did not intend for electors to be democratically elected (although they would not rule out the possibility), and it is even more apparent that however the electors were chosen they did not intend the method of choice to dictate how the electors would cast their ballots. Otherwise, why would the Constitution rule out federal officials as electors? Article II, Section 1 of the Constitution continues,

"The Electors shall meet in their respective States, and vote by Ballot for two Persons, of whom one at least shall not be an Inhabitant of the same State with themselves." The top vote getter would then become president if that person received votes from a majority of the electors, and the second-highest vote getter would become vice president. This provision was changed slightly by the 12th Amendment in 1804 so that the president and vice president were voted on separately, but the electoral college system remained essentially unchanged otherwise. The Constitution has never bound electors to vote for specific candidates, and the Constitution makes it clear that the founders envisioned electors using their discretion to select the best-qualified candidates in their view. That system remains intact at the beginning of the twenty-first century, and even though electors are associated with specific candidates, it has not been uncommon for an occasional elector to break ranks and vote for someone other than the candidate chosen by the state's voters.[8]

In practice, most presidents have won election by receiving a majority of the electoral votes, but at the time the Constitution was written the founders anticipated that in most cases no candidate would receive votes from a majority of the electors.[9] The founders reasoned that most electors would prefer candidates from their own states, so the typical elector would vote for one candidate from his own state and a candidate from another state, following the constitutional requirement, and it would be unlikely that voting along state lines would produce any candidate with a majority of votes. This state bias is reinforced by the fact that these electors are constitutionally charged to meet in their states and then forward their votes to the president of the Senate to be counted. There is much less of an opportunity for consensus under this system than under a system in which electors from all of the states gather together in a common location, making it even more likely that no candidate would receive a majority.

Today it is common to explain the constitutional provision that electors meet in their own states rather than gather in a central location simply as a result of the fact that transportation was much more difficult back then. Yet this provision served an important function, because it made it more difficult for the electoral college to arrive at a consensus in cases where there was no consensus candidate. Article I, Section 2 of the Constitution specifies that "if no Person have a Majority, then from the five highest on the List the said House shall in like Manner chuse the President." The founders envisioned that in most cases the president would end up being chosen by the House of Representatives from the list of the five top electoral vote recipients.

As it has evolved, the actual practice of electing a president is quite different from the way the founders intended. The founders intended electoral votes to be cast by electors who would be more knowledgeable than the general public rather than by popular mandate, and the founders envisioned that in most cases the final decision would be made by the House of Representatives rather than by the electors anyway. Furthermore, there was no indication that the number of electoral votes actually received should carry any weight besides creating a list of the top five candidates. The House could then use its discretion to determine who on that list would make the best president. Quite clearly, the process was not intended to be democratic, although it has evolved that way despite the fact that the constitutional provisions for selecting a president remain essentially unchanged. As specified in the Constitution, the election process should resemble the way in which a search committee might serve to locate a high-ranking corporate (or government or academic) administrator. The committee, like the electoral college, would develop a list of candidates, and the CEO (or bureau chief or university president) would then select his or her most preferred candidate from the list. As it actually has evolved, this multistep process has been set aside in favor of popular elections.

The electoral college system envisioned by the founders was designed to select a chief executive for the nation from a candidate pool composed of an elite group. Successful candidates would have to be well known and viewed as highly qualified in many states to get enough electoral votes to make the final list and would have to have enough respect within the House of Representatives to be chosen from a list of five finalists. Those involved in the selection process would be an elite group of Americans, and the process was engineered to produce a president that came from the upper echelons of the American elite. The process was not intended to be democratic.

The Selection of Presidential Electors

The current selection of electors is by a restricted general ticket, which allows voters only to vote for a bloc of electors who represent a specific candidate. But this method of election was chosen by the states and is not specified in the Constitution. The general ticket method of selecting electors was not well established until at least three decades after

presidential elections began, and the most common method for selecting electors early in the nation's history was to have state legislatures
do it. In the first presidential election, only two states, Pennsylvania
and Maryland, used general ticket elections to select their presidential
electors. In the second presidential election in 1792, there were 15
states: three used general ticket elections, 10 chose their electors in the
state legislature, and two had district elections for electors. In the election of 1800, which elected Thomas Jefferson to his first term, there
were 16 states, and only one used a general ticket election while 10 had
their state legislatures choose their electors.

The selection of electors by state legislatures remained common
through 1820, when James Monroe was elected to his second term of
office. In that election, 9 out of 24 states chose their electors in the state
legislature, while eight used general ticket elections. After 1820 the
selection of electors through general ticket elections became rapidly
more common. In 1824, 12 of the 24 states used general ticket elections
and only six selected electors in their state legislatures. By 1828, 18 of
24 states used general ticket elections and only two chose electors in the
legislature. By 1832 only South Carolina chose their electors in the legislature, one state had district elections, and the other 22 used general
ticket elections. In 1836 all states but South Carolina used general
ticket elections. South Carolinians did not vote directly for their electors until after the War between the States.[10]

The movement toward democratic elections for president in the
nation's early history is striking. States used a variety of methods for
selecting their electors, but up until 1820 the most common method of
selecting electors was through the state legislature, without direct voting. By 1832, just twelve years later, direct voting was used almost
nationwide. The design of the Constitution makes it apparent that the
founders did not intend to have the president elected by direct vote, but
they left it up to the states to determine exactly how presidential electors would be chosen. The result was that, despite the retention of the
electoral college, the president is effectively chosen by direct vote and
has been since the 1820s. The movement toward the democratic election of the president also corresponds with a more democratic notion
of the office itself, beginning in the 1820s.

The Elite Presidency: 1789–1829

When the founders at the Constitutional Convention were designing
the office of the president, one factor underlying the discussion was the

assumption that George Washington would be elected the first president. Washington, revered today, also commanded a huge amount of respect after the Revolution, and the office was designed in part with the thought that he would set the precedent for the details of the office that were left out of the Constitution.[11] Design of the government would have been more difficult, and might have proceeded along different lines, had there not been such an obvious and popular candidate to become the first president.

The founders were wary of the potential for tyranny that majorities could exert in a democratic government and tried to guard against the exploitation of a minority by a majority in several ways. The role of democratic decision making was severely limited both by insulating the new government from direct voting and by constitutionally limiting the scope of the government. In addition, the founders wanted to guard against the emergence of factions to prevent citizens from viewing their interests as being represented by one group of political candidates rather than another. Especially with regard to the presidency, the system was designed to select the most qualified individual to head the executive branch of government rather than to select a candidate who represented some citizens more than others.

The Constitution makes no reference to political parties, and the methods of selecting federal officials were designed to prevent them from playing a major role. Modern sources tend to cite party affiliations for all past presidents, but political parties in the modern sense did not assume any importance in presidential elections until 1828, when Andrew Jackson was elected.[12] Candidates for the office came from a political elite, and because of widespread selection of electors by state legislatures candidates needed to win the support of others in the political elite to win the office. Despite the rapid emergence of factions in American government, prior to 1828 parties did not campaign for presidential candidates. There was no reason to undertake campaigns aimed at citizens, as is done today, because state legislators chose the members of the electoral college, and those electors were the people who voted for president.

George Washington and John Adams, the first two presidents, are associated with the Federalist party, a distinction that became crucial during Adams's term as president. Washington remained unchallenged as head of state during his two terms as president and had a solid enough following that his vice president, John Adams, was elected president when Washington chose not to serve a third term. In contrast to Washington who was not seriously challenged during his two elections, Adams won his election by a margin of only two electoral votes over Thomas Jefferson, a member of the Democratic-Republican party, who then, following the rules of the original Constitution, became vice president.

By the time of Adams's election in 1796 there had developed some serious philosophical differences regarding the way the federal government should evolve. At the center of much of the controversy was Alexander Hamilton, Washington's secretary of the treasury. Hamilton served as much more than just the secretary of the treasury during Washington's administration; indeed, one historian referred to him as effectively the "prime minister," partly because the Treasury Department was so large compared to the rest of the government at that time and partly because Hamilton took it upon himself to strengthen the position of the federal government whenever the opportunity presented itself.[13] One of the issues that created a considerable amount of controversy was the creation of the first Bank of the United States as a federally chartered corporation. As secretary of treasury, this was Hamilton's project, but among its significant opponents were James Madison and Jefferson. Despite opposition, in 1791 the first Bank of the United States was given a 20-year charter.

The Bank of the United States was but a part of Hamilton's broader vision of the role of the U.S. government. At the Constitutional Convention, Hamilton had argued that all communities can be divided into the few that are rich and well born and the remaining mass of people. Their interests are often at odds, he argued, but the masses are seldom good judges of what is right. Thus, Hamilton wanted a constitution that would ensure the "rich and well-born their distinct, permanent share in the government."[14] As secretary of treasury, he tried to design a government that would protect and promote industry. Hamilton's "Report on Manufactures," written while he was secretary of treasury, promoted government policy that encouraged government protection of industry, and Hamilton advocated an internal improvements program that would spend enough to maintain the national debt. Hamilton viewed the debt as creating a tie among the interests of financial groups, businesses, and creditors with the federal government. "A national debt, if not excessive, will be to us a national blessing," Hamilton said.[15]

Madison, who had strongly opposed parties and factions in the *The Federalist,* no. 10, revised his opinion as a reaction to the Hamiltonian expansion of the scope of government and along with Jefferson created the Democratic-Republican party to try to counter the growing power of the federal government that they viewed was occurring in the Washington administration. After Adams was elected president in a close election against Jefferson—whose electoral vote total was almost equal to that of Adams—Jefferson was able to create an unpleasant political environment for Adams, who was the first one-term president and was unseated by Jefferson in the election of 1800. The problems created by having a president and vice president from different parties laid the foundation for the 12th Amendment, which created separate electoral balloting for the offices of president and vice president.

Jefferson's two terms were followed by his fellow Democratic-Republicans Madison and Monroe. While their political alignments originally arose in opposition to Hamilton's vision of a U.S. government that would promote elite commercial and business interests, their policies drifted toward Hamilton's. Interestingly, despite Madison's leadership in the opposition to the first Bank of the United States, whose charter ran out in 1811, the Second Bank of the United States was chartered in 1816, also for 20 years, during Madison's presidency. Madison had decided that a nationally chartered bank was not such a bad idea after all. As Arthur Schlesinger Jr. notes, "The approval of the Second Bank of the United States in 1816 by the man who twenty-five years before had been the ablest opponent of the First Bank was an appropriate commentary on the breakdown of the Jeffersonian idyl."[16] What appeared to be a fissure between factions that created the Democratic-Republican party in hindsight did not result in a great division, especially in comparison to the political divisions that would appear within a few decades.

The first six presidents were members of America's political elite, chosen by America's political elite. After a close election for his first term, Jefferson received 162 out of 176 electoral votes to win his second term, in the first election in which the vice president was selected from a separate ballot. Madison and Monroe, the fourth and fifth presidents, each won two terms in office with electoral landslides, making the elite nature of the office uncontroversial. Outside of Washington, Monroe might lay claim to the title of the least partisan of all American presidents.[17] But controversy erupted in the election of 1824, when John Quincy Adams was selected by the House of Representatives to be the nation's sixth president.

Four candidates received electoral votes for president in 1824.

Andrew Jackson received the highest number of electoral votes with 99, followed by John Quincy Adams with 84, William H. Crawford with 41, and Henry Clay with 37. Because no candidate had a majority, following the rules modified by the 12th Amendment, the House of Representatives had to choose the president from the top three vote recipients. Rather than choose Jackson, a war hero but a political outsider, the House chose Adams, the son of the nation's second president and a member of the political elite. Adams's election followed the rules, but Jackson's supporters were outraged by the choice, believing that Adams was chosen only because of a "corrupt bargain" between Adams and Henry Clay in which Clay was appointed secretary of state in exchange for Clay's support of Adams's candidacy.

The Formation of the Democratic Party

The dissatisfaction of Jackson's supporters is consistent with the increasing democratization of American government at the time. Presidential elections were increasingly being decided by popular vote, with the big transition occurring in the 1820s. In the election of 1820, nine states still chose their electors in their state legislatures, but by 1824, when John Quincy Adams was elected, only six did so. In 1828, when Jackson unseated Adams to become president, only two states had their legislatures choose their electors. The increasingly democratic election methods came along with the formation of the Democratic party, which was organized for the specific purpose of electing Jackson to the presidency. Jackson's supporters, led by Martin Van Buren, formed the Democratic party after the election of 1824 to ensure that in the next election Jackson would get a majority of the electoral votes and could not be denied the presidency by an elitist House of Representatives.

The efforts of Jackson's supporters to form the Democratic party began even before John Quincy Adams was inaugurated as president. Although Adams's bargain to appoint Clay as secretary of state seemed reasonable to Adams, and there was no doubt that Clay was eminently qualified, Van Buren was quick to paint Adams as undertaking partisan activity. In contrast to presidents over the previous two decades, Adams had a very narrow base of political support, which in itself created political opposition and enhanced the appearance of factionalism. Adams could only appeal to his supporters to accomplish anything while in office, enhancing the appearance of governance by a political elite. Although the "corrupt bargain" between Adams and Clay gave them the immediate reward of the presidency, it also initiated the process that unseated Adams four years later, gave rise to the party system that has since dominated American politics, and greatly accelerated the movement of the United States toward democracy as its fundamental principle.[18]

Well-defined factions had existed within American government for decades. It was in Washington's administration, after all, that Jefferson and Madison formed their political party to oppose what they viewed as an unwarranted expansion of government power. In contrast to the elitist notion of party that had characterized American politics and that had placed John Quincy Adams in the White House, Van Buren began to promote a new and more positive view of political parties. His idea was that "Parties should be democratic associations, run by the majority of the membership."[19]

Van Buren was well aware of the American tradition opposing political parties, whose origins could be traced back through *The Federalist,* no. 10, and which was supported in word by all six of the first presidents. But Van Buren, a senator from New York, perceived legitimate political differences among politicians that could be expressed along party lines. More significant, he viewed the opposition that incumbents had to organized parties as support for the continuance of political dominance by America's aristocratic elite. Without organized opposition, the elite could continue to dominate American government indefinitely. Parties served the legitimate interest of organizing political opposition, resisting the concentration of power in an elite group, and providing a broader representation of the political views of most Americans.

Van Buren did not misperceive the role that his new Democratic party would play. Indeed, the founders tried to insulate the federal government from democratic control for what they believed were good reasons and had no notion that the president would be chosen by the popular vote of American citizens. Yet the Democratic party had formed to do just that. The efforts of Van Buren and the Democrats were an unqualified success, and Jackson won the presidency in 1828, defeating the incumbent president by an electoral total of 178 to 83. The modern party system was born, as both the Democrats and their opponents recognized that, after Jackson's election, a party organization would be necessary to win the presidency. After Jackson's two terms as president, Van Buren was elected president for one term but was unseated by his Whig challenger, William Henry Harrison, in 1840. The American two-party system has evolved since then, but it has not fundamentally changed.[20]

Democratic Elections and the Two-Party System

One can gain a greater understanding of American politics by reflecting on the operation of the two-party system. The Constitution says nothing about parties, and there is nothing to stop additional parties from arising, which they do, with startling regularity. Yet a three-party system does not survive. Either the fledgling third party passes out of existence or, if it gains sufficient strength, puts one of the prior two parties out of existence, as happened when the Republican party displaced the Whigs.

In a modern context, one can visualize party platforms as existing on a single-dimensioned continuum, from political left to political right. While the details of party platforms may be more complex, voters tend to view candidates running for office somewhere along this continuum. Democrats such as Franklin D. Roosevelt, Hubert Humphrey, and Ted Kennedy are viewed at the left end of the spectrum, while Barry Goldwater and Ronald Reagan are viewed at the right. Most successful politicians of the twentieth century have fallen somewhere in between. George H. W. Bush[21] and Bill Clinton fall toward the center of the continuum; Bush had a reputation as being a relatively liberal Republican, while Clinton was viewed as a relatively conservative Democrat.

Voters tend to see their own views as falling somewhere along the political left-right continuum and want to vote for candidates who are closest to their own views; in this manner political competition means that candidates will have to choose their own platforms in such a way as to get a majority of the votes. In a two-party system, this means locating near the middle of the left-right continuum. If this simple view of the political process were all there was to it, in a two-candidate election the candidate whose position was closest to the median voter would win the median vote and all votes to one side of the median. This would guarantee that candidate the victory. In reality, the electoral process is a little more complicated, but this simple description captures much of the essence of electoral competition. There is a political left-right continuum, and successful candidates tend to be those who have platforms close to the center.

President Nixon gave a clear statement of this when, in response to vocal protests to some of his policies, including but not limited to U.S. involvement in the Vietnam War, he proclaimed that he was not attempting to please these vocal protesters, who made up a small part of the total population, but rather aiming his policies at the "silent majority." Academics are not nearly so colorful in their language and refer to the process just described as the median voter model. In this model, politicians try to aim their policies at the median voter, because the candidate who gets the median vote wins the election.[22]

A common lament of voters is that all candidates tend to look alike. As earlier noted, both Clinton and Bush, whom Clinton defeated in the 1992 election, are viewed as holding positions toward the middle of the political spectrum. In the 1976 presidential election, Gerald Ford and Jimmy Carter were viewed as very similar, and Carter won by a slim margin. Candidates do tend to look alike because they have to in order to be competitive. They are competing for the vote of the median voter. President Reagan took advantage of a shift in voter preferences to win by a large margin in 1980 and also in 1984, when his positions were quite different from his opponents. Similarly, George McGovern, viewed as an extreme left-wing candidate, and Barry Goldwater, perceived as being on the extreme right wing, both lost by landslides. Extreme candidates cannot win elections because they are too far away from the median voter.

One of the implications of this view of democratic electoral competition is that third parties are not viable. With two parties, one party locks up the votes to the right tail of the distribution of voters and the other locks up the left. Competition takes place for those voters near the center, who are close to the median voter. A third party must take a position somewhere on the political spectrum, to one side or the other of the median, and when it does it takes most of its votes from one party but not the other. This makes both parties on that side of the median unviable, and to become competitive again one of them must fold, or they must combine, or one must accept enough of the views of the other to make it an insignificant political force. The Constitution does not specify that the United States should have a two-party system, but because of the way the electoral system was designed, a two-party system is the only stable political system that could exist.

This theory of democratic elections assumes that electoral choices can be arrayed in a single-dimensioned political continuum and that political instability might arise if this assumption is violated. The assumptions underlying this median voter model of representative democracy have been the subject of much study, and for decades most studies of the theory of democratic decision making have concluded that the underlying conditions of the model were approximately met.[23] In theory, it can be demonstrated that, if political issues cannot be collapsed into a single-dimensioned issue space, political instability will result.[24] However, in practice democratic institutions tend to be very stable, suggesting that this median voter model is a good description of the general operation of democratic political institutions.[25]

One reason this model of democracy may be descriptive of actual democratic decision-making processes is that studies examining political coalitions and issues find that, despite the fact that there are many political issues, most important issues can be placed on a single-dimensioned continuum such that voters who find themselves in agreement with a certain coalition on some issues tend to find agreement with that same group on other issues. In the United States this has produced the left-to-right political spectrum that is commonly understood by voters and theorists alike, but similar one-dimensional issues spaces tend to characterize other voting bodies as well.[26] Another factor leading to political stability is that even when voting by itself would not produce any clear majority winner, bargains can be struck, within a legislature or between the legislature and the executive, so that individuals can trade away their votes on issues they have relatively weak preferences for in exchange for political support on issues they care most about. In such instances, political exchange produces the same results as market exchange, leading to a stable political outcome.[27]

The operation of the democratic electoral system does not guarantee an orderly democratic process, but theory does suggest that, when the major political issues can be ordered on a one-dimensional continuum such as the left-to-right continuum within which contemporary political opinions are cast, the process will tend to be stable and orderly. Furthermore, it suggests why we have a two-party system and suggests that American political opinion will tend to be aggregated through the electoral process to represent the median voter.[28] Thus, with some theoretical background, one can understand more clearly the operation of the American political system.

Jacksonian Policy

Andrew Jackson's vision of American politics at the time he was elected fits firmly within the single-dimensioned model of political competition just described. Jackson viewed himself as following a Jef-fersonian tradition, both in opposing the status quo of the previous administration and in trying to limit the powers of the federal govern-ment and loosen the grip of the political elite over American govern-ment. The federal government remained relatively limited in scope, but under Jackson's predecessors its power had been slowly but steadily growing and was controlled by elites, allowing the broader population little say in the operation of their government. Jackson wanted to move in the other direction along the continuum: to limit the powers of the federal government and to move from government by elites to govern-ment by democracy. The founders had intended for the federal gov-ernment to be controlled by elites rather than to respond to the masses, placing Jackson's populist ideas at odds with his predecessors, but the founders just as clearly intended for the federal government to be strictly limited in scope, making Jackson's ideas in this area more in harmony with the founders.

One of the significant issues that Jackson pursued was the Second Bank of the United States, which he opposed as an institution that cen-tralized power and shackled the growth of the American economy. Jackson believed that the policies of the Second Bank perpetuated monopoly in the banking industry, giving privilege to the few at the expense of the many. Despite an attempt by Congress to extend the bank's charter, Jackson was able to veto the bank, and it passed out of existence in 1836, the last year of Jackson's second term.[29] Jackson's philosophy of government came from a group of successful business-men who pushed laissez-faire ideas.[30] While monopolistic business practices could prove harmful, the Jacksonians, following Adam Smith, believed that government was more often the source of monop-olistic business practices rather than the solution.[31] Rather than try to get the government involved in the economy, Jackson attempted to pull back, in the case of the Second Bank and in the case of government regulation and support of the economy more generally.

Jackson wanted to dilute the economic power wielded by Amer-ica's business elite, and he viewed that much of that power was driven by government policy, including policies of incorporation. In Jack-son's day, banks were the corporations that wielded the most economic power, and he wanted to eliminate bank notes and move to a system of hard money to remove some of the power of banks. Banks were only a part of the incorporation problem, however. Often corporate charters were granted for projects that conveyed some monopoly power, such as the building of toll roads and bridges, and Jackson wanted to extend the ability to incorporate so that anybody would be allowed to create a corporation following general laws rather than have to specifically be granted a corporate charter. General incorporation laws at the state level, following the Jacksonian idea, began to spread prior to the War between the States and became universal after the war. Corporate forms of business are so common today that it is difficult to imagine business without it, but the modern corporate form is "a direct legacy from Jacksonian democracy."[32]

Another important issue for Jackson was the federal funding of internal improvements. Jackson was against it, not just as a matter of policy but as a constitutional issue. Jackson saw no allowance within the Constitution for the federal government to engage in public works and believed that, if the people wanted the government involved, they should either petition their state governments to undertake the projects they desired or amend the Constitution.[33] This was an issue in which Jackson stood in stark contrast to John Quincy Adams, who in his first State of the Union address proposed a stunning array of public works, including roads and canals, a national university, and federal support for the exploration of the western territories.[34] These activities should be undertaken for the good of the nation, regardless of popular opinion, Adams argued. Adams had inadvertently given Jackson two issues that clearly differentiated the two men and created a clear contrast for the presidential election of 1828. The first issue was directly related to the federal government's involvement in public works, but the second, larger issue was the role of popular opinion as a guide to government policy.

Jackson's first major move against public works was his Maysville veto in 1830 against a bill that would have provided federal funding for a road that was to be built entirely within Kentucky. The bill's supporters argued that the road would be an important link in the federal transportation system, but Jackson viewed this argument as irrelevant. The federal government had no constitutional authority to finance internal improvements, regardless of whether they were national in character.[35]

Jackson also believed that the courts, and the law itself, were too inaccessible to most citizens and favored codification and simplification of law to remove some of the power of the courts.[36] Jackson would not have prevented the courts from interpreting the law but believed the Supreme Court was substantially overstepping their constitutional bounds whenever it attempted to divine the true meaning of ambiguous parts of the Constitution.[37] To do so made the actions of the other branches of government subordinate to the interpretations of the judiciary, which was contrary to Jackson's vision of the Constitution's design.

In contrast to Hamilton's view, Jackson opposed the national debt and by 1835 had retired it entirely, an accomplishment in which he took pride.[38] He also wanted the federal government to give up its ownership of public lands.[39] Jackson claimed to be a Jeffersonian republican, committed to the idea of limited government and determined to turn around what he viewed as the expansion of federal government power under his predecessors. His policies were consistently laissez-faire, and he left his mark on the nation by successfully limiting the scope of government in many ways. At the same time, Jackson viewed the federal government as a necessary check on the power of state governments and believed that this balance was necessary to preserve liberty. He opposed the attempts of states to try to nullify federal law within their borders,[40] and when South Carolina threatened secession in 1833 Jackson made it perfectly clear that he would use military force, if necessary, to preserve the Union, setting a precedent upon which Lincoln called less than three decades later.[41]

Jacksonian Democracy

The public policy positions taken by Jackson were consistently aimed at the goal of reducing the scope and power of the federal government, but in addition to these policy ends Jackson also believed in democracy as a means to control the federal government. The top officials in the government should be elected directly, Jackson believed, including senators and the president, to make them more accountable to the people, and once elected they should heed the wishes of the electorate. Through democracy, Jackson wanted to remove the federal government from the control of the political elite that had overseen it since the approval of the Constitution.

As an outsider, a war hero, and a person who had worked his way up to national prominence rather than having been born into privilege, Jackson found a sympathetic audience in the electorate. As one historian put it, "it was much in Jackson's favor that he was an ignorant man, fully as devoid as the average citizen could be of all the training, through books or practice, which had theretofore been commonly regarded as constituting the odious superior qualifications of a detestable upper class."[42] In short, Jackson's ideas were not the product of thoughtful scholarship and an in-depth understanding of political theory but rather were a reaction to his perception that a government established to protect the liberty of its citizens had been accumulating power in the hands of a political elite. Democracy was the mechanism Jackson favored for redistributing power away from this elite and returning it to the people.

Interests in Jackson's Administration

Within the context of the growth of federal government power, Jackson's presidency had two opposing effects. As noted in the previous section, Jackson favored a smaller federal government with less power and with less oversight over the activities of state governments. This return to Jeffersonian principles had the immediate effect of reducing the scope and power of the federal government. Pulling in the other direction, however, was Jackson's desire for more democratic representation in the federal government and his assigning of federal government positions based on political patronage. The fledgling civil service system that existed when Jackson was elected was done away with by him. Prior to Jackson's administration there was the notion that, as long as civil servants performed their duties well, they were entitled to keep their jobs. Jackson saw things differently. He believed that the jobs were not so demanding that people of reasonable intelligence could not perform them and argued that more was lost by giving people a guarantee of continuing employment than was gained by retaining an experienced workforce. Thus, Jackson replaced many government workers after his election.[43]

Jackson's argument about giving government workers an incentive to perform has some merit and found a sympathetic hearing in his day, but one by-product of Jackson's actions was the transformation of government jobs into political patronage awards. Jackson's political supporters ended up getting government jobs and had an incentive to continue supporting Jackson if they wanted to keep their jobs. Political appointments have a certain logic behind them, because if government workers perform poorly then incumbent politicians are more likely to lose the next election and those workers are likely to lose their jobs. Thus, political appointees have an incentive to make the government look good. But it was also apparent that many government employees had their jobs only because they supported the Democratic party.

This aspect of political parties is almost inevitable, although civil service reform that began at the end of the nineteenth century has curbed the process somewhat. When presidents were selected by political elites from a group of political elites, they did not accumulate political debts and were not compelled to act in a partisan fashion. But when a president is elected because of the support of a political party, the president owes his election to the party and is pressured to repay the favor by giving benefits to his political supporters. With a limited federal government early in the nineteenth century, the major kind of benefit that could be tendered was government employment. Thus, Jacksonian democracy brought with it political patronage and reinforced the idea that, in a political competition, to the victor belongs the spoils. The nation had taken another step away from liberty and another step toward democracy.[44]

The scope of the federal government during Jackson's administration was limited, which meant there were limited opportunities for political interests to receive benefits. Most of the nation's revenues came from tariffs, and in this area there was interest group activity. The southern states, which always felt that the tariff worked against them, wanted low tariffs but especially favored low tariffs on manufactured goods. Southerners believed that, because tariffs were imposed on imports but not exports by constitutional design, the South, which imported manufactured goods but sent much in the way of raw materials to the North for manufacture and export, bore the brunt of tariffs. Southerners paid tariffs on their imported manufactured goods and exported raw materials to the North. Northerners, therefore, did not pay tariffs on their imports from the South and were able to export their manufactured goods duty-free.

The tariff was a major issue of the time, and while Jackson was philosophically in favor of lower tariffs, he also wanted to keep tariff revenue flowing to retire the federal debt. In 1828 Jackson sought to maintain political support by adjusting tariff rates on different goods, producing a tariff with so many different rates tailored to special interests that it has since been called the "tariff of abominations."[45] Federal tariff policy became one of the issues over which the southern states argued they should secede from the union. In 1832 most of the "abominations" were eliminated from the tariff in a new bill that reduced rates. Still, the tariff was one of the earliest issues in which interest groups became involved in distributive politics.[46]

While Jackson viewed himself as aligned with Jeffersonian political ideals, his election campaign had little to do with issues and everything to do with personalities. The Democratic party was formed to elect Jackson, and for that Jackson owed a debt to those who supported him. Jackson repaid his supporters with federal government positions. Jackson's avowed motives were in line with the tenets of his Democratic party. He believed that replacing a complacent elite group of federal employees with a new group of citizens would enhance the democratic nature of government and would improve the efficiency of its operation. The result was to establish political patronage as a method of rewarding those who supported victorious politicians. Although during the first eighteen months of his administration Jackson only replaced 919 people out of 10,093 on the federal payroll,[47] he did so in a more deliberate manor than his predecessors. As Schlesinger notes, "Jackson ousted no greater a proportion of officeholders than Jefferson, though his administration certainly established the spoils system in national politics."[48]

After Jackson, before the War

The establishment of the Democratic party was a pivotal event in American politics, and it changed the course of American government. Jackson created the modern presidency by being elected with the support of a political party, by promoting the principle of democracy both as a method of selecting government leaders and as a principle by which public policies should be pursued, and by incorporating the spoils system into American politics and supporting the idea that, in exchange for political support, interests could petition the government for benefits. Much has changed in the course of American history, but in one sense there is more similarity in the office of the presidency between the terms of Andrew Jackson and George W. Bush than there was between the terms of John Quincy Adams and Jackson.

Jackson remained a popular president, one result of which was his ability to pick Martin Van Buren, the architect of the Democratic party, to succeed him in office. But after Jackson's administration, it was apparent that any candidate for the presidency would have to have the support of an actively campaigning political party to hope to claim the White House. The presidents following Jackson were considerably less popular; the next president reelected to a second term was Lincoln. The Whig party had arisen to counter the Democrats, and Whig candidate William Henry Harrison unseated Van Buren, only to die in office a month after his inauguration. John Tyler took over the office, but the Whigs nominated Henry Clay as their candidate in 1844, yet Clay lost to the Democrat James Polk. Because of the succession of one-term presidents[49] and the overriding issues that led to the War between the States, the terms between those of Jackson and Lincoln saw a relative lull in the evolution of American democracy.

Interests and the Post Office

The Constitution specifies relatively few activities that are allowed to the federal government, but one is the establishment of a post office. In the nation's first few decades, the Post Office was financed internally from revenues it raised by charging for the delivery of mail. That did not prevent it from being used for political interests, however. When Jackson was elected, the U.S. postmaster general, John McLean, objected to Jackson's attempts to remove local postmasters who had supported Adams from their postmaster positions. Jackson's remedy for McLean's reluctance was to offer McLean a position on the Supreme Court, which McLean accepted. McLean's replacement, William Barry, was more compliant, and although the operations of the Post Office continued profitably, Jackson's appointments of supporters made it an extension of his political empire.[50]

Running the Post Office as a revenue-generating operation changed in 1851, when after much debate in Congress an act was passed that greatly overhauled the nature of mail delivery. The 1851 act lowered postal rates for letters to three cents for delivery up to 3,000 miles and to six cents for delivery beyond that limit. This was the first step toward eliminating distance as a factor in postal rates, and by 1863 all letters were delivered for the same price. The act also specified that "No post office now in existence shall be discontinued, nor shall the mail service on any mail route in any of the states or territories, be discontinued or diminished in consequence of any diminution of revenues that may result from this Act and it shall be the duty of the Postmaster General to establish new offices and place the mail service on any new mail routes, established, or that may hereafter be established, in the same manner as though this Act had not passed."[51] This act marked the transition of the Post Office from a profitable public enterprise into a subsidized activity that transferred benefits from taxpayers in general to the recipients of subsidized mail delivery.

The biggest beneficiaries were residents on the Pacific coast. In 1857 and 1858, under the direction of Postmaster Aaron V. Brown, the

Post Office established new routes to the West Coast that showed expenses of more than $2 million but that raised only $339,000 in revenues.[52] In 1859, when Joseph Holt of Kentucky took over as postmaster, he attempted to reverse the subsidies but ultimately was unsuccessful. In 1865 the Post Office established new routes between Utah and California with an annual cost of $750,000 that yielded revenues of only $23,900.[53] The guiding principle of the Post Office became the provision of service without regard to the revenue it generated.

Because of the extended services at lower costs, the Post Office began losing money and required congressional appropriations to continue its operations. Additional extensions of service became the subject of congressional debate, pitting West Coast interests against those in the more populous East.[54] Once the principle was established that postal services would be offered at low prices regardless of the cost of the service, the opportunity for rent seeking presented itself, and western states availed themselves of the opportunity to obtain services below cost. Thus, the services of the Post Office began evolving from a type of public service paid for by the beneficiaries into one of the first federal programs in which explicit transfers were made, benefiting some Americans by using tax dollars collected from everyone.

The use of the Post Office in this way, as a mechanism for transferring benefits to a subset of the population, is not so important for the amount of subsidy that went to western states as for the precedent it set. Patronage in the Jackson administration gave favor to his supporters over others for federal employment but did not alter the scope or nature of the federal government. The transfer element of the Post Office established the clear precedent that federal programs could use general tax dollars to benefit identifiable subgroups of the population.

Conclusion

The government of the United States was significantly different by the mid-1800s than it was envisioned by its creators. As designed in the Constitution, the U.S. government was not intended to be a democracy. There was little room for direct democratic input from American citizens, and the founders went to great lengths to see that public policies were not designed by the will of the majority. The Constitution originally provided for direct citizen voting only for members of the House of Representatives and even then left it up to the states to specify who had the right to vote. Senators were chosen by the state legislatures, and the president was to be chosen by an electoral college or by the House of Representatives. The Constitution did not, and still does not, specify how members of the electoral college are to be chosen, instead leaving that up to the states to decide. Throughout the nation's early history the most common method of choosing electors was to have them selected by the state legislatures, in the same manner as senators were selected. That method changed quickly in the 1820s, leading to direct voting for electors and for the president.

Andrew Jackson had a profound effect on American government and was the most important figure in the promotion of democracy before the War between the States. Even before his election, however, the nation had moved significantly down the road to democracy, especially in the area of presidential elections. Because popular voting for the president became increasingly common, and also because Jefferson, Madison, and Monroe won their elections by such significant margins, Americans had several decades of experience leading them to believe that the presidential candidate most popular with the voters would be the president. Thus, despite that John Quincy Adams's selection as president by the House of Representatives was done following both the letter and the spirit of the Constitution, it created the appearance of impropriety and led to the establishment of the Democratic party for the specific purpose of guaranteeing Jackson an electoral majority in the next presidential election.

Jackson's Democratic party was appropriately named, for Jackson believed that liberty could be protected only by allowing the people to govern through majority rule.[55] The increased scope of democracy over American government was something Jackson favored. He favored direct election of the president and senators and even favored democratic oversight of the Supreme Court.[56] Jackson saw democracy and liberty as self-reinforcing, because democratic oversight of the government would guard against its being taken over by a political elite and would prevent the elite government from pursuing policies that would benefit the elite few at the expense of the masses. The founders felt otherwise, for two reasons. First, they did not believe that most people had the capacity to make thoughtful and informed decisions about their government. Second, they believed that rule by majority could be just as tyrannical as rule by a king or by any elite group. Thus, they designed the government to be run by a political elite but constrained in its actions by the Constitution.

Jackson fought for democracy as a method of limiting the scope and power of the federal government, but, ironically, the result of making the nation's government more democratic has been to increase the scope and power of government in response to popular demands for government programs. This was the result the founders foresaw and tried to guard against by limiting the role of democracy in their new government. Jackson was a strong president and was able to accomplish many of his immediate goals while in office, but the results of his presidency do not look as good, judged by his own goals, over a longer time horizon. Although Jackson wanted to limit the powers of the federal government and succeeded in doing so during his own administration, the more democratic government that he created laid the foundation for future government growth. The growth of government as a direct result of Jacksonian democracy after Jackson left office more than offset the reductions in the scope of government that Jackson presided over during his eight years in the White House.

CHAPTER 6

The Impact of the War between the States

Without doubt, the single most important event in the transformation of American government was the War between the States. Prior to the War between the States, state governments were viewed as the primary governments and the federal government was viewed, as its name implies, as a federation of state governments. After the war, there was no doubt that the federal government was supreme and that the state governments were subservient to the federal government. Prior to the War between the States, the United States was used as a plural term in recognition of the many states. Because of their differences, the United States were headed for the most destructive war in their history, and as a result of it, after the war they were more firmly under the power of the federal government although in many ways more divided than ever.

Abraham Lincoln referred to the War between the States as a civil war in his Gettysburg Address, and while the term has the advantage of being a more concise description than War between the States, it inaccurately describes the conflict. Civil war normally refers to a conflict in which different parties are fighting for control over a nation's government, whereas in this case one part of the nation was trying to gain independence from another part. Had the Confederate States of America been victorious, the war surely would have been remembered as the war of Confederate independence. As remembered at the dawn of the twenty-first century, the War between the States often is simplistically seen as the result of Lincoln's crusade to free the slaves in the Southern states. Slavery was a major issue, but, as explained later, it was peripheral to the actual cause of hostilities, which was Lincoln's determination not to allow the Confederate States to secede from the Union. Lincoln's success firmly established the federal government's absolute power over the states.

The effects of the War between the States on government in the United States and the direction that the Confederate States had planned for their new government, as indicated by the Confederate Constitution, are an interesting contrast. The lasting legacy of the War between the States was a federal government that established itself as dominant over the state governments and that increased the scope of its power in many ways. In contrast, the Confederates intended to design a federal government more constrained than the U.S. government, especially with regard to the federal government's ability to benefit special interests. In the end, special interests won out over the general public interest, as this chapter and the next one show. Perhaps the most obvious place to start is with the issue of secession itself.

Secession

The issue of secession had been considered long before Lincoln's election and long before the creation of the Republican party. As chapter 5 noted, South Carolina had considered seceding during Jackson's administration, and there was also discussion of secession among the Northern states because of their opposition to slavery. In 1840, John Quincy Adams argued that, if Texas, which allowed slavery, became a state, that would justify the dissolution of the United States,[1] and other Northerners argued that Southern slavery was able to survive only because of costly enforcement measures imposed on Northern states. The nation's Fugitive Slave Law required nonslave states to patrol their states for fugitive slaves and return them to their owners. Opponents to slavery argued that, if the North seceded and no longer had to enforce the South's laws, slaves could then escape to the North and Southern slavery would rapidly collapse.[2] The point is that secession was considered as a serious possibility by both Northerners and Southerners and was even declared justified (under certain conditions) by a former U.S. president. Secession was not a new idea in 1860.

Many actions that were not taken have been discussed in the abstract. For example, one important issue is whether secession, once the Confederate States seceded, is allowed under the Constitution that united the states in the first place. Using the Constitution as a guide, the clear answer is yes. Article VII of the Constitution states, "The Ratification of the Conventions of nine States, shall be sufficient for the Establishment of this Constitution between the States so ratifying the Same." With thirteen states unified and governed by the Articles of Confederation, this article provides for the secession of up to four states if nine agree to the new Constitution. Thus, any state that did not want to be governed by the Constitution was given the option of leaving the Union. The Constitution specifically and explicitly allows states to secede from the United States in Article VII, so the Constitution was written envisioning the possibility that some states might want to leave the Union if they did not agree with the decisions of others in this specific circumstance.

The 10th Amendment to the Constitution reads, "The powers not delegated to the United States by the Constitution, nor prohibited by it to the States, are reserved to the States respectively, or to the people." The Constitution does not give the United States the power to prevent states from seceding and even allows secession under the conditions specified in Article VII, so the United States clearly does not have the constitutional power to prevent states from leaving the Union. The power of secession by states is not prohibited by the Constitution, such that power should therefore be reserved to the states, following the 10th Amendment. A literal reading of the Constitution in no way prevents secession and in one case specifically allows it.[3]

Secession had been contemplated for decades by the time the Confederate States actually seceded. It appeared to be accepted as a possible remedy for the rift that had grown between the Northern and Southern states, and it appeared to be constitutionally allowable. One result of the War between the States was to establish that states did not have the right to secede, and this by itself vested the federal government with more power. After the war, it was clear that states did not have the option of withdrawing from the Union if they viewed the costs of membership to be greater than the benefits. Secession did appear to be possible before the war, and this change alone gave the federal government more power in its dealings with the states.

Slavery and Emancipation

Nations have a tendency to tell their histories in a way that makes the nation, as an entity, appear as virtuous as possible. Americans have criticized the Japanese for portraying themselves as victims in World War II when in fact they engaged in a campaign of conquest and initiated hostilities. Similarly, they have criticized the Swiss for not admitting their compliance with the Germans during World War II, especially in their role as bankers who hid assets stolen from Jews. The story of the War between the States, as told by Americans, similarly slants the picture toward the virtue of the nation by depicting it as a war to free the slaves. That story is false. The Confederate States tried to secede from the Union to preserve their states' rights from domination by the federal government. Lincoln initiated the war to preserve the Union, not to free the slaves.[4]

Slavery was, of course, the overriding issue that led to the division between the North and South and ultimately that precipitated the war. However, Lincoln's aim was to preserve the Union, and he was willing to tolerate slavery to do so. In his inaugural address in 1861, Lincoln stated, "I have no purpose directly or indirectly to interfere with the institution of slavery in the United States where it exists. . . . I believe I have no lawful right to do so, and I have no inclination to do so."[5] Lincoln reiterated this opinion in 1862, shortly before issuing his Emancipation Proclamation: "My paramount objective in this struggle *is* to save the Union, and is *not* either to save or destroy slavery. If I could save the Union without freeing *any* slave I would do it, and if I could save it by freeing *all* the slaves I would do it; and if I could save it by freeing some and leaving others alone I would also do that."[6]

The Emancipation Proclamation, issued on September 22, 1862, gave the Confederate States until the end of that year to end their fighting and rejoin the Union. Then, "within any State [or] part of a State [that had not rejoined the Union], all persons held as slaves . . . shall be then, and thenceforward, forever free."[7] For states that met Lincoln's deadline, he proposed compensation of slave owners and resettlement of former slaves, perhaps in Central America. The Emancipation Proclamation did not apply to the four border states of Delaware, Maryland, Kentucky, and Missouri, which were all under Union control at that time, or to those areas of Tennessee, Virginia, and Louisiana that were under Union control. Thus, the Emancipation Proclamation applied only to slaves in those areas that continued to fight for their independence from the United States. Slaves located within the control of the Union were not freed by the Emancipation Proclamation, further reinforcing Lincoln's claim that his only motive in interfering with slavery was to save the Union.

Lincoln was opposed to admitting any new slave states into the United States. Hence, Southerners did envision becoming outnumbered as the nation inevitably granted statehood to western territories, which was a major factor in the decision of the Confederate States to secede. Slavery was, indeed, an issue for the Confederates, but the war was not fought to free the slaves, and Lincoln was agreeable to allowing slavery to remain in the Southern states if they remained in the

Union. However, his Emancipation Proclamation was a huge leap in the exercise of presidential power. The Constitution at that time explicitly recognized the institution of slavery, yet Lincoln, in complete disregard of the Constitution, proclaimed some slaves to be free, not based on any moral argument but as a retaliatory measure against states that did not give up their war for independence. The slaves that Lincoln proclaimed freed were not in the areas controlled by the Union, so the Emancipation Proclamation did not actually free any slaves. Slaves in areas that were under the control of Lincoln's government were not freed because the Emancipation Proclamation did not cover them, and slaves outside those areas were not freed because Lincoln's government did not control them.

When the Constitution was written, slavery was not an exclusively Southern institution. The census of 1790 counted slaves in every state except Massachusetts. There was a significant retreat prior to the War between the States, and Jeffrey Rogers Hummel claims that market institutions and the advance of manufacturing put slavery on shaky grounds. Even before the war some slave owners found it more profitable to have their slaves employed for wages in nonagricultural jobs and then to split the wages with the slave. Foreseeing a continuation of this trend with free blacks working alongside slaves for wages, slavery could not last, Hummel argues. The War between the States accelerated the trend through the increased flow of blacks into wartime manufacturing and the recruitment of Southern blacks into the Union army.[8] As a result, Hummel argues, slavery probably would have ended after the War between the States regardless of which side won.

Hummel's argument must be tempered by the realization that it would have been harder to end slavery in the South than in the North. When states abolished slavery, slave owners did not set their slaves free. Rather, they sold them to others in states where slavery remained legal. For example, in New York a law was passed in 1788 prohibiting the importation or sale of slaves within the state, and another law was passed in 1796 declaring that any children born from slaves after July 4, 1799, would be free.[9] On the face of it, this would cause the slave population to decrease, and eventually disappear, as existing slaves grew old and died. But because the children of slaves would be free, this drastically reduced the value of slaves in New York; therefore, slave owners had the incentive to ship them southward and sell them where they would be worth more. The state laws that eliminated slavery in Northern states allowed slave owners to get market value for their slaves, which made the laws more politically palatable but did not free any slaves. Rather, they provided a mechanism for keeping slaves enslaved and for selling them to new owners in the South. Northern states found a politically easier way to abolish slavery than to free their slaves, but obviously every state could not use the same solution, for eventually there would be no states left in which people could buy the slaves.

Although the process took place over many decades, Northerners first sold their slaves to Southerners and then forced Southerners to set them free without compensation, which is worth noting for several reasons. First, the race relations problems that the nation faced were concentrated in the South because Northerners had shipped their slaves there rather than freeing them and letting them stay as free citizens. Indeed, state laws in Northern states tended to be very discriminatory against blacks, discouraging them from staying and preventing them from being equal members of society. Second, it mitigates somewhat the Northern claim of moral superiority on the slavery issue, because it was only in the Southern states that slaves were actually freed. Northern slave owners received market value for their slaves, while Southern slave owners received nothing.

Two main points (and a third intriguing conjecture), therefore, emerge when considering the impact of slavery on the transformation of American government. First, the War between the States was not fought to free the slaves, even though that was one of the results. Second, Lincoln's Emancipation Proclamation represented a major development in the growth of presidential power. A third point worth considering is Hummel's conjecture that slavery would not have survived long in the South anyway.

Reconstruction

Reconstruction refers to the period of time from the end of the War between the States until 1877, when federal troops occupied the Southern states. The occupation began as a part of the war, when Union troops occupied the Confederate territory they had captured, so complete occupation was simply an extension of the process that occurred during the war. As a part of his war powers, Lincoln appointed military governors to the captured territories. While occupied by federal troops, the former Confederate States found themselves in political limbo. Both Presidents Lincoln and, after him, Andrew Johnson recognized the states, but Congress refused to seat their representatives. The 13th Amendment, outlawing slavery, received its two-thirds majority of both houses of Congress without representatives from the Southern states, yet they were acknowledged as states for purposes of counting the three-fourths of the states needed for ratification, and the amendment was ratified only because ten of the eleven former Confederate States voted for ratification.

Union troops closely supervised Southern elections, disallowing many white voters as Confederate sympathizers while encouraging the registration of blacks. This led to many black officeholders and temporarily enhanced the strength of the Republican party in the South. With Republicans in control of both Congress and the White House, one can see the advantages of such policies to those who created them.[10] From a constitutional standpoint, during Reconstruction the War between the States was viewed as the result of actions of individuals who were disloyal to the federal government rather than of actions of the states themselves. Thus, states always were recognized as a part of the Union, even if their citizens were not.[11] After Reconstruction, however, blacks were effectively disenfranchised and the South became solidly Democratic. There was no legacy of black voting rights from the episode, but Reconstruction did permanently raise the size of federal military forces and established the precedent, unimaginable before the War between the States, of having federal troops enforce federal laws within the nation's borders.

It goes without saying that Reconstruction had a huge impact on the postwar South and was instrumental in shaping the next century of American politics. It also had a huge impact on the scope of federal government power over the states. The War between the States established that states do not have the right to secede from the Union; Reconstruction established that the federal government has the power to station its troops in states to enforce federal law. Southern whites were not in a hurry to end occupation because, with so many whites disenfranchised, an end to occupation would result in the election of many blacks, and Southern whites often preferred the military rule of Northern whites to that of Southern blacks.[12] The political power of blacks quickly eroded after Reconstruction ended, and whites regained the right to vote.[13]

One consequence of the political environment the North imposed on the South was that, because Southerners did not object strenuously to the military occupation of their states, this expanded the scope of government power that citizens accepted as legitimate. The federal government was originally formed as a federation of states to undertake activities in their mutual interests. In less than a century it had become a central government that would use military force to enforce its laws, even to the extent of directing the operations of state governments.

The 14th Amendment

The ratification of the 14th Amendment to the Constitution in 1868 signaled a major change in the way states interacted with the federal government and brought with it a major advance in the powers of the federal government. While many factors have conspired to increase the scope and power of the federal government over its history, no amendment to the Constitution has conferred more power to the federal government than the 14th. The 13th Amendment, abolishing slavery, was ratified in 1865, but it became apparent to Northern observers that, while slavery per se may have been abolished, states were establishing a number of laws restricting the rights of the former slaves. Most Southern states denied blacks the right to bear arms or to assemble after sunset. Mississippi prohibited blacks from renting homes or land outside of cities.[14] This led to the Civil Rights Act of 1866, which guaranteed to blacks the right to enter into contracts and to buy and rent property and more generally provided blacks with the same rights as whites. However, the question remained as to whether the federal government had the constitutional power to enforce the act, which led to the demand for a constitutional amendment.

The constitutional question turned on what exactly was implied by the 13th Amendment. The first section of the amendment abolished slavery, and the second section gave Congress "power to enforce this article by appropriate legislation." One interpretation of the 13th Amendment was that it simply severed the bond between slaves and their owners but established no new rights. Following this interpretation, the Civil Rights Act was on shaky ground because it was designed to extend the rights of blacks. Another interpretation of the 13th Amendment was that it was intended to extend to everyone the same rights enjoyed by whites. The issues were not limited to Southern states. In Indiana, for example, blacks were not allowed to enter into contracts, to own real estate, to sit on juries, or to marry whites.[15] If the 13th Amendment was simply meant to free the slaves, it would have no effect on state laws such as those in Indiana. If it was meant to prevent the states from racial discrimination, its effects would be more far-ranging. The passage of the 14th Amendment made the question moot by explicitly preventing this type of discrimination.

Most of the text of the 14th Amendment deals with issues related to the War between the States. It discusses the rights of former Confederates to vote and hold office and affirms debt obligations of the U.S. government related to the war while repudiating Confederate debt. However, the most far-reaching provision of the 14th Amendment is that "No State shall make or enforce any law which shall abridge the privileges or immunities of citizens of the United States, nor shall any State deprive any person of life, liberty, or property, without due process of law; nor deny to any person within its jurisdiction the equal protection of the laws."

The 14th Amendment for the first time explicitly extends federal power to cover the actions of states. Prior to the 14th Amendment, it was presumed that the Constitution placed limits on the actions of the federal government but that it did not bind the states. Thus, the proponents of the Civil Rights Act questioned the degree to which it could be enforced. Quite clearly it would prevent the federal government from discriminating against blacks, but the question remained about whether the federal courts would view the law as under their jurisdiction or whether enforcement at the state level was a power reserved to the state governments under the Constitution. The 14th Amendment explicitly deals with the issue by stating that state governments are required to abide by federal law. In yet another way the War between the States led to a permanent increase in federal government power.

The wording of the amendments is significant, and it is worth comparing the wording of the 13th Amendment with those of the 14th and 15th Amendments. The 13th Amendment, abolishing slavery, reads, "Neither slavery nor involuntary servitude, except as a punishment for crime whereof the party shall have been duly convicted, shall exist within the United States, or any place subject to their jurisdiction."[16] The 14th Amendment says, "No state shall make or enforce any law which shall abridge the privileges or immunities of citizens of the United States"; the 15th Amendment reads, "The right of citizens of the United States to vote shall not be denied or abridged by the United States or by any state on account of race, color, or previous condition of servitude." Thus, while the 13th Amendment is a general declaration of rights, the 14th and 15th Amendments are aimed directly at states, clearly making the power of states subservient to that of the federal government.

The attempt to enhance the power of the federal government over the states was intentional and was an extension of the movement within the Republican party, begun under Lincoln, to firmly establish the supremacy of the federal government over the states.[17] Constitutional scholars of the time believed that Congress overstepped its constitutional authority when trying to enforce the right of Southern blacks to vote, because enforcement of such laws fell clearly within the realm of powers reserved to the states.[18] Indeed, as discussed in chapter 5, Article I, Section 2 of the Constitution explicitly gave states the power to determine who was eligible to vote in federal elections. Thus, any federal law establishing voting rights of individuals was questionable on constitutional grounds. The 14th and 15th Amendments overcame this problem by giving the federal government constitutional authority over state government activity.

In the context of twenty-first-century America, it is easy to focus on the effect of the 14th Amendment in extending equal rights to all citizens. It is also easy to overlook the fact that the amendment fundamentally altered the relationship of states to the federal government and in the process massively expanded the federal government's powers. The *New York World,* an influential newspaper at the time, argued that the amendment would "confer upon Congress all the powers now exercised by the state Legislatures, and reduce the States to the condition of counties."[19] Yet ultimately it was approved by three-quarters of the states, but not without debate. In several states the concern was raised that the amendment would take away from the states their right to determine who was a citizen of the state (which, of course, it did), but this was simply a special case of the overall issue of whether federal laws had supremacy over state laws.[20] The debate shows that Americans were well aware of the fundamental compromises to the sovereignty of states that the 14th Amendment would bring, and so they chose to ratify it with at least some awareness of its long-run potential for changes in American government. Indeed, constitutional scholar Raoul Berger says that the 14th Amendment "is probably the largest source of the [Supreme] Court's business and furnishes the chief fulcrum for its control of controversial policies."[21]

The 15th Amendment and the Right to Vote

The emancipation of the slaves was more of an unintended by-product of the War between the States than a consequence that had been anticipated. Lincoln had, after all, reiterated many times that he did not intend to interfere with slavery, except if it would help hold the Union together, and even offered to peacefully let the Confederate States back in the Union, slavery intact, if they would just cease their secession attempt. But they did not, and the result was that, at the end of the war, the slaves were free. But if these newly freed slaves were counted as citizens, it would raise the number of representatives to which the former Confederate States were entitled and would raise the number of electors they had in the electoral college, giving the South substantially more representation in the federal government than they had before the war. Recall that according to the Constitution slaves were counted as three-fifths of a person for the purpose of allocating seats in the House of Representatives. Extending former slaves the right to vote would have reduced the political power of the North and the power of the Republican party.

The Civil Rights Act of 1866 extended to former slaves the rights to life, liberty, and property but failed to mention the right to vote. Indeed, it was unclear that anybody had a constitutional right to vote, because Article I, Section 2 of the Constitution reserves to states the power to determine who has the right to vote. The 14th Amendment was even more explicit: "when the right to vote at any election . . . is denied to any of the male inhabitants of such State . . . the basis of representation therein shall be reduced in the proportion which the number of such male citizens shall bear to the whole number of male citizens." In short, states determined the qualifications for the right to vote and even though the 14th Amendment guaranteed the rights of former slaves, but the right to vote was not among them. Yet if states did deny former slaves the right to vote, the numbers of representatives and electoral votes they would have would be reduced in proportion.

The 15th Amendment, ratified in 1870, less than two years after the 14th Amendment, changed that. The 15th Amendment in its entirety reads, "Section 1. The right of citizens of the United States to vote shall not be denied or abridged by the United States or by any State on account of race, color, or previous condition of servitude. Section 2. The Congress shall have the power to enforce this article by appropriate legislation." This extends to former slaves, in a limited sense, the right to vote. It did not prevent other requirements not based on race from limiting the qualifications for the right to vote, and, as will be discussed in chapter 11, many blacks were effectively disenfranchised until the 1960s. The 15th Amendment was an attempt, although not wholly successful, to eliminate race as a qualification for the right to vote, but it was significant for two other reasons as well.

First, it shifts the right to determine which citizens are qualified to vote from the states to the federal government, further enhancing the power of the federal government over the states. Second, it creates the perception that certain advantages, conveyed through government, go to those with political power. If the role of the government was limited to impartially protecting the rights of its citizens and maintaining a rule of law, the right to vote would not convey much political power to citizens. Indeed, as noted in chapter 5, the founders did not intend for the officials of the federal government to be chosen by its citizens, except in the limited case of the members of the House of Representatives, and they did not intend for the federal government's activities to be responsive to the demands of its citizens. Obviously that was less true after the War between the States. Federal troops occupied the former Confederate States after the war and had a heavy hand in running state governments. Indeed, the war itself pitted the interests of Northerners against the interests of Southerners, further showing that representation was important. It was made quite clear during Jackson's presidency that, in politics, to the victor belongs the spoils, so having the right to vote meant having the power to make policy demands on the government and having the right to share in the spoils. Thus, the 15th Amendment is significant for the power it gives the federal government, taken directly from the states, and it is significant as a visible manifestation of the nation's transformation from liberty to democracy.

The National Banking Act

One major impact of the War between the States was the reintroduction of the federal government into the control of banking. The United States had always had a relatively small presence in banking, but in their day the First and Second Banks of the United States were sources of controversy. When the Second Bank of the United States saw its charter expire at the end of Jackson's presidency—and as a direct result of Jackson's opposition to the bank—the nation entered an era of free banking, and the federal government had nothing whatsoever to do with the nation's money or its banking system. This was consistent with Jackson's laissez-faire philosophy and with the philosophy of the Democratic party up until the New Deal.

From 1836 until 1861 banks issued their own bank notes, redeemable in gold, with no federal oversight. The U.S. Treasury did mint coins, but money minted by foreign governments and even private mints circulated alongside government-minted coins and privately issued bank notes. Critics of the free banking era cite frequent problems with the monetary system, such as banks going out of business or the notes of questionable banks trading at below par against notes from other more reputable banks. Still, the free banking era survived unthreatened for 25 years, and the American economy continued to prosper. What brought the free banking era to an end had nothing to do with the merits of free banking as a monetary system but rather with the demands that war finance placed on the U.S. government.

In 1861 the U.S. Treasury sold $150 million in bonds to Northern banks to help finance the war. When people began to conjecture that the war would be long and costly, they questioned the ability of the government to redeem the bonds, which then began falling in value. Because banks were holding these bonds as assets, depositors began questioning whether their banks would be able to redeem the notes they issued and started turning in their notes for gold. As a result, the federal government suspended note redemption in 1861 to help avert a banking panic. Then, in 1862, the federal government began issuing its own currency, declaring by fiat that it was legal tender but not backing it by gold. These bills, green in color, became known as greenbacks because they were not backed by anything else. Although redemption of private bank notes had been suspended, their issuers were still obligated to redeem them once the suspension was lifted. Greenbacks carried no such promise.

An increase in the quantity of money leads to inflation, and the issuance of greenbacks into the nation's money supply was no exception. Because private bank notes did carry at least some promise of eventual redemption in gold, greenbacks began trading at a discount to bank money; in response Congress passed the National Banking Act of 1863, which created federally chartered banks and placed a 10 percent tax on transactions that used private bank notes. The idea was that this would drive all state banks out of business or make them apply for federal charters, thus replacing the existing system of state-chartered banks with a national banking system. This idea did not work exactly as planned because state banks began the more widespread use of demand deposits—checking accounts—and were able to survive. Thus, the National Banking Act was intended to replace state banks with federal banks, but due to a historical accident the state-chartered banks survived and the current dual system of state-chartered and federally chartered banks remains intact.

Nevertheless, by 1865 about 75 percent of the money in circulation in the United States was made up of greenbacks and other U.S. notes that were not backed in any other way.[22] By the end of the War between the States, the U.S. government had replaced the 25-year-old system of free banking with a system of federally issued currency, had begun federal regulation of the banking system, and had taken control of the money supply. This, by itself, represents another area in which federal power was enhanced as a direct result of the war and also is an area in which state government power was transferred to the federal government.

Republicans, Democrats, and Government Growth

One cannot escape concluding that a major impact of the War between the States was a massive increase in the power of the federal government. Because casual historical accounts of the war focus on the elimination of slavery and the subsequent racial problems of the South, they overlook this major legacy of Lincoln, the first Republican president. In contrast, Jackson, the first Democratic president, believed that his predecessors had been too complacent about the expansion in federal government power and successfully worked for a retrenchment in the federal government's activities. Judged by the actions of their first presidential officeholders, the Democrats were the party of limited government and states' rights and the Republicans were the party of government growth and federal government power. This characterization is roughly accurate up until the election of Franklin Roosevelt, who reversed the ideological positions of the parties. It is worth remembering that, when at the end of the twentieth century Republicans called for smaller government and Democrats were viewed as the party of big government, these associations were reversed until the New Deal, and even then Southern Democrats retained their identity with limited government and states' rights solidly into the 1970s.

While one would be hard-pressed to identify a twentieth-century politician with nineteenth-century political ideals, the Southern Democrats of the twentieth century retained the legacy of Confederate political ideals and defined the Democratic party until FDR. Some of the political ideas of the Confederates can be seen by examining the Confederate Constitution.

Distributive Politics before the War between the States

One of the Madisonian ideals for American government was to create a government free of factions, such that the apparatus of government was insulated from interest group politics. As the previous chapters have shown, American government before the War between the States had become increasingly factionalized. Perhaps the first important split occurred when Jefferson explicitly wanted to reverse the growth of government that he saw in the Washington and Adams administrations, spearheaded by Secretary of Treasury Alexander Hamilton. The creation of the Democratic party and the introduction of the spoils system into federal politics by Jackson mark another milestone. Of course, the divisions that led to the War between the States further factionalized the nation and led interests on both sides to see the federal government as a vehicle for furthering their own interests. Interest group politics, an accepted part of the political process at the end of the twentieth century, was something the founders recognized as a danger and tried to guard against.

When the Confederates were designing their new government, the constitution they created for their new government provides strong evidence that the authors of that constitution viewed the influence of special interests as a significant problem with American government. The Confederate Constitution was a slightly modified version of the U.S. Constitution, and the most significant modifications were intended to rectify the problems of interest group politics.[23]

The Confederate Constitution

The Confederate Constitutional Convention began in February 1861, and from the beginning those attending the convention intended to base the Confederate Constitution on the Constitution of the United States.[24] Robert Barnwell Rhett from South Carolina, who was called "the father of secession," both initiated South Carolina's secession from the Union and encouraged other states to secede. Rhett favored separate action by South Carolina if other states would not secede together, and initial inquiries produced unfavorable responses from

Virginia, Georgia, and Louisiana but favorable replies from Mississippi, Alabama, and Florida. Although those states were willing to secede, they did not want to be the first ones, which helped establish Rhett's leadership position. Once the states had decided to move cooperatively to form the Confederacy, Rhett was instrumental in calling the Constitutional Convention, and he promoted the idea that the Confederate Constitution should be based on the Constitution of the United States.

The convention consisted of 50 delegates elected from the seven seceding states. Rhett nominated Howell Cobb, a Georgia attorney and former Speaker of the U.S. House of Representatives, to preside over the convention, and the motion was approved by acclamation. Alexander Stevens, an influential delegate from Georgia, called Cobb the most active member of the convention. Cobb's notes on the convention credit Rhett and Robert Toombs, also of Georgia, as being the originators of most of the changes made to the document during the convention.[25]

As a whole the Georgia delegation was undoubtedly the most influential of the convention, but the general structure of the Confederate Constitution had already been determined because the delegates agreed with Rhett's suggestion of using the U.S. Constitution as its model. With its basic structure already determined, the Confederate Constitution was quickly completed and adopted by the convention on March 11, 1861.[26]

In outline and in language, the Confederate Constitution follows the Constitution of the United States almost exactly. It uses the exact same language unless it appeared that an obvious improvement could be made. Furthermore, the Confederate Constitution uses the exact same outline as the Constitution of the United States, except when there is an obvious reason to deviate. Thus, for example, Article I, Section 8 of both documents describes the powers of Congress, and both use the same wording except when the Confederate Constitution intends to deliberately change the meaning or interpretation of that section.

The similarities between the two documents make the differences stand out as perceived problem areas with the U.S. Constitution that became evident after more than seven decades of experience with the document. The following sections consider the differences between the two documents, and the comparison makes clear that the primary problem the Confederate Constitution was trying to address was the use of the legislature to engage in special interest politics.

It is worth noting that the preamble to the Confederate Constitution declares that the states are acting "in order to form a permanent federal government," which differs from the U.S. Constitution, and that Article VI, Section 3, of the Confederate Constitution declares that "This Constitution, and the laws . . . made in pursuance thereof . . . shall be the supreme law of the land," which is identical wording to the language of the U.S. Constitution. In other words, while the Confederate States were seceding from the Union, they intended to create a permanent federal government superior to the state governments. This point is important in addressing the argument that states' rights were a major issue. Undoubtedly the Confederate States were strongly supportive of states' rights, but by adopting a constitution almost identical to the U.S. Constitution, they indicated that the degree of protection of states' rights in the U.S. Constitution was sufficient.

Slavery and Rights

Because the War between the States is so closely identified with the issue of slavery, it is worth noting that the differences between the two constitutions on the issue of slavery are not large. Perhaps the largest difference is a more restrictive clause in the Confederate Constitution. The U.S. Constitution allowed the importation of slaves to continue through 1808 and does not specify what would happen beyond that date, but the Confederate Constitution explicitly prohibits the importing of slaves. While the Confederate provision might be seen as a special interest provision protecting the market value of slaves already in the country, the larger point is that both constitutions permitted slavery, although the Confederate Constitution clearly intended to perpetuate it. The Confederate Constitution explicitly states, "No bill of attainer, ex post facto law, or law denying or impairing the right of property in negro slaves shall be passed." But the explicit provisions in the Confederate Constitution simply preserved the status quo that had existed under the Constitution of the United States. The treatment of slavery in the two constitutions cannot be considered very different; the Confederate Constitution simply went the extra step toward more explicitly preserving the institution as it had existed under the U.S. Constitution.

The Bill of Rights constituting the first 10 amendments to the U.S. Constitution were a part of that document from its adoption. They are built into the body of the Confederate Constitution rather than appended to the end, but they use almost the same wording as the Bill of Rights. With regard to the Bill of Rights, there is a difference of form, but not of substance, between the two constitutions.

The General Welfare

A very significant difference exists between the two constitutions with regard to the omission of a few words. The Confederate Constitution does not refer to the general welfare. The U.S. Constitution gives Congress the power "To lay and collect Taxes, Duties, Imposts, and Excises, to pay the Debts and provide for the common Defence and general Welfare of the United States," while the parallel passage in the Confederate Constitution gives Congress the power "To lay and collect taxes, duties, imposts, and excises, for revenue necessary to pay the debts, provide for the common defense, and carry on the Government of the Confederate States." Quite clearly, reference to the general welfare had already become viewed as a potential open door for any type of governmental activity.[27]

It would seem that the proper interpretation of the general welfare in the U.S. Constitution would be to prevent governmental financing of activities that benefited particular groups or individuals rather than the nation in general. The term "general welfare" is in the sentence referring to taxation. Furthermore, if the intent was to have the government in general try to promote the general welfare, there would be no reason for the Constitution to enumerate the allowable activities of the federal government, because those activities would be in addition to anything else Congress thought would promote the general welfare. And it would be contradictory to restrict the government, as in the 10th Amendment, to those activities enumerated if one of the activities was to promote the general welfare in whatever way Congress saw fit.

Immediately following that clause in the Confederate Constitution is a clause that has no parallel in the U.S. Constitution: "but no bounties shall be granted from the Treasury; nor shall any duties of taxes on importations from foreign nations be laid to promote or foster any branch of industry." This clause directly addresses the use of tariffs to shelter domestic industries from foreign competition. The use of protective tariffs had been an important issue in national politics since they were first adopted in 1816. Southern states felt that they bore heavy costs from the tariffs, because they were used to protect northern manufacturing. Southern economies exported agricultural commodities and imported almost all the goods they consumed, either from abroad or from northern states. Either way, tariffs that protected northern industries raised the cost of goods in the southern states.

There was strong support among members of the Confederate Convention for free trade, but this was balanced against the desire to use tariffs as a revenue source.[28] The wording in the clause mentioned previously was the result of a compromise on the subject. Protective tariffs are one of the products of special interest politics, and by prohibiting protective tariffs the Confederate Constitution was designed to prevent a type of special interest benefit that was apparent in the United States well before the War between the States.

The Confederate Constitution prevents Congress from appropriating money "for any internal improvement intended to facilitate commerce," except for improvements to facilitate waterway navigation, but "in all such cases, such duties shall be laid on the navigation facilitated thereby, as may be necessary to pay for the costs and expenses thereof." Once again, the Confederate Constitution explicitly prohibits general revenues from being used for the benefits of special interests. These constitutional provisions are reminiscent of the ideas of Jackson, who thought it was unconstitutional for the federal government to appropriate expenditures for internal improvements. The idea becomes explicit in the Confederate Constitution.

While reference to the general welfare in the U.S. Constitution might have an ambiguous interpretation, the changes in the Confederate Constitution make clear the interpretation that the Confederate States intended to avoid. The Confederate Constitution's altered wording plainly states that tax revenues are only to be spent for programs that benefit everyone, not programs that benefit a specific segment of the population, and that, in those instances where allowed expenditures are targeted at a specific segment, taxes to pay for those expenditures must be targeted at the same specific segment. The problems of narrow special interests being able to use democratic government for their own private purposes have been well recognized in the twentieth century, but the changes in the Confederate Constitution when compared to the U.S. Constitution show that the problem existed, and was recognized, before the War between the States and that the Confederate States tried to construct their constitution in such a way as to reduce the problem.[29]

Taxation and Appropriations

The problems with taxation in the Union, as perceived by the authors of the Confederate Constitution, paralleled the problem of special interest spending, and the authors of the Confederate Constitution tried to design parallel solutions. One provision in this regard was just mentioned, and the document's authors clearly intended to implement the benefit principle of taxation in which taxes are paid by those who directly benefited from the government's expenditures. In other places the Confederate Constitution added to the Constitution of the United States by requiring that taxes not be levied on those who will not benefit from the expenditures and that expenditures for programs that benefit a narrow constituency be paid for by taxes on that constituency. Explicit redistributional programs in the United States were at that time several decades into the future, and even those in the Union could not envision the federal government becoming involved in transfer programs. The biggest redistributional issue that arose before the War between the States was the subsidization of western postal routes. Still, the Confederates recognized and tried to address the issue of taxing some citizens for the benefit of others.

The Confederate Constitution also tried to limit the special interest expenditures through the appropriations process. The Confederate Constitution gave the president a line-item veto with regard to appropriations: "The President may approve any appropriation and disapprove any other appropriation in the same bill."

Another important difference is that under many circumstances the decision rule for appropriations was two-thirds majority rather than simple majority. "Congress shall appropriate no money from the Treasury, except by a vote of two thirds of both Houses, taken by yeas and nays, unless it be asked and estimated for by some one of the heads of departments, and submitted to Congress by the President." In other words, without the president's request, a two-thirds majority of both houses would have been necessary for Congress to spend money. This fits well within the framework discussed in chapter 3 regarding the fact that larger majorities reduce the probability that one group can impose costs on others. The greater the consensus in collective decision making, the more likely it is that a collective decision will produce benefits in excess of costs. The two-thirds rule creates greater consensus, but it also raises decision-making costs. The logic of reverting to simple majority rule when the budgetary request is initiated by the president is that with the president in agreement there is greater consensus, so a less inclusive decision rule with lower decision-making costs can be used by Congress.

Another provision in the Confederate Constitution reads, "All bills appropriating money shall specify, in Federal currency, the exact amount of each appropriation, and the purposes for which it is made, and Congress shall grant no extra compensation to any public contractor, officer, agent, or servant, after such a contract shall have been made or such service rendered." The Confederate Constitution tried to make sure that there would be no open-ended commitments and no entitlement programs in the Confederate States. All expenditure bills would specify a fixed amount of money, and another bill would be needed to exceed the initial appropriation. All of these differences in appropriations procedures between the United States and the Confederate States were clearly aimed at controlling the ability of special interests to use the government for their benefit.

Other Differences

There are a number of other differences between the two constitutions that deserve remarks. Related to, but more general than, the subject of appropriations is the provision that "Every law, or resolution having the force of law, shall relate to but one subject, and that shall be expressed in the title." This prevents legislatures from tying together unrelated pieces of legislation in an attempt to get special interest benefits passed along with legislation that was more widely favored.

Another difference was that the president of the Confederate States would be elected to a six-year term and would not be eligible for another term. Another minor difference was that the Post Office was required to be financially self-sufficient. This had become an issue in the 1850s when Congress succeeded in subsidizing postal service to the west coast. Yet another difference was that, while the U.S. Constitution prohibits taxes on exports, the Confederate Constitution provided for export taxes if they were approved by a two-thirds vote of both houses of Congress. Other minor differences exist between the two documents, but the constitutions are similar by design because it was the intent of the authors of the Confederate Constitution to retain the U.S. Constitution except where they would be able to improve it with the benefit of more than seven decades of experience.

The Relevance of the Confederate Constitution

An analysis of the Constitution of the Confederate States of America provides a great deal of insight into the workings of the Constitution of the United States before the War between the States. The authors of the Confederate Constitution had enough respect for the U.S. Constitution that they were willing to adopt almost all of its general form and language, modifying only those areas in which they believed clear improvement could be made. Thus, an analysis of the differences can pinpoint specific problems that the founders of the Confederacy believed existed in the U.S. Constitution's design. Despite the hostilities between North and South, at least one Northern source, the New York *Herald,* argued on March 19, 1861, that the Confederate Constitution was an improvement over the U.S. Constitution and that whatever the outcome of the war the Union could benefit from adopting some Confederate ideas.[30]

Seen in this light, it is interesting to note that the problems the authors of the Confederate Constitution actually did address were overwhelmingly associated with the use of legislative powers to impose costs on the general public in order to provide benefits to narrow constituencies. The problems of interest group politics and the expansion of the federal government beyond what some perceived as its constitutionally limited boundaries were already apparent by 1860. The Confederate Constitution tried to address these issues, but the aftermath of the War between the States created a bigger, more powerful federal government that more clearly could dictate its policies to the states rather than a more limited government that the Confederates had envisioned.

Conclusion

The purpose of this chapter is not to glorify the Confederacy or argue that in some sense it was better than the Union. There are strong arguments to the contrary, the most obvious being the Confederate government's attempt to forever perpetuate slavery. Furthermore, even in its quest for independence, the Confederate government imposed what Hummel calls "Confederate war socialism" on its states.[31] Both sides relied on a military draft for a substantial part of their manpower, but unlike the Union, which allowed soldiers to return home after serving their time, the Confederacy often required soldiers to remain in service indefinitely. Both sides also greatly increased taxes, but unlike the Union the Confederacy imposed taxes in kind on farms and required farmers to sell to the government at fixed prices well below market prices. This amounted to a confiscation of agricultural products by the Confederate government. One Confederate farmer even suggested he was better off having the Union army nearby, despite the potential destruction, than the Confederate army, which was sure to take everything he had produced.[32] In fact, both the Confederate and Union governments saw an expansion in their scope of power well beyond anything that had been known in the United States previously.

The analysis of the Confederate Constitution in this chapter is not intended as a defense of the Confederate government. Rather, the analysis sheds some light on the way in which American government was viewed in 1860 as well as on the direction a new constitutional convention might have pointed. The analysis shows that even during that time period there was widespread sentiment that the federal government was too powerful and that it was too easy for interest groups to gain benefits from the federal government at the expense of the general public. The evolution from liberty to democracy was already obviously under way prior to the War between the States. The Confederate Constitution, which really was only an amended version of the U.S. Constitution, would have pushed the nation back in the direction of liberty. Instead, the aftermath of the war left a much more powerful federal government, and much more centralized government power, paving the way for future interest group activity and additional government expansion.

By establishing the right of the federal government to draft citizens into war, to place federal troops in the states to enforce the law under Reconstruction, and to regulate the banking and monetary system, the U.S. government clearly expanded its scope of power during the War between the States. Lincoln's Emancipation Proclamation represented a massive increase in the exercise of presidential power. The passage of the 14th Amendment changed the fundamental relationship between the federal government and the states. Prior to the War between the States the U.S. Constitution was viewed as a constraint on the power of the federal government but not on the states. The 14th Amendment allowed federal law to be imposed on the states. With the 15th Amendment the federal government for the first time asserted its right to determine qualifications for the right to vote, a power formerly in the hands of the states, and in so doing further pushed the fundamental principle of American government toward democracy. The War between the States clearly enhanced the power of the federal government and firmly established the supremacy of the federal government over the states.

CHAPTER 7

Interest Groups and the Transition to Government Growth: 1870–1915

If one looks only at expenditures, federal government growth really did not begin until the twentieth century. Prior to World War I federal expenditures were only about 2 percent of the gross national product (GNP) and had actually been shrinking as a percentage of income for decades, but by 1990 federal expenditures had grown to about 22.5 percent of the GNP. The contrast between the nineteenth and twentieth centuries is clearly shown in figure 3, which plots real per capita federal expenditures (in 1990 dollars) from 1800 to 1990. After more than a century of low federal expenditures and almost no growth up until World War I, the remainder of the twentieth century shows constant and substantial growth. Peaks in federal expenditures associated with the two world wars are clearly evident, but the most striking feature of figure 3 is not the peaks but rather the continued upward trend in the twentieth century, which contrasts so sharply with the relatively unchanging expenditures in the nineteenth century. The figure shows a sharp transition to federal government expenditure growth early in the twentieth century. This chapter describes how the activities of political interest groups between the War between the States and World War I laid the foundation for that transition to government growth.

The previous six chapters have already discussed the underlying causes of government growth. Since the American Revolution, which was fought for the cause of liberty, American political institutions have continually evolved away from the principle of liberty toward the principle of democracy. There were those leaders like Andrew Jackson, who viewed liberty and democracy as mutually reinforcing, but much of the impetus behind democracy was the push by interest groups to use the democratic political process to further their narrow interests. The War between the States had greatly increased the power of the federal government, which brought with it the opportunity for interest groups to use that power for their own ends. The activities of special

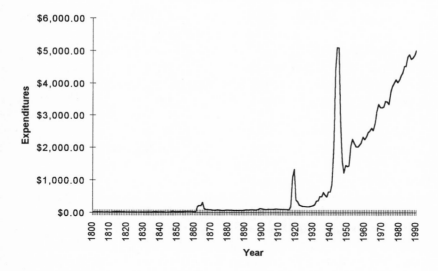

Fig. 3. Real per capita federal expenditures: 1800–1990 (in constant
1990 dollars)

interests after the War between the States up through the beginning of
the twentieth century transformed the relationship between the government and its citizens and laid the foundation for the massive government expenditure growth of the twentieth century.

Federal expenditures did grow during the nineteenth century but
much less than in the twentieth century. In 1800 federal expenditures
per capita were $16.87 and by 1900 had risen to $107.24, for an
increase of 636 percent. By 1990 federal expenditures were $5,010.82
per capita—an increase of 4,673 percent since 1900. (These dollar
figures, and all dollar figures in this chapter, are given in inflation-
adjusted 1990 dollars unless otherwise noted.) While federal government expenditures did grow by a significant amount in the nineteenth
century, the percentage growth was much less than that in the twentieth century.

The growth of federal expenditures in the nineteenth century looks
small relative to growth in the twentieth century, but it looks even
smaller when the data are examined in more detail. Most of the growth
in the nineteenth century came prior to and during the War between
the States. By 1861 federal expenditures were $30.33 per capita—

almost double what they were in 1800. They more than doubled again by 1870 to $79.76, but in 1895 they were $79.56, almost what they were 25 years earlier. By 1900 they were 35 percent higher than five years before, largely because of the Spanish-American War, but fell to $83.60 per capita by 1916. Inflation-adjusted per capita federal expenditures increased by less than 5 percent in the 45 years from 1870 to the beginning of World War I.[1]

The decline is even more dramatic when federal expenditures are viewed as a percentage of income. Federal expenditures were more than 4 percent of the GNP in 1870 and fell to 2.4 percent by 1880. By 1900 federal expenditures were 2.8 percent of the GNP and because of income growth had fallen to 1.9 percent by 1915.[2] From the end of the War between the States to the beginning of World War I federal expenditures were roughly the same in real per capita terms and had declined substantially as a percentage of income. This contrasts sharply with the period of government growth after World War I and demonstrates that twentieth-century federal government growth was a phenomenon in itself, not just an extrapolation of the growth of the previous century.

The transition to government growth came at the end of the Progressive Era, which is commonly dated from 1900 until the start of World War I, and this provides a possible explanation for the growth. Robert Higgs provides an excellent history of the period and ultimately concludes that there was a change in ideology around the turn of the century that led people to demand more government—and a government more oriented toward protecting and furthering its citizens' economic interests.[3] The conclusion that the government growth of the twentieth century was caused by a change in ideology is ultimately unsatisfying, however, because people do not change their ways of thinking for no reason.[4] A complete explanation should reveal why there was a change in ideology rather than treat the change as exogenous. This chapter examines the behavior of interest groups, and the following chapter considers the ideology of the period in more detail.

Similarly, one can cite the many institutional changes around that period of time as reasons for government growth. The most prominent of those was the 16th Amendment to the Constitution, ratified in 1913, which allowed the federal government to collect income taxes. While it is indisputably true that the federal government could not have grown nearly as much in the twentieth century without the income tax, the passage of the income tax must be viewed as a result of changing preferences for the size of government, and it was added to the Constitution to fund the increased demand for government expenditures. Why was the income tax amendment not passed sooner? Indeed, the United States used a temporary income tax from 1861 to 1871 to help finance the War between the States but repealed it. The income tax amendment did not cause the government to grow. It was passed in response to the demand for more revenues to feed a growing government.

This chapter identifies three major factors associated with the transition to government growth following the War between the States. (1) A growing economy produced a budget surplus, which in turn produced an opportunity for interest groups to lobby for federal transfers. Veterans were an organized interest group already receiving federal support, and during the transition veterans groups organized to become the first rent-seeking special interest to capture major transfer payments from the federal government. (2) The scope of the federal government's activities continued to be broadened from the protection of individual rights to include the promotion of the economic interests of its citizens. This is most clearly seen in the increase in federal regulatory activities. (3) The federal bureaucracy was transformed from a group of political appointees who owed their jobs and loyalties to the current administration into a civil service where jobs were objectively assigned based on civil service examinations and where principles of scientific public management were used to create a long-term workforce of career public-sector employees. Each of these changes led to the strengthening of interest groups that demanded a larger government to further their economic interests.[5]

Throughout most of the nineteenth century the transition from liberty to democracy as the fundamental principle underlying American government was a political phenomenon, not an economic one, because the government at that time had a relatively small impact on people's economic activities. It protected their rights but taxed them relatively little, spent relatively little, and engaged in little regulation. In 1860 government involvement in the economy was small and in many areas declining. Government involvement in banking was minimal, especially at the federal level, after 1836 with the demise of the Second Bank of the United States; government regulation of medical care was smaller than it ever had been;[6] and in most other areas people's activities were only peripherally affected by government. That changed substantially in the period from 1870 to 1915, when American democracy moved from being primarily a feature of the political system to being a significant feature of the economic system as well.

The Federal Budget between the Wars

The growth of federal government expenditures is only a small part of the transition to government growth, and even with regard to expenditures the most significant factor is not the level of expenditures themselves but rather the way in which a powerful interest group was able to gain enough political clout to produce a major increase in direct monetary transfers to group members. Veterans established the precedent that would be emulated by other interest groups as the government grew, changing the character of government expenditures. To see how veterans groups were able to organize to capture those transfers, some background on the federal budget after the War between the States is useful.

The War between the States had a profound effect on the federal budget between that war and World War I for several reasons. First, in overall level the magnitude of postwar expenditures was at least double the prewar outlays. Before the War between the States, federal outlays hovered in the neighborhood of $30 per capita, and after the war they gradually fell from about $80 in 1869 to a low of $60.44 in 1886. A substantial amount of this increase was directly war related, however. Subtracting military, veterans, and interest expenditures, federal outlays were roughly $20 per capita after the war, and military expenditures in the 1870s were about $15 per capita, placing expenditures in the 1870s roughly in the same range as they were before the war. Some of these military expenditures were directly related to the War between the States, because federal troops occupied the South during Reconstruction, which ended in 1877. Thus, the apparent ratcheting up of federal expenditures after the War between the States was primarily due to additional expenditures that were directly related to the war.

Federal outlays remained relatively stable until the late 1870s, when they began to increase substantially. Figure 4 shows real per capita federal expenditures from 1870 to 1915 to illustrate the change. The solid line in the figure shows total per capita outlays, which is identical to the 1870–1915 segment of figure 3. The dashed line shows total outlays less interest expenditures. After the war the federal government debt topped $2.5 billion, and budget surpluses up through the early 1890s lowered the debt to about $1 billion and with it lowered interest payments on the debt, as is apparent in figure 4. Total expenditures look relatively stable until the late 1880s because higher expenditures on federal programs were being offset by lower interest payments. The dashed

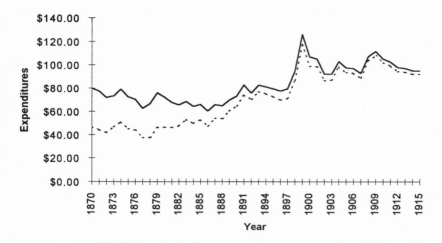

Fig. 4.   Real per capita federal expenditures: 1870–1915 (in constant 1990 dollars). (The solid line represents total expenditures; the dashed line represents total expenditures minus interest on public debt.)

line in figure 4 shows that, when interest payments are subtracted, federal expenditures declined slightly through the late 1870s and then began a sustained growth that lasted until the turn of the century.

Noninterest federal expenditures were $37.67 per capita in 1878. Ten years later they had increased 43 percent to $53.86 per capita, and by 1898, just prior to the Spanish-American War, they were $86.82, a 61 percent increase in a decade and a 230 percent increase when compared to 1878. The spike in federal expenditures in 1899 is due to military expenditures associated with the Spanish-American War, and expenditures were once again relatively stable after the turn of the century up to the beginning of World War I. Within this longer period is a remarkable increase in noninterest expenditures in the seven-year period from 1886 to 1893. Expenditures were $47.73 per capita in 1886 and increased 61 percent to $77.01 by 1893. Noninterest federal expenditures were relatively stable through the 1870s and grew only modestly during most of the 1880s before beginning that substantial growth in 1886. This suggests that if the transition to government growth is identified as a point in time—rather than a range of years—then, using expenditures as an indicator, that point would be in the mid- to late 1880s.

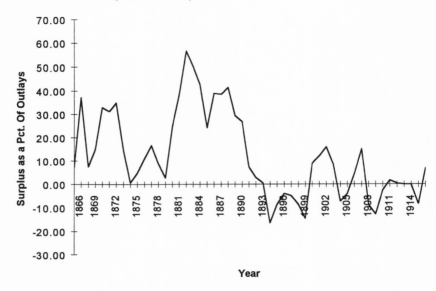

**Fig. 5.   U.S. federal government surplus as a percentage of outlays.
(Note: A federal income tax was in effect from 1861 to 1871 and again
beginning in 1913. The economy suffered a substantial depression in
1893–94.)**

The stabilization of expenditures after the turn of the century is
due to the revenue constraints faced by the federal government. Figure
5, depicting the federal budget surplus, shows that throughout the
1880s and up to 1893 the federal government ran a substantial budget
surplus that provided the resources for rising federal expenditures. The
substantial growth stopped in 1893, at the same time that the budget
was approximately balanced. As figure 5 shows, the budget remained
approximately in balance up until the beginning of World War I.
Faced with this revenue constraint, federal expenditures had to stop
growing until more revenues could be found.[7] If the underlying growth
before 1893 reflects the demand for increased federal expenditures, this
explains the derived demand for a federal income tax to provide additional revenues that would allow continued growth.

Figure 5 illustrates that throughout the 1880s the federal government had more than enough revenues to meet the demand for federal
expenditures. The surplus was used to pay down the public debt not
because there was a mandate to do so but because the supply of revenues exceeded the effective demand for expenditures.[8] While the debt

from the War between the States remained substantial, it was scarcely reduced during the 1870s. In 1870 the public debt stood at $2.4 billion and was reduced to $2.3 billion by 1879. The change was barely noticeable. By 1893 the public debt was down to $961 million. If the populace had an urgent desire to see the public debt reduced, that reduction should have started right after the end of the war. It was not until 15 years after the War between the States ended that the debt began to be rapidly reduced, not because money was expressly set aside for debt reduction but because income and population growth generated the revenues that allowed debt repayment.[9]

The surpluses of the 1880s cannot be explained as a result of debt repayment, therefore. There was almost no repayment in the 1870s, and after 1893 the public debt began increasing again, despite that only about 60 percent of it had been paid off. Figure 5 shows an excess supply of federal revenues that rapidly eroded as federal expenditures increased through the 1880s. Early in the 1890s the balanced budget constraint was reached, which temporarily halted the growth in federal expenditures until the income tax amendment was passed in 1913.

Components of the Federal Budget

The noninterest federal outlays shown in figure 4 are broken down into three components in figure 6. The solid line represents civilian outlays, calculated by subtracting outlays for interest, military, and veterans from total outlays. Civilian expenditures per capita declined through most of the 1870s and stood at $17 in 1880. By 1891 they had increased by 72 percent to $29.21. Thus, civilian outlays mirror the overall trend in outlays, beginning their transition to growth in the 1880s. Military expenditures, represented by the dashed line, barely increased until the 1890s. In the 1870s military expenditures per capita were $18 and were $18.26 in 1897. They ratcheted up due to the Spanish-American War, and while they are the lowest of the three components in 1897, after that time military expenditures far exceeded the other three components up through World War I.

Outlays on veterans show the most remarkable growth of the three components. Despite the decline in the number of veterans during the period due to the deaths of veterans of the War between the States, and despite the rapid population growth of nonveteran taxpayers, per capita veterans expenditures continued to increase from $7.20 in 1870 to $15.38 in 1880 to $24.61 in 1890, peaking at $34.39 in 1893. Veterans compensation and pensions were the earliest major U.S. transfer

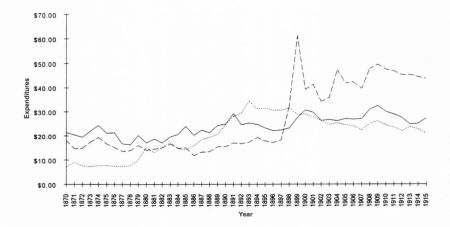

Fig. 6.   Components of federal outlays: 1870–1915 (real per capita expenditures in 1990 dollars). (The solid line represents civilian expenditures; the dashed line represents military expenditures; the dotted line represents veterans compensation and pensions.)

programs, and veterans formed a powerful interest group, so they were able to maintain generous benefits through the political process. A transfer program like this, once started, is difficult to slow, and the increase in payments to veterans mimics the increased payments to retirees through Social Security and Medicare in the late twentieth century.[10] Once the balanced budget constraint was hit in 1893, per capita expenditures on veterans began to decline.

Veterans Expenditures during the Transition

The increase in veterans benefits paid after the War between the States is an important part of the transition to government growth for several reasons. Most obviously, this category of federal expenditures grew more rapidly than any other from the mid-1870s to the mid-1890s. These expenditures are more significant, however, because they represent the most substantial interest group expenditure undertaken by the federal government prior to the twentieth century. The growth of veterans benefits was entirely a result of organized interests working through the political system to produce benefits for their members and paved the road for the domination of interest groups in American government.

Veterans made up more than 5 percent of the total population after the War between the States, but because of the restricted franchise they made up a much larger fraction of the voting population. The presidential election of 1864 pitted Lincoln, running for reelection, against Democrat George McClellan, an army general whom Lincoln had removed from command, and both sides fervently pursued the vote of soldiers as a group. After the war, there was little in the way of assistance for veterans, but in 1865 a group called the United States Soldiers and Sailors Protective Society was formed for the purpose of aiding veterans. This nonpolitical group hoped to further the interests of veterans through "mutual confidence and mutual help."[11]

The next year, in 1866, Union veteran Dr. Benjamin Stephenson founded a more formidable veterans group called the Grand Army of the Republic (GAR), which was explicitly set up to be a political group. The GAR was not organized along military lines but was more like a political party, with precincts and statewide headquarters, and rapidly became a substantial political force.[12]

Federal benefits to veterans of the War between the States were defined by acts of Congress in 1865 and 1866. Payments went to disabled veterans and to surviving widows and children of those killed in the war according to specific schedules. Veterans who survived the war uninjured were not entitled to pensions.[13] To try to control the level of expenditures on pensions, an act in 1868 specified that, to be eligible for a disability pension, the disability had to have occurred in the line of duty.[14] Soldiers injured while in the army, but not injured in the line of duty, were not entitled to pensions. Pensions had to be claimed within five years of the disabling injury for the claim to be valid, although there was an appeals process that allowed exceptions to the five-year time limit.[15] Veterans benefits at the end of the 1860s were intended to help out the soldiers who were injured or killed in the war and their dependents, and those who were disabled in the war but eventually recovered were expected to give up their pensions.

Veterans made up a substantial interest group, and with the political organization provided by the GAR they became a potent political force. In 1872 there were 1.8 million veterans and 6.5 million votes cast in the presidential election. Without veteran turnout data it is hard to say what percentage of voters were veterans, but veterans divided by votes gives a fraction of 0.28, suggesting the substantial political power of veterans. The GAR was instrumental in establishing Memorial Day as a national holiday in 1869 despite widespread sentiment that the holiday would hinder the reunification of the nation[16] but had the broader agenda of increasing federal veterans benefits to its members. Instrumental in the effort to increase benefits was the influence of a substantial number of pension attorneys in the GAR who became quite active in pursuing pension cases for individual veterans.[17]

There was relatively little veterans legislation through most of the 1870s, but, encouraged by pension attorneys, veterans continued to apply for disability pensions through the appeals process (because the five-year time limit for application had expired). As the commissioner of pensions noted in 1871, when an appeal was filed it often was difficult to tell whether the disabling injury was actually a result of the war.[18] Furthermore, veterans whose injuries had healed continued to collect pensions in violation of the law, but violations were difficult to detect, and it was often a subjective determination as to whether the veteran had actually recovered.

The Arrears Act of 1879 was a major turning point for veterans benefits. Prior to the Arrears Act, veterans would begin receiving pension benefits at the time of application. After passage of the act, benefits commenced from the time of discharge from the army or, for dependents, from the time of death. Those already receiving pensions were due arrears, but what is more significant is that new applicants would also receive arrears if their appeal was successful. This substantially increased the value of appealing to receive a pension, increasing the number of applications tremendously and also increasing the number of fraudulent applications.[19] Prior to the Arrears Act about 1,600 pension claims were filed each month. After the act passed new claims rose to more than 10,000 a month.[20] The average arrears payment was about $1,000, which was a substantial sum because at that time the average earnings of nonfarm workers in the United States was about $400 a year.[21] As figure 6 shows, federal expenditures on veterans benefits skyrocketed in the 1880s.

For veterans who were denied pensions, or who were not disabled, they could pursue another route to receive a pension—through a special bill requiring the approval of the president. Grover Cleveland, first elected as president in 1884, signed 1,453 such bills in his first term, making him popular with veterans. Nevertheless, when in 1887 he vetoed the Dependent Pension Bill, which would have provided pensions to all disabled veterans regardless of whether their disabilities were war related, he lost his bid for reelection, in no small part because of opposition from the GAR.[22]

When considering the GAR specifically, and veterans in general, as an interest group, one must recognize the link between veterans interests and the Republican party. The Republicans, the party of Lincoln, victorious in the War between the States, had their political strength in the North, whereas the South was a Democratic stronghold. If this was not enough to create regional differences in party strengths, Confederate veterans were not eligible for federal pensions, meaning that veterans benefits were a transfer from taxpayers in general to recipients in Northern states.[23] Thus, there was a natural alliance between veterans groups and the Republican party. In the twentieth century the Democratic party was often viewed as having close ties with organized labor, but the natural bonds that linked organized veterans groups with the Republican party in the late nineteenth century were considerably stronger. The Republican party relied on veterans for electoral support and paid off their supporters with increasingly generous veterans benefits.

Benjamin Harrison, the Republican who defeated Cleveland, understood the importance of veterans support. One of the leading figures in the GAR was James Tanner, commander of the GAR's New York department. Tanner campaigned for Harrison, and his support in helping Harrison win the presidential election was repaid when Harrison appointed Tanner pension commissioner. Harrison instructed Tanner to "Be liberal with the boys," to which Tanner replied, "I will drive a six-mule team through the Treasury."[24] In 1890 veterans benefits were broadened further to provide benefits to disabled veterans and survivors benefits to widows of veterans regardless of whether they were injured in the war and regardless of need.[25] Thus, a veteran who became mentally or physically disabled after the war was entitled to a pension, as was any widow of a veteran. In practice, few claims were denied, and "large numbers of persons, seemingly in normal health, have discovered in themselves ailments which would have passed unnoticed but for the pension laws."[26]

Benefits to veterans of the War between the States became a major political issue as Tanner managed to transfer increasingly large sums from the Treasury to veterans. Charles William Eliot, president of Harvard College, argued in a public speech, "I hold it to be a hideous wrong inflicted upon the republic that the pension system instituted for the benefit of the soldiers and sailors of the United States has been prostituted and degraded by a whole series of Republican administrations. As things are, gentlemen, one cannot tell whether a pensioner of the United States received an honorable wound in battle or contracted a chronic catarrh twenty years after the war."[27]

Late in the nineteenth century the conventional wisdom was that during normal times the government should run a budget surplus to offset deficits that would inevitably occur during wars and other emergencies. But, as figure 5 shows, by 1893 the surplus had been completely eroded, and one Republican loyalist lamented, "If Tanner does not go soon, the surplus will—and the Republican party after it."[28] Tanner's successes on behalf of veterans were not uniformly appreciated by the general public, as the preceding quotation indicates, and Tanner resigned after only six months as commissioner. Nevertheless, Cleveland, defeated in 1888 by Harrison after one term, ran again and won in 1892. This is especially noteworthy because, after the election of Lincoln, the first Republican president, in 1860, Cleveland was the only Democrat elected to the White House until the election of Woodrow Wilson in 1914.[29]

Veterans as an Interest Group

The historical details are worth reviewing to understand how veterans interests became so successful after the War between the States. These details support a straightforward interest group story. After the war veterans made up a substantial share of the voting population, and because of the political entrepreneurship of Benjamin Stephenson they became a well-organized political force through the GAR. There was a natural alliance between the GAR and the Republican party because both had their strengths geographically concentrated in the North. The GAR supported the Republican party and in exchange was paid off with increasingly generous pensions during a period of Republican domination. Another enabling factor was that, due to the budget surplus, funds were available, allowing Republicans to compensate veterans in exchange for their support. Veterans were an organized group and were prepared to argue their case. The surplus provided an opportunity for them to succeed.

While maintaining the surplus was viewed as prudent public policy, it was unclear exactly how much of a surplus it would be prudent to keep. Eventually, increasingly generous veterans benefits eroded the whole thing. It is interesting to note from figure 6 that in the 1890s, when the surplus had disappeared, increases in veterans benefits also ceased. As long as there was a budget surplus veterans were able to garner increasing transfers, but once the surplus was gone the growth in veterans benefits ended too.

The veterans lobby after the War between the States was the first large-scale special interest group in the United States, and it paved the way for future interest group activity. As the history of the period shows, benefits were viewed as payments to an interest group rather than as an activity furthering the common good. There was substantial political debate on the subject, and political campaigns consciously considered the payment of veterans benefits as a way to buy the support of that voting bloc.

Lobbying, today accepted as a normal part of the political process, was not viewed that way in the nineteenth century. Veterans, with the GAR as their political organization, set the stage for large-scale lobbying by openly promoting additional benefits for the members of their group. Seeing that example, other groups who wanted benefits from Congress could hardly resist following their lead. Rather than being reserved for certain well-defined public purposes, the federal budget was being transformed into a pork pie, and if some groups did not want to try to compete for a share, the budget would be spent on others.

The Increasing Scope of Government

Interest group activity did not begin with veterans from the War between the States, of course. Many writers have observed that individuals attempted to use government to further their own private interests well prior to the War between the States, and in many ways the scope of federal government activity in the United States began increasing from the time the nation was founded.[30] But the War between the States obviously strengthened the power of the federal government because it established the primacy of the federal government over the states.[31] While the monetary transfers garnered by veterans benefited them as an interest group, the transfers did not change the overall nature of the federal government's activities. In contrast, the federal government's regulatory actions in the late nineteenth century did.

Terry Anderson and Peter Hill date the birth of the transfer society at 1877, when the Supreme Court decided in *Munn v. Illinois* that the Illinois legislature could regulate grain elevator rates.[32] Anderson and Hill argue that Supreme Court decisions tracing back to *Munn v.*

Illinois were crucial in establishing the government as an institution designed to further the economic well-being of its citizens in addition to protecting their rights. This landmark case allowing transfer through regulation came at the same time that the growth in veterans benefits established the legitimacy of transferring income directly from the Treasury to a subgroup of the population. The *Munn v. Illinois* case gave a state government the right to balance the economic interests of citizens against one another, but it was not long before the federal government became significantly involved, changing the way in which citizens interacted with their governments. Perhaps the most significant area in which government grew prior to World War I was in regulation, and the most heavily regulated area of the economy was rail transportation.

Regulation

As the rail network grew after the War between the States, pushes for regulation came from two major directions. First, shippers, who were mainly farmers trying to move their products to market, wanted rate regulation to protect their economic interests from the potential monopoly power of the railroads. Second, the railroads themselves were concerned about excessive competition and wanted regulation as a way of protecting their economic interests against the forces of the market. While at first there may appear to be a contradiction, it is indeed possible that local shippers might fall prey to a local branch line monopolist, while on trunk lines there could be substantial competition. The more significant feature to note in both cases, however, is that individuals wanted regulation not to protect their rights or to secure their property but rather to further their economic interests.

State governments, in support of farming interests, passed legislation to try to encourage competition among railroads, to prevent price discrimination, and to try to keep rates low. The most significant action at the state level was the creation of the Illinois Railroad and Warehouse Commission in 1873.[33] While state legislatures had previously passed legislation to aid shippers, this was the first case in which an independent commission was established for that purpose, and the Illinois commission served as a model for the Interstate Commerce Commission (ICC) in 1887. While farmers supported railroad regulation, New York City shippers may have been the strongest single interest group favoring regulation to try to preserve the status of the port of

New York as America's dominant corridor through which goods came to and from European markets.[34]

The railroads themselves saw advantages to regulation. Unstable prices, disliked by rail customers, could also be detrimental to the railroads. A recession in 1884 led to the failure of a number of railroads, and the railroads wanted to undertake pooling arrangements for their mutual profitability. Thus, the railroad industry, which was very competitive, wanted the ICC to stabilize rates and regulate routes.[35] Essentially, the ICC cartelized the railroad industry, allowing it to be more profitable than it could have been in a more competitive unregulated environment. At the beginning of the twenty-first century it is well recognized that private business can use government regulation to make itself more profitable.[36] This same idea applied to the railroad industry in the late 1800s.

What matters for present purposes is that there were interest groups on both sides of the market that wanted regulation in order to further their own economic well-being. Interest group politics again were at work, but these regulatory changes also represent an expansion of the role of government to further individuals' interests as the federal government for the first time showed itself willing to intervene to further the economic welfare of specific groups rather than merely to protect their rights. In addition, the establishment of the ICC as a separate commission transferred the responsibility for regulation from the legislature to a separate administrative agency within the executive branch of government. This marked a significant change in the way interest groups were able to interact with their governments.

The Supreme Court decision of *Wabash, St. Louis, and Pacific Railway Co. v. Illinois,* delivered in October 1886, also pushed Congress toward the establishment of the ICC. In *Wabash,* the Court ruled that state regulatory agencies could not impose restrictions on interstate transactions without an act of Congress, pushing Congress toward the national regulation of commerce through the ICC.[37]

The ICC was a natural place for the federal government to begin regulation of the economy, because Article I, Section 8 of the Constitution explicitly gives Congress the right "To regulate Commerce . . . among the several States," but the ICC was the beginning of a major push for federal involvement in people's economic affairs. In 1890 the Sherman Act was passed, explicitly for the benefit of the economic interests of a subset of the population. The Pure Food and Drug Act was passed in 1906, the Federal Reserve was created in 1913, and the

Federal Trade Commission was organized in 1914. Throughout this period there were major amendments to the Interstate Commerce Act, and additional legislation passed explicitly to further the economic well-being of specific interest groups.[38]

At the beginning of the twenty-first century such government activities are taken for granted as a part of government's natural role, but at the end of the nineteenth century this was a radical departure, as a government that historically had been constitutionally limited to protecting the rights of its citizens began acting to further their economic interests as well. There was a change in philosophy and also a change in method, as Congress, starting with the ICC, established regulatory agencies independent of the legislative branch of government to further the economic interests of its citizens. At the beginning of the twenty-first century, when the government at all levels spends close to 35 percent of the gross domestic product (GDP), transfers of money and goods in kind (such as public housing and government health care) are common, but without a large supply of tax revenues to draw on, regulation can serve as a form of taxation by forcing individuals to provide benefits to others at their own expense. It is certainly clear that, if government expenditures are examined without considering regulation, the examination neglects a major part of the government's activity in the economy.[39] The Interstate Commerce Act in 1887 was the beginning of a new paradigm in government regulation.

Civil Service and the Science of Public Administration

The evolution of the federal government included not only the growth of interest groups, a radical change in the scope of government through regulation, and the participation of the legislature and the courts in designing these changes, but it also included fundamental changes in the administrative nature of government. While the idea of scientific management, both in the public and private sectors, was gaining currency throughout the second half of the nineteenth century,[40] the watershed event was the passage of the Civil Service Act of 1883, which established career civil service with formal criteria for hiring and a hierarchical professional structure for federal employees.

Civil service reform after the War between the States began in 1871 with a law that gave the president the authority to establish rules governing the hiring of and performance standards for government employees.[41] With the Republican party dominating the White House, many observers felt that civil service jobs were made on partisan political grounds, and appointments at the New York Customhouse were especially visible and especially criticized for their partisan nature. The New York Customhouse was significant because it accounted for more than half of the federal government's revenues in the 1870s.[42] Ohio Democrat George Pendleton proposed legislation that would award civil service jobs based on the results of competitive examinations, and while the legislation was not initially given much chance to pass, Republicans sensed their vulnerability on the issue, and the measure was belatedly passed in Chester Arthur's administration in 1883. Still, it was not enough to prevent the defeat of Arthur to Cleveland in 1884, making Cleveland the first Democrat elected to the presidency since 1856.[43]

Stephen Skowronek notes, "The most widely held interest in central administrative reform in the post–Civil War era was expressed in the idea of retrenchment."[44] He goes on to say that this meant cutting the excesses from wartime government, focusing government activities within a limited sphere of action, and increasing the efficiency of government. "Retrenchment" is not the first word that might come to mind to describe the evolution of government during the period. There were 53,000 civilian federal employees in 1871, and by 1901 civilian federal employment had grown to 256,000, so considering both the creation of the civil service and the substantial growth of employment during the period, government employment changed substantially both in its scope and in its nature.

Civil service reform in 1883 created a system whereby federal employees were hired in a nonpartisan way, based on objective test results. Throughout the remainder of the century, an increasing share of federal employees found themselves under the new system, and therefore an increasing share of employees did not owe their jobs to the current administration. More substantial change came after the turn of the century, when President Teddy Roosevelt created more nonpatronage positions out of positions formerly available as political appointments. He also passed stringent rules to create a "neutral" civil service that had stronger ties to the executive branch of government but whose ties to Congress and political parties were severed.[45] During Roosevelt's administration the civil service became more independent from political influences, but more substantial change occurred during the Taft administration, when in 1911 the Lloyd-LaFollette Act gave civil servants the right to organize and to petition Congress for their own interests and also set up a civil service procedure to evaluate the performance of civil servants.[46]

Thus, the period from the late 1870s until the beginning of World War I saw civil service transformed from a system of political patronage, controlled by party interests, into a system insulated from politics to a large degree. The new system was insulated because hiring and promotions were determined from within, following an objective set of rules, and federal workers had the right to unionize. Whereas prior to this time civil servants could expect their interests to be closely tied to the current administration, after this time a permanent civil service was created that could not be fired and could outlast administrations. This gave the civil service more autonomy to set policy and to disregard administration policy. Government bureaucrats could then become an interest group themselves, having an interest in the ongoing growth of the federal government rather than having their interests tied closely to the success of incumbent politicians. Thus, there is a close link between civil service reform and the incentives for those in government to act as an interest group that would promote growth in government expenditures.

The Army

After having explained how veterans became the first major interest group to redirect substantial federal transfers their way and how civil servants were able to transform federal employees from being dependent on the administration in power into being an autonomous and powerful element of federal government, the army during this period stands as an interesting contrast. As a clue in trying to answer the question of how government was transformed in the late 1800s, the army is like the dog that did not bark. Prior to the War between the States, most soldiers served in locally organized militias, which remained the case after the war as well. While there was a federal superstructure above the local organizations, and while those in the U.S. War Department wanted an increasingly professionalized army, such reform did not happen until the twentieth century.[47]

The reason this reform did not happen earlier is because local militias, with local leaders and local members, were more powerful as an interest group than those at the federal level. If soldiers had been federal employees, like civil servants, military reforms similar to civil service reforms might have occurred. Interest group politics leaned the other way, however, and the principles of scientific management that had permeated civil service were unable to produce meaningful reform in military service. Only in the twentieth century did international conflicts lead to a centralized and bureaucratic federal military establishment that would parallel the development of civil service.

The foundations for twentieth-century growth in military expenditures were laid in the late nineteenth century, with the purchase of ships for the navy that presaged the twentieth-century military-industrial complex. Shipbuilders thus became an interest group that favored more military spending and a more organized federal military force.[48] However, aggregate military expenditure data show that their main successes had to wait until the twentieth century. Following the Spanish-American War in 1898 the U.S. Military Academy at West Point stepped up its effort to professionalize the army, but the real transformation in the military did not come until World War I.

Such measures as civil service reform to vest more power and autonomy in federal employees and the growth of veterans programs were able to move forward in the late 1800s because of interest group politics. Military reform did not occur because of local interest groups who preferred the status quo over increased federal power.

The Post Office

One can see that conditions after the War between the States led to the growth of interest group expenditures, but, as previously noted, the problem of special interest politics was recognized prior to the war. One area in which the government began providing benefits to special interests prior to the War between the States was the Post Office. Mail delivery is one of the few activities of the federal government that is explicitly provided for by the Constitution, but before 1851 the Post Office was run as a revenue-generating operation. That changed in 1851, when after much debate in Congress an act was passed that greatly overhauled the nature of mail delivery.

The effects of the 1851 act were discussed in chapter 5. Recall that after the 1851 act mail delivery to western states was subsidized, but postal rates were not sufficient enough for profits from service in the East to cover the subsidy, so Congress appropriated money to cover the deficit. This meant that additional extensions of service became the subject of congressional debate and pitted West Coast interests against those in the more populous East.[49] Politics also entered the picture in the Lincoln administration in a big way when local postmasters were chosen. The Republicans were a new political party, and party loyalists were anxious for political favors. As a result, in the 1860s the only qualification needed to be appointed as a local postmaster was the recommendation of a Republican congressman. In fact, to reduce the political pressures he had to face, Postmaster General Montgomery Blair, who was appointed by Lincoln, openly recommended that applicants for local postmaster positions apply directly to their congressmen rather than to the Post Office Department.[50]

Interest group activity accelerated tremendously after the War between the States, but experiences at the Post Office show that the beginnings of interest group politics appeared before the war. Once the principle was established that postal services would be offered at low prices regardless of the cost of the service, the opportunity for rent seeking presented itself, and western states availed themselves of the opportunity to obtain services below cost. The special interest nature of the Post Office was aggravated by openly political appointments during the Lincoln administration. While the new policies only dated back to 1851, the Confederate States clearly saw the problems and attempted to correct them in their Constitution. The Confederate Constitution specified, as did the U.S. Constitution, that Congress would have the power "to establish post office and post roads" but added that the cost "shall be paid out of its own revenue."[51] The 1851 act may not have been intended to open the door of the federal Treasury to special interests, but it had that effect and provided a foundation on which veterans could build after the War between the States.

Interest Group Politics and the Transition to Government Growth

When the nation was founded the federal government was primarily a defender of the rights of its citizens, and the types of transfer programs that were taken for granted by the end of the twentieth century were regarded as improper government activities in the nineteenth century. Seeing the federal government increasingly turn toward the provision of special interest benefits, in 1887 President Cleveland argued, "A prevalent tendency to disregard the limited mission of [the government's] power and duty should be steadfastly resisted, to the end that the lesson should be constantly enforced that, though the people support the Government, the Government should not support the people."[52] The problem that Cleveland saw, anticipated by Tocqueville, was that in a democracy people have the political power to vote benefits to themselves. As the franchise expanded in the United States, more people were admitted to the group that could vote themselves benefits. As Tocqueville noted, "When a nation begins to modify the elective qualification, it may easily be foreseen that, sooner or later, that qualification will be entirely abolished. There is no more invariable rule in the history of society . . . no stop can be made short of universal suffrage."[53]

The expansion of the franchise is also linked to the metamorphosis of government from an institution that protects individual rights to an organization that enhances the economic well-being of its citizens. As interest groups such as veterans, farmers, rail shippers, and the customers and competitors of trusts are more able to use their political power for economic means, it becomes increasingly important for economic interests to be represented in the political process. Likewise, as the franchise expands, it becomes more important for elected representatives to be cognizant of the economic interests of their constituents.

When the history of the transition in government growth is examined, interest group politics plays a key role. The emergence of significant economic interests in the political process increased the demand for government expenditures (and government regulation) and laid the foundation for Progressive Era reforms that caused federal expenditures to transition from being relatively stable to continually increasing. The War between the States produced a well-organized interest group that seemed to have some legitimate claim to the Treasury's assets, and a budget surplus brought on by economic growth gave them resources to claim. These unique historical events, coupled with the propensity of interest groups to develop in a democracy, changed a stable government into a growing government.

Democracy and Economic Affairs

The period 1870–1915 saw a major transformation not only in the size and scope of government but also in the government's relationship to the economy. The changes in the scope of government mostly had to do with people's economic interaction with the government, in seeking direct transfers, in seeking regulatory protection, and in the overall philosophy that democracy has a role to play in the allocation of resources. If the government is protecting people from economic power, through antitrust laws and business regulation, and if government is providing benefits to some—whether postal patrons or war veterans—at the expense of others, somehow it must decide how these benefits are to be allocated. Civil service reform was intended to provide a more objective and less political way of allocating benefits, but ultimately the allocation of benefits would be made democratically. Thus, democracy became increasingly important as a method of allocating economic resources in addition to its role in political decision making. Early in the nineteenth century the implications of democratic government were almost entirely political. By the end of the nineteenth century democracy had become more of an economic system. The Populist and Progressive movements, which are the subjects of the following chapter, explain the linkage between democracy and economic affairs in more detail.

Conclusion

The idea that the role of government in the twentieth century is different from that of the nineteenth century has been observed and discussed by many others,[54] but increased federal government power did not immediately transform itself into increased federal spending. As figure 4 shows, spending increases only showed up around the 1880s. Figure 5 illustrates that there was not much in the way of excess federal revenues to be spent before then, but the nation did have an income tax from 1861 to 1871 and chose to repeal it and forego those revenues rather than continue the tax.[55] Exactly the opposite decision was made in 1913. The creation of a federal income tax was not the cause of government growth but rather a response to the demand for greater government expenditure and for greater involvement in the economic affairs of Americans. Significant changes occurred in the way Americans viewed their government in that span of less than 50 years. The government became more democratic, and democracy increasingly evolved from a political principle into a principle for guiding people's economic affairs.

CHAPTER 8

Populism and Progressivism

Americans have always had high expectations of their government. What, exactly, they have expected has changed considerably over the centuries, and how those changes have manifested themselves is the story of the transformation from liberty to democracy as the underlying ideology of American government. The high expectations that Americans have had came from the fundamental philosophy behind the American Revolution. That philosophy, revolutionary itself at the time, asserted that individuals have inalienable rights independent of the government and that the role of the government is to serve its citizens by protecting those rights. Prior to the American Revolution, political institutions divided people into the rulers and the ruled, and the rights of citizens were those that the government granted. Americans were familiar with political systems dating back to ancient Greece in which governmental decisions were made democratically and in which there was a great deal of equality among those granted citizenship, but even in those cases the people served the government rather than the government serving the people. The new American government was revolutionary because it was grounded on the new idea that the government was the servant of the people rather than the other way around, and this revolutionary idea raised the expectations of Americans.

The idea that the government should serve the people has become ingrained as a part of the American ideology. Government employees are referred to as public servants, although the implications of the term are rarely contemplated in depth. Public policies are intended to serve the public interest, not the interests of the crown. This American ideology helps promote the interests of the government by making compliant citizens, regardless of whether the government's interests are congruent with the public interest, but it also sets up expectations that government policy will further the public interest. Initially the public interest was viewed simply as liberty—freedom from government oppression. Andrew Jackson viewed democracy as a means to an end

161

and as a method of controlling the government and keeping it from gaining too much power. By the end of the nineteenth century, however, Jacksonian democracy had evolved to the point where democracy was an end in itself, and the appropriate role for government was viewed as protecting the interests of its citizens, whatever those interests might be, rather than just guarding their liberty.[1] Democracy became the method by which the interests of the nation's citizens were revealed.

After the War between the States and prior to World War I there were two major movements that exerted a crucial impact on the way Americans viewed their government and on the way they believed the government should interact with its citizens. Those were the Populist and Progressive movements. Briefly described, Populism was a movement to take control of the government away from elites and to provide citizens with more direct control over their government. Progressivism was a movement to provide more government control over the nation's economy and to use government policy to enhance the economic well-being of its citizens. Readers might object that these descriptions are overly simple, and such objections have some merit. Try, for example, to provide a short description of the twentieth-century Liberal or Conservative movements. Even members of those movements might disagree on the specifics. Nevertheless, these brief descriptions of the Populist and Progressive movements provide a starting point for analysis.

Populism

Political movements can have ideological foundations, but they cannot gain enough support to have an impact on the political landscape unless there are interest groups behind them who believe that, if the movement's political principles are adopted, those in the interest group will be better off. Populism drew its political support from the agricultural interests in the South and West. The United States was undergoing a massive economic transformation in the late 1800s, as the primarily agrarian economy was being eroded by a growing industrial sector. Manufacturing was growing at a breakneck pace, and the banking and financial sectors of the economy were prospering as a result. Railroads began linking the nation, providing transportation for both industrial and agricultural output. As most of the economy prospered, those in agriculture felt that they were being left behind.

In 1877 two major events changed the political climate in the United States. Only a few months after his election, President Rutherford B. Hayes announced the end of Reconstruction and withdrew federal troops from the South, more than 15 years after they first entered. Then, only a few months later, President Hayes sent troops to Martinsburg, West Virginia, in an attempt to try to end a railroad strike. Federal troops were withdrawn from the enforcement of political rights in the South, but the precedent was established for using them to protect the economic interests of powerful industrialists in the North. Meanwhile, that same year several fledgling agricultural groups began to organize to try to protect their interests against monied industrialists.[2]

Farm productivity was increasing in the late 1800s, but at the same time farm prices were sharply declining, especially after 1880.[3] Farmers were familiar with the theory that prices were falling because of overproduction, but they did not believe it. Demand for farm products was increasing, but the percentage of the population engaged in agriculture was steadily declining as the economy industrialized. Farmers believed that the culprits were the railroads. The nation's westward expansion in the second half of the 1800s could not have occurred without the railroads, and western farmers were completely dependent upon the railroads to bring their products to market. The railroads were able to expand because of federal land grants and were often heavily subsidized by local governments that wanted the railroad to run through their towns.[4] Furthermore, railroad attorneys often had direct control of the local political apparatus, especially in western states.[5] The intervention of federal troops in the 1877 rail strike made it clear that the federal government would even go so far as to use federal troops to support economic interests.

Farmers were also directly affected by the grain elevators that many of them had to deal with if they wanted to sell their produce, but they also viewed that anything they bought—from farm implements to clothing—was controlled by trusts that were able to monopolize their segments of the market and take advantage of the economically weaker farmers. The *Farmer's Alliance* of February 28, 1891, editorialized that the price fixing that victimized farmers was the "logical result of the individual freedom which we have always considered the pride of our system."[6] Yet another old issue was the tariff, which agricultural interests had always viewed as favoring industrial interests over agriculture. Farmers were also concerned about deflation. Withdrawal of greenbacks from circulation and a movement to a true gold standard caused the value of money to rise, which hurt farmers who had taken out mortgages and had to repay them with more valuable dollars than they had borrowed.

Agricultural interests faced many problems, and the most direct way to deal with them was to take control of the government away from elite interests and return it to the people. In the tradition of Jackson, the Populists saw their salvation in more popular control of the government. Government, after all, was behind many of the problems anyway, whether it was because of their support of the railroads, their reliance on the tariff, or their control over the money supply.

Populist Organizations

Farm interests manifested themselves in a number of ways in the political arena. Several political parties established in the late 1800s gained the sympathy and support of farm interests, including the People's Antimonopoly party and the National Greenback party. The interests of these parties and more were encompassed within the National Farmers' Alliance, which was not a political party per se but rather was intended to be a "political mouthpiece" through which the interests of farmers could be heard.[7] The National Farmers' Alliance spawned a number of derivative organizations representing smaller groups, sometimes organized by state and other times by region or other divisions, such as the Northern Alliance, the Southern Alliance, and the Colored Alliance. The key point is that Populist groups had begun organizing for the explicit purpose of influencing political decision making for their economic benefit.

Some Populists viewed the existing two-party system as working against their interests, and while the Populists did believe they could have some influence over the Democratic party in the South, they viewed the North as hopelessly hostile to their agenda. By 1890 they had organized their own political party, named the People's party. In 1892 the People's party ran James B. Weaver for president, who turned in a very respectable showing.[8] Weaver, a Union veteran and a former Republican who had joined the Greenback party and served several terms in Congress, was the Greenback party presidential candidate in 1880. Weaver ended up garnering 22 electoral votes and enough popular votes that his candidacy may have returned Democrat Grover Cleveland to the White House.

The Republicans had won every presidential election from 1860 until 1884, when Cleveland was elected to his first term due to a division within the Republican party. James Garfield, elected in 1880, died in office, and Vice President Chester Arthur was elevated to the presidency. But the Republicans did not nominate Arthur in 1884, and with veterans swinging their support toward the Democrats, Cleveland was elected. Cleveland was defeated by Benjamin Harrison in 1888, but in 1892 Cleveland became the only president to serve two nonconsecutive terms when he defeated Harrison by a comfortable margin. However, if the popular votes that went to Weaver had instead gone to Harrison, Harrison would have been reelected easily. The Populists would have preferred Harrison, but, ironically, by running their own candidate they may have taken enough votes away from Harrison to produce the election of their third choice.[9]

The Populists had more success in state governments,[10] but their lack of success at the national level plus their relative sympathies with the Democratic party relative to the Republican party led them to be absorbed into the Democratic party by the end of the 1890s. In the end, their most popular issue at the national level was monetary reform, which remained at the forefront. Populism also had an impact on the nation's electoral system.

The Money Issue

In the late 1800s the world moved toward a gold standard, and the United States moved with it. In international trade, a gold standard has the advantage that national currencies are a representation of a certain amount of gold and can always be redeemed in gold. Thus, those in one nation wanting to trade with those in another have an easy time determining the prices of goods across national boundaries. All essentially are denominated in gold. From a domestic standpoint, when a nation is on a gold standard, it prevents the money supply from being inflated. If those who issue money must redeem it in gold, the amount of money that can circulate is limited by the amount of gold that is available to back the money supply.[11] In the free banking era prior to the War between the States, banks issuing money without sufficient gold reserves to back it found their bank notes depreciating in value, placing the bank in peril. Thus, a natural limit was placed on the expansion of the money supply. After the war, the federal government had taken control of currency circulation in the United States but still would redeem its notes in gold, placing the same limits on the issuance of money.

If the government issued too much money, people would want to redeem it for gold, which would reduce the national gold stock and potentially could even deplete it entirely. Under a gold standard, the value of gold and the value of money remained in balance. People with gold who wanted money could exchange their gold for money, increasing the money supply, while people with money who wanted gold could redeem their money, reducing the money supply. In this manner, the quantity of gold regulated the money supply in the late 1800s. Rapid economic growth led to an increased demand for money, increasing the value of money and creating a steady deflation. From 1870 to 1900 prices in the United States declined by 34 percent. This was good for those wealthy individuals who had money and for creditors who were repaid in money more valuable than the money they lent; but for debtors, such as farmers with mortgages, the burden of repayment became increasingly heavy as deflation increased the value of money.

With the gold standard restricting the growth of the money supply, the popular opinion was that there was a shortage of money and that financial reform was needed to make more money available for the repayment of debts and for the expansion of commerce.[12] Because the federal government now controlled the money supply, this was clearly an issue of federal policy. The Greenback party pushed the issue by trying to get the government to issue paper money, but it was an issue with all minor parties. The popular belief was that the financial system was controlled by the same group of elite businessmen who controlled increasing parts of the entire economy. The solution was more democratic control of the money supply.

A major step was taken with the creation of the Federal Reserve System in 1913, and under the Federal Reserve monetary institutions continued to evolve throughout the twentieth century. In 1933 President Roosevelt continued dismantling the gold standard, and by 1971 President Nixon had severed the dollar's last tie with gold. The nation's monetary institutions evolved slowly, but the Greenback party platform was completely realized. Today there are no real assets backing the dollar, and the nation's monetary policy is completely under democratic control, run by the Board of Governors of the Federal Reserve System, who are appointed by the president.

Popular Elections

One of the lasting by-products of the Populist movement is a greater ability for direct citizen voting in American politics. Populism in this area was an extension of the movement toward popular voting for president, which had been virtually completed by the 1820s (discussed at length in chapter 5). Populist ideals were expressed by Jackson long before the Populist movement, but the idea that the people should have more direct control over their government took solid root toward the end of the nineteenth century.

One area in which this aspect of Populism was manifested was in the ability of citizens to place referenda on state ballots by citizen initiative. Citizens have often been asked to approve new state constitutions through referendum, and government through New England town meetings and similar institutions has provided forums through which citizens can have direct input into their governments. However, citizen initiatives to amend state laws and state constitutions did not exist until South Dakota allowed it in 1898, as a by-product of the Populist movement. Eighteen more states adopted citizen initiatives over the next three decades, allowing citizens direct control over the laws under which they were governed. As Populism faded from the political landscape, so did the demand for citizen initiatives, and only three states have implemented the citizen initiative process since 1918.[13]

Perhaps the most widely publicized voter initiatives have been the state property tax limitations led by California's Proposition 13 in 1978, but initiatives have been used much more widely and on other tax issues too. Several states have passed voter initiatives requiring voter approval of new taxes before they can take effect, and many states have also passed voter initiatives placing other tax or expenditure caps on state governments. In this area, the Populist goal of giving citizens more direct control of their governments has had a lasting impact. When reflecting on the fact that the Populist movement had greater electoral success and a more substantial impact at the state and local levels than at the federal level, it is worth recalling that at the end of the nineteenth century local governments had larger total expenditures than did either state governments or the federal government. Thus, the federal government did not yet dominate the other levels of government in the way it would in the twentieth century, and the influence of the Populists was more substantial than at first it might appear by only examining national politics.

The Direct Election of Senators

The U.S. Constitution originally specified that senators be chosen by state legislatures. The logic of choosing senators this way was discussed in chapter 5. Choosing members of the House and Senate by two different bodies of electors places an additional constraint on the types of legislation that can be passed. Simply put, under the old system, any legislation would have to meet the approval of both the representatives of the people and the representatives of the state legislatures to be passed, whereas when senators are elected directly by the electorate, both the House and the Senate represent the same interests. The selection of senators by state legislatures violated the Populist idea of direct citizen control over their government, and the Populists pushed for the direct election of senators. Their ultimate success on the issue came in 1913, when the 17th Amendment to the Constitution was ratified, mandating the direct election of senators.

Direct voting for senators actually began more than half a decade before the 17th Amendment passed, when in 1906 Oregon developed a plan whereby Senate candidates were nominated in party primaries and then a statewide referendum was held to choose among the party candidates. The state legislature then would select the candidate approved by the voter referendum. The Oregon plan proved so popular that 21 states had adopted it by 1913 and were already directly voting for their senators when the 17th Amendment was ratified.[14] Thus, even before the amendment, nearly half the states had adopted the Populist method of direct election.

While the Populist ideology provided one motivation for direct election of senators, there was another motivation as well. Many states had problems choosing senators because of political divisions within their state legislatures. Thus, at times states had only one senator, or sometimes even no senators, representing them, because the state legislatures were unable to agree on anyone. The lack of representation in the Senate, coupled with the political dissension that resulted, undoubtedly made states more open to the idea of another selection procedure. Still, although direct election of senators did predate the 17th Amendment, it did so by less than a decade and was clearly a result of Populist ideology and an attempt to give citizens more direct control over their government. The motivation for direct election was, in a word, democracy.

Progressivism

As the Populist movement was losing momentum in the 1890s, the foundations of Progressivism were being built. The basic idea behind Progressivism is that public policy should be used to protect and enhance the economic well-being of the nation's citizens in addition to just protecting their basic rights. Populism and Progressivism were distinct political movements, yet many of their objectives were consistent and overlapping. One distinction was that Populism was spearheaded by agricultural interests, whereas the leaders of the Progressive movement tended to be independent business people, lawyers, or editors.[15] Yet both movements shared the common goal of wanting to use government to control the economic power of big business.

While the Populists believed they were being exploited by the monopoly power of railroads and overcharged for manufactured goods by big business, and therefore wanted those economic abuses controlled, Progressives saw more fundamental problems that had arisen as the American economy industrialized. The half century following the War between the States brought with it increasingly concentrated economic power and produced a few men who had amassed fortunes that would have been unimaginable only a few years before. The generally held view was that their wealth came from exploiting others. Even a century later they are often referred to as robber barons, and it is surely true that early in the twentieth century John D. Rockefeller was the most despised person in America.

Part of the problem, Progressives believed, stemmed from the unavoidable evils of concentrated economic power. The Sherman Act, passed in 1890, was the first in a long series of laws that intended not just to have government regulate and control big business but also to limit the size and economic power of business. Herbert Croly, an influential Progressive (and in 1914 a cofounder of the *New Republic*), argued that the structure of government envisioned by the founders was inappropriate to secure the goals the founders sought because of the rise in concentrated economic power. Thus, revisiting a debate from a century earlier, Croly espoused the Jeffersonian goal of liberty but argued that, in light of the concentration of economic power, the Jeffersonian principle of noninterference must be abandoned and replaced by Hamiltonianism.[16] By Hamiltonianism, Croly meant the creation of a federal regulatory apparatus, staffed by experts, to oversee the activities of big business.

The problem was not solely with business, however. The Progressives also believed that government tended to be corrupt, that it was too often controlled by party bosses, especially at the local level, and that government policies actually helped businesses to exploit the general public. The solution was to have a stronger federal government, national in scope, to control businesses that now had become national in scope. The Progressives, recognizing the problems that had come from the influence of special interests over public policy and the effects of the spoils system in which interest groups supported politicians in exchange for political support of those interests, understood that a more powerful federal government would have to be controlled to benefit its citizens generally rather than powerful interests. They sought control in two ways. First, they wanted to reform the civil service to create a more professional government workforce, one chosen by merit rather than by political connections and one that would be relatively independent of electoral politics. Second, they wanted the government to become more democratic and therefore more accountable to the voters.[17]

The democratic impulses of the Progressives were no different from those of the Populists, and the 17th Amendment is as much a part of the Progressive agenda as it is a part of the Populist agenda. The same could be said of the regulation of railroads and, more generally, of business. But the Progressives had a more comprehensive view of government control over the economy and explicitly recognized their agenda as a departure from the past.[18] Their democratic impulses might be viewed as an extension of Populism and in turn an extension of Jacksonian democracy. But Jackson viewed democracy as a means to produce the limited government fought for by Jefferson, whereas the Progressives viewed democracy as a method of controlling a Hamiltonian government that, out of necessity, departed from the Jeffersonian vision.

The Progressive Ideology

Politicians consistently bring with them new ideas. The very nature of a political contest is that the ideas of one candidate are matched against the ideas of others. Yet in a broad sense, one might argue that there have been only two basic ideas upon which political platforms in the United States have been based and that all others are merely derivative of these two basic philosophies. One philosophy is that of liberty, which went essentially unchallenged for more than a century. The competing philosophy is that of Progressivism, which first began to be articulated in the late 1800s.

If one is to shoehorn American political debate into this framework, one can see that Jefferson campaigned for the cause of liberty against what he viewed as "Hamiltonian Progressivism." The term had not been used then, but Croly analyzed the split between Jefferson and Hamilton in just those terms.[19] Similarly, when Jackson ran on a Jeffersonian platform, it was in opposition to the yet unnamed Progressivism of his predecessors. And while Lincoln was willing to tolerate slavery to preserve the Union, the Republican party's opposition to slavery was based on the principle of liberty.[20] As chapter 6 argued, the ultimate effect of the War between the States was to enhance the power of the federal government and to move away from the principle of liberty—in other words, to further Progressivism. The freeing of the slaves was, of course, the major exception, but the slaves were freed not as a matter of principle but because Lincoln viewed it as a move of expediency to try to end the war.

Chapter 7 noted the rise of interest groups after the war, but again their intention was not to move away from the concept of liberty but, more narrowly, to have the federal government provide them with benefits. Even the Populists were simply trying to secure their freedom, which they viewed as being hampered by the railroads and other big business—with government assistance. The Populists had narrow objectives, whereas the Progressives brought with them a broad philosophy that stood in direct opposition to the philosophy of liberty that the founders espoused.[21] Liberty for the founders meant that the government would protect the rights of individuals but would have minimal involvement in their economic affairs. The Progressives viewed that notion as outmoded. The oppression that only the government could exert by force when the nation was founded was now being imposed by the trusts, and economic power had replaced political power as the oppressor of the people.

The bulk of American political debate in the twentieth century can be viewed as Progressivism versus this old-fashioned idea of liberty. Historian John Blum, with the title of his book, *The Progressive Presidents—Roosevelt, Wilson, Roosevelt, Johnson,* sums up the idea.[22] FDR's New Deal and Lyndon Johnson's Great Society were extensions of the Progressive ideology, and, by extension, Reagan's opposition to those initiatives was based on the old-fashioned idea of liberty. One can debate where, exactly, particular individuals or programs fall relative to these two fundamental ideas. Nevertheless, the philosophical foundations are clear. On one side is the original conception of liberty, which means a minimal government that protects the rights of individuals and does little more. On the other side is Progressivism, which means that the government, as a matter of public policy, will look out for the economic well-being of its citizens. The idea, mainly oriented toward legislation and public policy, can be extended even to the law. In the old view based on liberty, law exists separate from politics and public policy, whereas the more Progressive idea is that the legal system is an extension of politics and public policy and that the courts can be used in much the same way as the legislature for those who want to implement policy change.[23]

Progressivism, as an idea, found broad acceptance well before Theodore Roosevelt pushed Progressive policies so visibly. Cleveland was the last president to oppose on principle the foundations of Progressive ideology. Cleveland, with the distinction of being the only president to serve two nonconsecutive terms (1885–89 and 1893–97), also has the distinction of being the only Democrat elected to the presidency between James Buchanan, who left office in 1861, and Woodrow Wilson, who assumed office in 1913. As the previous chapter documented, the Republicans had overseen the rise in interest group activity following the War between the States to the point where interests could expect benefits in response to their political clout. In 1887, Texas farmers had secured the passage of the "Texas Seed Bill" through Congress to provide them with a modest $10,000 to buy seed and to ease their economic distress. Cleveland vetoed the bill, saying he could not find the authority for any such action by the federal government in the Constitution.[24] This was not the only time that Cleveland found himself at odds with the ascendant Progressive tendencies of the federal government. Prior to Cleveland's presidency, there had been 132 presidential vetoes issued. Cleveland issued 301 vetoes during his two terms and allowed another 109 bills die through his inaction.[25]

How was Progressivism able to transform itself into an ideology that was able to displace the revolutionary cause of liberty? One reason, undoubtedly, was public reaction to the growth of the trusts and the creation of an economic elite unlike anything the world had previously known. Prior to the rise of the American industrialists, economic power and political power went hand in hand. American government was run by those who had always known wealth and privilege. In the Progressive movement, the general public saw government as an institution that could protect them from exploitation, but at the same time those with political power saw the growth in economic power as a threat to their status. For the first time, those with the greatest economic power in the nation were not among the political elite. Thus, politicians used their power to counter economic power partly to retain their own status.[26] They were joined by an elite group of individuals with old wealth and professionals who found their relative status and influence waning in the face of the giant and growing fortunes of the new industrialists and financiers.

Another reason that Progressivism was able to develop into an ideology with national scope was that the press became an effective opponent of those with economic power. Just as pamphleteers had a substantial influence over the Revolution, so muckraking journalists had a substantial influence over the creation of the Progressive ideology. The rapid urbanization of America created new markets for newspapers. There were 574 daily newspapers in the United States in 1870, and that number grew to 1,610 by 1899 and to 2,600 by 1909.[27] With larger circulations and more revenues, editors began envisioning larger roles for themselves and went beyond reporting the news to doing investigative reporting, commentary, and analysis. Similarly, magazines with national circulations paid thousands of dollars to authors who wrote exposés of abuses of power in both the public and private sectors. The captains of industry provided a convenient target for which writers could gain a sympathetic readership. Thus, public opinion was turned toward an ideology that favored government control of the abuses and excesses of concentrated economic power.

Regulation of Economic Power

During the first half of the nineteenth century, the trend was to reduce government intervention into private economic activity. A reversal of this trend, toward more government intervention in the economy, began sometime after the War between the States. All such intervention was not aimed at big business. With the expiration of the charter of the Second Bank of the United States in 1836 the nation entered the free banking era, which lasted 25 years. The National Banking Act of 1862 gave the federal government control of the nation's currency, moving in the opposite direction and laying the foundation for the creation of the Federal Reserve System in 1913. Similarly, prior to the War between the States all states eliminated their restrictions on the entry into the practice of medicine, but this trend too was reversed as states created new requirements for certification of those who wanted to be physicians.[28] In many areas that had nothing to do with American industrialization, the government began taking more control over the economy.

Big changes occurred in areas where industrialization was having big impacts, however. In the watershed case of *Munn v. Illinois* in 1877, the Supreme Court decided that the State of Illinois could regulate grain elevator rates.[29] The case was important because for the first time it declared that it was legal for the government to set the terms of a private exchange between two individuals. The demand for regulation came from the expansion of the railroads and the resulting economic power that it gave to grain elevator operators over the farmers from whom they bought grain. From this point, it was a relatively modest extension of the principle to create the Interstate Commerce Commission in 1887 for the purpose of regulating railroads more generally.

The Sherman Act in 1890, the nation's first antitrust law, was intended to prevent the abuses of monopolies by giving the government the power to break them up into smaller competing companies, and it found an increasing scope of enforcement as the years went by. The Clayton Act, passed in 1914, enhanced the scope of antitrust action not just to existing monopoly power but to the prevention of actions that could lead to future monopoly power.[30] In 1903 the Department of Commerce was created at the urging of President Roosevelt and contained a Bureau of Corporations, which helped Roosevelt earn the reputation as a trustbuster.[31] The Bureau of Corporations increasingly gained influence as an antibusiness bureaucracy and laid the groundwork for the government's antitrust suit that broke up Standard Oil a decade later. It continued in existence until 1914, when it was superseded by the Federal Trade Commission.[32] The Pure Food and Drug Act was passed in 1906, eventually leading to the creation of the Food and Drug Administration in 1938. All were clearly aimed at regulating the market economy and controlling the economic power of the new captains of American industry.[33]

Progressives believed that their push to expand the role of government to protect the economic interests of its citizens was necessary because of the expansion of concentrated economic power in the decades following the War between the States. When the nation was founded, individuals could deal with each other under a situation of relative equality, but with the rise of corporations, because of both their size and their monopolization of certain markets, people could no longer deal with them as equals. Concentrated economic power of corporations required more concentrated power of the general public to maintain the balance.[34] In Jefferson's time, the tyranny of government was the largest threat to individual freedom, but the Progressives believed that, a century later, they were more threatened by economic power than by political power.

The Civil Service

Civil Service reform was an integral part of the Progressive movement. Jackson brought the spoils system to federal civil service without apology, arguing the merits of turnover in civil service jobs.[35] By the late 1800s, however, other nations were undertaking civil service reform, and there was the general idea that better personnel management practices, already proving themselves in business, could also be applied to government. In addition, blatant political favoritism was the frequent target of political attack, prompting reform as a defensive measure. Reform began in the late 1870s in the New York Customhouse, which was the largest source of federal revenues by far in the days before the income tax. Increasingly, jobs began being awarded on merit rather than as political favors, culminating in the Pendleton Civil Service Act of 1883. The Pendleton Act codified the merit system and also outlawed the requirment of compulsory political contributions from federal workers (although voluntary contributions were still allowed).[36] The act also prevented government workers for soliciting political contributions on government property (although it placed no restrictions on their activities off government property).

The spoils system was not entirely eliminated. In 1884 only 11 percent of federal jobs required civil service examinations for appointment, but by 1900, 46 percent were covered under civil service guidelines. This left ample room for continued political patronage but at the same time built a base of permanent civil service employees who were more insulated from the political process. Theodore Roosevelt was an integral part of the process. In 1889 he was appointed to the Civil Service Commission by the newly elected president Benjamin Harrison, where he pushed for reform, and after his ascendancy to the presidency himself in 1901 he actively shifted federal jobs from patronage to merit appointment.[37] When the process of civil service reform began in the late 1870s the scope of the federal government remained relatively limited, making its impact felt most heavily in customs and postal workers, but it laid the foundation for a civil service more independent of the current administration by the beginning of the twentieth century, when the scope of the federal government was poised for rapid expansion.

The need for civil service reform in the Progressive agenda was apparent. If the government was to expand its role to look out for the economic well-being of its citizens, the government workforce had to be free of the influence of special interest groups that were politically connected to the administration. The potential problems that could arise otherwise were already apparent in the way Republican administrations had catered to veterans interests after the War between the States. Union vets who were disabled as they fought to defend their nation were obviously deserving of both sympathy and support, but as chapter 7 showed, patronage and the political power of their interests transformed veterans pensions from a payment to deserving individuals into a wholesale transfer program that was criticized widely by both Republicans and Democrats. If the federal government really was to get more involved in the economic welfare of its citizens—which was a controversial new idea late in the 1800s—it would have to find a way to insulate government programs from politics, and civil service reform was viewed as the key.

The political demands for a more professional civil service were buttressed by academic developments in economics, management, business administration, and social work. Principles of scientific management that were being implemented in business could also be used in government. Developments in economics held out the promise that government policy could be used to strengthen the economy, and social work moved from charitable activities mainly run by volunteers to a professional activity. Philanthropies had a large hand in the professionalization of social work initially, but the government increasingly stepped in.[38] The foundation that was established early in the century enabled a vast superstructure of bureaucracy to be built during World War I, further distancing twentieth-century government bureaucracy from the patronage system of the nineteenth century.[39] The 1920s saw further developments, many under the guidance of Herbert Hoover, who was secretary of commerce from 1921 until he was elected president in 1928. Hoover's role as an engineer by training and a believer in the scientific management of the economy is discussed further in chapter 9.

Progressivism brought with it a complete transformation in the relationship of federal employees with their employer. The spoils system of political patronage evolved into a professional bureaucracy, chosen by merit and given job security beyond the tenure of the current administration. The professional interests of civil servants evolved from being completely tied up in the success of the current administration to being a function of the funding available to the federal government generally and their own agencies more specifically. As a result, civil servants became more interested in the budget allocations of their own agencies, because their personal interests became more congruent with their agencies' budgets.[40] Thus, civil servants became another interest group with an economic interest in larger government. The change in the incentive structure is a result of the creation of a federal bureaucracy largely independent of the elected officials who nominally run the government.

Interest Groups and Progressivism

The relationship that interest groups should have to public policy is ambiguous by nature within the Progressive ideology. Under the old ideology of liberty, ambiguity revolved around the nature of who should occupy government positions but did not extend to policy. Jackson explicitly introduced the spoils system to the federal government, justifying it by arguing that turnover in government positions was beneficial and that the jobs were not so demanding that newcomers could not perform them as well as veteran bureaucrats. Yet another justification was that, because government employees owed their jobs to the incumbent administration, they had an incentive to perform well to enhance the chances that the incumbents would be reelected so that they could keep their jobs. Nevertheless, one of the goals of civil service reform was to reduce party favoritism in the hiring of federal employees. Presumably, however, in Jackson's time the benefits that came with patronage jobs extended only to who got the jobs and not to the benefits of public policy that went to those outside of government. The mission of the federal government was constitutionally limited, suggesting that public policy would not favor some over others, regardless of who held the government jobs that implemented that policy.

Progressivism explicitly extended public policy not only to protect the rights of citizens but also to enhance their economic well-being. Under the old ideology, it was obviously inappropriate for one group to seek economic benefits at the expense of others, but Progressivism meant using the government to enhance people's economic well-being and sometimes meant providing some people with economic benefits at the expense of others. The regulation of railroads and grain elevator prices and antitrust legislation all were clearly targeted at enhancing the economic opportunities for some at the expense of others. These measures undoubtedly seemed fair to most people because the intended beneficiaries were far more numerous than the few individuals who held the concentrated economic power that was the target of such legislation. This is the way democracy in its purest form works. The majority has more political clout than the minority.

The founders intended for constitutional constraints to keep this type of democracy from determining public policy in the United States, but even without constitutional constraints democratic institutions do not always favor the side with the greatest numbers. Small groups can often benefit greatly from government policies that impose small costs on everyone to transfer concentrated benefits to a few. Most constituents have little incentive to become informed about such policies, because the costs imposed on them are small and because the likelihood that they would be able to change government policy is also small. This allows concentrated interests to use the political process for their benefit.[41] In such a setting, the general public will have relatively little influence over public policy and concentrated special interest groups can manipulate the political process for their benefit.[42] As noted in chapter 6, this problem was clearly recognized prior to the War between the States, and a Progressive method of dealing with part of the problem was to create a more professional civil service, insulated from political pressures, to carry out public policy. The fundamental problem remains, however, because the policies themselves are created by elected officials.

Although the influence of special interests was well known in the late 1800s, the extent to which interest groups influenced public policy shocked the general public when a series of newspaper articles on lobbying appeared in the *New York World* in 1913.[43] Professional lobbying was at that time an "open secret," but it was secret no more when a former lobbyist discussed how he had been paid by the National Association of Manufacturers to lobby on their behalf. The general public was outraged, but a number of senators denied any knowledge of lobbying. Constituents, including businesses, had always argued their interests, but the idea that a third party would lobby solely for financial gain, much as lawyers make the best arguments for their clients regardless of the merits of the case, was quite disturbing. Times change, however, and at the beginning of the twenty-first century this is considered an integral part of the political process.[44]

One might question what the role of interest groups ought to be under a Progressive government. Government provision of economic benefits steps well beyond the ideology of liberty but appears quite consistent with the ideology of Progressivism, and in a democratic government it may be that the best way to discover the economic interests of citizens is to let them state their cases directly. If public policy is intended to enhance the economic well-being of the nation's citizens, interest group politics, which so concerned James Madison and the other Founding Fathers, would seem to be a part of the new set of institutions that would replace the outmoded Jeffersonian ideals. One apparent problem is that often it is those with economic power who have the resources available to lobby effectively for benefits, so the interests who actually do receive economic benefits may not be those whom the Progressives had in mind. It is unlikely that such outrage would have been stirred in 1913 if it had been agricultural interests rather than the National Association of Manufacturers who had hired lobbyists.

Progressivism and Democracy

Progressivism and democracy are not the same things, and democracy does not necessarily further Progressivism, because democratic decision making too often results in the furtherance of narrow special interests rather than the general public interest. Progressives favored more democratic oversight over the government not as a method for furthering the will of the majority but as a method of providing oversight to prevent politicians from using their power to further the interests of those who already had economic power. Without democratic oversight, Progressives (and Populists) feared that those who had economic power would be able to buy government support of their agenda, and experience had borne them out. If they wanted the government to be more active in furthering the economic well-being of the general public, they believed that government officials would have to be accountable to the general public. That provided the role for democracy in the Progressive agenda.

As events unfolded, however, democracy, not Progressivism, ended up being the political ideology that survived the twentieth century, at least partly because of Progressive support. Herbert Croly, a prominent Progressive writer, argued that Progressivism implied a strong role for the president. He likened presidential elections to referendums of popular opinion and argued that strong executive leadership is necessary to implement Progressive policy. Croly viewed the president as more than just a passive conduit of public opinion, however, and viewed the president's role at least partly as that of an opinion maker.[45] Democracy was an integral part of the Progressive ideology and together with the notion that the government should work to further the economic well-being of its citizens hastened the transition of American ideology from liberty to democracy.

Democracy cannot lay claim to being the foundation for an ideology in the same way that liberty and Progressivism can. The idea of liberty places the protection of the rights of individuals at the foundation of government, and the idea of Progressivism places the protection of the economic well-being of individuals at the foundation. Democracy, by itself, means abiding by the will of the majority but offers no indication regarding what type of public policy the majority might favor. Progressives favored more democratic oversight of government as a means to control a government that would have more power and more discretion, but they did not believe that appropriate public policy was whatever the majority wanted. Indeed, Progressivism had clear ideas about what types of public policies were appropriate to the political and economic realities at the beginning of the twentieth century. Yet by the end of the twentieth century the Progressive ideas had faded into the background, and what remained was the concept that the nation is a democracy and that public policy measures are appropriate if they have the support of the majority. The concepts of liberty and Progressivism still battle in the political background, but the less ideological concept of democracy has become firmly entrenched as the fundamental principle of American government.

The Third-Party Dilemma in American Politics

As political parties, both the Populists and the Progressives illustrate a dilemma that faces third parties in a winner-take-all electoral system such as exists in the United States. Unless a new party completely displaces an existing party, the new party's successes are likely to result in outcomes that make the party's supporters worse off than if the party had never existed, in the short run anyway. If history provides a guide, it is possible for a new party to completely replace an existing party. The only time that has happened, however, was when the Republicans displaced the Whigs prior to the War between the States. Many new parties have tried to form in the century and a half that has passed since the creation of the Republican party, but the achievement of the Republican party remains unique, and it is at least partly due to the way the electoral system in the United States is organized.

Voters in all federal elections in the United States elect only one candidate from the slate of those running. This pushes the political system toward a two-party system. An alternative is to have proportional representation, where parties have representatives in the legislature in proportion to the number of votes they receive. In a proportional representation system, a party that garners 15 percent of the votes gets 15 percent of the seats, making it worthwhile to support such a minority party. In a winner-take-all system, a party that gets 15 percent of the votes loses the election, lessening the incentive to support minor parties.

Political ideas in the United States can be viewed as existing on a single dimensioned continuum from political left to political right. Political commentary often refers to political ideas in just this way, and candidates are often compared by saying one is to the left of the other. Although it is conceivable that political issues might be more multidimensional, all of the empirical evidence on voting shows that this one-dimensional political continuum is a good description of the way voters perceive candidates and issues.[46] Voters tend to favor candidates who are closer to them on this political left-right continuum, and as a part of political competition candidates try to position their image on this continuum in such a way as to be able to capture a majority of the votes. Because of this, all candidates have an incentive to move toward the political center of this left-right continuum. It is easily understandable why candidates all seem to look alike, as they compete for the center of the political spectrum, and why extreme candidates cannot win elections.

If a third party arises within this setting, the party will be perceived as existing more toward the left or right of the political spectrum and will take votes away from the candidate closest to that end of the spectrum. As noted earlier in this chapter, when James B. Weaver ran as a candidate of the People's party in 1892, the former Republican stole enough votes from incumbent Republican Benjamin Harrison that Grover Cleveland was able to regain the presidency. Likewise, when former Republican Teddy Roosevelt ran with the progressive Bull Moose party, he was able to divert enough votes from incumbent Republican William Howard Taft to put Woodrow Wilson in the White House. In 1992 Ross Perot mounted an independent campaign that eroded the support of incumbent George Bush and allowed Bill

Clinton to win the presidency, and in 2000 the third-party votes for Ralph Nader surely took enough votes from Al Gore, Clinton's vice president, to send George W. Bush to the White House.

The irony is that in each case most voters for the third-party candidate would have preferred the major party candidate who lost the election to the one who won. When viewing political platforms as existing on a single-dimensioned left-right continuum, it is clear why this is the case. Voters tend to vote for candidates closest to their position. Thus, third-party candidates take more votes away from the major party candidate to whom they are closest, giving a greater edge to the other major party candidate. In such a setting, third-party candidates can never win. They are always in the unhappy situation of dividing the votes on one side of the political spectrum with the major party candidate with whom they have most in common. Still, they can have an influence by changing the platforms of the major parties as they respond to the demands of an organized third party. If the third party becomes strong enough, it could even replace one of the major parties, as the Republicans replaced the Whigs, but three major parties cannot survive in American politics.

The U.S. Constitution makes no reference at all to political parties, and there is no indication that the founders had in mind the creation of a two-party system. Yet that is what has evolved because of the winner-take-all nature of American elections. Perhaps if the electoral college had worked as the founders had originally envisioned, more political parties would have been viable. The founders were wary of factions and certainly would not have deliberately created a political system that would stabilize with two dominant political parties. However, as the American political system is currently structured, it will support two parties, but no more.

Congressional Committees and Government Growth

The evolution of congressional institutions also greatly eroded any potential influence of third-party members by the end of the nineteenth century. When the federal government was more limited in scope, Congress had a limited number of issues with which to deal, and Congress could rightfully be called a deliberative body. As the scope of the federal government increased throughout the nineteenth century, there was more business to be taken care of and less possibility of deliberation. The problem was exacerbated by the growth of the committee system. Rather than Congress dealing with issues as a whole, increasingly matters began being delegated to committees. While committee output could be amended, the job of the entire body became more one of evaluating the work of committees rather than undertaking legislation as a whole group.

The rise of the committee system had the effect of reducing the efficiency and accountability of legislation passed in Congress for several reasons. First, it allowed members to sort themselves into committees in such a way that they could find themselves in committees overseeing areas for which they had a high demand for government intervention. Bills that emerged from committee would then likely call for more government intervention than the median member of Congress would prefer, but as the system was designed the body was placed in an all-or-nothing situation, where it could either take the bill as designed by the committee or reject it and hope for something better the next time. In this situation, Congress would be likely to settle for something a little more interventionist from the committee than if the whole body had drawn up the legislation together.[47]

A second factor is that because legislation is coming from a committee, which contains only a minority of the members of the entire house but requires majority support to become law, committee members can engage in vote trading to get legislation they like passed. "I'll vote for your bill if you'll vote for mine." Such "compromise" is the way legislation gets passed, and because legislators are likely to be more strongly in support of legislation that gives them benefits than they will be opposed to legislation that gives benefits to someone else, the result is that through vote trading a series of bills can pass into law as a group when no one individual bill could get the support of a majority by itself. Again, bigger government is the result.[48] One of the causes of the growth of the federal government has been the growth of the committee system.

Third-Party Members in Congress

The committee system had another effect, which was to lessen the influence of third-party members of Congress. When Congress made more decisions as a whole, and was more of a deliberative body, every member would have a chance to become a part of the debate on legislation and to have an influence on the outcome. The committee system passed more control to party leaders, who could determine who would

serve on and chair the committees. As a result, members of third parties saw their influence dwindle in Congress. Members of third parties
have been relatively rare in the twentieth century, but from 1890 to
1900 the People's party elected 39 members to the House of Representatives, who served a total of 58 terms. They also elected nine senators.[49] Their influence was limited, however, because of the dominance
of the Republicans and Democrats.

One advantage that the Republicans had in establishing themselves as a party prior to the War between the States is that, because the
committee system was not developed at that time, individual Republicans could be elected as senators and representatives and could play a
prominent role in national politics. Representatives from third parties
could not enjoy that same prominence under the current system, where
congressional work is dominated by committees.

Conclusion

The founders attempted to preserve liberty by creating a government
with strict constitutional limits on its activities. If the limits the
founders had envisioned had survived until the end of the nineteenth
century, Progressive public policy would not have been possible,
because the Constitution would have prevented it. The main issues go
back to the nation's earliest days, when Jefferson ran for the presidency in 1800 in opposition to Hamilton's vision of a federal government with a broader scope of activities. Jackson again raised the issue,
running as a Jeffersonian trying to reign in the expansion of the federal
government. Changes in the role of the federal government were slight
before the War between the States but accelerated afterward. The federal government's relationship to the states was irrevocably changed as
a result of the war, Reconstruction created a precedent for the federal
government to direct the activities of state governments when they
were in conflict with federal policy, and the rise in interest group activity at the federal level after the war created the expectation that interest groups could hope to receive economic benefits from the federal
government.

As the role of the federal government evolved, giving it the ability
to exercise more power, the nation's economy also evolved, producing
concentrated economic power that created a demand for more government control of the economy. That demand arose from farmers, who
wanted protection from the economic power of the railroads, the grain

elevators, and the firms from whom they purchased goods. That demand arose from workers, who wanted protection from the monopsony power of their employers. That demand arose from small business people and professionals, who found their economic status increasingly threatened by big corporations. That demand also came from politicians, who found their power and status threatened by the substantial economic power of those who ran big business. Thus, the Jeffersonian ideology of a government strictly limited to the protection of individual rights gave way to the Hamiltonian ideology of a more active federal government that could use its power to help secure the economic well-being of the nation's citizens.[50]

Americans were already well aware of the political power that special interests could wield, and a more active government had to deal with the threat that its political power could be directed for the benefit of those who had economic power. Thus, Progressivism brought with it changes in the way the federal government was run. It created a more professional civil service, insulated to a large degree from the political pressures faced by elected officials. Progressivism brought with it the federal income tax to finance government expansion. The income tax might be viewed as the means that allowed such substantial growth in government expenditures in the twentieth century, but it would be more accurate to view the income tax as the result of the Progressive demand for more government expenditures rather than the cause.[51]

Progressivism also brought with it the ideology of democracy. The founders intentionally created a minor role for democratic input from America's citizens when they wrote the Constitution. The leaders of government should not be directly accountable to the citizenry, the founders believed, and they designed a government in which only members of the House of Representatives, half of one of the three branches of government, would have to answer directly to the voters. This was done intentionally to allow citizens some check on the activities of government, but having the other five-sixths of government selected in a different manner was also done intentionally. Jackson's major challenge to the founders' vision of the role of democracy was echoed by the Populists and the Progressives, who saw accountability to the electorate as the best way to give the power of government to its citizens, rather than vesting it in a handful of elites.

The enhanced role of voters in American democracy makes sense in the context of the Progressive agenda. When the government's role is limited to protecting the rights of individuals, democratic input from the masses is not necessary. Rather, to the extent that it is used, democracy is a means to an end—a way to select competent people to carry on the business of government and to remove them from office if they prove incompetent. When the role of government is expanded to further the economic interests of the population, democratic representation becomes crucial. Even at the beginning of the Progressive movement, the economic interests of some were pitted against the economic interests of others through economic regulation, and if citizens are to have any hope that the government will choose to further their interests they must have power over those in government. The idea that government could further the economic well-being of special interest groups was already clear, and citizens needed a way to ensure that the government would further their interests, not somebody else's.

In the Progressive Era, where the common vision was that big business stood against the common man, democracy meant that people would be represented in proportion to their numbers rather than their wealth. Thus, democracy, which served a limited role in the government that the founders had envisioned, became an indispensable part of Progressive government. Concerning economic interests, the sides were not as clearly drawn at the end of the twentieth century as they were at the beginning. Contrast the popularity of Bill Gates, the world's wealthiest man at the end of the twentieth century, with the public unpopularity of John D. Rockefeller, the world's wealthiest man at the beginning of that century. The ideals of Progressivism have lost some of their focus, replaced by the concept of democracy as the fundamental principle underlying American government. At the same time, democracy has evolved from a method for making group decisions to a method for allocating economic resources. Public policy increasingly means providing economic benefits to some at the expense of others, and who gives and who gets is determined by majority rule. At the beginning of the twenty-first century public policy is guided by popular opinion rather than by principle, and the general public accepts the idea that a government policy is legitimate if most people are in favor of it. This is the lasting legacy of Progressivism.

CHAPTER 9

The Growth of the Federal Government
in the 1920s

The growth in federal government expenditures in the United States
has been a twentieth-century phenomenon. In 1913, just prior to
World War I, federal government expenditures were 2.5 percent of the
GNP but by 1990 had risen to 22.5 percent of the GNP. The relatively
small size of the federal government prior to World War I shows that
it exhibited minimal growth in the nineteenth century, in stark contrast
with its tremendous growth in the twentieth century. It is worth returning to figure 3 to review the history of real per capita federal expenditures from 1800 to 1990. The difference between government growth in
the twentieth century and that in the nineteenth century is striking. A
close look at figure 3 shows a large percentage increase in federal
expenditures during the War between the States, followed by a higher
level of expenditures after the war, but minimal growth. Real per
capita federal expenditures were $79.76 in 1870 and were $79.56 in
1895 (again, all figures are in 1990 dollars unless otherwise noted). Figure 3 shows the growth in federal expenditures that began in the latter
half of the 1890s and clearly reveals the wartime peaks of World Wars
I and II. But the most notable characteristic of this graph of government expenditure growth is not the peaks that are associated with wars
but the steady growth throughout the twentieth century, which is in
stark contrast to the absence of growth in the nineteenth century.[1] The
goal of this chapter is to contribute toward an understanding of government growth in the twentieth century by examining a period in that
century—the 1920s.[2]

The previous eight chapters have shown that an examination of
expenditure growth alone would present a very incomplete picture of
federal government growth in the nineteenth century. When the nation
was founded, its leaders envisioned a very limited scope of activity for
the federal government, and throughout the nineteenth century the
scope of the federal government continued to expand. Andrew Jackson

was alarmed by the expansion in the scope of the federal government in the 1820s, and despite his efforts to return to the Jeffersonian ideal of a limited federal government, his push to make the federal government more democratic set the stage for a major expansion in federal government power. The War between the States had a tremendous effect on redefining the role of the federal government, and the political activities of organized interest groups after the war, ranging from veterans who raided the Treasury for increasingly generous pension benefits to farmers who clamored for federal regulation of railroads, transformed the federal government from a protector of individual rights into an institution that promised to look out for the economic well-being of its citizens.

Interest group activity dates back to the nation's earliest days, but toward the end of the nineteenth century the Progressive Era brought with it a change in ideology such that the appeal of interest groups for assistance from the federal government was no longer viewed as an attempt for some to get government benefits at the expense of others, as it would have been just a few decades before. Rather, the Progressive ideology was an explicit break with the past that redefined the role of government to include the protection of the economic welfare of its citizens. Democracy had evolved from a strictly political concept into a method of readjusting the allocation of economic resources. Rather than paying lip service to the ideas of the founders, the Progressives openly recognized their departure from the old-fashioned Jeffersonian ideals.

While the scope of the federal government expanded throughout the nineteenth century, the growth of federal expenditures was limited by revenue constraints. Running a surplus during normal times was viewed as prudent public policy, but by the 1890s the federal budget was balanced and there was no more revenue to be spent. The passage of the 16th Amendment allowing the creation of a federal income tax provided the revenues to fuel the federal expenditure growth of the twentieth century, but the income tax did not cause the expenditure growth. Rather, it was instituted as a response to the demand for a larger federal government. Figure 3 dramatically shows the result.

The decade of the 1920s deserves special attention as a part of the history of the growth of the federal government for two reasons. First, as figure 3 shows, government growth in the 1920s was less than in any subsequent decade, so any light shed on growth of government in the 1920s can help illuminate the entire process of government growth.

Second, the decade of the 1920s falls between two well-known eras of government growth: the Progressive Era prior to World War I and the New Deal of the 1930s. One is tempted to view the 1920s as an era of government retrenchment that, perhaps, would have produced a repeat of the nineteenth century had it not been for the Great Depression and the New Deal.

The history of the 1920s is often viewed this way (although not by all historians)[3] perhaps because the government of the 1920s is prone to be closely associated with the presidents of the 1920s. Warren G. Harding and Calvin Coolidge were major personalities of the 1920s by virtue of being presidents, but one must view the government of the 1920s more broadly than by just the presidents of that decade. Even so, however, an examination of the policies promoted by Harding and Coolidge (and Herbert Hoover at the end of the decade) shows that they were considerably more sympathetic toward growth in government programs and expenditures than general opinion suggests.[4]

The study of government growth in the 1920s is interesting in its own right, but the conclusions from an examination of this decade have more significant implications for the process of growth in the surrounding decades and, more generally, for the entire process of government growth in the twentieth century. Popular opinion often credits (or blames) FDR's New Deal for the major increase in federal government growth. This chapter shows that the foundations of the New Deal go back to the 1920s and before and that Roosevelt's initiatives were not a crucial turning point in the growth of American government.[5] As an extension of the trends begun during the Progressive Era, the 1920s is not a key decade in the growth of American government, but understanding the government growth of the 1920s is a key element in understanding the process of the growth during the twentieth century.[6]

The Administrations of Harding, Coolidge, and Hoover

At first glance, it might appear that the three Republican administrations of the 1920s sandwiched in between the Democratic administrations of Woodrow Wilson (1913–21) and Franklin Roosevelt (1933–45) brought with them a period of conservatism, in much the same way that Reagan's election in 1980 might be viewed as a reaction against the expansion of government programs and expenditures in the 1960s and 1970s.[7] However, before Roosevelt's administration, the

Republicans were the party of government activism and the Democrats the party of conservatism, which weakens the analogy. Furthermore, except for Wilson's election, which was the result of a temporary fracture of the Republican party into Republicans and Progressives, the Republicans, along with Republican ideas, had dominated the White House since the War between the States. After Lincoln's presidency, Wilson and Grover Cleveland were the only Democrats to hold the office until FDR. The ideas of Progressivism, found mostly in the Republican party, provided the intellectual foundation for the substantial growth of twentieth-century government.

Another factor relevant to the political environment in the 1920s was the relative balance of power between the president and Congress. During World War I, the balance of power tipped considerably toward the presidency, but the 1920s brought a reduced amount of power to the presidency and an increase in the power of the Republican-dominated Congress. After the 1920 elections, Republicans held a majority of 303 to 131 in the House and 60 to 36 in the Senate, and, particularly when compared to the previous two decades, the political agenda was more controlled by Congress than by the presidency.

Without strong presidential leadership or an aggressive presidential agenda, political initiatives from Congress became oriented more toward special interest programs that generated economic benefits for clearly identified groups, but this involved an expansion of governmental scope and power.[8] While some war-oriented programs were eliminated after the war, many were not, and the orientation of federal government activities changed substantially. The scope of government increased substantially during the Progressive Era and World War I, but the 1920s continued pushing the bounds of government. Ellis W. Hawley says the administrations of Harding and Coolidge were able to "lend credibility to claims that permanent peace and prosperity were in train and that ways had been found to realize the dreams of the progressive era while avoiding the evils feared by conservatives."[9] It was not a period of retrenchment or even of stabilized governmental activity.[10]

The theme of the Harding administration was a return to normalcy, which must have sounded especially desirable after World War I. This theme was immediately adopted by Coolidge after Harding's death in 1923. One feature of this return, and an indicator of the conservatism of the Harding and Coolidge administrations, was the slashing of income tax rates, which involved considerable congressional debate. When the income tax was established in 1913, the highest marginal tax rate was 7 percent, but it increased to 77 percent in 1916 to help finance the war. The top rate was reduced to as low as 25 percent in 1925, which was still substantially higher than the 7 percent rate prior to the war, and the income levels that defined the brackets were also lowered substantially from their prewar levels. The "normalcy" of the 1920s incorporated considerably higher levels of federal spending and taxes than those of the Progressive Era prior to World War I.

The Progressive movement and the Progressive party remained vital through the 1920s, the difference being that the Republicans had been able to regain the support of the Progressives. In 1924 the Progressive party ran Robert LaFollette, a Republican senator from Wisconsin, as its presidential candidate, who gained a respectable 13 percent of the popular vote. Despite the three-way race, Coolidge still won a 54 percent majority, which contrasts sharply with the 1912 election in which the Progressive party split the Republican vote and led to the defeat of the Republican incumbent. Normalcy, in the Harding-Coolidge sense, meant peace and prosperity, but it also meant a continuation of the principles of Progressivism, which enabled the Republican party to retain the support of its Progressive element. Despite the popular view of the 1920s as a retreat from Progressivism, by any measure government was more firmly entrenched as a part of the American economy in 1925 than in 1915 and was continuing to grow. Harding and Coolidge were viewed as probusiness,[11] and there may be a tendency to equate this probusiness sentiment with anti-Progressivism.[12] The advance of Progressivism during their administrations may have been slower than before the war or during the New Deal, but a slower advance is not a retreat.[13]

The Hoover administration, from 1929 to 1933, must be analyzed differently because of the onset of the Great Depression, but compared to his immediate predecessors it is much easier to make the case that Hoover was an active supporter of increased government involvement in the economy. Hoover served in the Wilson administration as head of the United States Food Administration beginning in 1917, and throughout the Harding-Coolidge administrations he served as secretary of commerce and was the most active cabinet member in pursuing increased government involvement in the economy. Under Hoover's administration, real per capita federal expenditures increased by 88 percent. Under Roosevelt's administration from 1933 to 1940, just prior to World War II, they increased by only 74 percent. Although Hoover started from a lower base, in percentage terms expenditures under Hoover increased more in four years than during the next seven New Deal years.[14] If a case can be made that federal policies under the Harding and Coolidge administrations were a solidification and extension of Progressive principles, the case is more easily made for Hoover's administration.

One might be concerned that looking at the data in real per capita terms, as is done in table 1 and figure 3, makes growth look more substantial than it actually was because it ignores the fact that the 1920s were relatively prosperous years, especially when compared to the 1930s. The picture is not much different if federal outlays are examined as a percentage of GNP, however, as figure 7 shows. As already noted, there is no absolute growth in federal outlays as a percentage of GNP during the 1920s, but there is also almost no growth after 1932, when FDR's New Deal began. The substantial growth shown in figure 7 occurred during the Hoover administration. One would not want to

TABLE 1.   Real Per Capita Federal Expenditures: 1915–35 (in constant 1990 dollars)

Year	Total	Total Minus Defense and Interest
1915	95.02	27.39
1916	83.60	22.75
1917	193.22	113.81
1918	1,067.31	518.37
1919	1,329.77	477.53
1920	390.98	170.15
1921	338.86	136.16
1922	232.95	78.62
1923	214.57	74.49
1924	194.85	70.36
1925	187.78	71.09
1926	184.80	76.57
1927	180.57	72.75
1928	186.56	79.89
1929	195.41	89.30
1930	211.13	101.81
1931	247.41	130.80
1932	286.39	183.98
1933	367.84	231.20
1934	498.88	361.02
1935	486.81	328.03

Source: Historical Statistics of the United States from Colonial Times to 1970 and author's calculations.

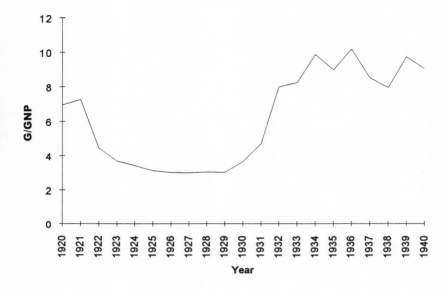

Fig. 7. Total federal government outlays as a percentage of GNP: 1920–40

argue, based on the aggregate expenditure data shown in figure 7, that the New Deal was not a period of substantial growth in government, although the data in the figure show little growth during the 1930s. This same reasoning applies to the 1920s. These aggregate data can conceal much, and they beg for a closer examination of both the 1930s and the 1920s.

Growth in Federal Spending

Table 1 shows real per capita federal expenditures for the years from 1915 through 1935, which brackets the 1920s by a half decade in each direction. The column that shows total real per capita federal expenditures are the numbers for 1915–35 that appear in figure 3. The next column shows that total less military, veterans, and interest expenditures in order to subtract out expenditures directly related to military activity. The relationship of military and veterans expenditures to the war is obvious, but in an era in which government budgets typically were in surplus, interest on the national debt during the 1920s was also almost entirely an expenditure related to the nation's involvement in World War I. In 1915, before the war, the national debt was $1.2 billion; by 1920, after the war, it had climbed to $24.3 billion.

An examination of the data in table 1 reveals several things about the growth of federal expenditures during the 1920s. First, note that nonmilitary expenditures prior to World War I were substantially less than $30 per capita but that the lowest year after the war (1924) had nonmilitary expenditures of more than $70 per capita—more than double the level of expenditures prior to the war. This lends some evidence for the ratchets hypothesis, which suggests that during times of crisis government expenditures are ratcheted up to deal with the crisis but never fall back down to their prior level after the crisis has passed.[15]

However, the table shows more than simply a ratcheting up of government expenditures. Following the ratchets hypothesis, one might expect military expenditures to soar during the war and decline afterward, but they would be offset somewhat by an increase in nonmilitary expenditures. Yet, nonmilitary expenditures also soared during the war and declined steeply afterward. Nonmilitary expenditures in 1924 were only 13.6 percent of their peak level in 1918. The second thing the data in table 1 suggest is that there are war-related expenditures in the government budget even after subtracting military, veterans, and interest expenditures. This makes it apparent that one cannot accept these nonwar expenditures as unrelated to the war (these expenditures will be analyzed at more length later in this chapter).

A third thing the data show is that after reaching their lowest postwar level in 1924 government expenditures began a relatively rapid growth. From 1924 to 1929, before depression-related expenditures would have found their way into the budget, nonmilitary expenditures increased by 27 percent, all during the Coolidge administration. If the decline in expenditures up through 1924 is attributed to a winding down of the war effort, there appears to be a considerable underlying growth in federal expenditures through the 1920s—growth worth examining more closely. What at first appears to be a relatively stable level of federal expenditures in the 1920s actually is substantial underlying growth, masked by a decline in war-related expenditures.

A fourth thing to consider is the appropriate benchmark for looking at government growth during the 1920s. The growth looks substantial if only the years since 1920 are considered, as just argued, but one could argue that it would be more appropriate to use the prewar year of 1916 as the benchmark and that if the 1920s really was a no-growth decade the government should have returned federal spending back to its prewar level. That federal spending always remained at more than double its prewar level does say something about growth in the 1920s, especially since the underlying trend was up.

Finally, the table shows that in percentage terms the Hoover administration undertook a massive increase in federal spending after the 1929 stock market crash and the onset of the Great Depression. From 1929 to 1933 (the final Hoover budget), nonmilitary federal expenditures increased by 259 percent. Total expenditures increased by a more modest 188 percent during that period because military expenditures were, in 1929, more than half of the federal budget. In percentage terms, growth in federal spending in the Hoover administration far outpaced the growth during Franklin Roosevelt's administration.

While a superficial look at the data suggests that the 1920s represent a lull in government growth between the Progressive Era and the New Deal, looking at the data in table 1 more closely raises several interesting issues and reveals that there was a substantial amount of underlying growth in government expenditures in the 1920s. It would be misleading to try to judge the growth of the federal government in the 1920s only by looking at aggregate expenditures. The next several sections look more closely at the decade to see how government growth manifested itself.

Expenditures by Function

Table 2 takes a more detailed look at federal expenditures in 1920, 1925, and 1930 to identify differences in budgetary growth among various categories of expenditures. The table shows that, when the decade is divided in half, the most substantial growth took place in the second half of the decade. General functions, which include the direct expenses of the legislative, judicial, and executive branches of government, remained stable through the first half of the 1920s but increased by 35 percent in the second half. Similarly, military expenditures, which fell substantially in the first half of the decade up through 1925, increased by 32 percent from 1925 to 1930. The majority of nonfunctional expenditures is interest on the federal debt, which is a relatively stable category. The category of civil functions is of most interest for current purposes.

In his analysis of federal expenditures, Carroll Wooddy breaks civil functions down into 20 categories, including land transportation and marine transportation.[16] Table 2 uses Wooddy's data but lists land transportation and marine transportation separately because changes in these two transportation categories so overwhelm the civil functions category. In 1920 there was a considerable wartime component to the transportation category because of the Merchant Fleet Corporation, which was established to aid in merchant shipping during the war, and because of the nationalization of the railroads during the war. Another major area of marine expenditures was the Coast Guard, which had substantial expenses associated with Prohibition. Because of wartime expenditures and Prohibition, the trends in marine transportation expenditures are not representative of government growth in general.

Civil functions less transportation in table 2 show relatively modest growth of only 18 percent from 1920 to 1925. In contrast, from 1925 to 1930 civil functions less transportation grew by 54 percent. Part of the reason for the relatively modest growth in the first half of the decade is that increases in some areas were offset by decreases in war-related civil expenditures in other areas. That is easy to document in the transportation category but is more difficult to see in other categories.[17] Federal relief, for example, declined from $48 million in 1920 to $3.5 million in 1930, undoubtedly because most relief expenditures in 1920 were war related.[18] But other areas increased substantially over the decade and deserve a closer look.

Table 3 lists a few areas that saw significant increases in federal expenditures over the 1920s. These areas are all subsets of the category

TABLE 2.   Expenditures of the Federal Government by Function: 1920, 1925, and 1930 (in thousands of 1930 dollars)

	1920	1925	1930
General functions	18,953	18,932	25,642
Military functions	1,966,358	1,099,711	1,455,093
Civil functions less trans.	426,964	504,891	775,298
Transportation	1,281,878	90,035	87,029
Nonfunctional	1,453,747	1,369,446	1,315,742
Total	5,147,900	3,083,016	3,658,804

Source: Author's calculations are from data in Carroll H. Wooddy, *The Growth of the Federal Government: 1915–1932* (New York: McGraw-Hill, 1934), 545–46.

Note: General functions are legislative, judicial, and executive expenditures. Military functions include military pensions. Nonfunctional expenditures include interest on the debt, investments, refunds, and deposits into trust funds.

of civil functions less transportation from table 2, and the final row in the table—the percentage of civil functions less transportation—shows the percentage of that category in table 2 that is made up of all of the categories in table 3. Thus, in 1920, the categories of table 9.3 are 36.5 percent of the category of civil functions less transportation in table 2, with the percentage increasing to 66.2 percent in 1925 and declining slightly to 62.7 percent in 1930. The last number in the "total" row shows that, taken together, these categories were 3.12 times as large in 1930 as they were in 1920. The substantial growth in these categories was partially offset by declines in some other categories, because the table 2 category was only 1.82 times as large in 1930 as in 1920. This suggests that the categories omitted from table 3 may reflect declines in war-related expenditures, although other factors may also have been at work.

The fourth column in table 3 gives the 1930 expenditure level divided by the 1920 level, so law enforcement expenditures in 1930 were 4.97 times as large in 1930 as in 1920. The last column gives the growth rate over that decade, so law enforcement expenditures grew at a 17.5 percent annual rate from 1920 to 1930. These categories cover nearly two-thirds of the category of civil functions less transportation from table 2, so they make up a significant component of nonmilitary federal expenditures. Table 3 shows that their average annual growth

TABLE 3. **Expenditures of the Federal Government, Selected Functions: 1920, 1925, and 1930 (in thousands of 1930 dollars)**

	1920	1925	1930	1930 ÷ 1920	Annual Growth Rate
Law enforcement	10,375	24,246	51,537	4.97	17.5
Public domain	15,402	24,994	37,789	2.45	9.4
Commerce	8,077	14,393	27,354	3.39	13.0
Agriculture	16,644	26,273	48,824	2.93	11.4
Labor interests	2,065	4,641	6,863	3.32	12.8
Immigration	2,953	5,541	9,512	3.22	12.5
Public education	5,405	10,483	14,295	2.64	10.2
Public improvements	73,481	183,411	241,387	3.29	12.7
Territorial & local govt.	19,964	38,228	46,367	2.32	8.9
Total	155,965	334,044	485,838	3.12	
Civil functions less trans. (%)	36.5	66.2	62.7		

Source: Author's calculations are from data in Carroll H. Wooddy, *The Growth of the Federal Government: 1915–1932* (New York: McGraw-Hill, 1934), 545.

rates were very high, so the categories in that table give some indication of where to look for government growth in the 1920s.

Law enforcement expenditures were almost five times as large in 1930 as in 1920, and much of this is related to Prohibition. Agricultural expenditures, which had an average annual growth rate through the 1920s of 11.4 percent, are discussed in more detail later. Immigration and naturalization expenditures more than tripled, partly representing greater selectivity in admitting immigrants. Immigration was sharply down in 1915 due to World War I, and legislation passed in 1917 restricted immigration after the war. In 1924 immigration quotas were established, further adding to immigration and naturalization expenditures.[19]

Federal expenditures on public education also increased substantially during the 1920s, funding programs such as land grant colleges and federal subsidies for vocational education. These expenditures were undertaken by grants to the states, but the federal government also contributed significant sums directly to some educational institutions, including Howard University and the Columbia Institution for the Deaf. The Library of Congress also falls within the education category and in 1930 accounted for $2.3 million of the $14 million education category. Two features of educational expenditures are relevant to the consideration of federal growth in the 1920s. First, education, which even in the early twenty-first century would normally be considered an activity undertaken primarily by the states, had considerable and rapidly growing federal involvement in the 1920s. Second, much of the federal government's expenditures involved grants to the states, leading to more federal financing and more federal control in areas traditionally administered by state governments.

Public domain expenditures include the Department of the Interior expenses to manage public lands and national parks; the Federal Power Commission, whose expenditures were largely related to hydroelectric projects; and the Forest Service, which was a part of the Department of Agriculture. About 70 percent of the public domain expenditures in table 3 are Forest Service expenditures, which went primarily for the construction of roads and trails and for grants to state governments to aid in their management of public lands, including road building and fire protection.

The Department of Commerce, headed up by Hoover through the Harding and Coolidge administrations, shows a remarkable 13 percent average annual growth rate through the 1920s, more than tripling in size. By 1930 about one-third of commerce expenditures were due to aviation, but that still leaves a substantial amount of the budget for nonaviation-related expenditures. The expenditures of the Patent Office increased substantially, as did those of the Bureau of Foreign and Domestic Commerce, which had as one of its main goals the promotion of American goods to foreign purchasers. Expenditures more than doubled in the Radio Commission and the Tariff Commission also. Increased expenditures and activity in the Department of Commerce through the 1920s may reflect the growth of commerce during that prosperous decade, but these expenditures grew under the guidance of Secretary of Commerce Hoover, lending some insight into Hoover's vision of government that would be applicable to evaluating his presidential administration.

The substantial increase in expenditures on labor interests cannot be assigned to a dominant area because these expenditures primarily represent the Department of Labor budget, which included a diverse set of activities. The Bureau of Labor Statistics and the United States Employment Service primarily provided information. The United States Board of Mediation helped to settle labor disputes. The United States Housing Corporation was created in 1918 to help facilitate the construction of housing in areas of critical wartime production but, despite its wartime motivation, lasted into the 1930s. The Harding and Coolidge administrations had a probusiness reputation, but expenditures on labor-related activities soared during the 1920s.

All of these areas might be explored in more detail, but this examination illustrates the primary point that, after omitting expenditures that are clearly related to World War I, there was substantial growth in underlying civilian federal expenditures in the 1920s. The next several sections select a few specific areas of government activity that have some special relevance to the nature of government growth in the 1920s.

Government-Owned Corporations

One of the methods by which the government expanded beyond its traditional bounds in the twentieth century is the establishment of government-owned corporations. The first wholly owned federal corporation was the Bank of the United States, chartered by an act of Congress in 1791. But after the charter of the Second Bank of the United States expired in 1836, another publicly owned corporation was not formed until 1904, to build the Panama Canal.

The next federally owned corporation was the Merchant Fleet Corporation, established in 1917 as a part of the war effort. After the war, the Merchant Fleet Corporation remained in business through the Great Depression, losing phenomenal sums of money over the decade of the 1920s.[20] Throughout the 1920s there were protests from members of Congress that the corporation was being run inefficiently, was unnecessary, and was a government-subsidized competitor of privately owned U.S. shippers. The corporation remained in business, however.

Also in 1917 the Food Administration Grain Corporation was established to help finance the sale of American wheat to Europe and pushed the frontiers of public corporations because its purpose was to aid private businesses (in this case farms) in selling their products, although admittedly in a manner related to the war effort. In 1918 the War Finance Corporation was established to help key industries borrow funds and pushed the frontiers even further. The War Finance Corporation aided businesses more generally, and in 1921, well after the war, its charter was extended so that it could undertake more general types of lending activity, including the making of agricultural loans. The War Finance Corporation continued in business through 1931.

Federally owned corporations, a rarity only a few years prior, began to proliferate in the late 1910s. The Federal Land Bank was established in 1917, and the Sugar Equalization Board, the United States Housing Corporation, and the Spruce Production Corporation were created in 1918. The war effort provided some impetus to these corporations, although some had a tenuous connection with the war. But the war ended in 1918. If these corporations were intended to help win World War I, they could have been dismantled after the war, but the corporations persisted and provided a model for government growth that continued through the 1920s.

In 1923 the Agricultural Credits Act created twelve federally owned banks to make agricultural loans. The Inland Waterways Corporation was created in 1924 to operate boats and barges on the Mississippi River. In 1929 the Federal Farm Board was created to support the prices of agricultural products. The use of public corporations to further the federal government's goals did not begin during World War I, but the late 1910s were transition years during which the government created more federally owned corporations than had ever been created previously. For the most part, they were not dismantled after the war but rather remained and became models for additional federally owned corporations that were established in the 1920s. Paul Johnson argues, "The war corporation of 1917 began one of the great continuities of modern American history, sometimes underground, sometimes at the surface, which culminated in the vast welfare state which Lyndon Johnson brought into being in the late 1960s."[21] Johnson's observation implies that the 1920s were a part of the continuing process of twentieth-century growth rather than a "return to normalcy" falling between the Progressive Era and the New Deal.

The goals of those corporations are significant. They were not formed to enhance national security or to protect the rights of individuals but to provide economic assistance to a subset of the U.S. population. These programs were small in scale when compared to the New Deal, but they were large in scale when compared to federal programs prior to World War I. They were built on the philosophy that the federal government has a direct role to play in enhancing the economic well-being of its citizens. The New Deal changed the scale of federal programs when compared to those of the 1920s but did not change the underlying philosophy.

Federal Aid to States

Federal aid to states was relatively small through the 1920s but grew rapidly. In 1915 federal aid to states totaled $6 million and had increased to $109 million by 1930. Though small in amount (with 48 states, the average state would have received $2.3 million), the percentage increase was substantial, and federal aid rose to $198 million in 1931 and $234 million in 1932. In examining the growth of the federal government from 1915 to 1932 Wooddy concludes, "There seems little doubt that the development of this device for permitting federal participation of the activities of state and local governments contributed substantially to the growth of the period."[22] For present purposes, the magnitude is not of as much interest as is the precedent.

The Post Office

The establishment of post offices and post roads is one of the activities of the federal government explicitly given in the Constitution. By charging for its services, the Post Office has been able to operate in a relatively businesslike manner, even though it was not, until recently, a publicly owned corporation. Through 1851 the Post Office operated under an implied balanced budget constraint, but legislation in 1851 specifically prevented the Post Office from diminishing any of its existing services while encouraging continued expansion. As earlier noted in chapters 5 and 7, in 1857 and 1858 the Post Office established new routes to the Pacific coast costing considerably more than the revenues they generated.[23] The 1850s marked the beginning of a postal policy designed to keep rates low to expand its service, which it was able to do thanks to the backing of the U.S. Treasury.

While postal deficits were not uncommon, in the years prior to World War I the Post Office was able to roughly balance its budget and during the war years showed a substantial surplus. The apparent financial success of the Post Office during the war years was bolstered by two factors. First, much mail was carried by the military during the war, and, second, postal rates increased during the war. But military assistance in carrying the mail never reduced the expenditures of the Post Office. In 1915 the Post Office spent $299 million, and with increases every year, expenditures were $454 million in 1920.[24] Despite some cost advantages due to the war, the Post Office delivered all mail of military personnel without postage and added to its responsibilities by selling war-savings certificates in 1917. More than 80 percent of these war-savings certificates were sold through post offices.

In the Wilson administration, Postmaster General Albert Burleson, appointed in 1913, ruled the Post Office with a heavy hand, trying to do away with unions and to increase the efficiency of the Post Office by controlling costs.[25] Burleson's explicit goal was to have the Post Office operate at a surplus, and he succeeded.[26] In 1917 postage for first-class letters was increased to 3 cents and for postcards to 2 cents, which increased Post Office revenues. In 1919, however, these increases were reversed, creating substantial losses for the Post Office.

Postmaster General Burleson was not popular with postal employees. After being elected, Harding appointed several postmaster generals, all of whom were considerably more sympathetic to postal employees than Burleson. But under Harding, postal expenditures increased tremendously. Expenditures of $454 million in 1920 were followed by expenditures of $621 million in 1921 and a huge postal deficit. While expenditures fell back to $546 million in 1922, they were still 20 percent larger in 1922 than in 1920, and the Post Office showed a deficit every year after 1919, when the rates were lowered to their prewar levels.

Despite the lowering of rates, in 1920 the salaries of letter carriers were raised from $1,400 a year to $1,800 and were raised again in 1924 to $2,100. Harding's first postmaster general, Will H. Hayes, explicitly stated that the Post Office did not exist to make a profit but rather to provide service. Further, Hayes wanted to "humanize" the postal industry, arguing that labor is not a commodity, which was a very Progressive sentiment. The result was not only higher wages but an expansion in the role of the Post Office. It expanded rural free delivery and established more city delivery offices. The Post Office also issued many more money orders and increased its sales of savings bonds (an activity that began in 1917 and continued through 1931). Postal deficits in the 1920s were due to the expansion of postal services and the provision of many services without charge or considerably below cost.

The deficits in the 1920s might be looked at as a return to the idea that, because of its service to the public, postal deficits should not be considered objectionable. However, this is in stark contrast to Postmaster Burleson's ideas, which were more in line with the contemporary vision of limited government and bureaucratic accountability and were the status quo for eight years under the Democratic Wilson administration. If the Harding-Coolidge administration was a return to limited government, it could have continued Wilson's businesslike approach. The Post Office under the Harding-Coolidge administration, however, shows a turn away from the conservative principles in the Wilson administration and a turn back toward the Progressivism that preceded it.

Prohibition

Prohibition corresponds almost exactly to the Republican administrations of Harding, Coolidge, and Hoover. After the passage of the 18th Amendment to the Constitution, Prohibition became effective in 1920 and continued until it was repealed in 1933 by the 21st Amendment. While Prohibition itself slightly predates the Harding administration, the way in which it was enforced was a function of the executive branch of government. Enforcement really goes back to the Harrison Act of 1914, which regulated the use of narcotic drugs. Because taxes were supposed to be paid on legal narcotics, the enforcement of the Harrison Act was undertaken by the Bureau of Internal Revenue, within the Treasury Department. Because there were also limited legal nonbeverage uses for liquor, the Bureau of Internal Revenue also was charged with enforcing Prohibition.

Expenditures to enforce Prohibition extended beyond the Bureau of Internal Revenue, because the Customs Service, Coast Guard, and Department of Justice were also involved. As table 3 shows, federal law enforcement expenditures increased by nearly 400 percent in the 1920s, more than doubling from 1920 to 1925 and then more than doubling again from 1925 to 1930. However, while there may be some debate about how costs of agencies such as the Coast Guard and the Department of Justice should be associated with Prohibition, it is interesting to note how rapidly expenditures of the Bureau of Internal Revenue were affected.[27] In 1920 a Prohibition Unit was established in the Bureau of Internal Revenue, and in 1927 a separate Bureau of Prohibition was created within the Treasury Department. The Treasury's Prohibition-related activities were obviously not intended to generate revenue, as table 4 shows. In no year did the Treasury Department collect more revenues from the enforcement of Prohibition than it expended in enforcement activities. This does not include expenditures undertaken by the Department of Justice, Customs Service, or the Coast Guard.

The revenues in table 4 include fines, penalties, and taxes collected as a result of enforcing Prohibition, and the expenditures include only Treasury Department expenditures. Note that revenues are never higher than in 1924, when they still fall short of expenditures by about

TABLE 4.   Treasury Revenues and
Expenditures from Enforcement of Prohibition
(in thousands of current dollars)

Year	Revenues	Expenditures
1920	1,149	2,060
1921	4,571	6,301
1922	4,356	6,544
1923	5,095	8,135
1924	6,538	7,509
1925	5,873	9,203
1926	5,647	9,573
1927	5,162	11,685
1928	6,184	11,610
1929	5,475	12,328
1930	5,357	13,507
1931	4,138	9,624
1932	3,954	11,058

Source: Data from Carroll H. Wooddy, *The Growth of the Federal Government: 1915–1932* (New York: McGraw-Hill, 1934), 101.

$1 million, but expenditures continue to increase substantially up through 1930. These expenditures are likely to represent less than one-third of total Prohibition-related federal expenditures. The government's powers related to Prohibition expanded as rapidly as its expenditures, and the creation of a separate Bureau of Prohibition was an initiative of the Coolidge administration to better enforce Prohibition. This is yet another area in which the government expanded its powers during the 1920s and did so with the approval of the Coolidge administration.[28]

Agriculture

In the 1920s American agriculture did not fare as well as American industry, creating the impression of an agriculture versus industry antagonism and the impression that the Harding and Coolidge administrations favored industry over agriculture.[29] Much of the blame for agricultural problems must be placed on increased worldwide production, which created a glut on world markets. The industry could have been allowed to adjust to market conditions, creating more transitionary hardship among farmers, but it was not. With regard to government policy in the 1920s, tariffs on farm products were passed by Congress in 1921; the Capper-Volstead Act was passed in 1922, exempting agricultural cooperatives from antitrust laws; and in 1926 the Division of Co-operative Marketing was set up in the Department of Agriculture with the warm endorsement of President Coolidge.[30] The Agricultural Credits Act of 1923 made it easier for farmers to get intermediate credit from the Federal Farm Loan Board.

Looking at the facts, one has to conclude that government intervention for the assistance of the agricultural industry was significant in the 1920s, and in no case was any government protection or assistance taken away from farmers. But farmers wanted more than they got from Coolidge. After much debate and substantial controversy, the McNary-Haugen Bill passed Congress in 1927, which would provide government support prices for agricultural commodities. Coolidge vetoed the bill, but it was redesigned and passed again the next year but again vetoed by Coolidge. After Hoover's election, the Agricultural Marketing Act of 1929 was passed, creating a Federal Farm Board with the power to buy and store "any quantity" of agricultural commodities for the purpose of supporting prices.[31]

The government did not treat farmers as generously as they

wanted to be treated in the 1920s, but despite the "industry versus agri-culture" impression that some historians have of the period, the 1920s saw no reversals of government policy to aid agriculture and there was a substantial growth in new agricultural policies. Benjamin M. Ander-son has argued that the original introduction of the McNary-Haugen Bill in 1924 marks the true beginning of the New Deal.[32] Beginning in 1924, legislation was increasingly designed to help control the econ-omy and to support the economic interests of well-defined interest groups, and farmers were major beneficiaries. As table 3 shows, in 1920 federal expenditures on agriculture were approximately $17 million (in 1930 prices) and had increased by 193 percent to nearly $49 million by 1930. Whether evaluated with regard to finances or programs, the 1920s saw considerable government growth in the agricultural industry and laid the foundation for more federal involvement that was to fol-low in the New Deal.

Antitrust

Expenditures are the easiest measure of the size of government, but they only tell a part of the story of government growth. Government regulation also has a substantial impact but is harder to measure.[33] Starting with the Sherman Act in 1890, the federal government began its antitrust activity to try to limit the economic power of businesses. Only 22 antitrust cases were brought before 1905, but the pace started picking up later in that decade, when 39 cases were brought between 1905 and 1909. From 1910 to 1919, a total of 134 cases were brought, showing increasing antitrust enforcement. There was little slowdown in the 1920s, which saw a total of 125 cases.[34]

As Thomas McCraw notes, "by the 1920s antitrust had become a permanent part of American economic and political life."[35] One might anticipate, after an increase in cases, that firms would be more cautious in their activities to avoid antitrust cases being brought against them. But McCraw further notes that in the 1920s a large proportion of antitrust cases were brought against firms that were not normally regarded as being highly concentrated.[36] Antitrust enforcement in the 1920s was vigorous and increasingly broad in scope. Antitrust enforce-ment is another dimension in which the federal government was exer-cising increased power in the 1920s, despite the conventional wisdom of the 1920s as a decade friendly to business.

Academic Influences

In a famous passage, John Maynard Keynes remarked, "the ideas of economists and political philosophers, both when they are right and when they are wrong, are more powerful than is commonly understood. Indeed, the world is ruled by little else."[37] Reinforcing the ideas of Progressivism, the academic concept of scientific management was gaining currency early in the twentieth century and enhanced the interface between academic institutions and public policy. The creation of the National Bureau of Economic Research (NBER), which owes its origin to the Progressive technocratic reform movement that wanted to use government to improve the economy's ability to produce and distribute income, was one manifestation of an increasing influence of academic institutions on government.

With private funding and support from both the public and private sectors, the NBER was established in 1920 with Wesley Clair Mitchell as its first director. Mitchell's goal was "to organize the bureau's research program around questions that were, first, of primary social importance, and second, capable of the statistical resolution needed to surmount social science's internal crisis of scientific legitimacy."[38] The NBER worked closely with the Department of Commerce, and Secretary Hoover was very interested in making the government more actively involved in economic policy. Indeed, many of the new Keynesian ideas of the 1930s were a part of the accepted wisdom of American economists in the 1920s.[39] The 1920s saw an alliance of academic institutions, private foundations, and government to create organizations like the NBER that furthered the scientific aspects of social science and provided data and ideas for government management of the economy.

Conclusion

The 1920s, falling between the Progressive Era and the New Deal and directly following World War I, may appear as a decade of stable government sandwiched between major episodes of government growth. In some sense, this is true. Government expenditures were declining dramatically from their peak levels during the war, and Calvin Coolidge, president during most of the decade, was not acting aggressively to expand the scope of government. But in other ways the 1920s was a decade of increasing government activity—in expenditures, in regulation, and in attitude—as the federal government was increasingly willing to expand its role in the economic lives of its citizens. Indeed, the foundation for the New Deal was established in the 1920s, and it certainly would be wrong to conclude that, were it not for the New Deal, government would have remained more confined later in the twentieth century. The New Deal was really an extension of the type of government growth that occurred in the 1920s.

Were it not for the Depression, government growth would have been slower in the 1930s, because there would have been no call to respond to a national economic crisis. But the government expanded its programs, its powers, and its budget during the 1920s in the relatively passive presidential administration of Calvin Coolidge as a part of the trend of government growth that had begun with the Progressive Era around the turn of the century. If the trends of the 1920s had continued, federal government growth would have been substantial with or without the Great Depression and with or without the New Deal. For Coolidge, being probusiness did not mean being antigovernment (or antilabor or antiagriculture), and he supported the expansion of government in almost every area, although not to the degree desired by some of his critics.

This chapter sheds some light on the remarkable phenomenon of government growth in the twentieth century by closely examining the decade that saw the least government growth in the century. By looking at the decade prior to the New Deal, it is apparent that neither the New Deal nor the nation's response to the depression triggered the growth of the federal government. The seeds were sown in the Progressive Era prior to World War I, and the 1920s served to reinforce those principles of government established during the Progressive Era by continuing to expand the government's reach. The 1920s did not represent a plateau in government activity that was reversed by the New Deal; rather, the foundations for the New Deal were established by the increasing scope of federal government activity during the 1920s.

Well prior to the New Deal, three trends were clearly apparent in the evolution of American government. The most obvious—because it is the most easily quantified—was the growth in government expenditures. This expenditure growth was accompanied by growth in government regulatory activities and by a transition toward transfers, which were viewed as an illegitimate activity for government as late as the 1890s but were viewed as an integral part of the activities of a progressive government by the early twentieth century. Government growth also brought with it an increasing centralization, as the federal government became more significant relative to state and local governments. This particular aspect of government growth can be traced at least as far back as the War between the States. In addition to government growth, the second trend was the increasing democratization of government. The Progressive Era marks the turning point here, as the fundamental principle directing public policy evolved from protecting individual liberty to furthering the will of the majority. The third trend that was apparent prior to the New Deal was the increasing reliance on democracy as a guide to rights and to economic resource allocation.

Prior to the Progressive Era, democracy was a method of political decision making, but the limited government of the time had relatively little impact on people's economic affairs. In contrast, such policies as government regulation of business, antitrust laws that could actually force individuals to divest themselves of their property, higher taxes, and explicit transfer programs such as farm subsidies were democratically chosen to affect the allocation of economic resources. Democracy had evolved from a political decision-making mechanism into an economic system for resource allocation. This transformation clearly predates the New Deal, and the history of the 1920s shows that even in a period of relative normalcy the transformation continued to take place. The 1920s was a decade of growing government, where government policy was increasingly determined by democracy rather than by the principle of protecting individual liberty, and a decade in which democracy increasingly became an integral part of the nation's economic system as well as its political system.

CHAPTER 10

The New Deal and World War II

One of the trade-offs involved in the design of government is between consensus in collective decision making and the scope of governmental activity. American constitutional history, even before the Declaration of Independence, shows that there has been a constant movement away from consensus in collective decision making, which has allowed the scope of governmental action to increase. The Iroquois constitution, discussed in chapter 3, required consensus among all citizens for almost all collective decisions, and one consequence was that the scope of Iroquois government was very limited. The Constitutional Convention was held to broaden the powers of the federal government, as chapter 4 described, because the founders believed that the activities of the federal government were too constrained by their existing constitution, the Articles of Confederation. In the process, political decision making moved further away from consensus toward collective action based on the approval of a simple majority. The Great Depression and World War II were generally viewed as crises that required extensive government action in response, and the demand for increased government action in response to these crises came with a willingness among citizens to allow less consensus in the collective decision-making process that would respond to the crises.

World War I had established a precedent for government action that went beyond the previously accepted limits of government power. During that war, businesses were nationalized by the government, tax rates were increased substantially, citizens were drafted into military service, and federal policy pushed government into virtually every area of the economy in furtherance of the war effort.[1] As chapter 9 showed, many of those increases in the scope of government remained after the war was over. When Franklin Delano Roosevelt ascended to the presidency in 1933, the World War I experience provided precedent for government action to expand the scope of government and to narrow the reliance on consensus in collective decision making. There was also the ideological sentiment from the Progressive movement that made citizens sympathetic with the idea that part of government's role is to look out for the economic interests of its citizens. Thus, the constitutional limits on the scope of government were substantially eroded during the New Deal and were further eroded because of the participation of the United States in World War II.

An obvious effect of the New Deal and World War II was a substantial increase in the level of government expenditures and in the types of activities in which the federal government was involved. That growth in government programs and expenditures has been extensively documented and is well known to anyone with even a casual familiarity with the period so will not be the main focus of this chapter. Rather, this chapter will focus on the erosion of constitutional constraints on government during these decades and on the replacement of constitutionally limited governmental powers as a guide to government action with the democratic idea of government policy in response to the desires of the majority. Government did get bigger during this period—much bigger. But the nature of government also changed in a fundamental way. The Progressive ideology that began to modify the role of the federal government in the 1890s had finally triumphed by the time Eisenhower assumed the presidency in the 1950s.

During the 1930s and 1940s Americans ceded many of the constitutional limits on government power, allowing government to act more unilaterally, with less consensus, in exchange for enhancing the scope of government to deal with the crises of war and depression. At midcentury, looking back, government had largely succeeded. The Depression was over, and the war was won. There was another looming crisis, in the form of the cold war, that cried out for continued strong government, but there was also peace and prosperity following two decades of extraordinary growth in the scope of government. This chapter looks not so much at the actual changes in government spending and government programs but rather at the ideological shifts that enabled those changes to occur. After World War I Americans were more willing to increase the power of government to respond to crisis situations. After World War II Americans were more willing to give government power over their lives in normal times, as a method of enhancing their economic well-being.

Partly this meant providing a safety net for those who are least fortunate in society. More significant is that this meant giving the government the responsibility for maintaining an economic environment within which people can prosper economically. In the 1890s this mostly meant regulating the economic behavior of those with concentrated economic power. In the 1950s this meant regulating economic activity in general and providing a macroeconomic environment conducive to prosperity. Under the old ideology of liberty, government activity was limited to the protection of individual rights, allowing individuals to pursue prosperity on their own. Under the new ideology, if government is looking out for the economic well-being of its citizens, then those citizens find it more important to have a voice in determining the actions of government to ensure that the government does not short-change them in the process of furthering the economic well-being of others. Thus, democracy is a natural extension of government involvement in the economy.

Roosevelt's Hundred Days

When Roosevelt's presidency began, the nation's economy was bordering on collapse. More than three years after the stock market crash of 1929, the economy continued its decline, and neither President Hoover nor Congress appeared to be capable of doing anything to stop the decline. Roosevelt was inaugurated on March 4, 1933, and on March 5 called a special session of Congress to meet on March 9, which began his Hundred Days. On March 5, he ordered a national banking holiday and only allowed banks to reopen their doors after they had been individually inspected and approved. Even at that time, many argued that closing the banks was unnecessary and that it created an atmosphere of crisis.[2] But by creating the appearance of a crisis and by taking decisive steps to deal with the crisis, Roosevelt accomplished two things. First, he enhanced his appearance as a leader and a man of action, standing in contrast to Hoover and Congress, who appeared paralyzed in the face of the nation's economic problems. Second, the appearance of crisis increased the popular demand for government action, making citizens more willing to accept Roosevelt's initiatives without waiting for some type of political consensus to affirm them.

In Roosevelt's inaugural address he argued that the Depression was a crisis as serious as war and called for drastic measures to respond to this national emergency. His banking holiday served the dual purpose of showing strong leadership in responding to the emergency and of accentuating the crisis. Economic activity is much more difficult to undertake without banks. Roosevelt's quick and drastic action established his ability to decisively lead the nation in crisis and generated popular support. He created the foundations for the New Deal in his Hundred Days, when he asked Congress to cooperate with him to pass fundamental New Deal legislation. Roosevelt succeeded with minimal opposition, and the New Deal was under way. Those Hundred Days saw the passage of foreign exchange controls, housing programs, new labor laws, the creation of the Civilian Conservation Corps and the Tennessee Valley Authority, and the passage of the Agricultural Adjustment Act and the National Industrial Recovery Act.[3] The legislation itself is significant, but equally significant is the fact that it was so readily supported by Congress and that the general public was so accepting of such broad increases in government authority.

The Regulation of Banking and Finance

The onset of the Great Depression is normally placed at October 29, 1929, the date of the stock market crash. From this initial meltdown of financial markets, the crisis spread throughout the rest of the economy. Part of the problem was that banks had made loans for individuals to buy stock, and when the value of the stock fell borrowers were unable to pay their loans. The problem was exacerbated by the nature of fractional reserve banking. Everyone knows that banks lend out the money they receive in deposit, and so no bank could possibly repay all of its depositors immediately. The system counts on the fact that most of the time deposits and withdrawals roughly balance each other out. But when depositors panic, as they did after the onset of the Depression, and many want their money right away, even the most solid bank will have to turn some depositors away.

The Federal Reserve Bank (Fed) was established in 1913 to mitigate just such a crisis, but for a number of reasons it failed to support the banking industry during the Depression. One reason was that the Fed was established as a lender of last resort for solvent banks. To borrow from the Fed, banks had to show that they had loans coming due in the future with which they could pay off their debt to the Fed. Bad loans did not count. Thus, if banks faced a temporary liquidity crisis, the Fed would help out, but if banks made bad loans and became insolvent, that was the bank's problem. Another problem the Fed faced was that the nation was still on the gold standard, and if it did prop up the banking system by creating new money there was the risk that the new money would cause gold to flow overseas, undoing the Fed's policy and causing a loss of U.S. gold at the same time. Perhaps the Fed could have acted to shore up the banking system and the economy, but it did not.[4]

The failure of the banking system led to a host of regulations on banking and finance. In 1933 the Glass Steagall Act was passed, which separated commercial banking from investment banking. Thus, commercial banks, and the nation's money supply, would be more substantially insulated from problems that might arise in financial markets. To further aid the stability of the banking system, the Federal Deposit Insurance Corporation was established in 1934 to provide federal insurance to depositors who kept their assets in commercial banks. In addition, the Fed assumed much greater control over the banking industry, including instituting controls on allowable interest rates. It also became more difficult to charter a bank, because the government did not want new banks entering the industry to threaten the stability of existing banks.

The Securities and Exchange Commission (SEC) was also created in 1933 as the agency to oversee the securities industry as specified in the Securities Act of 1933. Americans correctly viewed that speculation in the stock market in the 1920s had led to the crash of 1929, so found merit in regulating the issuance and trading of securities. While the cause of the speculation in stocks goes beyond the scope of this volume, it is worth remarking that many observers would place much of the blame on the Fed for allowing the credit expansion that provided the money to engage in speculation, suggesting that the stock market crash was a failure of public policy rather than a breakdown of the market.[5] But it does not matter. The main issue here is the response to the stock market crash rather than its underlying causes. The SEC was given broad powers to require disclosure of substantial amounts of financial information at the time a security is issued. Furthermore, it was given substantial powers to regulate the types of bargaining that could take place in the securities industry and the mandate to prevent insider trading of securities, which was made illegal. Benjamin Anderson has argued that these laws went well beyond what was necessary and compared American securities regulation with British regulation, which is far less restrictive yet apparently equally effective.[6]

The point here is not the effectiveness of the legislation but rather the degree to which the public was eager to allow the federal government to dictate the terms of securities transactions. Whatever their benefit, heavy regulations have made it much harder to take a company public and have reduced the freedom of individuals to undertake business in a mutually agreeable manner. Complete disclosure is important in publicly traded securities, beyond a doubt; financial markets could not operate effectively without it. Yet disclosure could be enforced through common law rules against fraud or even through less restrictive regulation. But the public was, understandably, favorably disposed to heavy regulation of the securities industry, because the stock market crash was viewed as the initial cause of the Depression. Thus, they were happy to sacrifice some liberty to undertake financial transactions in exchange for more democratic control through federal regulation.

One aspect of this expanded regulation of banking and finance was the expansion of government power that it entailed. But two more aspects of banking regulation are relevant also. First, the regulation was politically popular and serves as another example of public policy being determined based on the demands of the majority rather than on any reference to the constitutional limits of governmental power. Second, because banking stands as the central industry in any economy, acceptance of such far-reaching banking and financial regulation is further acceptance of the role that government should play in looking out for the economic well-being of the nation rather than merely protecting its liberty.

The Supreme Court and the Constitution

The U.S. Constitution, with its three branches of government and a system of checks and balances, found itself overwhelmed by a charismatic president, a compliant Congress, and popular opinion supporting a call to action. The Constitution, as originally written, provided the federal government with substantial insulation from popular opinion. The president was intended to be chosen by an electoral college and by the House of Representatives, the Senate was to be chosen by the state legislatures, and the members of the Supreme Court were chosen by the president. The founders intended that only members of the House of Representatives would be directly accountable to public opinion. By the 1930s both the president and Congress were directly accountable to popular opinion, leaving only the Court insulated from the pressures of democracy. Accordingly, it was the Supreme Court that provided the biggest impediment to the New Deal.

The Supreme Court had advanced into the Progressive Era along with the rest of the nation and was not inclined to undo Progressive reforms or to turn back the clock to the earlier era of liberty. Thus, when a Minnesota law that mandated a moratorium on mortgage fore-closures was challenged, the Court ruled that the law was constitu-tional,[7] and when New York established a board to regulate the milk industry and set legally mandated prices, the Court again ruled in favor of the state.[8] Precedent for such government intervention into the eco-nomic affairs of Americans had been set decades ago, and the Court was, if anything, willing to go beyond previous precedent in situations designed to mitigate the effects of the Depression. But the Court is, by design, a conservative institution, in the sense that its operation pre-serves the status quo and allows legal change to take place only slowly. Thus, the Court rejected many of the major parts of the New Deal.

In 1935 the Court signaled its skepticism toward New Deal pro-grams by declaring legislation designed to give the president broad powers to regulate the petroleum industry unconstitutional.[9] The law gave excessive power to the president, the Court ruled, and set the stage for further Court-produced setbacks for New Deal programs. The Court's most severe blow to the New Deal came when it declared the National Industrial Recovery Act (NIRA) unconstitutional in a unanimous decision.[10] The NIRA was a key part of Roosevelt's New Deal and was politically popular, supported by both business and labor interests and by Republicans as well as Democrats.[11] The NIRA gave the president broad powers to design codes of fair competition to be adhered to by industries, gave all employees the right to collective bargaining, and allowed the president to set minimum wages, maxi-mum hours of work, and other conditions of employment. These pres-idential powers were temporary, approved for only two years under the act, but they were far-reaching, and the Court decided that the NIRA delegated legislative powers to the executive branch, which vio-lated the Constitution.

In 1936 the Supreme Court declared the Agricultural Adjustment Act (AAA), another key component of the New Deal, to be unconsti-tutional.[12] The AAA was unconstitutional for tax reasons, the Court determined, because it collected taxes from the population at large to finance a benefit to a specific group of individuals. In its decision, the Court explicitly addressed the general welfare clause of the Constitu-tion and interpreted it liberally to state that it gave Congress the power to pass legislation to further the general welfare, over and above the enumerated powers granted in the Constitution. This liberal interpretation of the general welfare clause, written in the majority opinion, did seem to acknowledge the philosophy behind the New Deal. Nevertheless, the Court still found that the AAA exceeded the taxing powers granted in the Constitution.

In addition, during the first three years of the New Deal, the Supreme Court and lesser federal courts issued well over 1,000 rulings in opposition to New Deal legislation.[13] The Court acted as a roadblock to many New Deal programs, which became a campaign issue for Roosevelt's opponents when Roosevelt ran for reelection in 1936. Roosevelt was trying to use his presidential power unconstitutionally, his opponents argued, and they used the Supreme Court decisions that went against him as evidence.[14] Roosevelt himself had little to say about the Court in his campaign, but popular opinion was with him, as he won his bid for reelection in a landslide. In his State of the Union message to Congress on January 6, 1937, he mentioned the need for judicial reform to enable more progress to be made against the problems that faced the nation.

Roosevelt believed that the problem he faced with the Court was not so much the legal system itself but that the Court was populated by enough conservative justices to thwart his initiatives. Even though the Court was aging, the justices seemed intent on remaining in order to oppose Roosevelt. During his first four years in office, no justice stepped down, preventing Roosevelt from making any appointments to the Court. On February 5, 1937, Roosevelt took action against the Court by sending a message to Congress suggesting that he be able to add justices to the Court to ease their workload. Roosevelt noted that many of the justices were older than the "retirement age" of 70 and suggested that he be able to appoint an additional justice to the Court for each justice older than 70 who had not retired. Roosevelt's proposal could have added as many as six new Supreme Court justices, enough to give his backers a majority on the court.[15]

Roosevelt's plan met with immediate opposition from the Court. The justices spoke publicly against it and testified before Congress. Of course, new justices could not be appointed without the approval of Congress, and Roosevelt's bold initiative died. Roosevelt failed in his attempt to pack the Court, but he won the larger battle. The Court seemed more willing to approve New Deal programs during Roosevelt's second term. The retirement of a justice early in Roosevelt's second term did allow him a new appointment, but more significant is that the existing justices seemed more willing to go along with Roosevelt's New Deal. In 1937 the Court handed down a host of decisions that reversed its previous opposition to the New Deal. The Court sustained the constitutionality of an amended Railway Labor Act, which it had previously declared completely unconstitutional;[16] it reversed its previous opinion on a revised Frazier-Lemke Act, which provided debt relief to farmers;[17] and it reversed earlier decisions to declare minimum wage laws constitutional. While the Court earlier had ruled that such laws interfered with freedom of contract, Chief Justice Hughes declared, "The Constitution does not speak of freedom of contract. It speaks of liberty and prohibits the depravation of liberty without due process of law."[18] Thus, the Court underwent a remarkable transformation in 1937, enabling the New Deal to move ahead largely without the judicial opposition it had faced in its first four years.

What caused the Court to reverse its course and support the New Deal? Undoubtedly the justices continued to be motivated to put their duty to the Constitution ahead of politics, but the Constitution always has been a matter of interpretation, and several factors weighed in favor of the Court's movement. One was that the nation's economic problems continued, and there might have been some merit in the argument that a more modern interpretation of the Constitution would help the government deal with the nation's problems more effectively. Another factor was the demonstrated popularity of Roosevelt's initiatives after his strong victory in the presidential election of 1936. Surely popular opinion sided with Roosevelt's New Deal initiatives, if not his Court-packing plan. And although Roosevelt's attempt to pack the Court had failed, the justices may have sensed that hostility toward their opposition to New Deal programs threatened the viability of the Court. Along these lines the Court's ideological change has been referred to as "the switch in time that saved nine."[19] Yet another factor was the reality that the existing justices eventually would be replaced by others more sympathetic to the president, even if the aging justices were determined to hold onto their seats until death. Indeed, Roosevelt appointed five new justices by 1940, before the end of his second term, and a total of eight during his entire presidency. Only George Washington had appointed more Supreme Court justices.[20] Whatever the reasons for the Court's reversals, the end result was a Court more inclined to take into account popular opinion in its rendering of its decisions. Thus, in the 1930s the Supreme Court made a substantial movement from liberty to democracy.[21]

Social Security

The erosion of constitutional constraints on the power of the federal government occurred gradually and began well before the New Deal. Yet the New Deal remains significant because it so firmly established the role of the federal government in promoting the nation's economic well-being. Many of the New Deal programs were temporary, however, and explicitly of an emergency nature. While it might be difficult to assign one New Deal program with the responsibility for fundamentally transforming the constitutional role of the federal government, the single program that would make the most persuasive candidate is Social Security. Unlike some entitlement programs, such as Aid to Families with Dependent Children (which was created as a part of the Social Security program) or food stamps, Social Security is not aimed at the needy, despite the tendency of the elderly to be needy in the 1930s. Unlike other entitlement programs, such as farm price supports, Social Security was not aimed at the regulation of commerce. It was designed as a compulsory retirement system, pure and simple. The 10th Amendment to the Constitution plainly states, "The powers not delegated to the United States by the Constitution, nor prohibited by it to the States, are reserved to the States respectively, or to the people." Nowhere in the Constitution is there the slightest hint that the federal government has any power to establish a compulsory retirement program, yet the Supreme Court ruled it constitutional. If the Constitution, thus interpreted, gives the federal government the power to run a compulsory retirement program, it is hard to see that there are any constitutional limits on the programs that the federal government is permitted to undertake.

If the Supreme Court had not changed course in 1937, Social Security never would have been able to survive judicial scrutiny. In 1934 Congress passed the Railroad Retirement Act, which created a mandatory pension system for railroad workers. In 1935 the Supreme Court ruled the act unconstitutional, not on the basis of any specific provisions of the act but rather on the grounds that Congress did not have the power to pass any compulsory retirement system to cover railroad workers.[22] In a dissenting opinion, Chief Justice Hughes argued that the Court's ruling was too extreme because it prevented Congress from remedying any defects in the retirement system and from creating any type of railroad pension system. But the majority of the justices clearly believed that a compulsory federal retirement system overstepped the federal government's constitutional limits.

In light of the judicial challenges that New Deal programs had faced in the past, Congress tried to design the Social Security program to withstand judicial scrutiny. The Social Security program was designed with three separate components, with the thought that if parts of it were declared unconstitutional the remainder of the program might survive.[23] First, the program provided old age and survivors benefits to those who had paid into the system. Second, it provided aid to dependent children and to other needy individuals. Third, it created a federal unemployment compensation program with the option to allow states to run their own programs instead. Despite the fears of the president and Congress, the Court supported the Social Security program in its entirety and rendered three decisions favorable to Social Security on May 24, 1937.[24] In its decisions, the Court ruled that the compulsory Social Security tax used to finance retirement benefits was a legitimate exercise of the power of Congress to tax in order to promote the general welfare, that Congress could provide money from the general Treasury for those in need, and that its unemployment compensation program did not unduly infringe on states' rights.[25] While the Court's earlier ruling on the AAA went against Roosevelt, that decision did expand the notion of the general welfare beyond the powers of government enumerated in the Constitution,[26] opening the door for a favorable ruling on Social Security. Thus, the general welfare, as referenced in the Constitution, had evolved to mean whatever Congress thought was in the best interest of the citizens. The Constitution had been completely transformed.

New Deal Expenditures and Democracy

When the reach of governmental power extends beyond protecting the rights of individuals and into looking out for their economic well-being, it becomes important for citizens to be represented in the political process. This is because economic benefits are likely to flow toward political power. New Deal programs were to a substantial degree designed to provide economic relief to those hardest hit by the Depression, but the evidence shows that, while resources did tend to flow toward those whose economic conditions were worst, benefits also went toward those areas of the country that had senior senators and representatives, that had representation on key committees, and that had supported the New Deal in their popular voting.[27] In other words,

New Deal expenditures had a substantial component of special interest expenditures.[28]

It is not hard to see why this might be the case. For some types of expenditures there is much discretion as to where, exactly, the money should be spent. For example, New Deal expenditures included highway expenditures that could have been taken throughout any part of the nation. Because the location at which such expenditures will take place is a political decision, it is not surprising that political power played a role in determining the allocation of those expenditures. Stepping back to look at the larger picture, there are many types of relief programs that could be undertaken. Obviously, representatives from rural areas would be more in favor of farm relief, while those from urban areas would prefer unemployment compensation and aid aimed at specific industries in their districts. There was much discretion as to how New Deal expenditures would be undertaken, and political power played a significant role in determining the geographical distribution of New Deal expenditures.

The substantial increase in government programs, government expenditures, and especially government monetary transfers during the New Deal tends to be the focus of attention for both the New Deal's supporters and its detractors. Less noticed is the way in which the New Deal transformed how the nation's collective decisions were made. During the 1930s not only had the Progressive idea that the government should look out for the economic interests of its citizens become more firmly entrenched, but the idea that democratic decision making was an appropriate way to determine public policy was also established. In part, this move toward democracy came because of the popular support for Roosevelt's initiatives that greatly expanded the economic role of government, and in part this move came from the acquiescence of the Supreme Court to the opinions of the popular majority. Thus, by the time World War II arrived, the idea that it was appropriate to determine public policy based on the will of the majority had become firmly established.

The Rise of the Federal Government

When the nation was founded, the federal government was a federation of state governments, and the intent of the Founding Fathers was to leave most of the activities at the state or local level. The federal government would deal with issues involving the interaction of the nation with other nations and the interactions of states with each other. Limits on the federal government were put in place both by having the Constitution enumerate the government's powers and, with the 10th Amendment, by limiting the government's actions only to those enumerated powers. By design, the federal government was subordinate to the states. That subordinate position was clearly reversed as a result of the War between the States, but in many ways the federal government remained a minor presence in the lives of its citizens until the twentieth century.

Before the New Deal, the role of the federal government began to grow because of the rise of the Progressive ideology, because of the leap forward in government programs during World War I, and because the federal income tax provided a new source of revenues to fund this expansion. Still, at the beginning of the New Deal, local government expenditures were substantially larger than either federal or state government expenditures. By 1940, federal government expenditures exceeded state government expenditures and local government expenditures.

The War Economy

The entry of the United States into World War II after the Japanese attack at Pearl Harbor on December 7, 1941, was much more popular than the nation's entry into World War I, and understandably so. But the nation was also well prepared to enter the war prior to the Japanese attack. The Selective Training and Service Act of 1940 required all males from ages 21 to 35 to register for the draft and gave the president the discretion to draft individuals into military service regardless of whether the nation was at war. The act went further than just enabling the draft; it also allowed the president to place orders for military materials and equipment that would take precedence over other business and allowed the government to seize any noncomplying facility.[29] While the nation was not at war, it was clear that in deference to popular sentiment Congress was willing to legislate a substantial sacrifice in individual liberty to further the nation's collective goals.

After the United States entered the war, Congress granted substantially more power to allow the executive branch of government to direct the economy to further the war effort. The First War Powers Act was passed on December 18, 1941, and gave the president the power to enter into any contracts he saw fit to facilitate the nation's involvement in the war, including making advance payments to contractors and amending and modifying contracts in any way he saw fit. The Second War Powers Act, passed on March 17, 1942, gave the executive branch even more far-reaching economic powers, including the power to take possession of any property that might further the war effort either by purchase or by outright appropriation. If the president foresaw a shortage of any material, the act gave him the right to allocate it as he saw fit, and it also created a link between the Treasury and the Federal Reserve Bank that essentially would allow for the printing up of new money to finance the war.[30]

Price Controls and Rationing

As the government entered the war, inflation started heating up, prompting Congress to pass legislation to control wages, rents, and prices in January 1942. Congress did so by establishing the Office of Price Administration (OPA), run under the direction of an appointed administrator. Congress offered two justifications for the price control legislation. First, controlled wages and prices would make sure that defense appropriations were not eaten up through rising prices. This meant that sellers would be called upon to help subsidize the war effort, but this should seem like a small sacrifice to those working in the civilian economy, considering that others had been drafted to fight a dangerous war overseas. The second justification was to try to protect those whose incomes were fixed or relatively limited. Once again, the government was following the Progressive principle of looking out for the economic well-being of its citizens. With price controls, it is clear that if one person pays a lower price another person receives a lower income, so the effect is clearly redistributive. It is telling that this second justification did not have to be offered at all. Why not just justify the controls based on the war effort? Yet the role of the government to protect economic interests was offered, despite the clearly redistributive nature of the policy. Again this emphasizes the importance of democratic representation in a nation that makes policy according to the will of the majority.[31]

There were exceptions to the authority of the OPA's administrator, and two major exceptions are telling. Employee compensation was partially excepted, as were agricultural products. Thus, the political power of labor unions and of the farm lobby was evident.[32] Organized labor had close ties to the Democratic party, which helped their cause, and agriculture has always been disproportionately represented as an industry. This is because many congressional districts are primarily agricultural, whereas few other districts are so heavily represented by one industry. Again one sees that, when economic resources are allocated democratically, the success of a group depends on how well its interests are represented in the political process.

The wage and price controls rapidly brought with them shortages, because, with prices held down, purchasers wanted to buy more of almost everything than sellers wanted to sell. The result was a potentially inequitable allocation of goods, as merchants saved items for their friends or allocated them in other ways besides selling them to whomever placed the highest value on the good. As a result, the OPA began rationing a number of necessities and organized the rationing program by establishing thousands of local boards to administer the rationing. Despite substantial regulations and red tape, this merely transferred the authority to sell from the sellers to a board, and the results were generally unsatisfactory. The price controls had eliminated market prices as a signal of how to allocate resources, and the economy became increasingly chaotic as a result. Seeing the problems, President Roosevelt argued, much as he had early in his first term, for increasingly broad presidential powers to command order in the economy. In response, Congress passed the Economic Stabilization Act of 1942, giving the president broad powers to set prices and wages, including those that had been exempt under the legislation passed the previous year.[33]

The wage and price controls and the accompanying rationing system was a wartime program, of course, and was accepted as such by Americans. But it set a precedent, and when President Nixon mandated wage and price controls on August 15, 1971, his move was very popular. Roosevelt's price controls provided the precedent, but Nixon's price controls came only in response to rising inflation, without any other associated crises. A move that was justified by war in 1942 was justified only because it was popular in 1971, despite that such controls clearly limit freedom of contract and exchange and thus compromise the liberty of the nation's citizens. The widespread acceptance of Nixon's wage and price controls clearly shows the triumph of democracy over liberty.

Withholding and the Income Tax

War-related expenditures took up an incredibly large share of the economy, and the government worked to finance them in every way it could. It borrowed and implied that it was the patriotic duty of citizens to buy war bonds; it printed up new money with the compliance of the Fed; and it substantially increased taxes. In 1939 most Americans did not pay income taxes because the personal exemption was high enough to exclude most people from the tax. That ended with the onset of the war, when the personal exemption was lowered substantially and tax rates were increased substantially. The personal exemption in 1939 was $1,000, meaning that a family of four would have $4,000 of income exempt from income taxation, which was well above the median income in 1939. In addition, the lowest tax bracket in 1939 was 4 percent, so even if that family earned a bit more than the exemption, they paid only 4 percent of any additional income in income taxes. By 1944 the personal exemption had been cut in half, to $500, and the lowest income tax bracket had been raised to 23 percent.[34]

Even with this substantial increase in income tax rates, the federal government still ran a large budget deficit and was looking for ways to raise additional revenues. One initiative to do so was to institute income tax withholding. Prior to World War II, those citizens whose incomes were high enough to be taxed were supposed to make estimated quarterly income tax payments and then settle up any differences after filing their annual returns. While this system had satisfactory results prior to the war, the increase in tax rates and the decrease in the personal exemption created some problems for income tax collections. First, because the newly covered taxpayers were less well off than those who paid income taxes before the war, it was more likely that they would have trouble putting together the money needed to pay their taxes on a quarterly basis, because it would require saving over a period of three months to make the quarterly payment. If they underestimated their tax liabilities, this could create the additional hardship of trying to put together enough money to make up the difference on April 15. It is easy to imagine that, as more people were covered, some people with average incomes would not have the financial discipline to set aside enough money to pay their tax liabilities. The problem was further aggravated by the much higher marginal tax rates that the lowest-income taxpayers faced.

Withholding helped taxpayers set aside sufficient funds by having employers withhold estimated tax payments and send them directly to the federal government.[35] At the end of the year taxpayers could then settle up and pay only the difference or get a refund if too much had been withheld. Surely, without withholding, many taxpayers would have found themselves financially unable to meet their tax liabilities because they would not have had the financial discipline to save enough for their future tax liabilities.

Another smaller but real advantage to withholding was that it provided a steady stream of tax revenues into the Treasury. Rather than wait several months for quarterly tax payments, the Treasury would receive the revenues almost as soon as the money was earned by employees. In a government strapped for funds, any little bit helped, and withholding reduced somewhat the need for the Treasury to borrow.

Withholding also had the major advantage of providing the federal government with a method of policing taxpayers. When the lowest tax bracket was 4 percent and most taxpayers did not even make enough to pay income tax, cheating was not a big problem. For those well off enough to pay income taxes, sending 4 percent of their taxable income to the federal government was not a big burden, so compliance was likely to be high. Even if some people cheated, the rate was low enough that, except for very high-income cheaters (who were more likely to be spotted and so less likely to cheat), the Treasury would not lose much revenue anyway. With higher rates and the addition of lower-income taxpayers into the tax base, there was both a bigger incentive for cheating and a bigger potential revenue loss to the Treasury.

The requirement that employers withhold tax payments from employee paychecks provides a good mechanism for controlling cheating among employees. The employers have no incentive to disregard the law. To do so would bring legal penalties on them, without giving them anything in return. Surely an employer could not offer to pay employees a little less in exchange for not withholding taxes, because the knowledge of this would be widespread enough that the employer would be found out. Once the income is withheld, the Treasury knows the identity of the taxpayer, so is better able to make sure that taxpayers file returns and pay any additional taxes they owe.

The creation of withholding has greatly enhanced the federal government's ability to collect income taxes for several reasons. First, it creates a system of monitoring that cuts down on cheating. Second, it provides a mechanism of forced saving so that taxpayers have no choice but to set aside sufficient funds to meet their tax liabilities. Surely many taxpayers who would want to comply would find themselves unable to do so without withholding. This leads to a third advantage of withholding. By creating the impression that most taxpayers are complying with the system, it encourages other taxpayers to go along and pay their fair share. If, in contrast, people had the impression that cheating was widespread, those who were paying would be more tempted to cheat, thinking that they had no moral obligation to pay when many others were evading their taxes. In wartime, when patriotic ideology is strong, this is surely the case, but it applies any time people have an ideological commitment to their government. Even U.S. citizens who dislike the income tax and the Internal Revenue Service still typically have a patriotic affinity for the ideals of American government, and those people will be encouraged to pay taxes if only because they view the tax system as a legitimate product of the democratic institutions that are at the foundation of the nation.[36]

The evolution of the federal income tax during World War II had several significant effects on the development of American democracy after the war. First, it provided an increased flow of revenues for the federal government. Taxes remained much higher in the 1950s than they were in the 1930s, and it is unlikely that Congress would have been able to enact such tax increases in the absence of a major crisis. Second, it made most Americans income taxpayers for the first time.[37] Those who were paying into the system would have the feeling that they should have some say in how the resulting revenues were spent and rightly so. Prior to World War II, any democratic decision on how to spend the nation's income tax revenues would have been a decision on how the revenues collected from the nation's upper-income elites should be spent. After World War II, any decision on how those revenues should be spent was a decision on the part of voters on how the money they themselves contributed should be spent. Because it was their money, they had every right to have a say in how it would be used.

Other factors with regard to the income tax were the increased ability of the government to keep track of the financial affairs of Americans, the presumption in tax law that one is guilty until proven innocent, and the acceptance of the idea that the federal government could garnish everyone's wages in anticipation of their future income tax liabilities. The scope of government power, democratically authorized through Congress, had increased substantially and was generally accepted by Americans. Surely this was the result of a willingness on the part of Americans to give up some of their liberties to aid in the war effort, but those liberties were not restored after the war. In contrast, there were several attempts in the 1980s to institute income tax withholding on interest and dividend payments, but all of these attempts failed to be approved through the political process. Most interest and dividend income is earned by those in the upper 10 percent of the income distribution, so one could envision support for the proposal among many Americans who would not be covered by the legislation, yet the same type of withholding that every wage earner has to comply with as a legacy of World War II was rejected for interest and dividend earners when no crisis was underfoot.

In the process of collecting income taxes, the Internal Revenue Service also collects a substantial amount of information on the business affairs of all Americans. While libertarians might view this as an invasion of privacy, it apparently does not constitute an unreasonable search "of persons, houses, papers, and effects," following the Fourth Amendment to the Constitution, at least according the popular opinion and the learned opinion of the Supreme Court. Furthermore, when a taxpayer is challenged by the Internal Revenue Service, the taxpayer must prove his innocence rather than leave the burden of proof on the IRS to prove that the taxpayers is guilty. While it is generally recognized that this is one area of law in which the accused is presumed guilty until proven innocent, again this appears to be generally accepted by Congress, the Supreme Court, and the population at large. One could make a convincing argument that, were this not so, the federal government would not be able to collect nearly as much in income tax revenue as it does and that noncompliance would be rampant. This is perhaps so, but this perversion of the law shows the willingness of a democratic society to sacrifice liberty in exchange for the demands of the majority.

The Roosevelt Era

When President Roosevelt died in 1945, the U.S. government was substantially different from the one he had taken command of in 1933. The growth in the scope and power of the federal government and the expansion of government programs during the Roosevelt era were well known. Perhaps because of this growth of government the transformation in the ideology supporting the government has been relatively neglected. In response to the Great Depression and World War II, Americans willingly turned over to democratic control a substantial amount of their liberties that had formerly been guaranteed by the Constitution and that had been a part of the American ideology. The changes that occurred were an extension of those begun during the Progressive Era and sustained during the 1920s. Americans had bought into the Progressive idea that it was appropriate for their government to look out for their economic well-being in addition to protecting their rights, and the Depression was a period in time during which their economic well-being was threatened. Thus, Americans accepted increased government control through regulation of the economy, through taxation in order to spend more on government programs, and through restrictions on individual liberties for the good of the nation, as determined by the desires of the majority.

The increased scope of government in response to crisis is one thing. The increasingly democratic ideology that developed along with growing government is a related, but different, phenomenon. For more than a decade Americans had become acclimated to increased democratic control of their society, giving up individual liberty in exchange for policies designed to aid their economic well-being and to protect the nation and the world. By 1945 the Depression was over, and the United States had emerged victorious after World War II. The government had faced two major crises and after substantial struggle had emerged victorious in both. Despite any lingering Jeffersonian ideals, Americans wanted a government that would continue to intervene in their lives when it could have a positive influence.

The Employment Act of 1946

Any doubt about the government's responsibility to promote the economic well-being of its citizens must be erased by the passage of the Employment Act of 1946. The Great Depression had not completely ended until the United States entered World War II, and the common view was that it was the government's demand for military output that finally pulled the economy out of its slump.[38] With the war over, there was the real fear that the economy would slip back into its prewar depression. But it did not have to do so, according to the nation's academic economists. Through active aggregate demand management, the federal government had the power to maintain full employment with low inflation. The intellectual foundation for the idea appeared in John Maynard Keynes's *The General Theory of Employment, Interest, and Money,* published in 1936, and by the end of World War II Keynes's ideas had been enthusiastically adopted by the nation's leading academic economists.

The Employment Act of 1946 states,

> The Congress hereby declares that it is the continuing policy and responsibility of the Federal Government to use all practicable means consistent with its needs and obligations and other essential considerations of national policy, with assistance and cooperation

of industry, agriculture, labor, and State and local governments, to coordinate and utilize all its plans, functions, and resources for the purpose of creating and maintaining, in a manner calculated to foster and promote free competitive enterprise and the general welfare, conditions under which there will be afforded useful employment opportunities, including self-employment, for those able, willing, and seeking to work and promote maximum employment, production, and purchasing power.[39]

The act tries to cover many bases and is vague about what, exactly, the government might do to promote maximum employment, but this vagueness is due both to the potential for disagreements regarding what the appropriate policy would be and the uncertainty that the government really has the power to do anything to prevent unemployment anyway.

The Employment Act of 1946 may be more symbolic than anything, but what it symbolizes is a wholesale acceptance of the Progressive ideology as a part of federal government policy. The act plainly states that it is the responsibility of the federal government to promote maximum employment, production, and purchasing power, and the tenets of the act have remained a part of the basic ideas of economics through the beginning of the twenty-first century. Students are taught in their college economics classes how federal government policy can be used to keep the economy near full employment and with low inflation.[40] Armed with this knowledge, citizens continue to adhere to the idea that the federal government has the responsibility for keeping the economy healthy and for promoting their economic welfare. In response to the crises of war and depression, Americans accepted an increase in democratic control over their lives and a resulting sacrifice in their liberties. The Employment Act of 1946 symbolizes the extension of this acceptance from crisis times into the postcrisis era. Thus, the events of the Great Depression and World War II further facilitated the transformation of the national ideology from liberty to democracy.

Conclusion

The presidency of FDR, encompassing both the Great Depression and World War II, has the reputation of being both an era of substantial government growth and the era in which the welfare state was born. The creation of major transfer programs such as Social Security and

Aid to Families with Dependent Children justifies that reputation, but the impact of the era on the future of American government is understated if one focuses only on the growth in government programs, taxes, and expenditures. That era saw the growing acceptance of democracy as a principle upon which to base government policy and a corresponding decline in the principle of liberty. People were increasingly willing to give up their personal liberties in exchange for government programs aimed as securing their economic well-being, and people increasingly viewed democratic decision making as the mechanism for determining appropriate public policy. Democracy in a time of crisis, when the scope of government was growing, also meant a move away from consensus in collective decision making. FDR was democratically elected, and the popular mandate registered in democratic elections enabled Roosevelt to implement public programs without additional democratic input. The underlying principle was democracy, not consensus, and even though the majority went along there was always a vocal discontented minority.

Increasingly, American democracy became an economic system in addition to a political decision-making mechanism. The major changes made during the period included increased regulation of private commerce, government restrictions on private contracts, a massive expansion in government transfer programs, increases in taxation, and income tax withholding. The Supreme Court, final guardian of the Constitution, was at first reluctant to go along with the sacrifices in liberty that accompanied Roosevelt's interventions, but in his second term the Court was more agreeable and in the process substantially changed America's constitutional rules. The United States, still predominantly a market economy, moved unmistakably in the direction of economic democracy, where resources are allocated according to the will of the majority rather than to the Lockean principles of liberty that had been the foundation of the economy in the previous century. The nation was in dire straits when Roosevelt took office. When he died, the nation was prosperous again and victorious in war. Americans did not want to give that up. Government had grown, but Americans saw some security in a big government that was charged with looking out for their well-being, and because of this they willingly accepted the further shift from liberty to democracy.

CHAPTER 11

Democracy Triumphs: The Great Society

The ratchets hypothesis of government growth argues that government grows in response to crises but after a crisis has passed never shrinks down to its precrisis level. Thus, government growth is an intermittent process, whereby a crisis appears and government ratchets up in response, shrinking somewhat after the crisis but remaining ever larger than before the crisis. Then another crisis comes along, ratcheting government up again. The process continues, and the government grows in response to each crisis. The hypothesis is credible and has been supported by academic research.[1] More cynical observers have even argued that those with government power engineer crises to aggrandize the state.[2] Indeed, much of the transformation from liberty to democracy over the history of the United States has been in response to crises. The War between the States was the major crisis of the nineteenth century, and the changes in American government as a result of the war had long-lasting effects. The twentieth century has been one of almost continual crisis, including two world wars, the Great Depression, and a cold war that lingered for half a century. Much of the growth of government documented in the preceding chapters can be traced to government reaction to some type of crisis. The Great Society programs initiated in the 1960s by Lyndon Johnson stand in contrast. These programs were initiated due to popular demand, not because of a crisis but despite one.

Johnson's Great Society was the triumph of democracy because, after a long transformation, public policy was determined not based on constitutional principles but rather on democratic principles. Programs were proposed and implemented based on the demand by the general public. Unlike the New Deal programs spawned during the Great Depression, there was no crisis motivating the government into action. Indeed, if there was a crisis during the period, it was the cold war, and Great Society programs actually diverted resources away from the crisis. The Great Society programs were aimed at helping those at the lower end of the income distribution but at a time when poverty was declining and the poor were becoming better off anyway. They were aimed at improving the availability of health care and educational opportunities but at a time when the population was becoming increasingly healthy and increasingly well educated anyway. The Great Society programs were not the response to a crisis, as could be argued about the New Deal programs, but rather were initiated even though the problems they were addressing were diminishing on their own. Unlike past initiatives of a similar scale, they were initiated because of their popular appeal, as a response of a democratic government to the desires of its citizens.

While one might make a similar argument about the Progressive movement, major changes were occurring at that time because of the increasing industrialization and urbanization of America. Those changes supported the argument that American society was undergoing a major transformation and that the role of government should change in response. The increased concentration of wealth and economic power in the hands of a few industrialists and financiers alarmed many people and prompted a demand for government action. Furthermore, those with political power would rationally try to maintain their power by curtailing the growing economic power of a group of people they could rightly view as competing for the leading roles in American society. Things were completely different in the 1960s. The cold war presented a crisis in the international arena, but as the 1960s began the nation was prosperous and optimistic and economic policy turned from trying to stabilize the economy and create an environment for full employment toward using the gains of prosperity to achieve public goals in addition to private goals. This was the contemporary liberal ideology endorsed by President Kennedy and increasingly supported by public opinion, especially among the nation's youth.

The Transition to the 1960s

The presidential election of 1960 pitted John F. Kennedy, a liberal senator from Massachusetts, against Richard Nixon, who had served as vice president during Eisenhower's two terms as president. The two candidates represented sharply contrasting political ideologies. Nixon represented a continuation of the conservatism of the Eisenhower years. Eisenhower was elected in 1952, when the nation still labored under a cloud of uncertainty about the future. As the nation's top general during World War II, Eisenhower was a hero and had a reputation as a strong leader. The Depression was slipping into the nation's memory, although concern remained even in the 1960s that a repeat of the 1930s could someday be on the horizon, partly because people still did not have a clear understanding about what caused the economic problems of the 1930s. World War II was also a memory, but the Korean conflict was under way as a part of a larger cold war that would pit the United States and its allies against the Soviet Union and its allies for decades to come. In light of the international situation, having a general at the nation's helm was reassuring.

On the economic front, the nation was experiencing unparalleled growth and prosperity during the 1950s. As automobile ownership became more common, Americans moved to the suburbs. America's love affair with the automobile was never stronger than during the 1950s and 1960s, when owning a car came within reach of most American families. In 1950 there were 40 million passenger cars registered in the United States, up from 26 million in 1945. By 1960 there were 62 million passenger cars, an increase of 55 percent since 1950 and an average of more than one car per family.[3] American automakers changed styles every year, and since Americans always wanted the latest model it was common to trade in a car well before it was worn out, just to get the newer model. This provided a ready source of used cars for those who could not quite afford a new one.

The automobile was not the only major lifestyle change that occurred during the 1950s. Television was rare in American households in 1950 but common by 1960. In 1949 only 50 television stations broadcast in the entire nation. That number nearly doubled the next year, to 97 stations in 1950, and increased to 517 stations in 1960, putting at least one television station within reach of most Americans. By 1960, 88 percent of American households had a television set, up from 67 percent just a few years earlier in 1955.[4] The increased wealth of the 1950s brought about not only a higher standard of living but a major change in lifestyle for many people, with the automobile, the television, and the migration to the suburbs leading the way. The economic strength of the United States, coupled with its military victories in the world wars, established it as unquestionably the leading nation in the world. The nation was brimming with optimism, with the cold war providing the only significant cloud on the horizon.

Despite this prosperity, few Americans would attribute their good fortune to the policies of President Eisenhower. While Eisenhower was well liked, he had the reputation for being relatively passive in the public policy arena, which was in stark contrast to Roosevelt, who had guided the nation through two decades of crisis. Eisenhower favored minimal government involvement in the economy and warned of the "military-industrial complex" that threatened to dominate the nation. If Nixon were elected in 1960, the nation could expect more of the same. Nixon had an advantage in the cold war era of looking more experienced in dealing with international affairs, but when faced with the choice, the nation chose Kennedy in 1960 by the slimmest of margins. The popular vote count gave Kennedy 34.2 million votes to Nixon's 34.1 million,[5] but once in office Kennedy was ready to push his agenda for American progress. What Kennedy lacked in international experience he made up for with a vision of a greater America at home. Working together, he argued, the nation would be able to do good things with its newfound prosperity. "Ask not what your country can do for you," Kennedy told his fellow citizens, "but what you can do for your country." It would be hard to think of a phrase that is more out of tune with John Locke's view of the role of government than Kennedy's call for Americans to ask what they can do for their country.

The Kennedy-Johnson Years

President Kennedy saw his administration as a significant enough break from the past to call it a New Frontier, evoking images of Roosevelt's New Deal but at the same time using terminology that implied progress on the horizon. Americans were used to progress in the private sector. After adjusting for inflation, average earnings had risen by 26 percent from 1950 to 1960,[6] but while the previous decade had shown substantial progress in the private sector, not much had changed in the public sector. It was easy to argue that some of the nation's newfound wealth should be put into public amenities to enhance the quality of life and to help out those who were really needy. Kennedy, a Harvard man both by education and by philosophy, drew inspiration from prominent liberal Harvard faculty members. Those ideas included empowering the government to make social change[7] and to use new techniques of economic policy to engineer the economy to full employment with low inflation.[8]

Despite the passage of the Employment Act of 1946, government policy toward employment had changed little until Kennedy took office. Until the 1960s the conventional wisdom on fiscal policy was that, except during emergencies, the government's budget should be balanced, and during the Eisenhower years the conventional wisdom ruled. Any deficits were small and unintentional. But the conventional wisdom had already been overthrown in academic economics, where Keynesian ideas had firmly taken hold and dominated the thinking on macroeconomic policy. The government could stabilize the economy by using functional finance, which meant running budget deficits when unemployment threatened, to stimulate the economy and keep it close to full employment, and running budget surpluses when inflation threatened, to reign in excess aggregate demand and prevent the economy from overheating. Kennedy brought in a new set of economic advisers who preached the Keynesian gospel. The first major policy move was the tax cut of 1964, designed specifically to stimulate an economy that appeared to be sliding into recession.

While the effectiveness of this tax cut can be debated, for present purposes it is more important to note that even the magnitudes of government taxes and expenditures were now being calculated to enhance the nation's economic well-being. Before 1960 federal taxes were viewed as a method of financing federal expenditures. The new view depicted them as a crucial tool for managing the economy to create full employment with low inflation. A look at any introductory economics textbook from the 1960s can confirm this. The discussion of federal taxes and expenditures takes place mostly under the heading of macroeconomics, where they are shown to be critical determinants of aggregate demand that determine whether the nation will have unemployment or inflation. The textbooks explain how taxes and expenditures can be adjusted to produce full employment, without ever considering what the government buys. In the textbook Keynesian analysis, what government buys with its expenditures is largely irrelevant.[9] The Employment Act of 1946 was based on these Keynesian ideas, but it was not until a decade and a half after the act's passage that the nation's voters chose policymakers who were truly committed to placing the ideas expressed in the act at the center of national economic policy.

Kennedy's New Frontier barely had time to get off the ground before he was felled by an assassin's bullet on November 22, 1963. On the international front, he had been distracted by the Cuban missile crisis the year before and the failed Bay of Pigs invasion to try to oust Castro from power. On the other side of the world, the Vietnam War was escalating. Meanwhile, at home, recession threatened, causing Kennedy to focus on macroeconomic policy more than microeconomic policy.[10] But Kennedy had ideas. In 1961 Congress passed the Area Redevelopment Act targeting funds to those areas of the United States that were most impoverished, and in 1962 the Manpower Development and Training Act was passed. Both were supported by Kennedy as federal programs that would directly address the economic well-being of those Americans who were least well off. Kennedy's vision of a greater America, propelled by federal government programs to enhance the nation's well-being, was picked up by his successor. Kennedy and Johnson were not friends, as was well known, and during Kennedy's brief presidency Vice President Johnson stood in Kennedy's shadow. As president, Johnson was determined to rise above his predecessor, and he formulated his Great Society programs to eclipse Kennedy's New Frontier and to extend the programs the Democrats had established during the New Deal.[11]

Johnson had his distractions, to be sure. The war in Vietnam was escalating out of control, and Johnson was at a loss as to how to deal with it. The civil rights movement was a component of the Great Society, as Johnson made an effort to extend to all Americans the same rights enjoyed by whites. But progress was slower than some would have liked, and demonstrators and rioters, sensing an opportunity, protested both the nation's racial problems and its involvement in the Vietnam War. The nuclear arms race continued, and the cold war remained a serious concern. The space race was also on in response to the Soviet Union's launching of a satellite into space in 1957, ahead of the United States; the Soviet Union continued its dominance in 1961 by being the first nation to put a man in orbit. President Kennedy pledged to land a man on the moon before 1970, and Johnson supported that effort as well. Johnson had a full agenda handed to him, but he added to it his Great Society programs in an effort to further transform the role of the federal government, extending Progressivism and the New Deal.

The Great Society

In March 1964, a few months after assuming the presidency, Johnson initiated a cornerstone of his Great Society by calling for a "war on poverty."[12] The War on Poverty was optimistic in its outlook. While income transfers had been at the heart of most poverty programs, the War on Poverty envisioned providing economic opportunity to the poor. Job training would help them earn their own incomes, and investment in health, nutrition, and education programs for the children of the poor would enable them to rise out of poverty to join mainstream America. The Office of Economic Opportunity was created, and a host of new programs with optimistic titles like Upward Bound, Job Corps, and Head Start were begun to change the culture of poverty and to bring the advantages of a thriving economy to every American. The philosophy behind the War on Poverty was built on the Progressive idea that through scientific management the findings of social science can be applied to attack the causes of poverty at its roots and that as the programs succeeded the need for them in the future would be continually reduced.[13] The War on Poverty, it goes without saying, is an example of government working to enhance the economic well-being of its citizens, not to protect their liberty.[14]

One of the key elements in the War on Poverty was the provision of enhanced educational opportunities for everyone. The poor could benefit, obviously, but a more educated society could improve everyone's well-being. Thus, Johnson formally introduced his Great Society at the University of Michigan in a speech he gave on May 22, 1964. He had tested the term on smaller audiences previously, but in Michigan he used it in a major policy speech that defined the ideas of his presidency and created his own identity, separate from his predecessor.[15] Johnson reorganized the Office of Education, then a part of the Department of Health, Education, and Welfare; passed legislation to provide federal funding for education in Appalachia; provided federal revenues for vocational education; sharply increased the budget of the National Science Foundation; created federal scholarships for students; and opened the opportunity for college students to get federally guaranteed student loans. Despite the distractions of Johnson's presidency, he continued to push successfully for additional federal aid to education.[16] Education was important because it was the key to economic opportunity, and the Great Society was all about enhancing the economic well-being of Americans.

Perhaps the biggest legacies of the Great Society are Medicare and Medicaid, two health care programs designed to extend government financing of medical care to the elderly and to the poor, respectively. At the time, the United States was alone among industrialized nations in having neither socialized medicine nor some form of national health insurance. Attempts had been made previously to try to create a similar program in the United States, but the American Medical Association (AMA) opposed the efforts. FDR wanted to include socialized medicine along with the Social Security program but foresaw that political opposition would threaten the whole program. An attempt was made in 1950 to create national health insurance, but that too failed. During the Eisenhower years no new initiatives were floated, but Johnson saw an opportunity to make national health care a part of his Great Society. The AMA was adamantly opposed to any government involvement, and health insurers were understandably concerned that the government was going to drive them out of business. On the other side, organized labor, headed by the AFL-CIO, was strongly in favor of national health care. Johnson believed that such a program would be politically viable if it was limited to providing health care to the poor and the elderly. The poor lacked health insurance anyway, lessening some of the political opposition, and the elderly were a high-risk group for insurers. The insurance industry mounted little protest, and despite AMA opposition both programs were passed in 1965.[17] The Great Society was well under way.

The Great Society and Democracy

A major component of the Great Society was the civil rights movement and, in particular, the legislation that was passed to eliminate discrimination based on race. Despite the ideal of liberty that was at the foundation of the Revolution, slavery is explicitly recognized in the Constitution, and in its first two centuries the nation's progress in eliminating differential legal treatment based on race had been painfully slow. Progress accelerated in the 1960s, which was one way the Great Society unambiguously furthered the ideal of liberty. One must keep in mind, however, that much of the discrimination based on race that existed as the 1960s began was legally sanctioned and even legally mandated.[18] The Supreme Court had begun dismantling the vestiges of segregation, most notably with the landmark *Brown v. Board of Education* case in 1954,[19] but the Court is by nature a conservative institution and can only modify the law in response to cases brought to it. Congress, under President Kennedy's leadership, enacted the Civil Rights Act of 1964 to speed the progress. It mandated desegregation of public education and required that all accommodations open to the public, including restaurants, motels, stores, and places of entertainment, could not discriminate based on race.

In addition to other provisions, the Civil Rights Act mandated that completion of the sixth grade was sufficient proof of literacy for purposes of voting in federal elections.[20] The voting component of the act intended to reduce the barriers that discouraged blacks from voting, but Johnson viewed it as insufficient and the next year pushed the Voting Rights Act of 1965 through Congress. Because the Civil Rights Act had only been passed a year before, the Voting Rights Act cannot be viewed as a response to any demonstrated failure of the Civil Rights Act. Rather, it took additional measures to try to increase black turnout, including suspending literacy tests altogether in counties where less than 50 percent of those eligible to vote were registered, doing away with poll taxes that discouraged those with low incomes from voting, and extending the act's provisions to all elections, not just federal elections.[21] Johnson's attempt to extend voting rights to all Americans must be applauded, but his actions had a political element to them that also must be recognized.

Especially in southern states, whites went to great lengths to discourage black voters, both by legal means like poll taxes and literacy tests and by more subtle means.[22] Everybody recognized that these blacks who were discouraged from voting were a natural constituency of the Democratic party. Johnson's push for civil rights, his War on Poverty, and indeed his more general vision of the Great Society made blacks a natural constituency, and anything Johnson could do to increase voter turnout among blacks would surely increase his political support. While the principle of liberty may have been at the foundation of much of the Great Society, the principle of democracy was at work in the 1965 Voting Rights Act, because Johnson, his supporters, and his opponents recognized that public policy would be determined by the tenor of public opinion and supporters of the Great Society realized that they could increase support for their agenda by extending the franchise toward those who would support their programs. With public policy determined by public opinion, the object of the Voting Rights Act was ultimately to get more voters who would support Johnson's initiatives.

This link between voting and the support of Progressive social programs was also recognized by the nation's largest foundations, who were strongly supportive of the War on Poverty. The Ford Foundation, in particular, funded voter registration drives in the 1960s aimed specifically at registering blacks for the purpose of increasing the political constituency for the programs it supported. A Ford Foundation voter registration drive undertaken exclusively in black neighborhoods has been credited with getting Carl Stokes, Cleveland's first black mayor, elected. Because of the overtly political nature of some foundation activities, Congress passed legislation in 1969 to limit the ability of foundations to engage in political advocacy.[23] The ideology of democracy had taken firm root, and individuals on all sides recognized that public policy would be determined based on the demands of the voters, not the principles behind the Constitution.

The Legacy of the Great Society

President Johnson was committed to pushing forward his Great Society programs, but the nation's attention was focused in large part on the war in Vietnam. Civil rights struggles were a part of the daily news as well, but it is not hard to imagine that President Johnson could have let his domestic agenda slide in order to focus on international issues. Indeed, this is not hard to imagine because Nixon, Johnson's successor, did just that. Nixon's response to vocal protestors on civil rights policy and the Vietnam War was to say his policies were aimed at the "silent majority" rather than the vocal minority of disenchanted Americans. Johnson, however, pushed ahead with his Great Society.

One of the problems the Vietnam War posed to Johnson was that military resources diverted to the war were resources that would not be available to further his domestic agenda, which in itself put a constraint on Johnson's ability to fully implement the Great Society. In 1960 military expenditures composed more than half of the federal government's budget, as table 5 shows. By 1965 military expenditures had fallen to 42.8 percent of the budget. Outlays on human resources, which include Social Security and other income security programs, health programs (including Medicare and Medicaid), education, and veterans benefits, were 28.4 percent of the federal budget in 1960 and had risen to 30.9 percent by 1965. These human resource programs were the expenditure programs that made up the core of the Great Society. By 1968, as table 5 shows, expenditures on both defense and human resources had increased as a share of the budget, with defense expenditures up to 46 percent and human resources expenditures up to 33.3 percent of the budget. Johnson was able to devote about 10 percent more of the budget to human resources, even though military expenditures were rising due to the Vietnam War.[24] If the level of expenditures is used as a measure of the degree to which Johnson had been able to establish his Great Society, there is only slight evidence of the Great Society in the budget. But Johnson was able to get the Great

Society legislation through Congress, laying the foundation for growth in Great Society programs.

After Johnson left office, President Nixon focused his attention more on international events than domestic policy, and with a Democratic Congress and the winding down of the Vietnam War the Great Society programs began to take hold. From 1968 to 1975, military expenditures declined from 46 percent of the federal budget to 26 percent of the budget, due largely to the end of the Vietnam War and discontent on the part of the general public for channeling expenditures to the military. This reduction of about 20 percent in the defense share of the federal budget was offset almost exactly by an increase in human resources expenditures, from 33.3 percent of the federal budget in 1968 to 52.1 percent in 1975. If one were to try to look at the change in federal expenditures to determine which president was responsible for ushering in the Great Society, it is apparent that the major increases in Great Society expenditures came in Nixon's administration, not Johnson's. This was, of course, not because Nixon supported the Great Society but because he was powerless to stop it. The programs were already in place, Congress wanted to allocate more federal expenditures to human resources, and the end of the Vietnam War provided a source of revenues to do so.

The expansion of the federal government was not limited to social programs or to redistributive activities. Rather, government programs expanded into all areas of the nation's economy. The Environmental Protection Agency (EPA) was created in 1970, following the National

TABLE 5.   Federal Outlays on National Defense and Human Resources

Year	Percentage of Total Federal Outlays	
	Defense	Human Resources
1960	52.2	28.4
1965	42.8	30.9
1968	46.0	33.3
1975	26.0	52.1
1980	22.7	53.0
1989	26.6	49.7
1997	16.4	62.5

Source: Author's calculations are from data in the *Statistical Abstract of the United States, 1997* (117th ed.), 334.

Environmental Policy Act of 1969, which required any public or private institution that received federal funds to file an environmental impact statement prior to the beginning of any construction project. The National Highway Traffic Safety Administration was created in 1970 to set safety requirements for automobiles, and the Consumer Product Safety Commission was created in 1970 and given substantial powers to regulate the safety of consumer products. The Occupational Safety and Health Administration (OSHA) was created in 1970 to regulate workplace safety.[25] The idea that the government was responsible both for looking out for the economic well-being of its citizens and for protecting them from being harmed by business, as workers and as consumers, was readily accepted by the general public, and democracy was further extended from a method for making political decisions to a method for determining the allocation of economic resources.

By 1980 defense expenditures had fallen to 22.7 percent of the federal budget and human resource expenditures had risen to 53 percent. When the allocation of federal expenditures in 1980 is compared with the allocation in 1960, it is interesting to note that in 1960 slightly more than half of federal expenditures went to national defense and a little more than a quarter of federal expenditures went to human resources. This allocation was almost reversed 20 years later, when slightly more than half of federal expenditures went to human resources and slightly less than a quarter went to national defense. If national priorities can be judged by the way the federal government allocates its resources, in 1960 the role of the federal government was primarily to defend the nation, and by 1980 the role of the federal government had shifted to the protection of the economic well-being of the nation's citizens. In this span of two decades, there was a major transformation in the role of the federal government, pushed ahead by the Great Society.

The budget figures in table 5 show that the Reagan revolution did put a temporary brake on the Great Society. Reagan wanted a stronger national defense, and defense expenditures grew from 22.7 percent of federal expenditures in 1980, the year Reagan was elected, to 26.6 percent of expenditures in 1989, the year he left office. Meanwhile, human resources expenditures were crowded out only slightly, falling from 53 percent of the budget to 49.7 percent. If the change in the allocation of government expenditures is used to judge revolutions, it would be more fitting to talk of a Nixon revolution that shifted expenditures from defense to human resources than of a Reagan revolution that changed the status quo only slightly. But in 1989 Reagan left office and the Berlin Wall fell, signaling the end of the cold war. During the Bush-Clinton years defense expenditures fell, to just 16.4 percent of federal expenditures by 1997, while expenditures on human resources rose from 49.7 percent of outlays in 1989 to 62.5 percent of outlays by 1997. The increase in Great Society expenditures took a breather during the Reagan years but resumed its climb after Reagan left office.

There is a tendency to overlook the remarkable transformation in the nature of federal expenditures following the Great Society because the level of federal expenditures, measured as a percentage of GDP, has not increased substantially. Table 6 shows that from 1960 to 1990 federal expenditures as a percentage of GDP rose from 17.8 percent to 22 percent, an increase of 4.2 percentage points over a 30-year period. During the 1950s federal expenditures as a percentage of GDP rose by 2.2 percentage points, from 15.6 percent to 17.8 percent of GDP. When just total expenditures are examined, federal spending grew faster in the 1950s than in any of the subsequent decades. But most federal expenditures in 1960 were military expenditures, and the growth in federal expenditures represented a buildup in response to the cold war. Military expenditures had always been a major component of federal expenditures, and the buildup in the 1950s, although unprecedented during peacetime, still fit with the founders' vision of the role of the federal government. With a tax system in place to finance this level of federal expenditures, the shift toward human resources brought with it only a slight increase in federal outlays from year to year but a major shift in the nature of federal expenditures. The relative constancy in the level of federal expenditures over the decades tends to mask the major transformation in federal expenditures that occurred in the 1970s and that continued through the end of the twentieth century.

TABLE 6. Federal Outlays as a Percentage of GDP

Year	Outlays (percentage of GDP)
1950	15.6
1960	17.8
1970	19.4
1980	21.7
1990	22.0

Source: Statistical Abstract of the United States, 1997 (117th ed.), 332.

An examination of the federal budget after Johnson left office shows the legacy of the Great Society. In 1960 the federal government spent 5 percent of the GDP on human resources. By 1997 it spent 13 percent of the GDP on human resources. In the context of the Progressive notion that the role of government should be extended to looking out for the economic well-being of its citizens, by looking only at federal expenditures it is clear that most of the federal government's Progressive activities have been initiated since 1960. Johnson, envisioning a great society in which a compassionate government would extend assistance to those in need, put the Great Society programs into place. Although most of the expenditures that resulted from this compassion came after Johnson left office, his legacy is a federal government that finds its largest mission by far the transferring of income (or the providing of in-kind benefits) from taxpayers to those who, following some criteria, are deserving of the government's economic assistance. Democracy is an economic system that allocates a substantial share of the nation's income, following the will of the majority.

The Triumph of Democracy

How does a nation determine what activities its government will undertake? Different nations may use different mechanisms. Dictatorships place ultimate authority in the dictator, for example. And the same nation may use different mechanisms at different times in its history. In the United States, the original principle upon which the activities of government were determined was liberty, but at the end of the twentieth century the principle upon which American government rests is democracy. The government undertakes those activities that the majority of the citizens want it to undertake, and the preferences of the majority are measured through the electoral process.

In 1993 President Clinton undertook a campaign to try to create a system of national health insurance, and both he and First Lady Hillary Rodham Clinton traveled around the country promoting the plan. The Clintons claimed that the program should be supported because the American people wanted the kind of health security that their plan could provide. The opponents of the Clintons' plan claimed that the plan would not work as advertised but, more tellingly, also claimed that the Clintons were mistaken about the popular appeal of their plan and that in fact most Americans were opposed to it. In the end, Clinton's opponents were correct. Most Americans did oppose the plan, and seeing the opposition, the Clintons abandoned it. That debate on national health insurance revealed as much about the principles of American politics by what was not said as by what was said. The issue ultimately came down to one of popularity. Did people want it or not? Never was the issue of whether the program was within the constitutional bounds of the federal government considered, and never was the issue of whether it would have an adverse impact on the liberty of Americans considered. The old constitutional principles had been left by the wayside, and the notion that the fundamental role of government is to protect the liberty of its citizens was never even considered. The issue was simply one of democratically determining what public policy the American citizenry wanted.

An analysis of the American political process that produces this kind of democracy is straightforward. Those who make public policy must be elected by the citizenry. The right to vote when those who are elected are expected to shape public policy in order to further people's economic interests is crucial, of course. Those competing for elected office must win votes, so the people whose interests they will favor will be voters. Thus, the continual expansion of the franchise since the nation's founding has been an integral element in the creation of democracy as the guiding principle of American government. The franchise has been expanded not only by extending it to people who previously did not have the right to vote but also by allowing citizens to vote for government officials who originally were beyond the direct reach of the electorate. As the founders envisioned it, the only federal officials who would be elected directly by the citizens were members of the House of Representatives, allowing the people some check on the activities of their government. That check was simply that legislation cannot be passed without the approval of the House. But most of the federal government would be run by individuals beyond the direct reach of the electorate, with the idea that public policy would be insulated from democratic pressures and the will of the majority. Senators were chosen by their state legislatures until 1913, and the president was to be chosen by an electoral college and the House of Representatives, as the founders originally envisioned the process. Supreme Court justices would be appointed by the president. By 1913 only the Supreme Court remained out of the direct grasp of the electorate.

In such a system, those running for election must cater to the opinion of the majority, because if they do not the electorate will choose someone else. The result of this electoral competition is public policy aimed at voters who are at the center of public opinion.[26] This conclusion must be tempered somewhat, because most voters will not be well informed about most issues, allowing special interests, who have an incentive to be informed and who will undertake expenditures to lobby for their positions, to have disproportionate influence. Therefore, the result of this democratic system is to produce public policy geared more toward special interest groups than toward the general public interest. The details are worthy of analysis in their own right,[27] but the larger point is that the principle by which public policy is determined is democracy—whatever most people want. Liberty is a concern only insofar as there is a demand for it rather than as a principle of government, and the Constitution is relevant only because at times it acts as an impediment to the implementation of the will of the majority. However, once Social Security was judged within the bounds of the federal government's constitutional power, it would seem that there are no practical constitutional limits to the scope of federal government activity.

The Great Society represents the ultimate triumph of democracy because for the first time there was a major expansion in the scope of government power, based on the demands of the electorate, with no extenuating circumstances. The Progressive movement, which explicitly called for a shift in the role of government, asking the government to look out for the economic well-being of its citizens in addition to protecting their rights, arose in response to a substantial increase in the concentration of economic power toward the end of the nineteenth century. Progressives argued that the nation was not the same one the founders envisioned governing more than a century before and that changes in government were required to respond to changes in the character of the nation. The old Jeffersonian ideal of limited government should be retired, they argued, and instead the Hamiltonian vision of more extensive government power should be adopted. Changes that the nation was undergoing demanded changes in the nation's government. In the twentieth century, the two world wars and the Great Depression were national emergencies that created the demand for more government action in response to those situations. Despite the philosophical undertones, government action was a pragmatic response to conditions rather than an acceptance of the fact that the role of government had changed.

The Great Society was different. Its push for the War on Poverty and a commitment to civil rights came despite the fact that progress was being made on both fronts. The protection of civil rights for minorities was already increasing, and the incidence of poverty had been falling for two decades prior to Johnson's Great Society programs. The progress was too slow for many, of course, which was why Johnson initiated the Great Society. But unlike the New Deal, which was initiated to counteract the setbacks and misfortunes that had befallen many Americans, the Great Society was designed to further assist those whose fortunes already were improving. There was no crisis and no emergency, unless one wants to count the protests, riots, and demonstrations of those who wanted government policy to go their way. But even those demonstrations help to prove the larger point. By appealing to popular sentiment and making the intensity of their desires known, the demonstrators hoped to push the democratic decision-making process to further their interests.

Before the Great Society, the federal government had been willing to sacrifice some liberty to further the will of the majority. But past sacrifices in liberty were in response to changes that threatened the well-being of Americans, and the government's response was intended to push American society back toward the prior status quo by offsetting the effects of recent events. The Great Society was an attempt to change the status quo in response to the demands of the electorate. Some people were in favor and some were opposed, but the issue came down to what the majority wanted, not whether the liberty of Americans was threatened. When Barry Goldwater ran for president against Johnson in 1964, he was labeled an extremist and retorted, "Extremism in the defense of liberty is no vice." The American electorate did not buy it, and Goldwater was solidly trounced by Johnson. In a nation that is run based on the principle of democracy, extremism in any manner is a political vice, because public policy is determined by the demands of the majority. President Nixon, who won two presidential elections, had a better read on the American political system when he said he was aiming his policies at the "silent majority." In a democracy, the majority rules.

As the twenty-first century begins, there is an ongoing debate about the proper scope of government in the United States (and around the world). Some people want more government, others want less, and some are content with the status quo. But democracy has won out over liberty, and the issue is not what type of government would best preserve the liberty of Americans but rather what type of government the majority favors. The Great Society firmly established democracy as the underlying principle of American government by promoting its programs as a response to public demand. Of course, President Johnson believed that his Great Society was the right thing for America, but not because it promoted the liberty that the founders created the nation to protect. Much of the Great Society—Medicare, Medicaid, the jobs programs, and educational initiatives—worked against the concept of liberty as envisioned by the founders. Rather, with public opinion on his side, Johnson pushed the Great Society to enhance the economic well-being of Americans, following the Progressive ideology.

In response to crises, it had previously been demonstrated that Americans would sacrifice their liberty in exchange for government action to try to regain the status quo. Government action in response to crises had to be designed, aimed, and controlled by some process, and that process was democracy. In Jacksonian terms, democratic control of public policy was a way to protect against government programs run for the benefit of the elite. When crises arose, Americans would allow the demands of the majority for government action to dominate the concept of liberty. The Great Society demonstrated that during normal, prosperous times democracy remained the underlying principle of American government. Indeed, if there were crises during the 1960s, they were the cold war and the Vietnam War, and the Great Society forged ahead not because of these crises but in spite of them. International events were not a sufficient distraction to disrupt the Great Society, and President Johnson's unpopularity due to the Vietnam War was not enough to derail the Great Society programs that the majority desired.

Perhaps the continual inroads that democracy made over liberty during the crises of the twentieth century enabled it to be accepted unconsciously as a replacement for the principle of liberty; or perhaps Americans were satisfied at the way democracy had worked during crises and were willing to entrust themselves more to the will of the majority. At the beginning of the twenty-first century, the term *liberty* has an almost quaint ring to it, and the liberties that Americans still enjoy are often taken for granted. No, worse. There is a utilitarian undercurrent in the nation that is willing to weigh the costs of sacrificing a little more liberty in exchange for other goals. Liberty is not taken for granted; it is willingly sacrificed. Democracy and prosperity are the goals promoted by the American ideology, not liberty. The Great Society signaled the final acceptance of democracy as the fundamental principle of American government.

CHAPTER 12

The Dangers of Democracy

By 1980 democracy had completely replaced liberty as the fundamental principle of American government. Liberty remained as something valued by Americans and something worth protecting but only to the extent that it met with the approval of the majority. Lyndon Johnson's Great Society brought with it a sense of optimism about what the government could accomplish, if only the nation would be willing to devote sufficient resources to it. A decade and a half later, Ronald Reagan questioned the efficacy of the government to solve the nation's problems, and public opinion on the desirability of government intervention fell, largely because the actual experience of government intervention did not live up to its promises. The Reagan revolution, as it was then called, was brought about not by an ideological or philosophical change in the American people but rather by the realization that government intervention did not work as well as advertised.

The proponents of smaller government objected to wasteful programs that were unable to achieve their goals and to taxation and regulation that interfered with the productivity of the private sector, making everyone poorer as a result. The objections to government were pragmatic and utilitarian, based on the argument that government intervention did not work as its proponents had hoped. And it was democratic. Taxation and regulation were attacked because most people thought they were overtaxed and overregulated. Unlike the revolution in 1776, which was based on the principle of liberty, the so-called Reagan revolution was based on the principle of democracy and moved forward because most people favored less government intervention. The argument was not that government should be reduced to further the cause of liberty but that it should be reduced because the majority wanted smaller government.

Perhaps future historians will see 1980 as a turning point, because the decade of the 1980s brought with it major changes both in world affairs and in political attitudes toward government.[1] The govern-

ments of Margaret Thatcher in Britain and Ronald Reagan in the
United States were both based on the policy goal of limiting the scope
and power of government. In fact, the governments in both the United
States and in Britain were little different in most respects at the end of
the 1980s than they were at the beginning of that decade.[2] Thatcher
and Reagan promoted the idea of limiting government, but at best they
were able to stop the growth of their governments, not reverse the
trend and shrink government. They also did not change the underlying
democratic philosophy of government. Any retrenchment of government during the Reagan and Thatcher eras was because popular opinion favored it, not because people wanted to reclaim liberty as the
underlying principle of government. Philosophically, the United States
had become a democracy, and in a democracy popular opinion directs
public policy.

The ascendancy of democracy as the fundamental principle of
American government raises important questions about whether
democracy is a political system capable of ensuring a stable government and a prosperous economy or whether democracy itself is even
capable of surviving over the long term. Francis Fukuyama has argued
that the ascendancy of democratic government and the market economy signals the end of history in the sense that political democracy will
be the final form of government and the market economy will be the
end point in the evolution of economic systems.[3] Fukuyama's optimistic view contrasts with Joseph Schumpeter's argument a half century earlier that democracy plants the seeds of its own destruction,
because it allows citizens to actively dissent and to vote away their freedoms.[4] While one might argue that the case for democracy is strong,
because it has survived for more than two centuries in the United
States and because by the end of the twentieth century it was spreading
around the world, the history recounted in this volume suggests that
the evidence is not as strong as it first appears.

Democracy in the United States has always been tempered by a
constitutionally limited government, and even at the beginning of the
twenty-first century constitutional constraints still retain some force.
Furthermore, it has only been since the 1960s that democracy has
become firmly entrenched as the fundamental principle of American
government. Earlier in the twentieth century, concessions were made
to the principle of liberty in response to the crises of wars and depression, and only more recently did Americans demonstrate that they
were willing to agree to give up some liberty to further the desires of the

majority during normal times. The United States has not experienced two centuries of democratic government. Rather, the United States began, in 1776, as a government dedicated to the principle of liberty, with a very limited role for democracy. Until the Progressive Era that began at the end of the nineteenth century, one could easily claim that democracy was a means to an end, but by the end of the twentieth century it had become an end in itself. In addition, until the Progressive Era, democracy played the limited role of a political decision-making mechanism, but starting with the Progressive Era democracy has increasingly supplanted the market economy as a method of allocating economic resources. Democracy in this role is relatively new and relatively untested, but it is easy to see how, once the constitutional constraints on government action have eroded, it becomes inevitable that democracy will play a larger role in the economic system. People have a natural tendency to use their political power to try to secure economic gains.

Andrew Jackson was a strong democrat, but he favored democracy as a means of controlling the power of political elites and of curbing the growth of government. Despite his hope that democracy would be a tool to limit the power of government, Jackson's democratic ideals were used to expand government. The right to vote was viewed as important enough after the War between the States to be embodied in the Constitution via amendment, but it was the Populists and Progressives who philosophically turned democracy from a means to an end into an end in itself, promoting the idea that public policy should be determined by the will of the majority and that the government should expand its role to protect the economic well-being of its citizens. Even in the twentieth century, the expansion of democracy came largely as a response to the crises of wars and depression, only finally emerging in the 1960s as a principle of government that stood on its own. In that sense, American democracy at the end of the twentieth century was less than half a century old and the world's experience with true democratic government is limited.[5]

The world's political and economic future is uncertain, but in many aspects future events are under the control of the world's citizens. Collectively, they will decide much of the future evolution of political and economic institutions. Government institutions, including legal systems and the rules that define the parameters of economic activity, are in large part the result of human design, so modifications are worth examining carefully. John Maynard Keynes, in his 1936 landmark economic treatise, *The General Theory of Employment, Interest, and Money,* wrote,

> the ideas of economists and political philosophers, both when they are right and when they are wrong, are more powerful than is commonly understood. Indeed the world is ruled by little else. Practical men, who believe themselves to be quite exempt from any intellectual influences, are usually the slaves of some defunct economist. Madmen in authority, who hear voices in the air, are distilling their frenzy from some academic scribbler of a few years back. I am sure the power of vested interests is vastly exaggerated compared with the gradual encroachment of ideas.[6]

Thus, as the principle of democracy overtakes the principle of liberty as the fundamental principle of American government, it is worth considering both the merits and the drawbacks of democratic decision making.

Problems with Democracy

The problems with democracy fall into two categories. First, as a method for making group decisions democracy is most likely to fail when it is most needed. Democracy is a great system for making collective decisions when there is a substantial consensus of opinion among those in the decision-making group, but it tends to break down when there is not general agreement. Second, as a method of allocating resources, democratic allocation is inefficient. If democracy creates problems as a political system, it creates even more problems as an economic system. With a Lockean system of private property, where owners of economic resources are free to determine how those resources are used, individuals pursuing their own interests are led by an invisible hand to do what is best for everyone, as Adam Smith observed in *The Wealth of Nations* more than 200 years ago. When resources are allocated democratically, everyone has a potential claim on the productivity of everyone else, enticing some to use the political process to take resources from others and forcing others to enter politics to protect the wealth they have produced.

When everyone is given a say in how resources are allocated through the democratic decision-making process, private ownership is transformed into collective ownership and the incentives to preserve the value of resources and to enhance a nation's wealth are destroyed. By the end of the twentieth century, the advantages of market economies over centrally planned economies—and of private ownership over government ownership—were well recognized. What was not so well recognized is that the mandates of democratic governments— whether they are zoning laws or land use regulations that dictate how property owners can develop their property, or regulations restricting certain types of products from being sold, or regulations requiring products to have certain features, or labor laws that dictate some of the terms under which people can exchange their time for money—all take a step toward collective ownership of resources. Freedom of exchange is replaced by government mandate. As the founders envisioned it, democracy was a component in the political decision-making process, not a method for determining how people can use their economic resources.

Agreement in Politics and in Markets

In politics, one must be careful about choosing alliances, because people who have common interests in some issues may find themselves disagreeing on others. Thus, when choosing with whom to cooperate, it is important to consider the views of potential allies on all issues, not just issues on which there are common views. For almost everybody, supporting one candidate or one platform over another will be a compromise in which the supporter agrees with the candidate or platform on many issues but not all issues. Supporting a candidate because one agrees with the candidate on many issues also helps the candidate advance issues with which the supporter disagrees. One may agree with a candidate's views on taxation, for example, but may not support the candidate because one disagrees with the candidate's views on abortion. A supporter, therefore, must evaluate potential candidates and parties not based on whether they have one issue in common but rather how close their views are on all issues. This creates an obvious source of conflict, because party supporters who agree with their colleagues on many issues will always have the incentive to try to push for a change in party position on issues where the supporters are in disagreement with their party. Politics, by its very nature, fosters conflict, even among people who agree about almost everything.

In markets the situation is just the opposite. People cooperate only when they gain from trade on some specific issue. When a person buys

gasoline at a gas station, for example, whether the gas station atten-
dant favors higher or lower taxes is irrelevant to the transaction. Similarly, nobody makes a transaction at a department store contingent on
whether the cashier has the same views on abortion as the purchaser.
The only relevant issues are whether the purchaser wants to make this
particular purchase and whether the seller is willing to sell. Nobody
asks, or even cares, about the political views of those with whom they
do business. Their interests are simply to complete the transaction as
easily as possible. Market exchange, by its very nature, fosters cooperation, even among people who disagree about almost everything.

In the market, purchasers are free to support the Coca-Cola Company by buying Sprite, if they prefer it to other lemon-lime soft drinks,
but they are also free to support the Pepsi-Cola Company by buying
Pepsi, if they prefer it to Coke. Similarly, purchasers can buy their vans
from the Ford Motor Company and their sedans from General
Motors, if that is what they prefer, supporting only those elements of a
company that they actually prefer. In politics, however, supporting a
party means supporting all of a party's positions. As long as there is
substantial consensus, this may not be a problem, but when there is not
consensus, disagreements can arise that cause the collective decision-
making process to function less smoothly. In other words, the more
important it becomes to make collective decisions to resolve disagreements, the less well democracy is able to function as a collective decision-making mechanism.

In the market, people can disagree about most things and yet still
cooperate in areas where they agree, typically without even being
aware of areas of disagreement because any areas of disagreement are
of no consequence to the transaction at hand. This is not so in politics.
Supporting a candidate on one issue strengthens that candidate's
impact on all issues, leaving much room for conflict even among people who agree about most things. Market decision making is designed
to find common ground and to limit controversy and conflict. Political
decision making highlights differences among people and fosters controversy and conflict.

Consensus and Democracy

When a group of people are in agreement about most things, democratic decision making works well but is of minor importance. Democratic decision making will produce decisions that reflect the opinion of

the group, but this would also be the case if all of the group's decisions were made by one of its members or if a small committee made all collective decisions for the larger group. In groups where people join together for a common purpose, such as clubs or homeowners' associations, democratic decision making is a sensible way of assessing the group's opinion, because the group is designed so that the interests of their members are largely homogeneous and the scope of collective decision making is very limited. However, when members of a group have homogeneous interests, it is relatively unimportant how that group arrives at its collective decisions.

When there is not consensus among a group's members, democratic decision making tends to break down and is unlikely to be a good reflection of the group's preferences. Thus, as a mechanism for making group decisions, democratic decision making has the flaw that it is most likely to break down precisely when it is most needed.[7] When areas of disagreement surface in a collective decision-making group, it is natural for members of the group to ally themselves with others in the group who have similar views, creating factions within the group. But as noted previously, people who are allies on one issue may well disagree on others, again creating tension within the group and impeding the collective decision-making process. With heterogeneous views, any outcome will be less than completely satisfactory. Either one side or the other wins, leaving the other side dissatisfied. Alternatively, the outcome could be a compromise, in which case nobody is completely satisfied and everybody has an incentive to continue the political conflict to push the outcome a little more toward their preferences. The problem is that the political decision is imposed on everyone in the group. In contrast, market transactions occur only among those who agree to them, so nobody is forced to participate in a market exchange if for any reason the person does not view it as satisfactory.

This problem with democracy can be limited to a degree by creating more consensus in collective decision making. But, as discussed in chapter 3, creating more consensus means limiting the scope of collective decision making, thus reducing the role of democracy. Consensus can be increased by explicitly limiting the scope of collective action, as the founders intended to do by designing a constitutionally limited government. Their idea was that democratic decision making would not be strained by creating a government that only undertook actions that produced benefits for everyone. Thus, there should be a consensus of opinion that democratic decision making should be able to identify.

Consensus can also be produced by requiring a more inclusive decision rule—unanimity at the extreme—but this also would effectively serve to limit the scope of collective activity. One can also create more consensus by subdividing groups into smaller, more homogeneous, units, but the evolution of American government has gone the opposite way. National decision making has replaced state and local decision making on many issues, and the constitutional limits on the scope of government have been eroded so that the government deals with more issues on which there is a diversity of opinion. Thus, democracy has become a less satisfactory way of making collective decisions because the scope of democratic decision making has expanded beyond those areas on which there is a substantial consensus of opinion. When there is consensus, almost any collective decision-making procedure will arrive at a satisfactory outcome. When there is not consensus, democracy tends to break down, just when the need for a satisfactory collective decision-making procedure is the greatest.

Problems with Majority Voting

Democracy, as a political system, is much more than just majority rule voting. Still, majority rule decision making is at the foundation of contemporary democracy and also is at the foundation of popular opinion about the way democracy operates as a governing principle. This section focuses more narrowly on the problems that occur with majority rule voting, while the next section considers democratic political institutions more broadly.

The first problem with collective action determined by majority rule is that those in the minority end up having to accept the outcome preferred by a majority. If a group is voting on whether to drink Coke or Pepsi, if a majority votes for Coke, then those who prefer Pepsi get Coke. In a market system, those who want Pepsi get Pepsi, those who want Dr Pepper get Dr Pepper, and those who want 7UP get 7UP. If a democratic government is deciding on the characteristics of public schools, the preferences of the majority are imposed on the minority. In a market system that produced schools in the private sector, there is no reason to think that the variety of schools would be any less great than the variety of soft drinks the market produces, allowing those in the minority to have their preferences satisfied too.

A second problem with majority voting is that it does not allow for voters to register their preference intensities. Thus, a majority may only slightly prefer one alternative, whereas a minority has a strong preference for another alternative. In a market system, the intense minority could pay the majority enough so that everyone would agree to the minority preference, but under strict majority rule the majority could easily impose costs on the minority that exceed the benefits reaped by the majority. The next section considers important exceptions to this problem that result from political bargaining, but political bargaining raises other issues, and in many cases bargaining for political outcomes is not feasible. In general elections, for example, including those for candidates for office, for ratification of constitutional amendments (more frequently done at the state than the national level), and for referenda on expenditures, voters can try to persuade each other but will not have any opportunity to bargain meaningfully with each other. The majority rules, even if the benefits to the majority are less than the costs imposed on the minority.

Unless political decision making is unanimous, some people can impose costs on others, and the possibility that the resulting collective decision creates total costs in excess of total benefits increases as the decision rule becomes less inclusive. The reason why a less inclusive decision rule, like majority rule rather than unanimity, is often used is to reduce the decision-making costs involved in arriving at a collective decision. But this points to a third problem with majority rule decision making—the collective decision-making procedure itself is costly. Of course, there are costs to market exchange also, but market exchange eliminates the necessity of having to get a group of people to agree. In most cases, transactions are between two parties, and if they have a mutual interest they can reap the gains of their exchange without having to convince others that it is a good idea.

Political theorists who have studied majority rule decision making have run into an even more vexing problem. In many circumstances it may be that there is no single outcome that can command the approval of a majority of voters against all other possible outcomes. In its simplest form, this problem is called the cyclical majority and is illustrated by the hypothetical example in table 7. There are three voters, numbered 1, 2, and 3, and the table shows their rank-order preferences for three alternatives, A, B, and C. For example, voter 1 prefers A to B and B to C. Now consider a majority rule vote to determine whether the group will choose A, B, or C. If A is voted on against B, then A gets the vote of voters 1 and 3, so A defeats B. If C is voted on against A, then C gets the votes of voters 2 and 3, so C defeats A. But in an election of

B against C, then B gets the votes of voters 1 and 2 to defeat C. Thus, B defeats C, A defeats B, but C defeats A. No matter which outcome is chosen, there is another that is preferred by a majority.[8]

This is a problem with majority voting because it implies that majority voting has no rational way of choosing one of the three alternatives. The problem vanishes if it is possible to rank everyone's preferences on a single-dimensioned continuum,[9] but this is an academic technicality. The real problem is that voters have no way to express their preference intensities. If they could, the optimal outcome could easily be selected. Assume for the moment that each person values its first preference at $3, its second preference at $2, and its third preference at $1. Then all three outcomes would be worth $6 in total, and any one would be just as good from the group's standpoint. Now change that assumption only slightly, so that A is worth $100 to voter 1 but that all other values are the same. Now outcome A is worth a total of $103, and if voters could express their intensities of preferences it would be easy to choose A over B and C. For example, if voter 1 could buy the votes of other voters, it would be easy for that person to pay the other voters to assure that A got a majority of votes. In a market system, where people can express their preference intensities by offering to pay more for things that are worth more to them, the optimal outcome tends to be chosen. In a majority rule decision, where each person gets one vote, there is no guarantee that majority rule will produce any particular outcome, let alone the one that voters value most highly.

For many reasons, when there is not a consensus of opinion, majority rule voting is not an effective mechanism for selecting a group preference. In many cases it will not choose the alternative the group values most highly, and in some cases the result of majority rule voting will produce an arbitrary result. When there is diversity of opinion it can lead to political instability, of which the cyclical majority is a sim-

TABLE 7. The Cyclical Majority (rank order of voter preferences)

Voters		
1	2	3
A	B	C
B	C	A
C	A	B

ple example. It also imposes the preferences of the majority on the minority. Of course, if everyone agrees on which outcome is best, that outcome will be selected by majority rule but also by any other political decision-making mechanism. Problems arise when there is not agreement, such as in the cyclical majority example just discussed. This reinforces the idea that, as a collective decision-making mechanism, democracy fares worst when it is needed the most.

Democratic Institutions

Democratic decision making is more complex than simply taking a majority vote on issues that arise. Thus, the problems that arise with majority voting must be placed within a context of democratic political institutions in order to fully understand their implications. Sometimes democracy is implemented through voting rules other than simple majority voting, such as those (unusual) cases where two-thirds approval is needed to make a decision. More significant is that political decisions are made within an institutional framework that affects the decision-making process, and political institutions can have a bigger impact than the type of voting rule that is used. Legislation is not simply produced by a majority vote of the electorate. Rather, the electorate elects representatives who produce legislation, and in the U.S. Congress much of the initial work takes place within congressional committees. The process of selecting committee members influences the type of legislation that committees produce, and the fact that legislation is drafted by committees rather than by Congress as a whole also has implications for the type of legislation that is produced. The president and the courts also play a role. In short, democracy means more than just majority rule voting, and political institutions have a substantial impact on the activities of democratic government.

Democracy has had a profound impact on the way political institutions operate, because it ultimately makes those who design the institutions and make the decisions accountable to the electorate. As emphasized throughout this volume, the founders tried to insulate governmental decision making from the pressures of democracy, but from the very beginning American political institutions have become increasingly democratic. If Congress were a deliberative body insulated from democratic pressures and used the Constitution as its first guide for public policy, its decisions would be much different from the situation at the beginning of the twenty-first century, where legislators think of their elected offices as lifetime occupations but where the actions they take must be made with an eye toward reelection to keep their jobs. This means that democratic pressures are always an important motivation behind legislative decision making. Similarly, if the president were a chief executive selected by an electoral college insulated from popular opinion, as originally intended by the founders, the president would be sheltered from democratic pressures rather than directly accountable to the electorate, as has been the case throughout most of American history.

This democratic accountability—the quest for popular support—is what drives the political decision-making process in the United States. Ultimately, elected officials need votes to retain their positions, but most voters have only the vaguest notion about most of the decisions legislators make, and rationally so. Even legislators themselves are unaware of many of the details of the legislation on which they vote, relying on their staffs to evaluate the merits of the legislation they must consider. There is just too much legislation passed for any one person, no matter how dedicated, to be aware of the details of all of it. Indeed, some people in the private sector have full-time jobs just trying to keep abreast of small components of legislation, such as tax law or environmental law. It would not be possible for a voter to be aware of all of it.

Not only would it not be possible, but it also would not be rational. An individual voter has a negligible impact on the legislative process. People rationally concentrate their efforts on doing their own jobs and on allocating the incomes they earn from their work. Voters who take some time to understand the differences among local restaurants or the differences among makes of automobiles can improve their lives by making better choices. Voters who take the time to understand the details of various trade agreements may be better informed, but the government will make the same decisions on trade agreements regardless of what any one individual voter thinks. Similarly, because elections—even close ones—are always determined by more than one vote, a voter has almost no chance of changing the outcome of an election. Voters collect information about political candidates because they are interested, just as they collect information about sports teams, but that information has a negligible impact on the outcome of an election or the determination of any issue. Thus, as was discussed at length in chapter 1, voters remain rationally ignorant about most of what the government does.

The simple fact is that, in a democratic election, the vote of one voter does not count in the sense that it will not change the outcome of the election. Voters realize this, so they tend to be uninformed. Those in government try to convince them otherwise. Of course, all votes taken together determine the outcome of an election, so in that sense every vote counts. But elected officials preach the message that every vote counts and that citizens have a patriotic duty to vote because those in elected positions have an incentive to get high voter turnout. Higher voter turnout implies more support for elected officials and so conveys more legitimacy to the election result. Thus, government officials encourage people to vote, even though they know that the people they are encouraging to vote are relatively uninformed about the alternatives they face.[10] Candidates then face the challenge of how to get a majority of the votes from this poorly informed electorate.

In contrast to the electorate, interest groups are well informed about those issues that affect their interests directly. Farmers are informed about farm policy, waterway shippers are informed about federal policy toward navigable waterways, and businesses and industry associations are informed about tax provisions that affect their industries specifically. Interest groups support candidates based on their positions on issues that directly affect their group and pay little attention to candidates' positions on other issues. Because so much is at stake for these groups on special interest issues, they keep abreast of those issues, hire lobbyists, and offer support in the form of campaign contributions and favorable publicity for those legislators who promote their agendas. Thus, legislators hear much from special interests about provisions that have a large effect on them but hear little from the general public, which will feel only a small impact.

A program of dairy price supports, for example, will have a relatively small impact on most individuals, costing them a few dollars a year in the form of more expensive dairy purchases. Thus, most voters will be uninformed about such a program because it would not pay the voter to invest in collecting information and approaching a legislator about legislation that has such a small impact on the individual. Dairy farmers, on the other hand, have a big incentive to become informed and make their preferences known, because a few dollars from every consumer means thousands of dollars in extra income to every dairy farmer. Dairy farmers will tend to support candidates based on the candidates' support for their industry, while most people will be uninformed about how candidates vote on dairy issues.

The same thing is replayed in every industry. Thus, legislators interact with special interests while the general public is uninformed about most legislation. The legislator can help the interest group, collecting campaign contributions and political support in exchange, or can decline to help the interest group, creating an adversary group. In either case, the general public will be uninformed about the legislator's actions. Thus, there is a strong bias for legislation to favor benefits for special interests over the general public interest.[11] How can one make sense of a federal government policy that claims a policy goal of greatly curtailing tobacco use yet subsidizes tobacco farmers? It makes complete sense if one views tobacco farmers as an interest group that has an incentive to promote its interests before the legislature, while the general public has only a slight interest in the outcome.

Democratic institutions act as a filter on public opinion, filtering out small costs and benefits that are spread among the population at large and focusing instead on concentrated costs and benefits that have large impacts on narrow interests. For this reason, democratic political institutions favor policies that impose small costs on most people, who are rationally ignorant about the policies, to finance large benefits to smaller groups. Thus, despite the potential problems with majority rule voting, political institutions distort the process even more so that the preferences that are transmitted to the legislature are not those of the general public but rather those of narrow concentrated interest groups. American legislative institutions have always worked this way, and in 1861 the authors of the Confederate Constitution tried to create impediments to interest group politics in their new government, as discussed in chapter 6. But the problem has become worse as the constitutional constraints on government have been eroded and as the philosophy of American government has migrated from liberty to democracy.

As noted previously, support for a politician on one issue strengthens that politician's position on all issues, and because political issues are bundled to parties and candidates it is difficult to separate support on one issue from support on other issues. If people choose to support candidates based on their positions on issues that are of special interest to them, then the support-maximizing politician will choose to side with concentrated special interests on all issues rather than the more diluted general interests. In this way, the special interest nature of modern democratic politics favors special interests rather than the general public interest. For example, dairy farmers may not agree with many positions a candidate takes on nonfarming issues, but they will support the candidate who offers their special interest the largest benefit, both by voting for the candidate and by offering political contributions. When contributions come through lobbying organizations, the only thing that matters is the special interest issue the organization represents. For this reason, it is unrealistic to think that the opinions of those who oppose interest groups will be weighted as heavily as those who do not.[12] Political support in the political marketplace ultimately goes to candidates, not to issues. When candidates look for support from groups of voters, they focus on the special interest issues that are likely to win their votes rather than weigh their opinions on all issues, which creates politicians who focus on producing benefits for special interests. Democracy demands it.

The Political Marketplace

In a democracy, elected representatives try to create public policy that will maximize the political support they receive, because they always must be looking ahead to the next election. Because the philosophy of democracy has replaced the philosophy of liberty, this outlook is easy to justify. Representatives represent the people and thus are responsible for being a conduit of public opinion and for crafting popular sentiment into public policy. If all voices were heard and if people were able to weigh in with an accurate representation of the intensities of their preferences, the process might work to generate a reasonably efficient outcome.[13] However, as noted, most voters do not even know most of what the legislature is doing, let alone make the effort to register their opinions on specific issues. One can think of the legislature as a political marketplace, where people bring issues of concern to the legislature and the legislature weighs the merits of various claims, supporting those it finds most meritorious. The problem is that interest groups routinely approach the legislature for legislation that would benefit them, but nobody represents the general public interest.

Thus, the legislative marketplace is populated by special interests and by legislators who can benefit those interests. The legislators exchange political benefits for electoral support and campaign contributions, resulting in democratic public policy that is skewed against the general public interest. Mancur Olson has persuasively argued that nations decline precisely because of this democratic political process,[14] and the founders anticipated these problems when they designed a government constitutionally limited in scope. According to Olson, as a nation ages, interest groups become more firmly entrenched, and it becomes increasingly profitable for people to seek income from government transfers rather than from productive activity. Transfers can come from taxing some people to pay for benefits to others or from regulation that imposes costs on some for the benefit of others.[15] This is the threat of public policy guided by the principle of democracy rather than committed to the principle of liberty. This points directly to the problems that emerge when democracy is employed as an economic system.

Economic Liberty versus Economic Democracy

The Industrial Revolution has brought with it such wealth that Americans almost take it for granted. The persistent question among those who study poverty is, "Why are some people poor?" Yet Thomas Malthus, writing in 1798, believed that poverty was destined to be the normal state of affairs for most people throughout time.[16] The more appropriate question should be, "Why are so many people rich?" The production of wealth is a difficult undertaking, and poverty would be the normal state of affairs were not some societies able to figure out how to produce an abundance of wealth. If one could figure out why many people are rich and apply this answer to the poor, the problem of poverty could be lessened. The answer clearly has to do with nations, not individuals. Poor people in the wealthiest nations are materially better off than almost everybody in poor nations.

The answer to this question has been known for hundreds of years. When Adam Smith published *The Wealth of Nations* in 1776, he described a laissez-faire economic system in which individuals pursuing their own self interests were led by an invisible hand to benefit the entire society. This type of economic system is what creates the wealth of nations. When individuals have economic liberty, as envisioned by John Locke, they own the fruits of their labor and are free to consume or exchange what they own with others. By combining their labor with unowned land, they can come to own land, and in the economic system Locke advocated, people have an incentive to use their resources productively and to add to the wealth of nations. Smith argued the limitless potential of economic liberty, and two centuries later economic historian David Landes has built on Smith, noting that the nations that have adopted a market economy have allowed freedom of exchange, have enforced an impartial rule of law, and have prospered; those nations that have not done so have remained in poverty.[17] The way to make everyone better off is to create an economic system based on liberty, where economic resources are privately owned and where the government protects the rights of individuals. This was the economic system envisioned by the American Founding Fathers.

By the end of the twentieth century it became common to view economic liberty as a situation in which everyone has a certain level of economic wealth or income, but to view it this way neglects the fact that wealth is difficult to produce and that to give income to some means to take it from others. This reduces the incentive to produce wealth and ultimately makes everyone poorer. By seeing liberty as Locke did, as the right to the product of one's labor, the economic system works to make everybody better off. Wealth production is not easy, but it is not a mystery either. By creating an economic and political environment that is fertile for economic growth, the modern world has produced a standard of living for typical citizens in nations that observe economic liberty that was unimaginable to people living a century before.

Economic democracy, in contrast, gives everybody some say in how people are able to use economic resources. It compromises economic liberty because people no longer are able to determine how the fruits of their labor are used.[18] The result is that resources are allocated by public opinion rather than by the desires of the producers of those resources. This blunts the incentive to be productive and creates the incentive for some people to try to control the production of others. The United States still allows resource owners considerable latitude to determine how resources they own are used, so the nation has not completely evolved to the extreme point of economic democracy depicted in the upper right-hand corner of figure 2. Yet it is moving in that direction, because the principle of democracy has been accepted as an appropriate way to make public policy decisions. Before analyzing the case further in the abstract, consider some examples.

Some Examples

One example is the minimum wage law, which makes certain exchanges of one's labor for money illegal. From the standpoint of liberty one can understand the minimum wage law as a straightforward infringement of freedom of contract. If two individuals arrive at a

mutually agreeable wage agreement, why should the government interfere? When looked at from the standpoint of democracy, the minimum
wage law takes on a more sinister appearance. Because the minimum
wage is low when compared to average wages, it covers only those
workers who have the lowest skills. Labor unions have been strong
supporters of minimum wage legislation, even though union wages
always exceed the minimum wage. The nominal reason for their support is that unions claim to have a policy of trying to improve the well-
being of all workers, not just their members. However, lower-skilled
nonunion workers can substitute for union workers and may be a good
buy because, due to their lower wages, an employer could hire several
nonunion workers in place of each union worker. Thus, the minimum
wage law keeps nonunion labor from looking as attractive when compared to union labor. It increases the employment of union workers
and decreases the employment of nonunion workers, especially of
nonunion workers with the lowest skill levels. In this way, the minimum wage law benefits union workers. It does not cover them, but it
does reduce the effectiveness of their competitors.

One can see by this example how economic democracy can be used
as a method of transferring resources from some to others, reducing
the productivity of the economy in the process. Union workers, who
are politically organized, can gain from a minimum wage law at the
expense of lower-skilled nonunion workers, who are not politically
organized. At the same time, people who might hire lower-priced
nonunion labor will be less likely to do so, creating an impediment to
exchange and reducing productivity. These workers who remain
unhired are harmed in two ways. Not only are they denied immediate
employment, but they also are denied job experience that can help
them get higher wages in the future. This infringement of economic liberty creates benefits for those who are already relatively better off at
the expense of another group of people who are relatively worse off.
The dangers of employing democracy in the allocation of resources are
apparent in this example.

In some nations (Italy, for example), collective bargaining sets
wages for certain occupations nationwide, extending democratic control of labor markets even more. Labor productivity tends to be higher
in northern Italy than in southern Italy, but because by law the same
wages must be paid for the same jobs, employers would rather hire
workers in the northern part of the country. Unemployment in southern Italy is much higher than in the north, but southerners are effec-

tively precluded from competing by offering lower wages to get jobs. So again the use of democracy and the compromise in liberty to set wages results in gains for some at the expense of others and reduces economic efficiency by keeping some potentially productive workers from working. A democratic economic system allows some to use the political process for their benefit but at a cost to others. While this level of economic democracy does not exist in the United States, one can see that developments in labor policy are pushing in that direction.

Another example of economic democracy is land use regulation. Until the last quarter of the twentieth century the most prominent example of land use regulation was zoning, but now many states and localities are creating additional types of land use regulation that attenuates property rights in land to a substantial degree. The progression from zoning to other types of land use regulation makes an interesting case study in the transition from liberty to democracy. Nominally, zoning can be justified based on the idea of separating incompatible uses of land. Thus, residential neighborhoods can be separated from industrial areas by zoning, and commercial uses of property can be kept from imposing costs on residences. Similarly, industrial uses of land, which might drive away customers, can be separated from commercial uses. Zoning laws for land were only introduced in the twentieth century. Prior to the widespread use of zoning, incompatible uses of property were prevented by applying the law of nuisance. The law of nuisance is very Lockean in its philosophy, for it allows people to use their property as they see fit, as long as they do not create a nuisance to their neighbors. Thus, someone who wanted to locate a cement plant next to a residential neighborhood would be prevented from doing so because the cement plant would create a nuisance to those living nearby. Using the law of nuisance to guide land use, people are at liberty to use their property as they see fit, without democratic oversight, as long as they do not infringe on the rights of their neighbors.

The law of nuisance remains as a part of the doctrine of common law, but its use has been substantially curbed because of government regulation. If someone wants to build a commercial facility near a residential neighborhood, the modern practice is to approach the zoning board to have the land zoned for commercial use, and with this political approval the determination is made that the land use complies with the law. A defense against nuisance then can be that the use of the property complies with zoning regulations. A good example of the narrowing of the scope of the law of nuisance comes from a lawsuit filed by Claude Kirk, a former governor of Florida, against a group of Florida sugar farmers who Kirk claimed were creating a nuisance by polluting the Everglades with runoff from their farms. The suit was dismissed, with the judge ruling that, because the farming activity was governed by the state's Department of Agriculture and Department of Environmental Protection, Kirk should take his complaints to those agencies rather than to the courts.[19] In other words, compliance with requirements of government regulatory agencies can insulate property owners from the legal liability of nuisances created by those regulated activities. Because the regulations are determined through the democratic political process, democracy crowds out liberty, as the will of the majority preempts private property rights.

If the idea of zoning and other regulations governing people's use of their land was originally intended to codify the common law notions that people are free to use their property as they desire, as long as they do not infringe upon the rights of others, that idea was abandoned by the end of the twentieth century. Government land use regulations are increasingly imposed to further the will of the majority rather than to prevent some people from violating the rights of others. At the state level, two of the leaders are Oregon, which established statewide land use regulations in 1973, and Florida, which passed statewide land use planning rules in 1985. In both cases the primary role for land use planning is to create what the planners believe is a desirable pattern of land use and property development. It is central planning, pure and simple.[20] All land use must comply with the government's comprehensive land use plan, which is democratically drawn up and approved by the state authorities. If a landowner wants to develop his or her property in a particular way, she or he can do so only if the state approves. The liberty to use one's property as desired, as long as the use does not infringe on the rights of others, is sacrificed and replaced by a democratic process whereby everybody can have some say in what others do with their property. One can debate whether the actual effects of this democratic land use planning improve the quality of life,[21] but beyond a doubt this is an example of democracy displacing liberty.

Income taxation provides another example. It is apparent at the outset that an income tax erodes economic liberty because it takes some of the compensation workers are paid for their labor and transfers it to others through government. If economic liberty means people are entitled to the fruits of their labor, there is no question that liberty is compromised through taxation. Yet as with the examples just mentioned, economic democracy has additional pernicious effects. When the allocation of tax dollars is determined by a democratic process, this allows some people to use the democratic process to acquire the resources of others. In the abstract, one can debate the merits of using the government to redistribute income, but when one examines the actual political process by which redistribution takes place it becomes apparent that, through the force of government, resources are transferred from those who have income and wealth to those who have political power.[22] In past centuries, this might have meant transferring resources to the British Crown, but citizens—including those in the American colonies—were on their guard to protect themselves from having the Crown take too much from them. In a democracy, political power comes from voting and income is not necessarily redistributed to those who need it most but rather to those who exert the most political pressure.

The largest redistribution program in the United States is Social Security, but the average recipient of Social Security benefits is wealthier than the average person who pays Social Security taxes. While this provides a good example of the idea that in a democracy transfers come from those who have income and goes toward those who have political power, it is also a good example of economic democracy, where people have a claim to the resources of others to the extent that such a claim is approved through the democratic political process.

Economists have often analyzed the pernicious effects of taxes and regulations but have rarely done so within the context of the economic system that generates these effects.[23] As the previous section argues in theory, and this section illustrates with examples, the problems discussed here arise as a result of creating a more democratic economic system and of compromising economic liberty in the process. An economic system of liberty has generated growth and prosperity in the nations that have adopted it for 250 years. Economic democracy is much more recent, but in nations where economic liberty has been sacrificed for economic democracy, economic growth has suffered.[24] The idea that American democracy has proven itself as a result of more than two centuries of good performance is, in an important sense, wrong. As this volume has documented, American democracy as it had evolved by the end of the twentieth century is a relatively recent phenomenon. Liberty, rather than democracy, was the fundamental principle of American government until the twentieth century, and democracy as the fundamental principle of American government was not firmly established until the 1960s.

Production versus Predation

The essential differences between economic liberty and economic democracy lie in the differences in the incentives the two systems provide for production versus predation. People can obtain income in two ways. They can produce goods and services, adding to the stock of wealth available to be consumed, or they can take goods and services from others, redistributing income but adding nothing to the total production. Economic liberty provides the incentive for production because the only way people can enhance their economic well-being is by providing goods and services that others want. Economic democracy provides the incentive for predation because it allows people to use the democratic political process to assert claims to the economic resources produced by others. Despite the inroads made by democracy in the twentieth century, a substantial amount of economic liberty remains. But because democracy has been so thoroughly accepted as a principle, the liberty that remains is threatened. If economic democracy were to become complete, nobody would have an incentive to produce anything, because anything they produced would be subject to appropriation by the majority.

This threat of appropriation was precisely the threat Thomas Hobbes saw more than 300 years ago, when he argued that government was necessary to protect property rights and to keep a society from becoming a war of all against all, where life was nasty, brutish, short, solitary, and poor.[25] The way Hobbes saw it was that, unless government protected property rights, there would be nothing to stop thugs from appropriating anything of value that they were able to find. But with banditry rampant, even the thugs would not be very well off. Nobody would have an incentive to produce any more than they could consume immediately, so there would be almost nothing for the thugs to steal. Hobbes's solution was to establish a government that would create law and order and would protect property rights to provide the incentive for productive activity. But there is a threat at the other end of the scale also. If government becomes too powerful, the government might violate the rights of individuals and appropriate their property. The American colonists, in their Declaration of Independence, claimed that they were rebelling against just such a government.

The American founders objected to the excessive government infringement of liberty imposed by the Crown, but democratic governments have that same capacity to infringe on the liberty of their citizens. The democratic government that Americans now take for granted was the very type of democracy the American founders were trying to prevent from occurring. The founders wanted to create a limited government that would protect the liberty of its citizens from the type of predation that Hobbes envisioned would occur in anarchy. But they also wanted to limit the scope of government so that the government itself would not become predatory and infringe on the liberty of its citizens.[26] They did not intend to create a democracy where some people could use the political process to appropriate resources from others or to dictate the conditions under which people could use or exchange the resources they owned.

As an economic system, the danger of democracy is that it creates incentives for people to gain wealth by using the political system for predation rather than by creating it through production. The founders wanted to create a government that prevented predation, but the democratic system that came to govern the United States in the twentieth century has increasingly encouraged predation. This predation through democratic government has the potential of creating a war of all against all, just as surely as the disorderly anarchy described by Hobbes centuries ago. When some people have the ability to take the resources of others by political means, whether the predators are kings or members of some political majority, the stability of the political system and the productivity of the economic system are threatened. Those are the dangers of democracy.

The Long-Run Problem with Anarchy

One alternative to democratic government is no government—in other words, anarchy. More than 300 years ago Hobbes argued that the problem with anarchy was that it would create a society of chaos and disorder. However, libertarian anarchists make a strong case that everything the government produces could be better produced through private markets, including education, infrastructure, police protection, and even courts and national defense. There is no need to recount those arguments here, but interested readers should follow up on them because orderly anarchy may be more feasible than it appears to those who have not considered it seriously.[27] For the sake of argument, assume that government is unnecessary to produce all of the goods and services that government now provides. A problem still remains because predators have an incentive to take the production of others rather than to engage in productive activity themselves.

The libertarian anarchist solution to this problem is that protective firms would emerge in the market system to protect the rights of their clients from predators and these firms would have an incentive to undertake their activities in a peaceful manner, entering into agreements with other protective firms to keep their costs down and to maximize profits. Indeed, in areas where governments are weak these types of firms do emerge and often coexist with governments. Throughout the world, the Mafia collects protection money from individuals and firms in exchange for assuring them that no harm will come their way. The major difference between protection by the Mafia and protection by a private security firm is that the Mafia will threaten potential customers with harm if they do not buy the service, but the main thing that keeps the Mafia (and private security firms) from more aggressively marketing its services in this way is that governments prevent it.[28]

Robert Nozick has argued that the market for private protection services is a natural monopoly and that the largest firm will eventually put all others out of business, creating a single protective firm.[29] At that point, Nozick argues, because the firm creates the public good of law and order, it is morally justified to force everyone to pay for its services. Thus, a minimal state, which collects taxes and protects individual rights, is created. When one looks at how governments are actually formed throughout the world, they are never the product of voluntary contracts with private firms, eventually resulting in a single monopoly. Rather, governments are created by some people conquering others by force and ruling over them or by an uprising of people within a nation taking over an existing government and imposing their rule by force. Even the U.S. government was created this way—by force. While there are some historical examples of groups of people living without government for a period of time, in every case a government was forcibly imposed on them by people who saw the opportunity for personal gain.

The fundamental problem with anarchy, even if the private sector can produce all government goods and services better than the government itself, is a variant of the Hobbesian threat of a war of all against all. In such a situation, bandits could prey upon people, taking everything they produce. However, there is a greater potential long-term profit if those bandits establish themselves as a permanent government. Thus, government is inevitable, not because it is necessary to produce public goods[30] but because some people find it in their advantage to rule over others and to use force to take a part of what they produce. There are many nations, including the United States, in which people are largely in agreement with the activities of their governments. Nevertheless, governments rule by force, not agreement, to which people who choose not to pay their taxes or violate other government rules can attest. No matter how much people like their governments or agree to go along, the government uses force to ensure compliance, and government is based on force, not agreement.[31]

Government raises its revenues from the production of its citizens, so once a government is created it has an incentive to protect its citizens, because by doing so it protects its own source of income. Competing governments from foreign countries, Mafias, and other bandits all could profit from predation on a government's citizens, but the government has an incentive to protect its citizens from the predators for selfish reasons. Citizens also want protection. Thus, there is a mutually advantageous exchange of protection for tribute that defines the fundamental nature of government.

The traditional economic explanation for government production of national defense is that it is a public good that the market would not efficiently produce. One problem with this explanation from an economist's point of view is that economists normally explain why people do things based on their own self-interests, whereas this explanation of government activity presumes that people in government act in the public interest. Once one realizes that national defense protects the government's own source of revenue, it is clear that those in government have an incentive to provide national defense for their own interests. Once it is in the protection business, government may find it profitable to expand its activities into other areas, but the fundamental activity of government, and the activity that creates the government in the first place, is the exchange of protection for tribute.[32]

The fundamental problem with anarchy, then, is that it is inevitable that some people will establish their rule over others by force, thus creating a government. The preservation of liberty requires a limited government to protect people from the threat that a less limited and more ruthless government will arise to compromise the liberty of its citizens. History is filled with examples of peoples who have been conquered by others and have had predatory governments imposed on them for the benefit of those in government. Throughout history, the most effective protection against this type of predation has been another government. Government may not be necessary, but it is inevitable, because without it predators will be in a position to impose one by force. The challenge is to create an exchange of protection for tribute that is tilted as much as possible toward the advantage of the government's citizens rather than those in government. Indeed, this was the challenge the American founders were trying to meet when they designed the government of the United States in the late 1700s.

The Ideology of Democracy

The American democratic political ideology views the role of government as transforming the preferences of its citizens into public policy. As its citizens view it, American government is a democracy in which those with political power implement the policies that citizens request through the political process. Yet, as this chapter argues, democracy is severely limited in its potential both as a political system and as an economic system. For democracy to work as a long-term component of government, its role must be strictly limited, as the Founders intended. American democracy was substantially different at the end of the twentieth century than it was at the beginning, so any claim that American democracy has proven itself because of its long record of success would be inaccurate. In fact, potential hazards have been created by the transformation of the fundamental principle of American government from liberty to democracy, and much of this transformation occurred in the twentieth century. To their credit, the American founders attempted to insulate their new government from the pressures of democracy, but much of the insulation they created has been removed over the subsequent two centuries.

The United States became an independent nation because the founders believed they were being oppressed by the government of England, and they declared their independence to protect the liberty of Americans. To them, liberty meant freedom from government oppression, because the clearest threat to liberty in those times came from government. The U.S. government was created as a limited government to protect against the threats of more oppressive governments. The founders recognized that their own newly created government had the same potential to threaten their liberty as did the British government they were trying to escape, so they created constitutional limits on the power of government to protect the liberty of its citizens and deliberately insulated the government from the democratic pressures of popular opinion. The insulation is now gone, and popular opinion drives the public policy process, partly because of conscious decisions that changed the nature of government but partly because popular opinion holds democracy in higher esteem as a political value than liberty. The dangers of democracy are not as readily apparent as the dangers of dictatorship, but they are just as menacing. Unfortunately, Americans do not appear to fully understand these dangers as they continue to push the foundations of their government away from liberty and toward democracy.

Notes

Preface

1. Alexis de Tocqueville, *Democracy in America* (New York: Alfred A. Knopf, 1963). The book was first published in French in 1835 and was translated into English that year.

2. Karl Polanyi, *The Great Transformation* (New York: Farrar & Rinehart, 1944); Raoul Berger, *Government by Judiciary: The Transformation of the Fourteenth Amendment,* 2d ed. (Indianapolis: Liberty Fund, 1997); Morton J. Horwitz, *The Transformation of American Law, 1870–1960: The Crisis of Legal Orthodoxy* (New York: Oxford University Press, 1992); Paul Starr, *The Social Transformation of American Medicine* (New York: Basic Books, 1982).

Chapter 1

1. "Democracy has become the battle cry of our day," proclaimed Carl J. Friedrich, professor of government at Harvard University, in the first sentence of his book, *Constitutional Government and Democracy,* rev. ed. (Boston: Ginn & Co., 1950).

2. See Roger Pilon, "Freedom, Responsibility, and the Constitution: On Recovering Our Founding Principles," *Notre Dame Law Review* 68, no. 3 (1993): 507–47, for a discussion of this theme.

3. For an explanation of why I use the term "War between the States" rather than the more conventional term "Civil War," see chapter 6.

4. For two excellent treatments of this topic, see Jeffrey Rogers Hummel, *Emancipating Slaves, Enslaving Free Men: A History of the American Civil War* (Chicago: Open Court, 1996), and Robert Higgs, *Crisis and Leviathan: Critical Episodes in the Growth of American Government* (New York: Oxford University Press, 1987).

5. Bruce Ackerman, *We The People 1: Foundations* (Cambridge, MA: Belknap, 1991), describes the evolution of American democracy, emphasizing the increasing dominance of the federal government over the states. Ackerman suggests that the notion of a government ultimately accountable to the people has led it to be increasingly democratic in its methods.

6. This statement is not universally true. For an excellent discussion of the evo-

lution of government institutions that is consistent with the one here, see Olson, *Rise and Decline of Nations.*

7. Tocqueville, *Democracy in America.*

8. Carl J. Friedrich, *An Introduction to Political Theory* (New York: Harper & Row, 1967), 4, makes a similar observation that in the United States there was an evolution from the idea of natural rights to the idea of civil liberties to the idea of personal freedoms that parallels the story told here. He goes on to note the irony that, whereas at one time Americans sought freedom from the oppression of government, they now seek freedom through the assistance of government (5).

9. This idea is discussed at length by Anthony Downs in *An Economic Theory of Democracy* (New York: Harper & Row, 1957), which provides a classic analysis of democratic decision making.

10. Dennis C. Mueller, *Public Choice II* (Cambridge: Cambridge University Press, 1989), 350, notes that others before him have used this example, citing B. F. Skinner, *Walden II* (New York: Macmillan, 1948), as the first.

11. This sentence was written prior to the 2000 presidential election, which apparently came down to a difference of only a few hundred votes. Even here, one or two votes would have made no difference, and the election was this close in only one state—Florida—so residents of other states had even less of a chance to cast the decisive vote. That election revealed something else about close elections: ultimately the outcome was determined by court challenges and by how the votes were (or were not) to be recounted, not by a few votes in one direction or another.

12. The founders intended for the electoral college to be more of a buffer between popular opinion and the selection of the president than it became by the mid-1800s, as chapter 5 describes. This is one way in which the nation has moved from liberty toward democracy.

13. See Christopher Lingle, *Singapore's Authoritarian Capitalism* (Fairfax, VA: Locke Institute, 1996), for a persuasive example.

14. Murray Edelman, *The Symbolic Uses of Politics* (Urbana: University of Illinois Press, 1964), makes this point well.

15. Tocqueville, *Democracy in America,* 57.

16. This theme has been developed by Douglass North. See, for example, "Ideology and Political/Economic Institutions," *Cato Journal* 8 (spring/summer 1988): 15–28, and *Structure and Change in Economic History* (New York: W. W. Norton & Co., 1981).

17. See Steven Kelman, "'Public Choice' and Public Spirit," *Public Interest* 87 (spring 1987): 80–94. Public choice analysis is explained and defended by James M. Buchanan, "Public Finance and Public Choice," *National Tax Journal* 28 (December 1975): 383–94.

18. Peter Laslett notes on page 3 of his introduction to John Locke, *Two Treatises of Government* (Cambridge: Cambridge University Press, 1967), that the first edition was dated 1690 on the title page.

19. See Bernard Bailyn, *The Ideological Origins of the American Revolution,* enl. ed. (Cambridge, MA: Belknap, 1992), 22–24.

20. Bailyn, *Ideological Origins,* discusses the pamphleteers and the contents of

their writing in detail. See also Paul Johnson, *A History of the American People* (New York: HarperCollins, 1997), 145, for a discussion of Locke's influence on Thomas Jefferson and other revolutionary writers.

21. See, for example, Murray N. Rothbard, *For a New Liberty* (New York: Macmillan, 1973), and David Friedman, *The Machinery of Freedom: A Guide to Radical Capitalism,* 2d ed. (La Salle, IL: Open Court, 1989).

22. Thomas Hobbes, *Leviathan* (1651; reprint, New York: E. P. Dutton, 1950), 142–43.

23. Hobbes, *Leviathan,* 143. Unless indicated otherwise, all emphases in quoted material are from the original.

24. Hobbes, *Leviathan,* 147.

25. Even this idea is not totally original. Sir Ernest Barker, *Social Contract* (New York and London: Oxford University Press, 1960), traces the origin of the social contract to Plato, and Harold J. Berman, *Law and Revolution: The Formation of Western Legal Tradition* (Cambridge: Harvard University Press, 1983), notes that when cities were being formed between 1050 and 1150 A.D. it was common practice to have all of the citizens gather in the center of the city and affirm their allegiance to the city's rules, providing a real-world historical antecedent to Hobbes's hypothetical social contract.

26. Locke, *Two Treatises of Government,* 287.

27. Locke, *Two Treatises of Government,* 289.

28. Locke, *Two Treatises of Government,* 306.

29. Locke, *Two Treatises of Government,* 341–42.

30. Locke, *Two Treatises of Government,* 344.

31. Locke, *Two Treatises of Government,* 348–49.

32. John Trenchard and Thomas Gordon, *Cato's Letters or, Essays on Liberty, Civil and Religious, and Other Important Subjects* (Indianapolis: Liberty Fund, 1995), 406–7.

33. Ronald Hamowy's introduction to the Liberty Fund edition of *Cato's Letters* provides some additional background.

34. Trenchard and Gordon, *Cato's Letters,* 747–53.

35. See Gordon S. Wood, *The Creation of the American Republic: 1776–1787* (Chapel Hill: University of North Carolina Press, 1969), who argues that the Revolution came about because of a transformation in Americans' habit of thinking that caused them to abandon the idea that governments have the right to oppress their citizens and to accept the idea that everybody has equal rights.

Chapter 2

1. Of course, exceptions to any generalization can be found. See, for example, R. G. Lipsey and Kelvin Lancaster, "The General Theory of Second Best," *Review of Economic Studies* 24 (1956–57): 11–32. Despite the innovative ideas in this article, the theory of second best never caught on and is not a part of neoclassical economics.

2. Francis Fukuyama, *The End of History and the Last Man* (New York: Free Press, 1992).

3. Examples include Friedrich A. Hayek, *The Road to Serfdom* (Chicago: University of Chicago Press, 1944); Joseph A. Schumpeter, *Capitalism, Socialism, and Democracy,* 3d. ed. (New York: Harper & Row, 1950); Milton Friedman, *Capitalism and Freedom* (Chicago: University of Chicago Press, 1962); Milton Friedman and Rose Friedman, *Free to Choose* (New York: Harcourt Brace Jovanovich, 1980); and Dan Usher, *The Welfare Economics of Markets, Voting, and Predation* (Ann Arbor: University of Michigan Press, 1992).

4. José Ortega y Gasset, *Invertebrate Spain,* trans. Mildred Adams (New York: W. W. Norton & Co., 1937), 125. Ortega goes on to remark, "The English revolution is a clear example of liberalism. The French, of democracy" (128).

5. Gottfried Dietze, *Liberalism Proper and Proper Liberalism* (Baltimore: Johns Hopkins University Press, 1985), 225, notes that the American founders were suspicious of democracy and discusses the inherent tensions between liberty and democracy (257–69).

6. Locke, *Two Treatises of Government,* second treatise, chap. 5, par. 27.

7. Friedrich, *Introduction to Political Theory,* 18, notes, "As Locke puts it in a number of places, property is all-inclusive. Life, liberty, and estate are involved in the broad meaning of property."

8. Karen Iverson Vaughn, *John Locke: Economist and Social Scientist* (Chicago: University of Chicago Press, 1980), 98–100, considers the argument that Locke had in mind some type of majoritarian control over the use of property and correctly rejects the idea.

9. C. E. Ferguson, *Microeconomic Theory,* rev. ed. (Homewood, IL: Richard D. Irwin, 1969), 28.

10. Neoclassical public goods theory is rigorously presented in two articles by Paul Samuelson, "The Pure Theory of Public Expenditure," *Review of Economics and Statistics* 36 (November 1954): 387–89, and "A Diagrammatic Exposition of a Theory of Public Expenditure," *Review of Economics and Statistics* 37 (November 1955): 350–56. Public goods theory is integrated more generally into a theory of market failure in Francis M. Bator, "The Anatomy of Market Failure," *Quarterly Journal of Economics* 72 (August 1958): 351–79. For a critique of public goods theory, see Randall G. Holcombe, "A Theory of the Theory of Public Goods," *Review of Austrian Economics* 10, no. 1 (1997): 1–22.

11. The neoclassical framework is often used to analyze situations in which property rights are not clearly defined, but when it is, the assumption remains that the property rights not explicitly assumed to be poorly defined have a clear definition. For example, one might analyze the problem of air pollution as a case where the property rights to the air are not clearly defined, but within that analysis the implied assumption is that all other property rights except those to air are clearly defined and always respected.

12. Again, the neoclassical framework has been used to analyze crime, but except for the explicitly assumed criminal behavior the other neoclassical assumptions remain intact.

13. Ferguson, *Microeconomic Theory,* is a standard college textbook that explains as well as any other the neoclassical framework. Ferguson was often thought of as the prototypical neoclassical economist, and the neoclassical economics described here corresponds with Ferguson's neoclassical economics.

14. Shays' Rebellion was motivated partly against government and taxes that pushed people into debt and partly against policies that favored some (merchants) over others (farmers), as explained by David P. Szatmary, *Shays' Rebellion: The Making of an Agrarian Insurrection* (Amherst: University of Massachusetts Press, 1980). Marion L. Starkey, *A Little Rebellion* (New York: Alfred A. Knopf, 1955), 5, refers to Shays' Rebellion as a class war with lasting consequences. See Robert A. Feer, *Shays's Rebellion* (New York: Garland, 1988), for a detailed analysis of Shays' Rebellion, the potential threat it posed to the new U.S. government, and the government's response to the uprising. In contrast to Starkey, Feer concludes that Shays' Rebellion probably had little lasting impact.

15. Richard D. Auster and Morris Silver, *The State as a Firm: Economic Forces in Political Development* (Boston: Martinus Nijhoff, 1979), argue that democracy is a way to control the monopoly power of the state. This idea is along the lines of Harold Demsetz, "Why Regulate Utilities?" *Journal of Law and Economics* 11 (1968): 55–65, and Gordon Tullock, "Entry Barriers in Politics," *American Economic Review* 55, no. 2 (March 1965): 458–66, who argue that monopoly power in markets and politics can be controlled by allowing competition for the right to be the monopolist.

16. Polanyi, *Great Transformation,* 234.

17. See Friedman, *Capitalism and Freedom,* chap. 12, for his proposal to create a negative income tax; and Alan Peacock, *The Political Economy of Economic Freedom* (Cheltenham, UK: Edward Elgar, 1997), chap. 6, for an even more extensive defense of redistributive taxation.

18. See Robert A. Goldwin and William A. Schambra, eds., *How Democratic Is the Constitution?* (Washington, DC: American Enterprise Institute, 1980), for a discussion on the degree to which the founders intended the nation to be democratic.

19. The paper, originally written in German, was published the following year. Mises continued writing on the subject, putting together a German-language book in 1929. A brief overview appears in Murray N. Rothbard, *Ludwig von Mises: Scholar, Creator, Hero* (Auburn, AL: Ludwig von Mises Institute, 1988). Mises's ideas on socialism appeared in English in *Planned Chaos* (Irving-on-Hudson, NY: Foundation for Economic Education, 1947) and in *Socialism* (New Haven: Yale University Press, 1951).

20. See, for example, Oskar Lange and Fred M. Taylor, *On the Economic Theory of Socialism* (Minneapolis: University of Minnesota Press, 1938), and Abba P. Lerner, *The Economics of Control: Principles of Welfare Economics* (New York: Macmillan, 1944).

21. Hayek's best answer to socialist economic theorists is found in his article, "The Use of Knowledge in Society," *American Economic Review* 35 (September

1945): 519–30. His book *Road to Serfdom* was aimed at a more popular audience and was a more general critique of socialism.

22. For an insightful analysis of incentives in public sector decision making, see William A. Niskanen, *Bureaucracy and Representative Government* (Chicago: Aldine-Atherton, 1971). A more recent analysis of the decline of socialism, largely siding with Hayek's arguments, is found in Joseph E. Stiglitz, *Whither Socialism?* (Cambridge, MA: MIT Press, 1994).

23. Paul A. Samuelson, *Economics,* 9th ed. (New York: McGraw-Hill, 1973), 883.

24. Geoffrey K. Fry, *The Growth of Government: The Development of Ideas about the Role of the State and the Machinery and Functions of Government in Britain since 1780* (London: Frank Cass and Co., 1979), discusses the philosophical foundations underlying the growth of government in Britain over the same time frame covered in this volume. Fry concentrates on British writers, but there was a considerable interchange of ideas between Britain and the United States, as was suggested in chapter 1.

25. For example, Polanyi, *Great Transformation,* 237, says, "The fascist solution of the *impasse* reached by liberal capitalism can be described as a reform of market economy achieved at the price of the extirpation of all democratic institutions, both in the industrial and in the political realm. The economic system which was in peril of disruption would thus be revitalized" (original emphasis). Yet a few pages later Polanyi indicates the vagueness of the concept of fascism: "There were no accepted criteria of fascism, nor did it possess conventional tenets" (239). Guenter Reimann, *The Vampire Economy: Doing Business under Fascism* (New York: Vanguard Press, 1939), illustrates that the fascist economy was highly controlled by the government, including dictating prices, dictating what materials businesses may use, controlling labor markets, and requiring bribes to undertake much ordinary business activity. Thus, German fascism in reality was quite different from the capitalist dictatorship as depicted in figure 1.

26. See Fareed Zakaria, "The Rise of Illiberal Democracy," *Foreign Affairs* 76, no. 6 (November/December 1997): 22–43, who argues that the biggest threat to democratic government is, as his title suggests, democratic governments that compromise personal liberty. Zakaria argues that democracy itself is a good thing and recognizes the tension between liberty and democracy but does not see it as an inevitable conflict.

Chapter 3

1. Adam Smith, *The Wealth of Nations* (1776; reprint, New York: Random House, Modern Library, 1937).

2. A political decision rule of unanimity does not produce the same outcome as market exchange, however, because politics allows everybody to participate in the decision, not just the parties to the exchange. If unanimous agreement from everyone (not just those engaging in an exchange) were required, many mutually beneficial exchanges would be prevented. For example, the owners of Burger

Kings would vote against allowing MacDonalds to open stores nearby, and environmentalists would vote against allowing soccer moms to buy gas-guzzling sport utility vehicles. For further discussion, see Russell S. Sobel and Randall G. Holcombe, "The Unanimous Voting Rule Is Not the Political Equivalent to Market Exchange," *Public Choice* 106, nos. 3–4 (March 2001): 233–42.

3. James M. Buchanan and Gordon Tullock, *The Calculus of Consent* (Ann Arbor: University of Michigan Press, 1962).

4. Buchanan and Tullock, *Calculus of Consent,* chap. 6.

5. John Rawls, *A Theory of Justice* (Cambridge, MA: Belknap, 1971), and James M. Buchanan, *The Limits of Liberty: Between Anarchy and Leviathan* (Chicago: University of Chicago Press, 1975). These theories based on some type of conceptual agreement rather than actual agreement are criticized by Leland B. Yeager, "Rights, Contract, and Utility in Policy Analysis," *Cato Journal* 5, no. 1 (summer 1985): 259–94.

6. This example is from Berman, *Law and Revolution.*

7. Donald J. Boudreaux and Randall G. Holcombe, "Government by Contract," *Public Finance Quarterly* 17, no. 3 (July 1989): 264–80, see enough of a parallel between homeowners' associations formed by restrictive covenants and traditional governments to refer to these associations as contractual governments.

8. In contemporary economic terms, one can think of the costs imposed on a minority by the majority in collective decision making as a political externality, analogous to economic externalities that arise when some people impose costs on others. James M. Buchanan, "Politics, Policy, and the Pigouvian Margins," *Economica,* n.s., 29 (February 1962): 17–28, uses this notion of political externalities.

9. This idea has been well known for a century and was emphasized by Erik Lindahl, "Just Taxation—A Positive Solution," in *Classics in the Theory of Public Finance,* ed. Richard A. Musgrave and Alan T. Peacock (1919; reprint, New York: St. Martin's, 1967), 168–76, and Knut Wicksell, "A New Principle of Just Taxation," in *Classics in the Theory of Public Finance,* ed. Musgrave and Peacock, 72–118.

10. A similar point is made by David Friedman, "Many, Few, One: Social Harmony and the Shrunken Choice Set," *American Economic Review* 70, no. 1 (March 1980): 225–32.

11. Higgs, *Crisis and Leviathan.*

12. This parallel between transactions costs in markets and decision-making costs in collective decisions is suggested by Oliver E. Williamson, "A Comparison of Alternative Approaches to Economic Organization," *Journal of Institutional and Theoretical Economics* 146, no. 1 (March 1990): 61–71, who considers public choice to be a part of the new institutional economics.

13. See Randall G. Holcombe, "Non-Optimal Unanimous Agreement," *Public Choice* 48, no. 3 (1986): 229–44.

14. Thus, William H. Riker, *The Theory of Political Coalitions* (New Haven: Yale University Press, 1962), talks of the advantages of a minimum winning coalition. See Randall G. Holcombe, *An Economic Analysis of Democracy* (Carbon-

dale: Southern Illinois University Press, 1985), for a discussion of the inefficiency of coalition decisions, even when everyone is in the coalition.

15. The five Iroquois nations were the Mohawk, Onieda, Onongaga, Cyuga, and Senica. The Tuscarora joined in the 1700s, but for most of its history the Iroquois confederacy consisted of five nations. Arthur C. Parker, in William N. Fenton, ed., *Parker on the Iroquois* (Syracuse: Syracuse University Press, 1968), book 3, p. 1, says that the sixth nation was added in 1724, but Donald A. Grinde, *The Iroquois and the Founding of the American Nation* (San Francisco: Indian Historian Press, 1977), places the date at 1735.

16. Bruce E. Johansen, *Forgotten Founders: Benjamin Franklin, the Iroquois, and the Rationale for the American Revolution* (Ipswich, MA: Gambit, 1982), reports these dates but notes that many Euro-American historians place the founding date around 1450. This still would mean that the Iroquois constitution was older in 1776 than the U.S. Constitution was at the end of the twentieth century.

17. One cannot be too critical of the Iroquois for not having a written constitution, because at the time that their constitution was developing there were no written constitutions anywhere in the world. As Paul Johnson, *History of the American People,* 105, notes, the first written constitution in the world was The Fundamental Orders of Connecticut, written in 1639, and Britain still has no written constitution.

18. For example, Terry L. Anderson and Peter J. Hill, *The Birth of a Transfer Society* (Stanford: Hoover Institution Press, 1980), argue that government involvement in income transfers began with Supreme Court decisions that changed the interpretation of the Constitution. The actual words of the Constitution remain the same, just as the Iroquois wampum remains physically unchanged, but the interpretation in each case can subtly change over time, in this case, following Anderson and Hill, apparently reversing the interpretation of constitutional provisions.

19. The Iroquois constitution is discussed by Jerry Mander, *In the Absence of the Sacred: The Failure of Technology and the Survival of the Indian Nations* (San Francisco: Sierra Club Books, 1991), 235–39, and by Fenton, *Parker on the Iroquois,* who has compiled and edited the work of Iroquois scholar Arthur C. Parker. Fenton's book, probably the best and most detailed description of Iroquois government, devotes 155 pages to a discussion of the Iroquois constitution and is the basis for much of this section.

20. In the academic literature, this idea of equal empowerment is embodied in the idea of the veil of ignorance popularized by John Rawls, *Theory of Justice.*

21. Quoted from Johansen, *Forgotten Founders,* 33. Jack Weatherford, *Indian Givers: How the Indians of the Americas Transformed the World* (New York: Crown, 1988), notes that the European colonists did not bring with them a tradition of liberty but rather lived in very hierarchical societies. The egalitarian democracy that exists in the United States is much closer in principle to the native American society that predated the American colonists.

22. Bruce L. Benson, "An Evolutionary Contractarian View of Primitive Law: The Institutions and Incentives Arising under Customary Indian Law," *Review of*

Austrian Economics 5, no. 1 (1991): 41–65, suggests that the organization of native American societies was also changed into more of a hierarchical structure following the immigration of Europeans into America.

23. This section is based on Randall G. Holcombe, "Constitutional Theory and the Constitutional History of Colonial America," *Independent Review* 3, no. 1 (summer 1998): 21–36.

24. Fenton, *Parker on the Iroquois,* relates a description of the Iroquois constitution by Arthur Parker, a well-known student of Iroquois institutions.

25. Barbara Graymont, *The Iroquois in the American Revolution* (Syracuse: Syracuse University Press, 1972), suggests that a part of the reason for the demise of the Iroquois nation in the face of the colonists was a general difference of opinion between the civil chiefs and the war chiefs as to how the advancing colonists should be dealt with. Consistent with contemporary notions of bureaucracy, the civil chiefs were more inclined to negotiate, while the war chiefs were more inclined to fight.

26. Daniel K. Richter, *The Ordeal of the Longhouse: The Peoples of the Iroquois League in the Era of European Colonialization* (Chapel Hill: University of North Carolina Press, 1992), 43–44.

27. Sarah Henry Stites, *Economics of the Iroquois* (Lancaster, PA: New Era, 1905), 98, discusses the idea of consensus in Iroquois decision making, noting that formal votes were not taken; rather, through discussion the sentiment of the group would emerge into a consensus opinion.

28. This is very similar to representation in the Continental Congress under the Articles of Confederation. Representatives to the Continental Congress were chosen by state legislatures and could be replaced at any time. Thus, representatives had to act as spokesmen for their states rather than as independent agents, or they would be replaced. Under the Constitution, legislators are elected for fixed terms, which gives them more discretion.

29. In this respect, tribal chiefs were more like United Nations ambassadors than U.S. congressmen. United Nations ambassadors are supposed to represent the opinions of their nations' administrations rather than do what they think is best and are subject to recall if they do not. Congressmen, on the other hand, serve fixed terms and have more discretion to act as they see fit.

30. See Fenton, *Parker on the Iroquois,* book 3, p. 10, for a more complete description.

31. Jared Diamond, *Guns, Germs, and Steel* (New York: W. W. Norton & Co., 1997), suggests that more primitive societies tend to be more egalitarian because there is less of a division of labor, making everyone's daily activities more similar, and because people produce little more than they need to survive, making it difficult for some people to live off the production of others. Similarly, Smith, *Wealth of Nations,* 15, suggests that differences among classes of people arise because of an increased division of labor that would not be present among primitive people. Following this line of reasoning, the relative equality among the Iroquois would be a result of their material conditions, not a result of their choosing.

32. Bailyn, *Ideological Origins,* 68–77, discusses the balance of power in Britain in the 1700s.

33. Quoted in Johansen, *Forgotten Founders,* 56. Franklin may have overestimated the degree to which the Iroquois were politically unified, however. Donald S. Lutz, "The Iroquois Confederation Constitution: An Analysis," *Publius* 28, no. 2 (spring 1998): 99–127, argues that there was more inequality and less political cohesiveness among the Iroquois than at first appears from a superficial analysis. He argues, "Even the American colonists, Benjamin Franklin among them, misunderstood the extent of Iroquois unity, and idealized the Five Nations as something it was not—a sovereign, unified, and politically coherent entity" (122).

34. See Johansen, *Forgotten Founders,* 67. There may have been more than just politics involved in the forging of alliances. Graymont, *Iroquois in the American Revolution,* 27, suggests that the Iroquois preferred dealing with the English over the French because English goods were cheaper.

35. Johansen, *Forgotten Founders,* 69–70.

36. Lutz, "Iroquois Confederation Constitution," argues that the Iroquois constitution cannot be viewed as a precursor to the Albany Plan of Union, nor to the Articles of Confederation, nor to the U.S. Constitution because of the substantial differences in them. There is no reason to take issue with Lutz here, because the argument of this chapter is built on a progression of constitutions, each one conforming less to the unanimity principle than the one before. The argument here does not depend upon one constitution being based on an earlier one. For example, looking ahead, one would not say the Constitution of the United States was based on the Articles of Confederation, because the Constitution was designed specifically to remedy the defects the founders saw in the Articles. Nevertheless, a chronological analysis is worthwhile, and surely an earlier document would influence the vision embodied in the new one, whether one is talking about the relationship of the Iroquois constitution to the Albany Plan or of the Articles of Confederation to the U.S. Constitution.

37. The Albany Plan of Union is reproduced as an appendix to Grinde, *Iroquois and the Founding.* For a description and analysis of the Albany Plan of Union, see Johansen, *Forgotten Founders,* 71–76.

38. The Articles might not have been ratified had France not insisted on it as a condition of receiving further aid in the American Revolution.

39. Karen A. Rassler and William R. Thompson, "War Making and State Making: Government Expenditures, Tax Revenues, and Global Wars," *American Political Science Review* 79, no. 2 (June 1985): 491–507, note that major wars tend to lead to the expansion of government power, extending the hypothesis of Alan T. Peacock and Jack Wiseman, *The Growth of Government Expenditures in the United Kingdom* (Princeton: Princeton University Press, 1961), on government growth.

40. It is interesting to note that, although the convention was called for the expressed purpose of amending the Articles of Confederation and although the Articles of Confederation required unanimous approval of the states for amendment, the Constitution states that it will become effective when approved by nine states. Thus, the principle of unanimity was abandoned, but at the same time the

importance of unanimity was recognized when the Constitution stated, "Done in Convention by the Unanimous Consent of the States present." In fact, no representatives from Rhode Island were present, and many delegates from other states did not approve of the document. Despite that only a majority of the delegates from almost every state agreed, the principle of unanimity was still considered important enough that the Constitution itself says that it was unanimously approved. The ratification of the new Constitution is discussed further in chapter 4.

41. Buchanan, *Limits of Liberty,* and Rawls, *Theory of Justice.*

42. See Charles A. Beard, *An Economic Interpretation of the Constitution of the United States* (New York: Macmillan, 1913), for a discussion of the Constitutional Convention in this regard, and Randall G. Holcombe, "A Contractarian Model of the Decline in Classical Liberalism," *Public Choice* 35, no. 3 (1980): 260–74, for a theoretical model based on Buchanan's analysis in *Limits of Liberty.*

Chapter 4

1. See, for a discussion, Anderson and Hill, *Birth of a Transfer Society,* who cite the role of Supreme Court decisions in loosening the constraints faced by governments at both the federal and state levels, and Higgs, *Crisis and Leviathan,* who recounts the loosening of constraints on government as a response to crises faced by the nation.

2. Diamond, *Guns, Germs, and Steel,* 290, notes that Germany had three failed attempts at unification, in 1848, 1850, and 1866, before France's declaration of war in 1871 prompted them to unify. Thus, the unification of both Germany and the United States may have only been due to external threats.

3. Some problems with the new government under the Articles are recounted by James M. Beck, *The Constitution of the United States* (New York: George H. Doran Co., 1924), whose analysis parallels the conventional wisdom on the weaknesses of the Articles.

4. See Keith L. Dougherty, *Collective Action under the Articles of Confederation* (Cambridge: Cambridge University Press, 2001), and Keith L. Dougherty and Michael J. G. Cain, "Marginal Cost Sharing and the Articles of Confederation," *Public Choice* 90, nos. 1–4 (March 1997): 201–13, for arguments that states would only pay their requisitions when they viewed it in their narrow self-interests to do so, leading to the argument that the revenue-raising powers of the federal government should be strengthened. However, Russell S. Sobel, "In Defense of the Articles of Confederation and the Contribution Mechanism as a Means of Government Finance: A General Comment on the Literature," *Public Choice* 99, nos. 3–4 (June 1999): 347–56, argues that the federal government was no less successful than other governments at the time at raising revenues it had legislated to collect.

5. Andrew C. McLaughlin, *The Confederation and the Constitution: 1783–1789* (New York: Collier Books, 1962), 53, suggests a related problem. The army should be paid by the federal government rather than by the states to reinforce the idea that soldiers' loyalty belongs first to the union rather than to the states.

6. See Merrill Jensen, *The Articles of Confederation* (Madison: University of Wisconsin Press, 1940), esp. 243–45, for an exposition of this idea and an attempt to understand the functioning of the Articles.

7. The text of the complete act appears in Alexander Hamilton, John Jay, and James Madison, *The Federalist* (Washington, DC: National Home Library, 1937), 577. The Articles of Confederation appear in that volume as appendix 2.

8. See Charles Warren, *The Making of the Constitution* (Cambridge: Harvard University Press, 1937), esp. 222. A standard reference of the proceedings of the Constitutional Convention is Max Farrand, *The Records of the Federal Convention of 1787*, rev. ed. in 4 vols. (New Haven: Yale University Press, 1937), who chronicles the debate through a thorough reconstruction of original notes taken at the convention.

9. A complete listing is given in Arthur Taylor Prescott, *Drafting the Federal Constitution* (Baton Rouge: Louisiana State University Press, 1941), 52–55. Prescott compares the Virginia and New Jersey plans on 55–60.

10. Both the Virginia and New Jersey plans are reproduced in appendixes to Beck, *Constitution of the United States.*

11. Dougherty, *Collective Action,* 159, suggests another reason: to circumvent the requirement for unanimous approval of amendments that existed in the Articles. The new Constitution was to take effect after the approval of nine of 13 states.

12. Paul Eidelberg, *The Philosophy of the American Constitution: A Reinterpretation of the Intentions of the Founding Fathers* (New York: Free Press, 1968), 42. This same quotation appears on page 3 of Jensen, *Articles of Confederation.* The constitutions Randolph is referring to are the state government constitutions.

13. Some of Mason's proposals are given in his own words in J. R. Pole, ed., *The American Constitution: For and Against* (New York: Hill and Wang, 1987), 126–32. For a sympathetic discussion of Mason's political views, see Robert A. Rutland, "George Mason: The Revolutionist as Conservative," in *The American Founding,* ed. Ralph A. Rossum and Gary L. McDowell (Port Washington, NY: Kennikat Press, 1981).

14. Only Pennsylvania and Connecticut had no property or wealth requirements for state office. Eidelberg, *Philosophy of the American Constitution,* appendix 1, table 2, lists the property qualifications for state office.

15. Beard, *Economic Interpretation.*

16. Robert A. McGuire and Robert L. Ohsfeldt, "Self-Interest, Agency Theory, and Political Voting Behavior: The Ratification of the United States Constitution," *American Economic Review* 79, no. 1 (March 1989): 219–34.

17. Grant McConnell, *Private Power and American Democracy* (New York: Alfred A. Knopf, 1966), documents the surprise and outrage that was expressed early in the twentieth century when the existence of paid lobbyists became public knowledge. This suggests an intellectual environment in which Beard's thesis would have been much more controversial than today, when, whether they like it or not, people accept the fact that interests pay professionals to try to alter legislation for their benefit.

18. See Beard, *Economic Interpretation,* 73, for a discussion.

19. Beard, *Economic Interpretation,* 176, mentions this but does not include items 1, 2, and 5 from the current list.

20. Buchanan and Tullock, *Calculus of Consent,* 96.

21. The importance of unanimity is also stressed in the frequently cited book by Rawls, *Theory of Justice.*

22. Vincent Ostrom, *The Political Theory of the Compound Republic,* 2d ed. (Lincoln: University of Nebraska Press, 1987), 62–65, discusses the importance of unanimity in the literature on constitutional decision making, citing writers from Hobbes to Madison to Buchanan and Tullock as sharing this idea.

23. Forrest McDonald, *Novus Ordo Seclorum: The Intellectual Origins of the Constitution* (Lawrence: University Press of Kansas, 1985), 279, explains that the Constitutional Convention recommended that the new Constitution be considered by conventions in each state as specified in the new document and that all thirteen state legislatures agreed to abide by this procedure, thereby voiding the unanimity requirement. McDonald goes on to argue that relying on state conventions rather than the state legislatures for ratification makes the document more valid, because it was agreed to by the people of the states (280). If it had been ratified by state legislatures, then it would be more a treaty among the states than a constitution for the people. Furthermore, McDonald argues that this makes it like a social contract and therefore indissoluble (281). This interpretation is open to question (and indeed was questioned in the text around this note) and will be questioned further in chapter 6.

24. Madison reiterates this defense that "To have required the unanimous ratification of the thirteen States would have subjected the essential interests of the while to the caprice or corruption of a single member" in *The Federalist,* no. 44.

25. Madison, often cited as the author of the Constitution, has often been accused of inconsistency in his principles. For example, he sided with Jefferson in opposing Hamilton's (successful) attempt to create the First Bank of the United States, yet after its charter expired the Second Bank of the United States was chartered during his presidency. As will be discussed further in chapter 5, Jackson ran for office on a Jeffersonian platform, arguing that the presidents following Jefferson (including Madison) had abandoned the principles of limited government on which the nation was founded. See Lance Banning, *The Sacred Fire of Liberty: James Madison and the Founding of the Federal Republic* (Ithaca: Cornell University Press, 1995), for a defense of Madison and an argument that he remained consistent and true to his principles.

26. Geoffrey Brennan and James M. Buchanan, *The Reason of Rules* (Cambridge: Cambridge University Press, 1985); Friedrich A. Hayek, *The Constitution of Liberty* (Chicago: University of Chicago Press, 1960); and Bruno Leoni, *Freedom and the Law* (Los Angeles: Nash, 1961). Hayek gave an updated and more complete statement of his views on the rule of law in his *Law, Legislation, and Liberty,* 3 vols. (Chicago: University of Chicago Press, 1973, 1976, 1979).

27. Prescott, *Drafting the Federal Constitution,* 57, notes when comparing the New Jersey plan to modify the Articles with the Virginia plan to draft a new constitution, "Stating the results of this comparison in general terms, the New Jersey

resolutions enumerate definite powers which Congress may exercise; the revised Virginia resolution, on the other hand, announces principles which are to determine future delegations of power."

28. See, for example, Holcombe, *Economic Analysis,* and Barry R. Weingast, Kenneth A. Shepsle, and Christopher Johnsen, "The Political Economy of Benefits and Costs: A Neoclassical Approach to Distributive Politics," *Journal of Political Economy* 89, no. 4 (August 1981): 642–64. For an opposing point of view, see Donald A. Wittman, *The Myth of Democratic Failure* (Chicago: University of Chicago Press, 1995), and for a summary exposition, see Donald A. Wittman, "Why Democracies Produce Efficient Results," *Journal of Political Economy* 97, no. 6 (December 1989): 1395–424.

29. Dwight R. Lee has proposed returning to this system of funding the federal government in "Reverse Revenue Sharing: A Modest Proposal," *Public Choice* 45, no. 3 (1985): 279–89, and "Reverse Revenue Sharing: A Return to Fiscal Federalism," *Cato Journal* 14, no. 1 (spring/summer 1994): 75–85.

30. William H. Riker, *Federalism: Origin, Operation, Significance* (Boston: Little Brown, 1964), 11.

31. James M. Buchanan and his coauthors have emphasized this theme. See, for example, Geoffrey Brennan and James M. Buchanan, *The Power to Tax* (Cambridge: Cambridge University Press, 1980), and James M. Buchanan and Richard E. Wagner, *Democracy in Deficit: The Political Legacy of Lord Keynes* (New York: Academic, 1977).

32. Pilon, "Freedom, Responsibility, and the Constitution," 507–47 and esp. 533–38.

33. Beard, *Economic Interpretation.*

34. Needless to say, after the passage of the 17th Amendment in 1913, which provided for the direct election of senators, senators were not accountable at all to the state legislatures.

35. This argument appears in Holcombe, "Contractarian Model," 260–74.

36. The changing concept of the general welfare is discussed in Richard E. Wagner, *To Promote the General Welfare: Market Processes vs. Political Transfers* (San Francisco: Pacific Research Institute, 1989).

37. One measure of government growth is growth in government expenditures, but as Robert Higgs notes in "Eighteen Problematic Propositions in the Analysis of the Growth of Government," *Review of Austrian Economics* 5, no. 1 (1991): 3–40, government growth encompasses much more than just expenditure growth and extends to regulatory growth and other government activities that limit individual liberty. See also William F. Shughart and Robert D. Tollison, "On the Growth of Government and the Political Economy of Legislation," *Research in Law and Economics* 9 (1986): 111–27, who show the correlation between government spending and government's legislative activity.

38. At the time the Constitution was adopted, the key issue was the additional powers that it gave to the federal government, not the constraints it placed on the states. See, for a discussion, Pole, *The American Constitution,* and John F. Manley and Kenneth M. Dolbeare, *The Case against the Constitution* (Armonk, NY: M. E. Sharpe, 1987).

39. Jensen, *Articles of Confederation,* argues that the primary benefit of the Constitution over the Articles of Confederation is that the Constitution more closely constrains the powers of the states.

40. The concept of intergovernmental competition as a constraint on government that pushes governments to satisfy citizen demands is found in Charles M. Tiebout, "A Pure Theory of Local Expenditures," *Journal of Political Economy* 64 (1956): 416–24.

Chapter 5

1. See Kenneth C. Martis, *The Historical Atlas of United States Congressional Districts: 1789–1983* (New York: Free Press, 1982), 2. This volume is the standard reference on the history of congressional districts, and material in this section comes from Martis unless otherwise referenced.

2. See Gordon Tullock, "The Transitional Gains Trap," *Bell Journal of Economics* 6 (autumn 1975): 671–78, for a discussion of some of the implications of government-produced monopoly profits for businesses. Gregg A. Jarrell, "The Demand for State Regulation of the Electric Utility Industry," *Journal of Law and Economics* 21, no. 3 (October 1978): 269–95, discusses the combining of competing local electric utility companies into government-regulated monopolies.

3. The idea that congressional districting creates a cartel among representatives is discussed by W. Mark Crain, "On the Structure and Stability of Political Markets," *Journal of Political Economy* 85, no. 4 (August 1977): 829–42.

4. See Tullock, "Entry Barriers in Politics," 458–66, and W. Mark Crain, Randall Holcombe, and Robert D. Tollison, "Monopoly Aspects of Political Parties," *Atlantic Economic Journal* 7, no. 2 (July 1979): 54–58, for a further discussion of political organization as a cartel.

5. Legislation is listed in table 5, p. 7, of Martis, *Historical Atlas.* Information in this section comes from this volume unless otherwise noted.

6. This idea is explained in detail in Buchanan and Tullock, *Calculus of Consent,* chap. 6.

7. Buchanan and Tullock, *Calculus of Consent,* chap. 16, discuss bicameralism in this context.

8. For example, in 1972, 1976, and 1988 electors cast votes for candidates other than those chosen by the voters of their states.

9. Forrest McDonald, *The American Presidency* (Lawrence: University Press of Kansas, 1994), 177–78, discusses this aspect of the Constitution.

10. Data on the methods of selecting electors are from *Historical Statistics of the United States from Colonial Times to 1970* (Washington, DC: Bureau of the Census, 1975), 1071.

11. See McDonald, *American Presidency,* 5, 143, and chap. 9.

12. See Richard P. McCormick, *The Second American Party System: Party Formation in the Jacksonian Era* (Chapel Hill: University of North Carolina Press, 1966), who discusses why parties after Jackson's presidency were different from those prior to it.

13. McDonald, *American Presidency,* 230, refers to Hamilton as "prime minis-

ter" (quotations in the original) and discusses Hamilton's role in the Washington administration at greater length in 225–43.

14. Quoted from Arthur M. Schlesinger Jr., *The Age of Jackson* (Boston: Little, Brown, 1945), 10. Schlesinger says, "The rock on which Alexander Hamilton built his church was the deep-seated conviction that society would be governed best by an aristocracy, and that an aristocracy was based most properly and enduringly on property" (12).

15. Schlesinger, *Age of Jackson,* 11.

16. Schlesinger, *Age of Jackson,* 19.

17. This is the evaluation of Ralph Ketcham, *Presidents above Party: The First American Presidency, 1789–1829* (Chapel Hill: University of North Carolina Press, 1984), 124.

18. Robert V. Remini, *The Legacy of Andrew Jackson* (Baton Rouge: Louisiana State University Press, 1988), 14.

19. Quoted from Ketcham, *Presidents above Party,* 141.

20. See Richard L. McCormick, *The Party Period and Public Policy: American Politics from the Age of Jackson to the Progressive Era* (New York: Oxford University Press, 1986), and McCormick, *Second American Party System.*

21. George H. W. Bush was the 41st president and is the father of George W. Bush, the 43rd president.

22. The classic exposition of the median voter model is found in Downs, *Economic Theory of Democracy.* The idea is older than this and was clearly if simply developed in Harold Hotelling, "Stability in Competition," *Economic Journal* 39 (March 1929): 41–57.

23. The possibility that no stable outcome might exist was explored in a well-known volume by Kenneth J. Arrow, *Social Choice and Individual Values* (New Haven: Yale University Press, 1951). Duncan Black, *The Theory of Committees and Elections* (Cambridge: Cambridge University Press, 1958), studied the electoral process in some detail, as did Downs, *Economic Theory of Democracy.* By the early 1970s academics took the model's conclusions seriously enough that a number of empirical studies in academic journals started with the assumption that the public sector reflected the median voter's preferences. See, for example, Robin Barlow, "Efficiency Aspects of Local School Finance," *Journal of Political Economy* 78 (September–October 1970): 1028–40; Thomas E. Borcherding and Robert T. Deacon, "The Demand for Services of Non-Federal Governments," *American Economic Review* 62 (December 1972): 891–901; and Theodore C. Bergstrom and Robert Goodman, "Private Demand for Public Goods," *American Economic Review* 63 (June 1973): 280–96.

24. Theoretical demonstrations can be found in R. D. McKelvey, "Intransitivities in Multi Dimensional Voting Models and Some Implications for Agenda Control," *Journal of Economic Theory* 12, no. 2 (June 1976): 472–82, and by the same author, "General Conditions for Global Intransitivities in Formal Voting Models," *Econometrica* 47, no. 5 (September 1979): 1085–1112. A more accessible model of instability in multidimensional political models appears in chap. 4 of Holcombe, *Economic Analysis.* See William H. Riker, "Implications from the Dis-

equilibrium of Majority Rule for the Study of Institutions," *American Political Science Review* 74, no. 2 (June 1980): 432–46, for a discussion by an eminent political scientist regarding the implications of models of political instability.

25. Gordon Tullock, "Why So Much Stability?" *Public Choice* 37, no. 2 (1982): 189–202, discusses some of the issues. For a further discussion of the applicability of the median voter model and the way it has been used in theory, see Randall G. Holcombe, "The Median Voter Model in Public Choice Theory," *Public Choice* 61, no. 2 (1989): 115–25.

26. With regard to the U.S. Congress, see a series of papers by Keith T. Poole and Howard Rosenthal, "A Spatial Model for Legislative Roll-Call Analysis," *American Journal of Political Science* 29, no. 2 (May 1985): 357–84; "Analysis of Congressional Coalition Patterns: A Unidimensional Spatial Model," *Legislative Studies Quarterly* 12, no. 1 (February 1987): 55–75; and "Patterns of Congressional Voting," *American Journal of Political Science* 35, no. 1 (February 1991): 228–78. Randall G. Holcombe and Russell S. Sobel, "The Stability of International Coalitions in United Nations Voting from 1946 to 1973," *Public Choice* 86, no. 1 (1996): 17–34, reports similar findings for voting in the United Nations.

27. James M. Buchanan, "Social Choice, Democracy, and Free Markets," *Journal of Political Economy* 62 (1954): 114–23, offers an insightful essay on this subject. Buchanan and Tullock, *Calculus of Consent,* discuss the issue more thoroughly. For more formal models of the political exchange process, see Kenneth J. Koford, "Centralized Vote Trading," *Public Choice* 39, no. 2 (1982): 245–68; Weingast, Shepsle, and Johnsen, "Political Economy," *Journal of Political Economy* 89, no. 4 (August 1981): 642–64; and Holcombe, *Economic Analysis.*

28. Nations such as Germany that support many political parties do so because of a fundamental difference in their electoral systems. Rather than having elections in which only one candidate wins, representatives are elected to the legislature in proportion to the votes their parties receive. This proportional representation tends to produce many political parties. This example shows the importance of political institutions in the production of political outcomes. Had the electoral college system worked as the founders originally envisioned, with many candidates receiving votes from their states and with most presidents being chosen by the House, more than two parties would be viable in the United States.

29. Schlesinger, *Age of Jackson,* 74–114, discusses Jackson's battle with those who supported the Second Bank in detail. Robert V. Remini, *The Life of Andrew Jackson* (New York: Harper & Row, 1988), 143, notes that Jackson, along with many others, viewed that corruption within the Second Bank was responsible for initiating the Panic of 1819 and the resulting economic collapse.

30. Jackson's advice often came from a group of "counsellors" who were paid well by the federal government but were not officially appointed to cabinet positions, thus giving rise to the term "Kitchen Cabinet." See Marquis James, *Andrew Jackson: Portrait of a President* (New York: Grosset & Dunlap, 1937), 191.

31. Schlesinger, *Age of Jackson,* 314–17, notes the influence of Adam Smith's *The Wealth of Nations* on the Jacksonian philosophy.

32. Schlesinger, *Age of Jackson,* 337.

33. Remini, *Legacy of Andrew Jackson*, 11.

34. Remini, *Life of Andrew Jackson*, 159.

35. Donald B. Cole, *The Presidency of Andrew Jackson* (Lawrence: University Press of Kansas, 1993), 63–65.

36. Schlesinger, *Age of Jackson*, 329–31.

37. See William Graham Sumner, *Andrew Jackson* (Boston: Houghton, Mifflin and Co., 1899), 218–19, and Remini, *Life of Andrew Jackson*, 305–6.

38. Remini, *Life of Andrew Jackson*, 295.

39. Sumner, *Andrew Jackson*, 229–36.

40. Sumner, *Andrew Jackson*, 246–64, discusses the nullification issue in detail. Some southern states wanted to establish their power to nullify federal laws, to which Jackson strenuously objected.

41. Remini, *Life of Andrew Jackson*, 244–51.

42. John T. Morse Jr., viii, in the introduction to Sumner, *Andrew Jackson*.

43. See Ketcham, *Presidents above Party*, 151–52, for a discussion. Also, Remini, *Life of Andrew Jackson*, 185–86, explains Jackson's point of view.

44. Sumner, *Andrew Jackson*, 188–92, discusses Jackson's use of the spoils system, noting that while it had previously been employed at the state level Jackson deserves the credit for bringing it to the federal level. Matthew A. Crenson, *The Federal Machine: Beginnings of Bureaucracy in Jacksonian America* (Baltimore: Johns Hopkins University Press, 1975), notes that, despite the spoils system that was introduced in the Jackson administration, the government became more bureaucratized and formalized during this time.

45. Sumner, *Andrew Jackson*, 243–46.

46. See Cole, *Presidency of Andrew Jackson*, 106–8.

47. Remini, *Life of Andrew Jackson*, 185.

48. Schlesinger, *Age of Jackson*, 47.

49. Even this is somewhat an overstatement. Zachary Taylor, who succeeded Polk, died in office, elevating Millard Filmore to the presidency, so they split a term. The next two presidents, Franklin Pierce and James Buchanan, were so unsuccessful that they were unable to be renominated by their parties to run for another term.

50. James, *Andrew Jackson*, 191.

51. Clyde Kelly, *United States Postal Policy* (New York: D. Appleton and Co., 1932), 63.

52. Kelly, *United States Postal Policy*, 67.

53. Kelly, *United States Postal Policy*, 70.

54. Le Roy R. Hafen, *The Overland Mail, 1849–1869: Promoter of Settlement, Precursor of Railroads* (Cleveland: Arthur H. Clark Co., 1926), 129–41.

55. Remini, *Legacy of Andrew Jackson*, 26.

56. Remini, *Legacy of Andrew Jackson*, 32–33.

Chapter 6

1. Hummel, *Emancipating Slaves*, 81–83.

2. Hummel, *Emancipating Slaves*, 52–56, discusses this.

3. McDonald, *Novus Ordo Seclorum,* 281, argues that Article IV, Section 3, of the Constitution prevents secession, but this interpretation is doubtful. That section consists of two paragraphs. The first reads, "New States may be admitted by the Congress into this Union; but no new State shall be formed or erected within the Jurisdiction of any other State; nor any State be formed by the Junction of two or more States, or Parts of States, without the Consent of the Legislatures of the States concerned as well as of the Congress." This paragraph deals with the formation of new states, so is not relevant to secession. The second paragraph reads, "The Congress shall have Power to dispose of and make all needful Rules and Regulations respecting the Territory or other Property belonging to the United States; and nothing in this Constitution shall be so construed as to Prejudice any Claims of the United States, or of any particular State." At best, this paragraph might apply to federally owned land within a state's boundaries but does not give the federal government any power over states and, indeed, in the last sentence places the claims of the federal and state governments on equal footing. Just because the federal government might own some property in a state does not affect the rights of the state governments, including their right to secede from the Union.

4. Jesse T. Carpenter, *The South as a Conscious Minority: 1789–1861* (New York: New York University Press, 1930), chap. 6, argues that slavery was a peripheral issue behind secession and cites numerous sources from the 1850s and 1860s to support his point.

5. Quoted in Charles Robert Lee Jr., *The Confederate Constitutions* (Chapel Hill: University of North Carolina Press, 1963), 203.

6. Quoted in Hummel, *Emancipating Slaves,* 207–8.

7. Quoted in Hummel, *Emancipating Slaves,* 210.

8. Hummel, *Emancipating Slaves,* 212–14.

9. Tocqueville, *Democracy in America,* 367.

10. See David Donald, *The Politics of Reconstruction: 1863–1867* (Baton Rouge: Louisiana State University Press, 1965), 18–19.

11. See John W. Burgess, *Reconstruction and the Constitution: 1866–1876* (New York: Charles Scribner's Sons, 1902), 9, for this argument.

12. Burgess, *Reconstruction and the Constitution,* 249.

13. At the same time whites regained the right to vote, blacks effectively lost it, because of organizations like the Ku Klux Klan and less organized efforts to disenfranchise them.

14. Hummel, *Emancipating Slaves,* 298.

15. Horace Edgar Flack, *The Adoption of the Fourteenth Amendment* (Glouchester, MA: Peter Smith, 1965), 14.

16. It is interesting to note that "United States" is used in the plural in this amendment.

17. Gretchen Ritter, *Goldbugs and Greenbacks: The Antimonopoly Tradition and the Politics of Finance in America* (Cambridge: Cambridge University Press, 1997).

18. Burgess, *Reconstruction and the Constitution,* 255.

19. Quoted from Flack, *Adoption of the Fourteenth Amendment,* 140.

20. Flack, *Adoption of the Fourteenth Amendment,* chap. 4, discusses the state ratification debates over the amendment.

21. Berger, *Government by Judiciary,* 3.

22. Michael R. Baye and Dennis W. Jansen, *Money, Banking, and Financial Markets* (Boston: Houghton Mifflin, 1995), 411.

23. This idea was developed in, and the next several sections are based on, Randall G. Holcombe, "The Distributive Model of Government: Evidence from the Confederate Constitution," *Southern Economic Journal* 58, no. 3 (January 1992): 762–69.

24. Lee, *Confederate Constitutions,* gives a complete history of the Confederate Constitution. Lee also reprints the Confederate Constitution and the U.S. Constitution side by side to facilitate a comparison.

25. Richard Barksdale Harwell, *The Confederate Constitution* (Athens: University of Georgia Libraries, 1979), gives a brief overview of the convention. A complete listing and brief biography of all 50 delegates are given in Lee, *Confederate Constitutions,* chap. 2. Of the 50 delegates to the convention, 23 had served in either the U.S. House or Senate and 42 were lawyers or "lawyer-planters" by occupation. One was a college professor. By political party affiliation, there were 31 Democrats and 17 Whigs.

26. By the end of 1861, 13 states had ratified the Constitution and had become a part of the Confederacy.

27. Wagner, *To Promote the General Welfare,* discusses this open door versus a constitutional view of government.

28. Lee, *Confederate Constitutions,* 93–94, discusses the debate on the tariff issue that occurred during the convention.

29. Jonathan R. T. Hughes, *The Governmental Habit* (New York: Basic Books, 1977), argues that special interests have always been ready and able to call on the government for favors.

30. This is reported by Russell Hoover Quynn, *The Constitutions of Abraham Lincoln and Jefferson Davis* (New York: Exposition, 1959), 297–99.

31. Hummel, *Emancipating Slaves,* chap. 9.

32. Hummel, *Emancipating Slaves,* 230.

Chapter 7

1. In 1865 per capita federal expenditures peaked at $306.55 because of the War between the States and did not surpass that peak until 1918, during World War I.

2. Federal expenditures as a percentage of GNP were calculated from GNP and government expenditure data from *Historical Statistics of the United States from Colonial Times to 1970.*

3. Higgs, *Crisis and Leviathan.*

4. Economists are reluctant to analyze any consumption changes as a result of changes in attitudes or preferences but would rather find an explanation for those underlying causes, such as changes in prices, incomes, or other constraints to behavior. See, for example, George J. Stigler and Gary S. Becker, "De Gustibus Non Est Disputandum," *American Economic Review* 67, no. 2 (March 1977): 76–90.

5. These themes are explored in Randall G. Holcombe, "Veterans Interests and the Transition to Government Growth: 1870–1915," *Public Choice* 99, nos. 3–4 (June 1999): 311–26.

6. Starr, *Social Transformation of American Medicine.*

7. Buchanan and Wagner, *Democracy in Deficit,* note that prior to the 1960s the federal government operated under an implied balanced budget constraint, except during wars and other emergencies.

8. Because public expenditures are bestowed on recipients at no cost, there is in a sense always an excess demand for them. However, there are also demands to limit public expenditures, and Congress weighs demands on both sides, as argued by Gary S. Becker, "A Theory of Competition among Pressure Groups for Political Influence," *Quarterly Journal of Economics* 98 (August 1983): 371–400. Becker's model suggests that the demands for limited government during the 1880s limited expenditures sufficiently for the federal government to run a surplus.

9. The U.S. population was 36 million in 1865, right after the war, and had increased to 50 million by 1880, so while the aggregate federal debt had not been reduced, the per capita debt had, because of population growth. Continued population growth provided a mechanism for reducing the per capita debt without paying it off, if the political climate demanded it.

10. Theda Skocpol, *Protecting Soldiers and Mothers: The Political Origins of Social Policy in the United States* (Cambridge, MA: Belknap, 1992), argues that veterans pensions served the same purpose as the social insurance pensions that had begun in the late nineteenth century in Europe, and the widespread availability of veterans pensions reduced the demand for more widespread social insurance in the United States. See also Ben Baack and Edward John Ray, "Federal Transfer Payments in America: Veterans' Pensions and the Rise of Social Security," *Economic Inquiry* 26, no. 4 (October 1988): 687–702.

11. Richard Severo and Lewis Milford, *The Wages of War: When America's Soldiers Came Home—From Valley Forge to Vietnam* (New York: Simon and Schuster, 1989), 153.

12. Severo and Milford, *Wages of War,* 156.

13. William Henry Glasson, *History of Military Pension Legislation in the United States* (New York: Columbia University Press, 1900), 70–79, provides a chronology of pension benefits due veterans from the War between the States. The first laws providing benefits to these veterans were passed in 1861, and later legislation extended and enhanced the benefits approved in earlier legislation.

14. Glasson, *History of Military Pension Legislation,* 82.

15. Glasson, *History of Military Pension Legislation,* 88.

16. Severo and Milford, *Wages of War,* 158.

17. Glasson, *History of Military Pension Legislation,* 128.

18. Glasson, *History of Military Pension Legislation,* 84–85.

19. Glasson, *History of Military Pension Legislation,* 96.

20. Skocpol, *Protecting Soldiers and Mothers,* 118.

21. Skocpol, *Protecting Soldiers and Mothers,* 116.

22. Severo and Milford, *Wages of War,* 174–75.

23. Because of migration, there were some beneficiaries in all states, but in states like Indiana and Ohio between 25 and 30 percent of the population age 65 and above received veterans pensions, whereas in the Carolinas, Georgia, and Alabama the percentage was below 5 percent, according to Skocpol, *Protecting Soldiers and Mothers,* 133. All Southern states did have their own pension systems for Confederate veterans, but they were considerably less generous than the federal pensions that went to Union vets (139).

24. Severo and Milford, *Wages of War,* 178.

25. Glasson, *History of Military Pension Legislation,* 114–16.

26. Glasson, *History of Military Pension Legislation,* 117.

27. Quoted from Severo and Milford, *Wages of War,* 180–81.

28. Severo and Milford, *Wages of War,* 180.

29. Even Wilson's election as a Democrat must be qualified by a footnote. He defeated incumbent William Howard Taft only because former Republican president Teddy Roosevelt was dissatisfied enough with Taft's performance to run against him as an independent, splitting the Republican vote, which allowed Wilson the victory.

30. See, for example, Hughes, *Governmental Habit,* and Holcombe, "Distributive Model of Government," 762–69.

31. Even at the turn of the century local governments spent far more than the federal government. As John Joseph Wallis notes in "The Birth of the Old Federalism: Financing the New Deal, 1932–1940," *Journal of Economic History* 44, no. 1 (March 1984): 139–59, local governments remained the biggest spenders until the 1930s, when the federal government replaced local governments as the top spender. Local governments saw their major growth after the War between the States, however. The nation was mainly rural in the mid-1800s but rapidly grew in the latter half of that century, and the growth led to rapidly expanding city government expenditures. See John B. Legler, Richard Sylla, and John J. Wallis, "U.S. City Finances and the Growth of Government," *Journal of Economic History* 48, no. 2 (June 1988): 347–56, for a discussion.

32. Anderson and Hill, *Birth of a Transfer Society.*

33. Stephen Skowronek, *Building a New American State: The Expansion of National Administrative Capabilities, 1877–1920* (New York: Cambridge University Press, 1982), 125–27.

34. Lee Benson, *Merchants, Farmers, and Railroads: Railroad Regulation and New York Politics, 1850–1877* (Cambridge: Harvard University Press, 1955), 212.

35. Gabriel Kolko, *Railroads and Regulation, 1877–1916* (New York: Norton, 1965).

36. The idea was popularized in the economics literature by George J. Stigler, "The Theory of Economic Regulation," *Bell Journal of Economics and Management Science* 2 (spring 1971): 3–21. Keith T. Poole and Howard Rosenthal, "The Enduring Nineteenth-Century Battle for Economic Regulation: The Interstate Commerce Act Revisited," *Journal of Law and Economics* 36, no. 2 (October 1993): 837–60, argue that those favoring regulation for their short-term gain came to see it in their long-run interest, making it a part of the ideological shift that was occurring during this time.

37. Skowronek, *Building a New American State,* 147–48.

38. Higgs, *Crisis and Leviathan,* 111.

39. This idea is developed in Richard A. Posner, "Taxation by Regulation," *Bell Journal of Economics and Management Science* 2 (spring 1971): 22–50.

40. The American Social Science Association (ASSA) was formed in 1865, for example. See Skowronek, *Building a New American State,* 43, for a discussion of the growth of scientific management principles.

41. Skowronek, *Building a New American State,* 57.

42. Skowronek, *Building a New American State,* 61.

43. Skowronek, *Building a New American State,* 64–68.

44. Skowronek, *Building a New American State,* 50.

45. Skowronek, *Building a New American State,* 179–84.

46. Skowronek, *Building a New American State,* 192–94.

47. Skowronek, *Building a New American State,* chap. 4, discusses military reform.

48. See Ben Baack and Edward Ray, "The Political Economy of the Origins of the Military-Industrial Complex in the United States," *Journal of Economic History* 45, no. 2 (June 1985): 369–75. See also their "Special Interests and the Nineteenth-Century Roots of the Military-Industrial Complex," *Research in Economic History* 11 (1988): 153–69, which shows that the military buildup in the late nineteenth century was centered on naval shipbuilding.

49. Hafen, *Overland Mail,* 129–41.

50. Gerald Cullinan, *The Post Office Department* (New York: Praeger, 1968), 79.

51. Kelly, *United States Postal Policy,* 65.

52. Quoted by Higgs, *Crisis and Leviathan,* 84.

53. Tocqueville, *Democracy in America,* 57.

54. See, for example, Polanyi, *Great Transformation;* Higgs, *Crisis and Leviathan;* and Paul Johnson, *Modern Times: The World from the Twenties to the Nineties,* rev. ed. (New York: HarperCollins, 1991). Skowronek, *Building a New American State,* 16, notes, "Scholars have long recognized political reform around the turn of the century as a watershed in the development of American government. They have differed largely on interpretations of the nature of this break with the past." Considering the break as an endogenous change naturally focuses attention on the decades preceding the turn of the century.

55. The income tax was originally passed as a temporary measure, but many temporary government measures become permanent. Higgs, *Crisis and Leviathan,* notes the large number of emergency wartime measures initiated during World War I that remained permanent features of government.

Chapter 8

1. Pilon, "Freedom, Responsibility, and the Constitution," 520, notes, "by the Progressive Era, toward century's end, we had come to think of government not as a necessary evil, to be guarded against at every turn, but as a positive good— indeed, as an instrument of good, an instrument for doing good."

2. See Robert C. McMath Jr., *American Populism: A Social History, 1877–1898* (New York: Hill and Wang, 1993), 3–8, for more detail.

3. John D. Hicks, *The Populist Revolt: A History of the Farmers' Alliance and the People's Party* (Minneapolis: University of Minnesota Press, 1931), 57–61, discusses the causes behind falling farm prices.

4. See Eric H. Monkkonen, *The Local State: Public Money and American Cities* (Stanford, CA: Stanford University Press, 1995), for a discussion of city finance of railroads in the late 1800s.

5. See Peter H. Argersinger, *Populism and Politics: William Alfred Peffer and the People's Party* (Lexington: University Press of Kentucky, 1974), 6–7.

6. Quoted from Hicks, *Populist Revolt,* 79.

7. Hicks, *Populist Revolt,* chap. 4.

8. Hicks, *Populist Revolt,* chap. 8, describes the emergence of the party and in chap. 9 describes the election of 1892. William A. Peffer, *Populism, Its Rise and Fall* (Lawrence: University Press of Kansas, 1992), is a reprint, with some new material, of a Populist U.S. senator's account of the movement originally published in 1899 as a series of articles in the *Chicago Tribune.*

9. Peter H. Argersinger, *The Limits of Agrarian Radicalism: Western Populism and American Politics* (Lawrence: University Press of Kansas, 1995), 9–10, discusses this election. See also chap. 10, where Argersinger discusses the evolution of political institutions in Congress that reduced the ability of legislators from minority parties to have much influence.

10. For a detailed discussion, see David B. Griffiths, *Populism in the Western United States: 1890–1900* (Lewiston, NY: Edwin Mellen Press, 1992).

11. Under fractional reserve banking, the quantity of money in circulation will be greater than the amount of gold backing it, but for present purposes this is an unimportant detail, because the amount of gold available to redeem bank notes and demand deposits still places a limit on monetary expansion.

12. Ritter, *Goldbugs and Greenbacks.*

13. See John G. Matsusaka, "Fiscal Effects of the Voter Initiative: Evidence from the Last 30 Years," *Journal of Political Economy* 103, no. 3 (June 1995): 587–623, for a discussion of the lasting effects of the initiatives. Matsusaka discusses the adoption of initiatives in the states on 591–93.

14. Some details, along with an explanation of state voting records for the amendment, are found in Lawrence Kenny and Mark Rush, "Self-Interest and the Senate Vote on Direct Elections," *Economics and Politics* 2, no. 3 (November 1990): 291–302.

15. Alfred D. Chandler Jr., "The Origins of Progressive Leadership," in *Progressivism: The Critical Issues,* ed. David M. Kennedy (Boston: Little, Brown, 1971), 74–78.

16. Herbert Croly, *The Promise of American Life* (New York: Macmillan, 1909), 152–53.

17. The role of democracy in the Progressive movement is discussed by William Allen White, *The Old Order Changeth: A View of American Democracy* (New York: Macmillan, 1910).

18. Benjamin Parke De Witt, *The Progressive Movement: A Non-Partisan, Comprehensive Discussion of Current Tendencies in American Politics* (New York: Macmillan, 1915), lists the three major items of the Progressive agenda as control of corporations, control of government, and relief for those in need, and he devotes a chapter to each of these topics.

19. Croly, *Promise of American Life.*

20. Arthur A. Ekirch Jr., *Progressivism in America: A Study of the Era from Theodore Roosevelt to Woodrow Wilson* (New York: New Viewpoints, 1974), chap. 5, characterizes Progressivism as a crusade for social justice, giving Progressivism something in common with the ultimate goals of the early Republican party.

21. J. Leonard Bates, *The United States, 1898–1928: Progressivism and a Society in Transition* (New York: McGraw-Hill, 1976), chap. 3, argues that Progressivism was a diverse movement harboring individuals and ideas that were sometimes in conflict.

22. John M. Blum, *The Progressive Presidents—Roosevelt, Wilson, Roosevelt, Johnson* (New York: Norton, 1980).

23. Horwitz, *Transformation of American Law.*

24. Higgs, *Crisis and Leviathan,* 84.

25. Henry Jones Ford, *The Cleveland Era* (New Haven: Yale University Press, 1919), 123.

26. Richard Hofstadter, *The Age of Reform: From Bryan to F.D.R.* (New York: Alfred A. Knopf, 1969), 135, suggests that this is one of the underlying forces that built Progressivism. See also chap. 4, where Hofstadter discusses divisions between old and new wealth and suggests why old wealth tended to throw their support behind Progressivism.

27. Hofstadter, *Age of Reform,* 187.

28. Starr, *Social Transformation of American Medicine.*

29. Anderson and Hill, *Birth of a Transfer Society.*

30. Benjamin J. Klebaner, "Potential Competition and the American Antitrust Legislation of 1914," *Business History Review* 38 (1964): 163–85.

31. See George E. Mowry, *The Era of Theodore Roosevelt: 1900–1912* (Harper & Brothers, 1958), chap. 7, for an outline of Roosevelt's "Square Deal."

32. Arthur M. Johnson, "Theodore Roosevelt and the Bureau of Corporations," *Mississippi Valley Historical Review* 45 (1959): 571–90.

33. Lewis L. Gould, *Reform and Regulation: American Politics from Roosevelt to Wilson,* 2d ed. (New York: Alfred A. Knopf, 1986), chap. 4, discusses the increased intensity of business regulation under Roosevelt, especially in his second term, when, Gould surmises, Roosevelt viewed his election as a mandate to continue the Progressive policies of his first administration.

34. See Hofstadter, *Age of Reform,* chap. 6, and Croly, *Promise of American Life,* chap. 7.

35. Crenson, *Federal Machine,* argues that despite the introduction of the spoils system by Jackson the federal government became more bureaucratized and more formalized during Jackson's administration.

36. See Skowronek, *Building a New American State,* 65–67.

37. Harold Howland, *Theodore Roosevelt and His Times: A Chronicle of the Progressive Movement* (New Haven: Yale University Press, 1921), esp. chap. 3.

38. This story is told well by Guy Alchon, *The Invisible Hand of Planning: Capitalism, Social Science, and the State in the 1920s* (Princeton: Princeton University Press, 1985).

39. Higgs, *Crisis and Leviathan,* chap. 7, discusses the development of the federal bureaucracy during World War I.

40. This idea is formalized by William A. Niskanen, "The Peculiar Economics of Bureaucracy," *American Economic Review* 58 (May 1968): 293–305. His ideas are further developed in his book, *Bureaucracy and Representative Government,* which had a more substantial impact. Niskanen further refined the ideas of his book in "Bureaucrats and Politicians," *Journal of Law and Economics* 18 (December 1975): 617–43.

41. This idea that voters have little incentive to be informed appears in Downs, *Economic Theory of Democracy.* Mueller, *Public Choice II,* notes that voters are more likely to be killed in an automobile accident on their way to vote than to cast a vote that changes the outcome of an election.

42. This idea is a fundamental part of the contemporary economic analysis of political institutions. See, for example, Holcombe, *Economic Analysis,* and Weingast, Shepsle, and Johnsen, "Political Economy," 642–64. For the opposite point of view, see Wittman, *Myth of Democratic Failure* and "Why Democracies Produce Efficient Results," 1395–1424.

43. McConnell, *Private Power,* chap. 1

44. The activities of lobbyists are regulated, however, both by the federal government and by state governments. Cynics might suggest that the regulation is more for the benefit of the legislature than for the general public, however. See Margaret F. Brinig, Randall G. Holcombe, and Linda Schwartzstein, "The Regulation of Lobbyists," *Public Choice* 77, no. 2 (October 1993): 377–84.

45. Herbert Croly, *Progressive Democracy* (New York: Macmillan, 1915), esp. chap. 15.

46. For a discussion and examples, see Kenneth J. Koford, "Dimensions, Transactions Costs, and Coalitions in Legislative Voting," *Economics and Politics* 2, no. 1 (1990): 59–82; Keith T. Poole and Howard Rosenthal, "Analysis of Congressional Coalition Patterns," 55–75; by the same authors, "Spatial Model," 357–84; and also by the same authors, "Patterns of Congressional Voting," 228–78. The same appears to be true in international voting. See, for example, Randall G. Holcombe and Russell S. Sobel, "Stability of International Coalitions," 17–34, and J. D. Hagan, "Domestic Political Regime Changes and Third World Voting Realignments in the United Nations, 1946–84," *International Organization* 43, no. 3 (summer 1989): 505–41.

47. This idea that committees tend to be staffed by high-demand legislators is found in Niskanen, *Bureaucracy and Representative Government.*

48. Buchanan and Tullock, *Calculus of Consent,* provide a theoretical foundation for analyzing the effects of vote trading. The inefficiencies that result from this

type of vote trading are discussed by Holcombe, *Economic Analysis,* and by Weingast, Shepsle, and Johnsen, "Political Economy," 642–64.

49. Argersinger, *Limits of Agrarian Radicalism,* 215.

50. Ballard C. Campbell, *The Growth of American Government: Governance from the Cleveland Era to the Present* (Bloomington: Indiana University Press, 1995), 39–44, argues that a fundamental cause of twentieth-century government growth was the reaction to the changing nature of the economy and in chapter 3 reviews the debate between those who wanted to retain the Jeffersonian ideal of limited government and those who believed that changing times warranted a fundamental change in the nature of government.

51. See Baack and Ray, "Special Interests," 607–25, and Randall G. Holcombe and Donald J. Lacombe, "Interests versus Ideology in the Ratification of the 16th and 17th Amendments," *Economics and Politics* 10, no. 2 (July 1998): 143–59, for discussions of interest groups behind the income tax amendment.

Chapter 9

1. Thomas E. Borcherding, in *Budgets and Bureaucrats: The Sources of Government Growth* (Durham, NC: Duke University Press, 1977), 45–70, examines the growth of the federal government from 1870 to 1970 and concludes that it has grown about twice as rapidly as one might have expected based solely on changes in underlying economic variables. By the same methodology he would surely have found government growing less rapidly than expected during the nineteenth century.

2. This chapter is based on Randall G. Holcombe, "The Growth of the Federal Government in the 1920s," *Cato Journal* 16, no. 2 (fall 1996): 175–99.

3. Neil A. Wynn, *From Progressivism to Prosperity: World War I and American Society* (New York: Holmes and Meir, 1986), 217, remarks, "Even the view of the Harding administration as 'conservative' is an oversimplification, and one not now generally accepted by historians. The new president had adopted a fairly liberal and sympathetic attitude to groups who had been dealt with quite harshly by the previous administration." A more extreme view comes from Benjamin M. Anderson, *Economics and the Public Welfare* (Indianapolis: Liberty, 1979), 125–27, who calls 1924 the beginning of the New Deal. Anderson calls the 1924 introduction of the McNary-Haugen Bill designed to protect farmers from foreign competition the first piece of the New Deal legislation that continued through FDR's presidency. (The bill was not actually passed until 1927.) See also Higgs, *Crisis and Leviathan;* Johnson, *Modern Times;* and Douglass C. North, "The Growth of Government in the United States: An Economic Historian's Perspective," *Journal of Public Economics* 28, no. 3 (December 1985): 359–82, who all see changes around the turn of the century as pivotal events in the history of government growth, thus suggesting a lesser role for the New Deal.

4. Robert R. Keller, "Supply-Side Economic Policies during the Coolidge-Mellon Era," *Journal of Economic Issues* 16, no. 3 (September 1982): 773–90, argues the similarities in the policies of Coolidge and Reagan—a similarity on which Rea-

304 Notes to Pages 189–91

gan himself tried to draw. In contrast, Jacob Metzer, "How New Was the New Era? The Public Sector in the 1920s," *Journal of Economic History* 45, no. 1 (March 1985): 119–26, agrees with the thesis of this chapter, arguing that public policy in the 1920s was a continuation of the prewar expansion of the federal government. For a more general treatment of the history of the time as being a part of a transformation to government growth, see Polanyi, *Great Transformation.* Also see Charles A. Beard and William Beard, *The American Leviathan: The Republic in the Machine Age* (New York: Macmillan, 1930), who approvingly refer to American government as a Leviathan and even dedicate their book "to the thousands of men and women who loyally serve the public on land and sea under the auspices of the Government of the United States."

5. In response to the depression, Roosevelt started many new programs, of which Social Security is the largest survivor. But Roosevelt also abolished many of the programs he started in response to the economic crisis. The Civilian Conservation Corps, the Works Progress Administration, and the National Youth Administration were among the programs that were terminated by FDR.

6. Wallis, "Birth of the Old Federalism," 139–59, sees a major change in the 1930s as federal government replaced local government as the dominant spending unit. Metzer, "How New Was the New Era?" in agreement with the current study, argues that the underlying government growth was present in the 1920s. Other writers, such as Solomon Fabricant, *The Trend of Government Activity in the U.S. since 1900* (New York: National Bureau of Economic Research, 1952), and Richard Musgrave and J. J. Culbertson, "The Growth of Public Expenditures in the U.S. 1890–1948," *National Tax Journal* 6, no. 2 (June 1953): 97–115, have noted the rising trend of government expenditures prior to the New Deal. M. Slade Kendrick, *A Century and a Half of Federal Expenditures* (New York: National Bureau of Economic Research, 1955), anticipates the ratchets hypothesis of Peacock and Wiseman, *Growth of Public Expenditures,* by arguing that wars become bridgeheads for maintaining larger postwar expenditures.

7. The parallel is noted by Keller, "Supply-Side Economic Policies."

8. Robert K. Murray, *The Politics of Normalcy: Government Theory and Practice in the Harding-Coolidge Era* (New York: W. W. Norton & Co., 1973), 41, says, "Almost by default, the Republican senatorial leadership attempted to speak for the party before Harding's inauguration in 1921." Murray goes on to describe the move toward government programs favoring special interests.

9. Ellis W. Hawley, *The Great War and the Search for a Modern Order: A History of the American People and Their Institutions* (New York: St. Martin's, 1979), 60.

10. As Wynn, *From Progressivism to Prosperity,* 219, notes, many of the goals that the Progressives had early in the century had been accomplished by the 1920s, which would naturally lead the movement to lose some of its force.

11. One political issue in the 1920s that is often cited as an example of Coolidge's probusiness leanings was his attempt to sell a hydroelectric plant and nitrate plant in Muscle Shoals, Alabama, to Henry Ford. Coolidge was blocked by Congress as Jules Ables, *In the Time of Silent Cal* (New York: G. P. Putnam, 1969), 70–71,

describes, and the facility later became the beginning of the Tennessee Valley Authority.

12. This impression may be furthered by the Progressive elements in the Republican party that continued to oppose Coolidge. See, for example, John D. Hicks, *The Republican Ascendancy: 1921–1933* (New York: Harper & Brothers, 1960), chap. 4.

13. Harding's cabinet is viewed by some as the strongest in American history. Of the four most prominent members, three—Charles Evans Hughes, secretary of state; Henry C. Wallace, secretary of agriculture; and Herbert Hoover, secretary of commerce—were associated with Republican Progressivism. Andrew Mellon, secretary of treasury, was the only major cabinet officer without Progressive leanings. See Hawley, *Great War,* 58–59.

14. In 1929 real per capita federal expenditures in 1990 dollars were $195.41 and increased to $367.84 by 1933, an 82 percent increase. By 1937, an equal number of years into the Roosevelt administration, per capita federal expenditures were $545.23, only a 48 percent increase, and had gone up to $638.78 by 1940.

15. This ratchets hypothesis, originally put forward by Peacock and Wiseman in *Growth of Public Expenditures,* plays a significant role in discussions of government growth by Rassler and Thompson, "War Making and State Making," 491–507, and by Higgs, *Crisis and Leviathan.* While these ratchets undoubtedly exist, Randall G. Holcombe, "Are There Ratchets in the Growth of Federal Government Spending?" *Public Finance Quarterly* 21, no. 1 (January 1993): 33–47, casts some doubt on this hypothesis as an explanation of government growth.

16. Carroll H. Wooddy, *The Growth of the Federal Government: 1915–1932* (New York: McGraw-Hill, 1934).

17. One category, listed by Wooddy, *Growth of the Federal Government,* 545, under "general and financial administration" as a subset called "other" declined from $8,672,000 in 1920 to $601,000 in 1930. One must suspect that there are some significant war-related expenses in this "other" category.

18. The total for 1925 was only $65,000.

19. See Wooddy, *Growth of the Federal Government,* 300–91.

20. The Merchant Fleet Corporation was originally established under the name United States Shipping Board. Additional details on its operation are given in James M. Beck, *Our Wonderland of Bureaucracy* (New York: Macmillan, 1932).

21. Johnson, *Modern Times,* 17.

22. Wooddy, *Growth of the Federal Government,* 552.

23. Kelly, *United States Postal Policy,* 63–65.

24. Figures on postal expenditures are from Wooddy, *Growth of the Federal Government,* unless otherwise noted.

25. One effect of Burleson's tenure as postmaster general was to reduce morale among postal employees. See Cullinan, *Post Office Department,* 124–40, for a discussion of Burleson's tenure as well as those who succeeded him during the Harding administration.

26. Kelly, *United States Postal Policy,* 83.

27. The Coast Guard's own figures on the subject show that more than half its

budget during the 1920s, amounting to about $15 million a year, went toward enforcing Prohibition, as Laurence F. Schmeckebier notes in *The Bureau of Prohibition: Its History, Activities, and Organization* (Washington, DC: Brookings Institution, 1929), 14. The Department of Justice estimated that about one-third of its budget, or about $10 million, would be spent enforcing Prohibition in 1930 (308).

28. Donald J. Boudreaux and A. C. Pritchard, "The Price of Prohibition," *Arizona Law Review* 36, no. 1 (spring 1994): 1–10, persuasively argue that the tax system and tax revenues had much to do with both the establishment of Prohibition and its repeal. After the income tax was passed in 1913, excise tax revenues from alcohol sales were no longer very important to the federal government, making it less costly to establish Prohibition. After the onset of the depression, however, revenues became scarce, making Prohibition more costly and leading to its repeal.

29. This impression was accentuated by Andrew Mellon's relative prominence as secretary of treasury, a position he held through the Harding and Coolidge administrations. Ables, *In the Time of Silent Cal,* calls the Harding-Coolidge administrations the "rule of Mellon."

30. Hicks, *Republican Ascendancy,* chap. 9.

31. See Hicks, *Republican Ascendancy,* 196–218. For a discussion of Hoover's role in agricultural policy both during his and Coolidge's administrations, see David A. Horowitz, "The Perils of Western Farm Politics: Herbert Hoover, Gerald P. Nye, and Agricultural Reform," in *Herbert Hoover and the Republican Era,* ed. Carl E. Krog and William R. Tanner (Lantham, MD: University Press of America, 1984), 220–43.

32. Anderson, *Economics and the Public Welfare,* 125–27.

33. Shughart and Tollison, "On the Growth of Government," 111–27, show a tremendous increase in bills introduced into Congress (and a less dramatic increase in laws enacted) prior to the 1920s, giving another measure to the size of government.

34. These statistics are from Richard A. Posner, "A Statistical Study of Antitrust Enforcement," *Journal of Law and Economics* 13, no. 2 (October 1970): 376.

35. Thomas K. McCraw, *Prophets of Regulation* (Cambridge, MA: Belknap, 1984), 145.

36. McCraw, *Prophets of Regulation,* 146.

37. John Maynard Keynes, *The General Theory of Employment, Interest, and Money* (New York: Harcourt, Brace, and Co., 1936), 383.

38. Alchon, *Invisible Hand of Planning,* 59.

39. J. Ronnie Davis, *The New Economics and the Old Economists* (Ames: Iowa State University Press, 1971).

Chapter 10

1. Higgs, *Crisis and Leviathan,* documents the expansion of government power during World War I. W. Elliot Brownlee, *Federal Taxation in America: A Short History* (Cambridge: Cambridge University Press, 1996), supports Higgs's idea that government expands in response to crisis by arguing that major changes in tax

systems instituted to raise revenues for wars have persisted after the wars, shaping postwar taxation in important ways.

2. Higgs, *Crisis and Leviathan,* 168–69, describes the events and makes this argument.

3. Higgs, *Crisis and Leviathan,* 173.

4. Milton Friedman and Anna Jacobson Schwartz, *A Monetary History of the United States: 1867–1960* (Princeton: Princeton University Press, 1968), argue that the Fed could have, and should have, acted to prevent the depression.

5. Ludwig von Mises, *Theory of Money and Credit* (New Haven: Yale University Press, 1953), originally published in German in 1913, warned of the dangers of credit expansion leading to economic downturns, anticipating the events of 1929 and their aftermath. Murray N. Rothbard, *America's Great Depression* (Kansas City: Sheed and Ward, 1963), discusses these same ideas after the fact, showing how the line of reasoning developed by Mises suggested that the Fed's credit expansion in the 1920s would lead to an economic downturn.

6. See Anderson, *Economics and the Public Welfare,* 449–56, for a fuller discussion.

7. *Home Building and Loan Association v. Blaisdell et al.,* 290 U.S. 398 (1934).

8. *Nebbia v. New York,* 291 U.S. 502 (1934).

9. *Panama Refining Co. v. Ryan; Amazon Petroleum Corp. v. Ryan,* 293 U.S. 389 (1935).

10. *U.S. v. A.L.S. Schechter Poultry Corporation,* 295 U.S. 495 (1935).

11. See Robert H. Jackson, *The Struggle for Judicial Supremacy: A Study of a Crisis in American Power Politics* (New York: Alfred A. Knopf, 1941), 109–14, for a discussion.

12. *U.S. v. William M. Butler et al., Receivers of Hoosac Mills Corporation,* 297 U.S. 1 (1936).

13. Higgs, *Crisis and Leviathan,* 180.

14. Jackson, *Struggle for Judicial Supremacy,* 176–77.

15. Jackson, *Struggle for Judicial Supremacy,* 187–89. See also Henry J. Abraham, *Justices and Presidents: A Political History of Appointments to the Supreme Court,* 3d ed. (New York: Oxford University Press, 1992).

16. *Virginian Ry. v. Federation,* 300 U.S. 515 (1937).

17. *Wright v. Vinton Branch,* 300 U.S. 440 (1937).

18. Quoted in Jackson, *Struggle for Judicial Supremacy,* 209.

19. See Abraham, *Justices and Presidents,* 211.

20. William F. Swindler, *Court and Constitution in the Twentieth Century,* vol. 2 (Indianapolis: Bobbs-Merrill, 1970), 81.

21. The Court's change has been referred to as legal realism, which is oriented toward interpreting law more so that government can enable individuals to accomplish their ends rather than just looking at law as a set of prohibited actions. See Paul L. Murphy, *The Constitution in Crisis Times: 1918–1969* (New York: Harper & Row, 1972), 103–7.

22. *Retirement Board v. Alton R. Co.,* 295 U.S. 330, 374 (1935).

23. See C. Gordon Post, Frances P. DeLancy, and Fredryc R. Darby, eds, *Basic Constitutional Cases* (New York: Oxford University Press, 1948), 239–41.

24. *Carmichael v. Southern Coal Co.*, 301 U.S. (495); *Helvering v. Davis*, 301 U.S. 619 (1937); and *Steward Machine Co. v. Davis*, 301 U.S. 548 (1937).

25. For an excellent discussion of the politics behind the Court's rulings, see John Attarian, "The Roots of the Social Security Myth," in *Essays in Political Economy* (Auburn, AL: Ludwig von Mises Institute, 2001).

26. Jackson, *Struggle for Judicial Supremacy,* 232.

27. Gary M. Anderson and Robert D. Tollison, "Congressional Influence and Patterns of New Deal Spending, 1933–1939," *Journal of Law and Economics* 34, no. 1 (April 1991): 161–75.

28. Kenneth Finegold and Theda Skocpol, *State and Party in America's New Deal* (Madison: University of Wisconsin Press, 1995), argue, however, that the continuation of programs was partly determined by their results. Using two programs as examples, they argue that the Agriculture Adjustment Administration was run by competent people and thus survived and was successful, while the National Recovery Administration was run by interests rather than experts, causing its rapid demise.

29. Higgs, *Crisis and Leviathan,* 200–201.

30. Higgs, *Crisis and Leviathan,* 205–6.

31. Higgs, *Crisis and Leviathan,* 207–8.

32. Higgs, *Crisis and Leviathan,* 208.

33. Higgs, *Crisis and Leviathan,* 209–10.

34. See Randall G. Holcombe, *Public Finance: Government Revenues and Expenditures in the United States Economy* (Minneapolis/St. Paul: West, 1996), 299.

35. See Charlotte Twight, "Evolution of Federal Income Tax Withholding: The Machinery of Institutional Change," *Cato Journal* 14, no. 3 (winter 1995): 359–95, for a discussion of the implementation of withholding.

36. Randall G. Holcombe, *The Economic Foundations of Government* (New York: New York University Press, 1994), chap. 10, discusses ideology and how it can foster agreement with policies that a citizen opposes.

37. There was, however, a great deal of uncertainty when the system was enacted as well as the fear that, with so many additional taxpayers, there might be widespread noncompliance. See Carolyn C. Jones, "Mass-Based Income Taxation: Creating a Taxpaying Culture, 1940–1952," in *Funding the Modern American State, 1941–1995: The Rise and Fall of the Era of Easy Finance,* ed. W. Elliot Brownlee (Cambridge: Cambridge University Press, 1996), 107–47.

38. See, however, Robert Higgs, "Regime Uncertainty: Why the Great Depression Lasted So Long and Why Prosperity Resumed after the War," *Independent Review* 1, no. 4 (spring 1997): 561–90, for a persuasive argument that the depression lingered on because of constant policy initiatives during the depression that created uncertainty for potential investors.

39. Quoted from Campbell R. McConnell, *Economics: Principles, Problems, and Policies,* 3d ed. (New York: McGraw-Hill, 1966), 252–53.

40. What the textbooks have actually recommended regarding government policy has evolved considerably over the years, however. Up through the 1960s economists focused on government taxes and expenditures—fiscal policy—as the most important tool available to government. Since then there has been an evolution

toward the idea that monetary policy—the control of the money supply, interest rates, and financial markets—is more important.

Chapter 11

1. See, for example, Higgs, *Crisis and Leviathan,* and Rassler and Thompson, "War Making and State Making," 491–507.

2. For example, Randolph S. Bourne, *War and the Intellectuals* (New York: Harper & Row, 1964), calls war the health of the state.

3. *Statistical Abstract of the United States, 1961,* 39, reports 45 million families in the United States in 1960. The number of passenger cars is reported on p. 557.

4. *Statistical Abstract of the United States, 1961,* 516, reports the number households with television sets and on p. 514 reports the number of broadcast stations. Even with the spread of television, the number of broadcast radio stations also increased substantially during the 1950s, perhaps because of the increased radio audience in cars.

5. *Statistical Abstract of the United States, 1961,* 349. The electoral vote total was not as close, with Kennedy winning by 303 to 219.

6. Earnings are reported in the *Statistical Abstract of the United States, 1961,* 323, and are deflated by the consumer price index reported on p. 334.

7. See, for example, John Kenneth Galbraith, *The Affluent Society* (Boston: Houghton Mifflin, 1958) and *The New Industrial State* (Boston: Houghton Mifflin, 1967).

8. The ideas behind Kennedy's economic policies can be found in Paul Samuelson's *Economics: An Introductory Analysis,* which first appeared in 1948. The fifth edition was published in 1961, and it was by far the most popular economics textbook at that time.

9. Samuelson's *Economics* is a good textbook to examine for this purpose. By the late 1960s his book was being overtaken in popularity by another Keynesian-oriented introductory text, Campbell R. McConnell's *Economics,* first published in 1960, with new editions continuing through the 1990s.

10. James T. Patterson, *America's Struggle against Poverty: 1900–1085* (Cambridge: Harvard University Press, 1986), 127, notes, "Before 1963 Kennedy and his top advisors were concerned mainly about sustaining economic growth and relieving unemployment."

11. Philip Reed Rulon, *The Compassionate Samaritan: The Life of Lyndon Baines Johnson* (Chicago: Nelson-Hall, 1981), chap. 8, describes Johnson as "In the Shadow of the New Frontier."

12. Patterson, *America's Struggle against Poverty,* 134.

13. Patterson, *America's Struggle against Poverty,* 136–37.

14. In hindsight, the Great Society did not live up to its promises. See Vaughn Davis Bornet, *The Presidency of Lyndon Johnson* (Lawrence: University Press of Kansas, 1983), chap. 10, for a discussion. But the end results do not affect the political foundations on which it was built.

15. The text of the speech and some background on the term "Great Society" are found in Rulon, *Compassionate Samaritan,* chap. 10. Doris Kearns, *Lyndon John-*

son and the American Dream (New York: Harper & Row, 1976), 219, suggests that Johnson had in mind not just eclipsing Kennedy but creating programs that went well beyond the New Deal. Johnson, Kearns says, was confident that the programs, once established, would succeed.

16. Rulon, *Compassionate Samaritan,* chap. 11, details the extensive education initiatives pushed by Johnson during his presidency.

17. The politics behind the passage of these programs are discussed in Irving Bernstein, *Guns or Butter? The Presidency of Lyndon Johnson* (New York: Oxford University Press, 1996), chap. 6, and in Charlotte Twight, "Medicare's Origin: The Economics and Politics of Dependency," *Cato Journal* 16, no. 3 (winter 1997): 309–38.

18. The Supreme Court established the legality of segregation in *Plessy v. Ferguson,* 163 U.S. 537 (1896), by supporting the provision of "separate but equal" facilities for different races.

19. *Brown v. Board of Education of Topeka,* 347 U.S. 483 (1954).

20. Bernstein, *Guns or Butter?* chap. 3, discusses the Civil Rights Act of 1964 in detail.

21. Bernstein, *Guns or Butter?* chap. 8, discusses the politics behind the 1965 Voting Rights Act.

22. An acquaintance of mine who lived in rural Florida through the 1950s and 1960s tells me that, at the polls for primary elections, when whites entered they were given a Democratic ballot and when blacks entered they were given a Republican ballot. Because blacks were outnumbered and the state was controlled by the Democratic party, blacks were effectively disenfranchised.

23. See Jeffrey Hart, "Foundations and Social Activism: A Critical View," in *The Future of Foundations,* ed. Fritz F. Heimann (Englewood Cliffs, NJ: Prentice-Hall, 1973), for a discussion of Ford Foundation activities in the 1960s. The role of foundations in social policy is discussed in detail in Randall G. Holcombe, *Writing Off Ideas: The Effect of Tax Laws on America's Non-Profit Foundations* (New Brunswick, NJ: Transaction, 1999).

24. It might be that the increasing importance of the military during the cold war and the Vietnam War increased the perceived legitimacy of government, helping Johnson's agenda. Robert Higgs, "The Cold War Economy: Opportunity Cost, Ideology, and the Politics of Crisis," *Explorations in Economic History* 31 (1994): 283–312, suggests that the cold war was more important to government activity during the period than is commonly recognized.

25. See Campbell, *Growth of American Government,* 130–31, for a discussion of these developments.

26. This idea is developed in detail by Downs, *Economic Theory of Democracy.*

27. The process by which special interests gain undue influence is discussed in Holcombe, *Economic Analysis.*

Chapter 12

1. Johnson, *Modern Times,* 697, calls the 1980s "one of the watersheds of modern history."

2. According to Organization for Economic Cooperation and Development (OECD) figures, total government outlays in Britain composed 44.9 percent of the GDP in 1980 and 42.3 percent in 1990, and in the United States they composed 33.7 percent of the GDP in 1980 and 34.8 percent in 1990. Measured by expenditures alone, there was only a slight decrease in the size of government in Britain in the 1980s and a slight increase in the size of government in the United States.

3. Fukuyama, *End of History.*

4. Schumpeter, *Capitalism, Socialism, and Democracy.*

5. See Ackerman, *We The People 1,* for a discussion of the role of democracy in the evolution of American government. Ackerman describes how a government accountable to the people has become more democratic in its operation because of that accountability.

6. Keynes, *General Theory of Employment,* 383.

7. This point is insightfully discussed by Russell Hardin, "Democracy on the Margin," in *Understanding Democracy: Economic and Political Perspectives,* ed. Albert Breton, Gianluigi Galeotti, Pierre Salmon, and Ronald Wintrobe (Cambridge: Cambridge University Press, 1997), 249–66.

8. While he did not discover this problem of the cyclical majority, it was brought to the attention of academics studying collective decision making by Arrow, *Social Choice.*

9. This idea was explored in depth by Black, *Theory of Committees and Elections,* but McKelvey, "Intransitivities in Multi Dimensional Voting Models," 472–82, showed that the problem is, in theory, quite general and that in most cases raw preferences cannot be so ranked.

10. This idea of rational ignorance on the part of voters is emphasized by Downs, *Economic Theory of Democracy.* If one is really concerned about the quality of government, which of these ideas would make more sense: encouraging everybody, regardless of how informed they are, to exercise their right to vote, as is done now, or encouraging people not to vote if they are relatively uninformed, thus leaving the pool of voters smaller but more informed and better able to make a good decision? Now consider this: why would it be unpatriotic to ask those who are uninformed not to vote on election day?

11. This interest group view of government is described in more detail in Holcombe, *Economic Analysis.*

12. See Wittman, *Myth of Democratic Failure,* and "Why Democracies Produce Efficient Results," 1395–424, for an argument on the other side.

13. See Becker, "A Theory of Competition," 371–400, and Wittman, *Myth of Democratic Failure,* for analyses suggesting that the process is reasonably efficient for just these reasons.

14. Olson, *Rise and Decline of Nations.*

15. This idea is explained in Posner, "Taxation by Regulation," 22–50.

16. Thomas Robert Malthus, *An Essay on Population* (1798; reprint, New York: E. P. Dutton, 1914).

17. David S. Landes, *The Wealth and Poverty of Nations: Why Some Are So Rich and Some So Poor* (New York: W. W. Norton & Co., 1998).

18. Zakaria, "Rise of Illiberal Democracy," 42–43, states, "Democracy without

constitutional liberalism is not simply inadequate, but dangerous. . . . Eighty years ago Woodrow Wilson took America into the twentieth century with a challenge, to make the world safe for democracy. As we approach the next century, our task is to make democracy safe for the world."

19. *Tallahassee Democrat,* "Judge Dismisses Former Governor's Suit against Sugar Growers," November 19, 1996, 4C.

20. These regulations are discussed more extensively in Randall G. Holcombe, *Public Policy and the Quality of Life* (Westport, CT: Greenwood Press, 1995), chap. 5.

21. I think not, for reasons I discuss in *Public Policy and the Quality of Life.* For more evidence that land use planning has had little effect, see Bernard H. Siegan, *Land Use without Zoning* (Lexington, MA: D.C. Heath, 1972), and by the same author, "Non-Zoning in Houston," *Journal of Law and Economics* 13 (April 1970): 71–147.

22. George J. Stigler has named this idea "director's law" in "Director's Law of Public Income Redistribution," *Journal of Law and Economics* 13, no. 1 (April 1970): 1–10.

23. A well-conceived exception to this is Usher, *Welfare Economics.*

24. For evidence, see James Gwartney, Robert Lawson, and Randall Holcombe, "Economic Freedom and the Environment for Economic Growth," *Journal of Institutional and Theoretical Economics* 155, no. 4 (December 1999): 643–63.

25. Hobbes, *Leviathan.*

26. The idea that liberty exists on a continuum between predation in anarchy and predation by excessive government can be found in Buchanan, *Limits of Liberty,* and Usher, *Welfare Economics.*

27. For good general treatises, see Rothbard, *For a New Liberty,* and Friedman, *Machinery of Freedom.* For an argument that law and law enforcement can be produced privately, see Bruce L. Benson, *The Enterprise of Law: Justice without the State* (San Francisco: Pacific Research Institute, 1990). For a discussion of public goods and social services, see Fred Foldvary, *Public Goods and Private Communities: The Market Provision of Social Services* (Brookfield, VT: Edward Elgar, 1994).

28. Note that government, like the Mafia, also threatens its "customers" with harm if they do not comply with government demands for payment.

29. Robert Nozick, *Anarchy, State, and Utopia* (New York: Basic Books, 1974).

30. See Holcombe, "Theory of Public Goods," 1–22, for a discussion of public goods theory and for the argument that public goods theory has little relevance to actual government activity.

31. This point is eloquently made by Yeager, "Rights, Contract, and Utility," 259–94.

32. See Holcombe, *The Economic Foundations of Government,* for an elaboration of this idea.

References

Ables, Jules. *In the Time of Silent Cal.* New York: G. P. Putnam, 1969.

Abraham, Henry J. *Justices and Presidents: A Political History of Appointments to the Supreme Court.* 3d ed. New York: Oxford University Press, 1992.

Ackerman, Bruce. *We The People 1: Foundations.* Cambridge, MA: Belknap, 1991.

Alchon, Guy. *The Invisible Hand of Planning: Capitalism, Social Science, and the State in the 1920s.* Princeton: Princeton University Press, 1985.

Anderson, Benjamin M. *Economics and the Public Welfare.* Indianapolis: Liberty, 1979.

Anderson, Gary M., and Robert D. Tollison. "Congressional Influence and Patterns of New Deal Spending, 1933–1939." *Journal of Law and Economics* 34, no. 1 (April 1991): 161–75.

Anderson, Terry L., and Peter J. Hill. *The Birth of a Transfer Society.* Stanford: Hoover Institution Press, 1980.

Argersinger, Peter H. *The Limits of Agrarian Radicalism: Western Populism and American Politics.* Lawrence: University Press of Kansas, 1995.

———. *Populism and Politics: William Alfred Peffer and the People's Party.* Lexington: University Press of Kentucky, 1974.

Arrow, Kenneth J. *Social Choice and Individual Values.* New Haven: Yale University Press, 1951.

Attarian, John. "The Roots of the Social Security Myth." In *Essays in Political Economy.* Auburn, AL: Ludwig von Mises Institute, 2001.

Auster, Richard D., and Morris Silver. *The State as a Firm: Economic Forces in Political Development.* Boston: Martinus Nijhoff, 1979.

Baack, Ben, and Edward John Ray. "Federal Transfer Payments in America: Veterans' Pensions and the Rise of Social Security." *Economic Inquiry* 26, no. 4 (October 1988): 687–702.

———. "The Political Economy of the Origins of the Military-Industrial Complex in the United States." *Journal of Economic History* 45, no. 2 (June 1985): 369–75.

———. "Special Interests and the Adoption of the Income Tax in the United States." *Journal of Economic History* 45, no. 3 (September 1985): 607–25.

———. "Special Interests and the Nineteenth-Century Roots of the Military-Industrial Complex." *Research in Economic History* 11 (1988): 153–69.

Bailyn, Bernard. *The Ideological Origins of the American Revolution.* Enl. ed. Cambridge, MA: Belknap, 1992.

Banning, Lance. *The Sacred Fire of Liberty: James Madison and the Founding of the Federal Republic.* Ithaca: Cornell University Press, 1995.

Barker, Sir Ernest. *Social Contract.* New York and London: Oxford University Press, 1960.

Barlow, Robin. "Efficiency Aspects of Local School Finance." *Journal of Political Economy* 78 (September–October 1970): 1028–40.

Bates, J. Leonard. *The United States, 1898–1928: Progressivism and a Society in Transition.* New York: McGraw-Hill, 1976.

Bator, Francis M. "The Anatomy of Market Failure." *Quarterly Journal of Economics* 72 (August 1958): 351–79.

Baye, Michael R., and Dennis W. Jansen. *Money, Banking, and Financial Markets.* Boston: Houghton Mifflin, 1995.

Beard, Charles A. *An Economic Interpretation of the Constitution of the United States.* New York: Macmillan, 1913.

Beard, Charles A., and William Beard. *The American Leviathan: The Republic in the Machine Age.* New York: Macmillan, 1930.

Beck, James M. *The Constitution of the United States.* New York: George H. Doran Co., 1924.

———. *Our Wonderland of Bureaucracy.* New York: Macmillan, 1932.

Becker, Gary S. "A Theory of Competition among Pressure Groups for Political Influence." *Quarterly Journal of Economics* 98 (August 1983): 371–400.

Benson, Bruce L. *The Enterprise of Law: Justice without the State.* San Francisco: Pacific Research Institute, 1990.

———. "An Evolutionary Contractarian View of Primitive Law: The Institutions and Incentives Arising under Customary Indian Law." *Review of Austrian Economics* 5, no. 1 (1991): 41–65.

Benson, Lee. *Merchants, Farmers, and Railroads: Railroad Regulation and New York Politics, 1850–1877.* Cambridge: Harvard University Press, 1955.

Berger, Raoul. *Government by Judiciary: The Transformation of the Fourteenth Amendment.* 2d ed. Indianapolis: Liberty Fund, 1997.

Bergstrom, Theodore C., and Robert Goodman. "Private Demand for Public Goods." *American Economic Review* 63 (June 1973): 280–96.

Berman, Harold J. *Law and Revolution: The Formation of Western Legal Tradition.* Cambridge: Harvard University Press, 1983.

Bernstein, Irving. *Guns or Butter? The Presidency of Lyndon Johnson.* New York: Oxford University Press, 1996.

Black, Duncan. *The Theory of Committees and Elections.* Cambridge: Cambridge University Press, 1958.

Blum, John M. *The Progressive Presidents—Roosevelt, Wilson, Roosevelt, Johnson.* New York: Norton, 1980.

Borcherding, Thomas E. "The Causes of Government Expenditure Growth: A Summary of U.S. Evidence." *Journal of Public Economics* 28, no. 3 (December 1985): 359–82.

———, ed. *Budgets and Bureaucrats: The Sources of Government Growth.* Durham, NC: Duke University Press, 1977.

Borcherding, Thomas E., and Robert T. Deacon. "The Demand for Services of Non-Federal Governments." *American Economic Review* 62 (December 1972): 891–901.

Bornet, Vaughn Davis. *The Presidency of Lyndon Johnson.* Lawrence: University Press of Kansas, 1983.

Boudreaux, Donald J., and Randall G. Holcombe. "Government by Contract." *Public Finance Quarterly* 17, no. 3 (July 1989): 264–80.

Boudreaux, Donald J., and A. C. Pritchard. "The Price of Prohibition." *Arizona Law Review* 36, no. 1 (spring 1994): 1–10.

Bourne, Randolph S. *War and the Intellectuals.* New York: Harper & Row, 1964.

Brennan, Geoffrey, and James M. Buchanan. *The Power to Tax.* Cambridge: Cambridge University Press, 1980.

———. *The Reason of Rules.* Cambridge: Cambridge University Press, 1985.

Breton, Albert, Gianluigi Galeotti, Pierre Salmon, and Ronald Wintrobe, eds. *Understanding Democracy: Economic and Political Perspectives.* Cambridge: Cambridge University Press, 1997.

Brinig, Margaret F., Randall G. Holcombe, and Linda Schwartzstein. "The Regulation of Lobbyists." *Public Choice* 77, no. 2 (October 1993): 377–84.

Brownlee, W. Elliot. *Federal Taxation in America: A Short History.* Cambridge: Cambridge University Press, 1996.

———, ed. *Funding the Modern American State, 1941–1995: The Rise and Fall of the Era of Easy Finance.* Cambridge: Cambridge University Press, 1996.

Buchanan, James M. *The Limits of Liberty: Between Anarchy and Leviathan.* Chicago: University of Chicago Press, 1975.

———. "Politics, Policy, and the Pigouvian Margins." *Economica,* n.s., 29 (February 1962): 17–28.

———. "Public Finance and Public Choice." *National Tax Journal* 28 (December 1975): 383—94.

———. "Social Choice, Democracy, and Free Markets." *Journal of Political Economy* 62 (1954): 114–23.

Buchanan, James M., and Gordon Tullock. *The Calculus of Consent.* Ann Arbor: University of Michigan Press, 1962.

Buchanan, James M., and Richard E. Wagner. *Democracy in Deficit: The Political Legacy of Lord Keynes.* New York: Academic, 1977.

Burgess, John W. *Reconstruction and the Constitution: 1866–1876.* New York: Charles Scribner's Sons, 1902.

Campbell, Ballard C. *The Growth of American Government: Governance from the Cleveland Era to the Present.* Bloomington: Indiana University Press, 1995.

Carpenter, Jesse T. *The South as a Conscious Minority: 1789–1861.* New York: New York University Press, 1930.

Chandler, Alfred D., Jr. "The Origins of Progressive Leadership." In *Progressivism: The Critical Issues,* ed. David M. Kennedy, 74–78. Boston: Little, Brown, 1971.

Cole, Donald B. *The Presidency of Andrew Jackson.* Lawrence: University Press of Kansas, 1993.

Crain, W. Mark. "On the Structure and Stability of Political Markets." *Journal of Political Economy* 85, no. 4 (August 1977): 829–42.

Crain, W. Mark, Randall Holcombe, and Robert D. Tollison. "Monopoly Aspects of Political Parties." *Atlantic Economic Journal* 7, no. 2 (July 1979): 54–58.

Crenson, Matthew A. *The Federal Machine: Beginnings of Bureaucracy in Jacksonian America.* Baltimore: Johns Hopkins University Press, 1975.

Croly, Herbert. *Progressive Democracy.* New York: Macmillan, 1915.

———. *The Promise of American Life.* New York: Macmillan, 1909.

Cullinan, Gerald. *The Post Office Department.* New York: Praeger, 1968.

Davis, J. Ronnie. *The New Economics and the Old Economists.* Ames: Iowa State University Press, 1971.

De Witt, Benjamin Parke. *The Progressive Movement: A Non-Partisan, Comprehensive Discussion of Current Tendencies in American Politics.* New York: Macmillan, 1915.

Demsetz, Harold. "Why Regulate Utilities?" *Journal of Law and Economics* 11 (1968): 55–65.

Diamond, Jared. *Guns, Germs, and Steel: The Fates of Human Societies.* New York: W. W. Norton & Co., 1997.

Dietze, Gottfried. *Liberalism Proper and Proper Liberalism.* Baltimore: Johns Hopkins University Press, 1985.

Donald, David. *The Politics of Reconstruction: 1863–1867.* Baton Rouge: Louisiana State University Press, 1965.

Dougherty, Keith L. *Collective Action under the Articles of Confederation.* Cambridge: Cambridge University Press, 2001.

Dougherty, Keith L., and Michael J. G. Cain. "Marginal Cost Sharing and the Articles of Confederation." *Public Choice* 90, nos. 1–4 (March 1997): 201–13.

Downs, Anthony. *An Economic Theory of Democracy.* New York: Harper & Row, 1957.

Edelman, Murray. *The Symbolic Uses of Politics.* Urbana: University of Illinois Press, 1964.

Eidelberg, Paul. *The Philosophy of the American Constitution: A Reinterpretation of the Intentions of the Founding Fathers.* New York: Free Press, 1968.

Ekirch, Arthur A., Jr. *Progressivism in America: A Study of the Era from Theodore Roosevelt to Woodrow Wilson.* New York: New Viewpoints, 1974.

Fabricant, Solomon. *The Trend of Government Activity in the U.S. since 1900.* New York: National Bureau of Economic Research, 1952.

Farrand, Max. *The Records of the Federal Convention of 1787.* Rev. ed. in 4 vols. New Haven: Yale University Press, 1937.

Feer, Robert A. *Shays's Rebellion.* New York: Garland, 1988.

Fenton, William N., ed. *Parker on the Iroquois.* Syracuse: Syracuse University Press, 1968.

Ford, Henry Jones. *The Cleveland Era.* New Haven: Yale University Press, 1919.

Ferguson, C. E. *Microeconomic Theory.* Rev. ed. Homewood, IL: Richard D. Irwin, 1969.

Finegold, Kenneth, and Theda Skocpol. *State and Party in America's New Deal.* Madison: University of Wisconsin Press, 1995.

Flack, Horace Edgar. *The Adoption of the Fourteenth Amendment.* Glouchester, MA: Peter Smith, 1965.

Foldvary, Fred. *Public Goods and Private Communities: The Market Provision of Social Services.* Brookfield, VT: Edward Elgar, 1994.

Friedman, David. *The Machinery of Freedom: A Guide to Radical Capitalism.* 2d ed. La Salle, IL: Open Court, 1989.

———. "Many, Few, One: Social Harmony and the Shrunken Choice Set." *American Economic Review* 70, no. 1 (March 1980): 225–32.

Friedman, Milton. *Capitalism and Freedom.* Chicago: University of Chicago Press, 1962.

Friedman, Milton, and Rose Friedman. *Free to Choose.* New York: Harcourt Brace Jovanovich, 1980.

Friedman, Milton, and Anna Jacobson Schwartz. *A Monetary History of the United States: 1867–1960.* Princeton: Princeton University Press, 1968.

Friedrich, Carl J. *Constitutional Government and Democracy.* Rev. ed. Boston: Ginn & Co., 1950.

———. *An Introduction to Political Theory.* New York: Harper & Row, 1967.

Fry, Geoffrey K. *The Growth of Government: The Development of Ideas about the Role of the State and the Machinery and Functions of Government in Britain since 1780.* London: Frank Cass, 1979.

Fukuyama, Francis. *The End of History and the Last Man.* New York: Free Press, 1992.

Galbraith, John Kenneth. *The Affluent Society.* Boston: Houghton Mifflin, 1958.

———. *The New Industrial State.* Boston: Houghton Mifflin, 1967.

Glasson, William Henry. *History of Military Pension Legislation in the United States.* New York: Columbia University Press, 1900.

Goldwin, Robert A., and William A. Schambra, eds. *How Democratic Is the Constitution?* Washington, DC: American Enterprise Institute, 1980.

Graymont, Barbara. *The Iroquois in the American Revolution.* Syracuse: Syracuse University Press, 1972.

Griffiths, David B. *Populism in the Western United States: 1890–1900.* Lewiston, NY: Edwin Mellen Press, 1992.

Grinde, Donald A. *The Iroquois and the Founding of the American Nation.* San Francisco: Indian Historian Press, 1977.

Gwartney, James, Robert Lawson, and Randall Holcombe. "Economic Freedom and the Environment for Economic Growth." *Journal of Institutional and Theoretical Economics* 155, no. 4 (December 1999): 643–63.

Hafen, Le Roy R. *The Overland Mail, 1849–1869: Promoter of Settlement, Precursor of Railroads.* Cleveland: Arthur H. Clark Co., 1926.

Hagan, J. D. "Domestic Political Regime Changes and Third World Voting Realignments in the United Nations, 1946–84." *International Organization* 43, no. 3 (summer 1989): 505–41.

Hamilton, Alexander, John Jay, and James Madison. *The Federalist.* Washington, DC: National Home Library, 1937.

Hardin, Russell. "Democracy on the Margin." In *Understanding Democracy: Economic and Political Perspectives,* ed. Albert Breton, Gianluigi Galeotti, Pierre Salmon, and Ronald Wintrobe, 249–66. Cambridge: Cambridge University Press, 1997.

Hart, Jeffrey. "Foundations and Social Activism: A Critical View." In *The Future of Foundations,* ed. Fritz F. Heimann. Englewood Cliffs, NJ: Prentice-Hall, 1973.

Harwell, Richard Barksdale. *The Confederate Constitution.* Athens: University of Georgia Libraries, 1979.

Hawley, Ellis W. *The Great War and the Search for a Modern Order: A History of the American People and Their Institutions, 1917–1933.* New York: St. Martin's, 1979.

Hayek, Friedrich A. *The Constitution of Liberty.* Chicago: University of Chicago Press, 1960.

———. *Law, Legislation, and Liberty.* 3 vols. Chicago: University of Chicago Press, 1973, 1976, 1979.

———. *The Road to Serfdom.* Chicago: University of Chicago Press, 1944.

———. "The Use of Knowledge in Society." *American Economic Review* 35 (September 1945): 519–30.

Heimann, Fritz F., ed. *The Future of Foundations.* Englewood Cliffs, NJ: Prentice-Hall, 1973.

Hicks, John D. *The Populist Revolt: A History of the Farmers' Alliance and the People's Party.* Minneapolis: University of Minnesota Press, 1931.

———. *Republican Ascendancy: 1921–1933.* New York: Harper & Bros., 1960.

Higgs, Robert. "The Cold War Economy: Opportunity Cost, Ideology, and the Politics of Crisis." *Explorations in Economic History* 31 (1994): 283–312.

———. *Crisis and Leviathan: Critical Episodes in the Growth of American Government.* New York: Oxford University Press, 1987.

———. "Eighteen Problematic Propositions in the Analysis of the Growth of Government." *Review of Austrian Economics* 5, no. 1 (1991): 3–40.

———. "Regime Uncertainty: Why the Great Depression Lasted So Long and Why Prosperity Resumed after the War." *Independent Review* 1, no. 4 (spring 1997): 561–90.

Hobbes, Thomas. *Leviathan.* 1651. Reprint, New York: E. P. Dutton, 1950.

Hofstadter, Richard. *The Age of Reform: From Bryan to F.D.R.* New York: Alfred A. Knopf, 1969.

Holcombe, Randall G. "Are There Ratchets in the Growth of Federal Government Spending?" *Public Finance Quarterly* 21, no. 1 (January 1993): 33–47.

———. "Constitutional Theory and the Constitutional History of Colonial America." *Independent Review* 3, no. 1 (summer 1998): 21–36.

———. "Constitutions as Constraints: A Case Study of Three American Constitutions." *Constitutional Political Economy* 2, no. 3 (fall 1991): 303–28.

―――. "A Contractarian Model of the Decline in Classical Liberalism." *Public Choice* 35, no. 3 (1980): 260–74.

―――. "The Distributive Model of Government: Evidence from the Confederate Constitution." *Southern Economic Journal* 58, no. 3 (January 1992): 762–69.

―――. *An Economic Analysis of Democracy.* Carbondale: Southern Illinois University Press, 1985.

―――. *The Economic Foundations of Government.* New York: New York University Press, 1994.

―――. "The Growth of the Federal Government in the 1920s." *Cato Journal* 16, no. 2 (fall 1996): 175–99.

―――. "The Median Voter Model in Public Choice Theory." *Public Choice* 61, no. 2 (1989): 115–25.

―――. "Non-Optimal Unanimous Agreement." *Public Choice* 48, no. 3 (1986): 229–44.

―――. *Public Finance: Government Revenues and Expenditures in the United States Economy.* Minneapolis-St. Paul: West, 1996.

―――. *Public Policy and the Quality of Life.* Westport, CT: Greenwood, 1995.

―――. "A Theory of the Theory of Public Goods." *Review of Austrian Economics* 10, no. 1 (1997): 1–22.

―――. "Veterans Interests and the Transition to Government Growth: 1870–1915." *Public Choice* 99, nos. 3–4 (June 1999): 311–26.

―――. *Writing off Ideas: The Effect of Tax Laws on America's Non-Profit Foundations.* New Brunswick, NJ: Transaction, 1999.

Holcombe, Randall G., and Donald J. Lacombe. "Interests versus Ideology in the Ratification of the 16th and 17th Amendments." *Economics and Politics* 10, no. 2 (July 1998): 143–59.

Holcombe, Randall G., and Russell S. Sobel. "The Stability of International Coalitions in United Nations Voting from 1946 to 1973." *Public Choice* 86, no. 1 (1996): 17–34.

Horowitz, David A. "The Perils of Western Farm Politics: Herbert Hoover, Gerald P. Nye, and Agricultural Reform." In *Herbert Hoover and the Republican Era,* ed. Carl E. Krog and William R. Tanner, 220–43. Lantham, MD: University Press of America, 1984.

Horwitz, Morton J. *The Transformation of American Law, 1870–1960: The Crisis of Legal Orthodoxy.* New York: Oxford University Press, 1992.

Hotelling, Harold. "Stability in Competition." *Economic Journal* 39 (March 1929): 41–57.

Howland, Harold. *Theodore Roosevelt and His Times: A Chronicle of the Progressive Movement.* New Haven: Yale University Press, 1921.

Hughes, Jonathan R. T. *The Governmental Habit: Economic Controls from Colonial Times to the Present.* New York: Basic Books, 1977.

Hummel, Jeffrey Rogers. *Emancipating Slaves, Enslaving Free Men: A History of the American Civil War.* Chicago: Open Court, 1996.

Jackson, Robert H. *The Struggle for Judicial Supremacy: A Study of a Crisis in American Power Politics.* New York: Alfred A. Knopf, 1941.

Jaggers, Keith, and Ted Robert Gurr. "Tracking Democracy's Third Wave with the Polity III Data." *Journal of Peace Research* 32, no. 4 (1995): 469–82.

James, Marquis. *Andrew Jackson: Portrait of a President.* New York: Grosset & Dunlap, 1937.

Jarrell, Gregg A. "The Demand for State Regulation of the Electric Utility Industry." *Journal of Law and Economics* 21, no. 3 (October 1978): 269–95.

Jensen, Merrill. *The Articles of Confederation.* Madison: University of Wisconsin Press, 1940.

Johansen, Bruce E. *Forgotten Founders: Benjamin Franklin, the Iroquois, and the Rationale for the American Revolution.* Ipswich, MA: Gambit, 1982.

Johnson, Arthur M. "Theodore Roosevelt and the Bureau of Corporations." *Mississippi Valley Historical Review* 45 (1959): 571–90.

Johnson, Paul. *A History of the American People.* New York: HarperCollins, 1997.

———. *Modern Times: The World from the Twenties to the Nineties.* Rev. ed. New York: HarperCollins, 1991.

Kearns, Doris. *Lyndon Johnson and the American Dream.* New York: Harper & Row, 1976.

Keller, Robert R. "Supply-Side Economic Policies during the Collidge-Mellon Era." *Journal of Economic Issues* 16, no. 3 (September 1982): 773–90.

Kelly, Clyde. *United States Postal Policy.* New York: D. Appleton and Co., 1932.

Kelman, Steven. "'Public Choice' and Public Spirit." *Public Interest* 87 (spring 1987): 80–94.

Kendrick, M. Slade. *A Century and a Half of Federal Expenditures.* New York: National Bureau of Economic Research, 1955.

Kennedy, David M., ed. *Progressivism: The Critical Issues.* Boston: Little, Brown, 1971.

Kenny, Lawrence, and Mark Rush. "Self-Interest and the Senate Vote on Direct Elections." *Economics and Politics* 2, no. 3 (November 1990): 291–302.

Ketcham, Ralph. *Presidents above Party: The First American Presidency, 1789–1829.* Chapel Hill: University of North Carolina Press, 1984.

Keynes, John Maynard. *The General Theory of Employment, Interest, and Money.* New York: Harcourt, Brace, and Co., 1936.

Klebaner, Benjamin J. "Potential Competition and the American Antitrust Legislation of 1914." *Business History Review* 38 (1964): 163–85.

Koford, Kenneth J. "Centralized Vote Trading." *Public Choice* 39, no. 2 (1982): 245–68.

———. "Dimensions, Transactions Costs, and Coalitions in Legislative Voting." *Economics and Politics* 2, no. 1 (1990): 59–82.

Kolko, Gabriel. *Railroads and Regulation, 1877–1916.* New York: Norton, 1965.

Krog, Carl E., and William R. Tanner, eds. *Herbert Hoover and the Republican Era.* Lanham, MD: University Press of America, 1984.

Landes, David S. *The Wealth and Poverty of Nations: Why Some Are So Rich and Some So Poor.* New York: W. W. Norton & Co., 1998.

Lange, Oskar, and Fred M. Taylor. *On the Economic Theory of Socialism.* Minneapolis: University of Minnesota Press, 1938.

Lee, Charles Robert, Jr. *The Confederate Constitutions.* Chapel Hill: University of North Carolina Press, 1963.

Lee, Dwight R. "Reverse Revenue Sharing: A Modest Proposal." *Public Choice* 45, no. 3 (1985): 279–89.

———. "Reverse Revenue Sharing: A Return to Fiscal Federalism." *Cato Journal* 14, no. 1 (spring/summer 1994): 75–85.

Legler, John B., Richard Sylla, and John J. Wallis. "U.S. City Finances and the Growth of Government." *Journal of Economic History* 48, no. 2 (June 1988): 347–56.

Leoni, Bruno. *Freedom and the Law.* Los Angeles: Nash, 1961.

Lerner, Abba P. *The Economics of Control: Principles of Welfare Economics.* New York: Macmillan, 1944.

Lindahl, Erik. "Just Taxation—A Positive Solution." In *Classics in the Theory of Public Finance,* ed. Richard A. Musgrave and Alan T. Peacock, 168–76. 1919. Reprint, New York: St. Martin's, 1967.

Lingle, Christopher. *Singapore's Authoritarian Capitalism.* Fairfax, VA: Locke Institute, 1996.

Lipsey, R. G., and Kelvin Lancaster. "The General Theory of Second Best." *Review of Economic Studies* 24 (1956–57): 11–32.

Locke, John. *Two Treatises of Government.* 1690. Reprint, Cambridge: Cambridge University Press, 1967.

Lutz, Donald S. "The Iroquois Confederation Constitution: An Analysis." *Publius* 28, no. 2 (spring 1998): 99–127.

Malthus, Thomas Robert. *An Essay on Population.* 1798. Reprint, New York: E. P. Dutton, 1914.

Mander, Jerry. *In the Absence of the Sacred: The Failure of Technology and the Survival of the Indian Nations.* San Francisco: Sierra Club Books, 1991.

Manley, John F., and Kenneth M. Dolbeare. *The Case against the Constitution.* Armonk, NY: M. E. Sharpe, 1987.

Martis, Kenneth C. *The Historical Atlas of United States Congressional Districts: 1789–1983.* New York: Free Press, 1982.

Marx, Karl. *Capital.* 1867. Reprint, New York: Modern Library, 1906.

Matsusaka, John G. "Fiscal Effects of the Voter Initiative: Evidence from the Last 30 Years." *Journal of Political Economy* 103, no. 3 (June 1995): 587–623.

McCaw, Thomas K. *Prophets of Regulation.* Cambridge, MA: Belknap, 1984.

McConnell, Campbell R. *Economics: Principles, Problems, and Policies.* 3d ed. New York: McGraw-Hill, 1966.

McConnell, Grant. *Private Power and American Democracy.* New York: Alfred A. Knopf, 1966.

McCormick, Richard L. *The Party Period and Public Policy: American Politics from the Age of Jackson to the Progressive Era.* New York: Oxford University Press, 1986.

McCormick, Richard P. *The Second American Party System: Party Formation in the Jacksonian Era.* Chapel Hill: University of North Carolina Press, 1966.

McDonald, Forrest. *The American Presidency.* Lawrence: University Press of Kansas, 1994.

———. *Novus Ordo Seclorum: The Intellectual Origins of the Constitution.* Lawrence: University Press of Kansas, 1985.

McGuire, Robert A., and Robert L. Ohsfeldt. "Self-Interest, Agency Theory, and Political Voting Behavior: The Ratification of the United States Constitution." *American Economic Review* 79, no. 1 (March 1989): 219–34.

McKelvey, R. D. "General Conditions for Global Intransitivities in Formal Voting Models." *Econometrica* 47, no. 5 (September 1979): 1085–1112.

———. "Intransitivities in Multi Dimensional Voting Models and Some Implications for Agenda Control." *Journal of Economic Theory* 12, no. 2 (June 1976): 472–82.

McLaughlin, Andrew C. *The Confederation and the Constitution: 1783–1789.* New York: Collier Books, 1962.

McMath, Robert C., Jr. *American Populism: A Social History, 1877–1898.* New York: Hill and Wang, 1993.

Metzer, Jacob. "How New Was the New Era? The Public Sector in the 1920s." *Journal of Economic History* 45, no. 1 (March 1985): 119–26.

Mises, Ludwig von. *Planned Chaos.* Irving-on-Hudson, NY: Foundation for Economic Education, 1947.

———. *Socialism.* New Haven: Yale University Press, 1951.

———. *Theory of Money and Credit.* New Haven: Yale University Press, 1953.

Monkkonen, Eric H. *The Local State: Public Money and American Cities.* Stanford, CA: Stanford University Press, 1995.

Mowry, George E. *The Era of Theodore Roosevelt: 1900–1912.* Harper & Bros., 1958.

Mueller, Dennis C. *Public Choice II.* Cambridge: Cambridge University Press, 1989.

Murphy, Paul L. *The Constitution in Crisis Times: 1918–1969.* New York: Harper & Row, 1972.

Murray, Robert K. *The Politics of Normalcy: Government Theory and Practice in the Harding-Coolidge Era.* New York: W. W. Norton & Co., 1973.

Musgrave, Richard, and J. J. Culbertson. "The Growth of Public Expenditures in the U.S., 1890–1948." *National Tax Journal* 6, no. 2 (June 1953): 97–115.

Niskanen, William A. "Bureaucrats and Politicians." *Journal of Law and Economics* 18 (December 1975): 617–43.

———. *Bureaucracy and Representative Government.* Chicago: Aldine-Atherton, 1971.

———. "The Peculiar Economics of Bureaucracy." *American Economic Review* 58 (May 1968): 293–305.

North, Douglass C. "The Growth of Government in the United States: An Economic Historian's Perspective." *Journal of Public Economics* 28, no. 3 (December 1985): 359–82.

———. "Ideology and Political/Economic Institutions." *Cato Journal* 8 (spring/summer 1988): 15–28.

————. *Structure and Change in Economic History.* New York: W. W. Norton & Co., 1981.

Nozick, Robert. *Anarchy, State, and Utopia.* New York: Basic Books, 1974.

Olson, Mancur. *The Rise and Decline of Nations.* New Haven: Yale University Press, 1982.

Ortega y Gasset, José. *Invertebrate Spain.* Trans. Mildred Adams. New York: W. W. Norton & Co., 1937.

Ostrom, Vincent. *The Political Theory of the Compound Republic.* 2d ed. Lincoln: University of Nebraska Press, 1987.

Patterson, James T. *America's Struggle against Poverty: 1900–1985.* Cambridge: Harvard University Press, 1986.

Peacock, Alan. *The Political Economy of Economic Freedom.* Cheltenham, UK: Edward Elgar, 1997.

Peacock, Alan T., and Jack Wiseman. *The Growth of Government Expenditures in the United Kingdom.* Princeton: Princeton University Press, 1961.

Peffer, William A. *Populism, Its Rise and Fall.* Edited by Peter H. Argersinger. Lawrence: University Press of Kansas, 1992.

Pilon, Roger. "Freedom, Responsibility, and the Constitution: On Recovering Our Founding Principles." *Notre Dame Law Review* 68, no. 3 (1993): 507–47.

Polanyi, Karl. *The Great Transformation.* New York: Farrar & Rinehart, 1944.

Pole, J. R., ed. *The American Constitution: For and Against.* New York: Hill and Wang, 1987.

Poole, Keith T., and Howard Rosenthal. "Analysis of Congressional Coalition Patterns: A Unidimensional Spatial Model." *Legislative Studies Quarterly* 12, no. 1 (February 1987): 55–75.

————. "The Enduring Nineteenth-Century Battle for Economic Regulation: The Interstate Commerce Act Revisited." *Journal of Law and Economics* 36, no. 2 (October 1993): 837–60.

————. "Patterns of Congressional Voting." *American Journal of Political Science* 35, no. 1 (February 1991): 228–78.

————. "A Spatial Model for Legislative Roll-Call Analysis." *American Journal of Political Science* 29, no. 2 (May 1985): 357–84.

Posner, Richard A. "A Statistical Study of Antitrust Enforcement." *Journal of Law and Economics* 13, no. 2 (October 1970): 365–419.

————. "Taxation by Regulation." *Bell Journal of Economics and Management Science* 2 (spring 1971): 22–50.

Post, C. Gordon, Frances P. DeLancy, and Fredryc R. Darby, eds. *Basic Constitutional Cases.* New York: Oxford University Press, 1948.

Prescott, Arthur Taylor. *Drafting the Federal Constitution.* Baton Rouge: Louisiana State University Press, 1941.

Quynn, Russell Hoover. *The Constitutions of Abraham Lincoln and Jefferson Davis.* New York: Exposition, 1959.

Rassler, Karen A., and William R. Thompson. "War Making and State Making: Government Expenditures, Tax Revenues, and Global Wars." *American Political Science Review* 79, no. 2 (June 1985): 491–507.

Rawls, John. *A Theory of Justice.* Cambridge, MA: Belknap, 1971.

Reimann, Guenter. *The Vampire Economy: Doing Business under Fascism.* New York: Vanguard Press, 1939.

Remini, Robert V. *The Legacy of Andrew Jackson.* Baton Rouge: Louisiana State University Press, 1988.

———. *The Life of Andrew Jackson.* New York: Harper & Row, 1988.

Richter, Daniel K. *The Ordeal of the Longhouse: The Peoples of the Iroquois League in the Era of European Colonialization.* Chapel Hill: University of North Carolina Press, 1992.

Riker, William H. *Federalism: Origin, Operation, Significance.* Boston: Little, Brown, 1964.

———. "Implications from the Disequilibrium of Majority Rule for the Study of Institutions." *American Political Science Review* 74, no. 2 (June 1980): 432–46.

———. *The Theory of Political Coalitions.* New Haven: Yale University Press, 1962.

Ritter, Gretchen. *Goldbugs and Greenbacks: The Antimonopoly Tradition and the Politics of Finance in America.* Cambridge: Cambridge University Press, 1997.

Rossum, Ralph A., and Gary L. McDowell, eds. *The American Founding.* Port Washington, NY: Kennikat Press, 1981.

Rothbard, Murray N. *America's Great Depression.* Kansas City: Sheed and Ward, 1963.

———. *For a New Liberty.* New York: Macmillan, 1973.

———. *Ludwig von Mises: Scholar, Creator, Hero.* Auburn, AL: Ludwig von Mises Institute, 1988.

Rulon, Philip Reed. *The Compassionate Samaritan: The Life of Lyndon Baines Johnson.* Chicago: Nelson-Hall, 1981.

Rutland, Robert A. "George Mason: The Revolutionist as Conservative." In *The American Founding,* ed. Ralph A. Rossum and Gary L. McDowell. Port Washington, NY: Kennikat Press, 1981.

Samuelson, Paul A. "A Diagrammatic Exposition of a Theory of Public Expenditure." *Review of Economics and Statistics* 37 (November 1955): 350–56.

———. *Economics.* 9th ed. New York: McGraw-Hill, 1973.

———. "The Pure Theory of Public Expenditure." *Review of Economics and Statistics* 36 (November 1954): 387–89.

Schlesinger, Arthur M., Jr. *The Age of Jackson.* Boston: Little, Brown, 1945.

Schmeckebier, Laurence F. *The Bureau of Prohibition: Its History, Activities, and Organization.* Washington, DC: Brookings Institution, 1929.

Schumpeter, Joseph A. *Capitalism, Socialism, and Democracy.* 3d ed. New York: Harper & Row, 1950.

Severo, Richard, and Lewis Milford. *The Wages of War: When America's Soldiers Came Home—From Valley Forge to Vietnam.* New York: Simon and Schuster, 1989.

Shughart, William F., II, and Robert D. Tollison. "On the Growth of Government and the Political Economy of Legislation." *Research in Law and Economics* 9 (1986): 111–27.

Siegan, Bernard H. *Land Use without Zoning.* Lexington, MA: D.C. Heath, 1972.

———. "Non-Zoning in Houston." *Journal of Law and Economics* 13 (April 1970): 71–147.

Skinner, B. F. *Walden II.* New York: Macmillan, 1948.

Skocpol, Theda. *Protecting Soldiers and Mothers: The Political Origins of Social Policy in the United States.* Cambridge, MA: Belknap, 1992.

Skowronek, Stephen. *Building a New American State: The Expansion of National Administrative Capacities, 1877–1920.* Cambridge: Cambridge University Press, 1982.

Smith, Adam. *The Wealth of Nations.* 1776. Reprint, New York: Random House, Modern Library, 1937.

Sobel, Russell S. "In Defense of the Articles of Confederation and the Contribution Mechanism as a Means of Government Finance: A General Comment on the Literature." *Public Choice* 99, nos. 3–4 (June 1999): 347–56.

Sobel, Russell S., and Randall G. Holcombe. "The Unanimous Voting Rule Is Not the Political Equivalent to Market Exchange." *Public Choice* 106, nos. 3–4 (March 2001): 233–42.

Starkey, Marion L. *A Little Rebellion.* New York: Alfred A. Knopf, 1955.

Starr, Paul. *The Social Transformation of American Medicine.* New York: Basic Books, 1982.

Stigler, George J. "Director's Law of Public Income Redistribution." *Journal of Law and Economics* 13, no. 1 (April 1970): 1–10.

———. "The Theory of Economic Regulation." *Bell Journal of Economics and Management Science* 2 (spring 1971): 3–21.

Stigler, George J., and Gary S. Becker. "De Gustibus Non Est Disputandum." *American Economic Review* 67, no. 2 (March 1977): 76–90.

Stiglitz, Joseph E. *Whither Socialism?* Cambridge, MA: MIT Press, 1994.

Stites, Sarah Henry. *Economics of the Iroquois.* Lancaster, PA: New Era, 1905.

Sumner, William Graham. *Andrew Jackson.* Boston: Houghton, Mifflin, and Co., 1899.

Swindler, William F. *Court and Constitution in the Twentieth Century.* Vol. 1, *The Old Legality, 1889–1932.* Indianapolis: Bobbs-Merrill, 1969.

———. *Court and Constitution in the Twentieth Century.* Vol. 2, *The New Legality, 1932–1968.* Indianapolis: Bobbs-Merrill, 1970.

Szatmary, David P. *Shays' Rebellion: The Making of an Agrarian Insurrection.* Amherst: University of Massachusetts Press, 1980.

Tiebout, Charles M. "A Pure Theory of Local Expenditures." *Journal of Political Economy* 64 (1956): 416–24.

Tocqueville, Alexis de. *Democracy in America.* 1835. Reprint, New York: Alfred A. Knopf, 1963.

Trenchard, John, and Thomas Gordon. *Cato's Letters, or, Essays on Liberty, Civil and Religious, and Other Important Subjects.* Indianapolis: Liberty Fund, 1995.

Tullock, Gordon. "Entry Barriers in Politics." *American Economic Review* 55, no. 2 (March 1965): 458–66.

———. "The Transitional Gains Trap." *Bell Journal of Economics* 6 (fall 1975): 671–78.

———. "Why So Much Stability?" *Public Choice* 37, no. 2 (1982): 189–202.

Turner, Frederick Jackson. "The Problem of the West." *Atlantic Monthly* 78 (September 1896): 289–97.

Twight, Charlotte. "Evolution of Federal Income Tax Withholding: The Machinery of Institutional Change." *Cato Journal* 14, no. 3 (winter 1995): 359–95.

———. "Medicare's Origin: The Economics and Politics of Dependency." *Cato Journal* 16, no. 3 (winter 1997): 309–38.

Usher, Dan. *The Welfare Economics of Markets, Voting, and Predation.* Ann Arbor: University of Michigan Press, 1992.

Vaughn, Karen Iverson. *John Locke: Economist and Social Scientist.* Chicago: University of Chicago Press, 1980.

Wagner, Richard E. *To Promote the General Welfare: Market Processes vs. Political Transfers.* San Francisco: Pacific Research Institute, 1989.

Wallis, John Joseph. "The Birth of the Old Federalism: Financing the New Deal, 1932–1940." *Journal of Economic History* 44, no. 1 (March 1984): 139–59.

Warren, Charles. *The Making of the Constitution.* Cambridge: Harvard University Press, 1937.

Weatherford, Jack. *Indian Givers: How the Indians of the Americas Transformed the World.* New York: Crown, 1988.

Weingast, Barry R., Kenneth A. Shepsle, and Christopher Johnsen. "The Political Economy of Benefits and Costs: A Neoclassical Approach to Distributive Politics." *Journal of Political Economy* 89, no. 4 (August 1981): 642–64.

White, William Allen. *The Old Order Changeth: A View of American Democracy.* New York: Macmillan, 1910.

Wicksell, Knut. "A New Principle of Just Taxation." In *Classics in the Theory of Public Finance,* ed. Richard A. Musgrave and Alan T. Peacock, 72–118. 1919. Reprint, New York: St. Martin's, 1967.

Williamson, Oliver E. "A Comparison of Alternative Approaches to Economic Organization." *Journal of Institutional and Theoretical Economics* 146, no. 1 (March 1990): 61–71.

Wilson, Joan Hoff. *Herbert Hoover: Forgotten Progressive.* Prospect Heights, IL: Waveland Press, 1992.

Wittman, Donald A. *The Myth of Democratic Failure.* Chicago: University of Chicago Press, 1995.

———. "Why Democracies Produce Efficient Results." *Journal of Political Economy* 97, no. 6 (December 1989): 1395–424.

Wood, Gordon S. *The Creation of the American Republic: 1776–1787.* Chapel Hill: University of North Carolina Press, 1969.

Wooddy, Carroll H. *The Growth of the Federal Government: 1915–1932.* New York: McGraw-Hill, 1934.

Wynn, Neil A. *From Progressivism to Prosperity: World War I and American Society.* New York: Holmes and Meir, 1986.

Yeager, Leland B. "Rights, Contract, and Utility in Policy Analysis." *Cato Journal* 5, no. 1 (summer 1985): 259–94.

Zakaria, Fareed. "The Rise of Illiberal Democracy." *Foreign Affairs* 76, no. 6 (November/December 1997): 22–43.

Index

Ables, Jules, 305, 306
Abraham, Henry J., 307, 308
Ackerman, Bruce, 277, 311
Adams, John, 97–98, 99, 129
Adams, John Quincy, 99–100, 101, 106, 116
Agricultural Adjustment Act, 216, 220
Agriculture, 198, 200–201, 205–6
Albany Plan of Union, 52–54, 61, 69
Alchon, Guy, 302, 306
Anarcho-capitalism, 33, 272–75
Anderson, Benjamin M., 206, 214, 307
Anderson, Gary M., 308
Anderson, Terry L., 151, 284, 287, 298, 301
Antitrust, 169, 206
Argersinger, Peter H., 300, 303
Arrears Act, 148
Arrow, Kenneth J., 292, 311
Articles of Confederation
    compared to the U.S. Constitution, 60, 67–78
    and democracy, 7, 25
    government under, 61–63
    provisions of, 54–56
    weaknesses of, 62, 69, 73
Attarian, John, 307
Auster, Richard D., 281

Baack, Ben, 297, 299, 303
Bailyn, Bernard, 278, 286
Ballot initiatives, 167
Banking holiday, 212
Banking regulation, 213, 215

Bank of the United States, 98, 99, 105, 126, 199
Banning, Lance, 289
Barlow, Robin, 279, 292
Bates, J. Leonard, 301
Bator, Francis M., 280
Baye, Michael P., 296
Beard, Charles A., 66, 74, 75, 78, 287, 288, 289, 304
Beard, William, 304
Beck, James M., 287, 288, 305
Becker, Gary S., 296, 311
Benson, Bruce L., 284, 312
Benson, Lee, xiii, 298
Berger, Raoul, 124
Bergstrom, Theodore C., 292
Berman, Harold J., 279, 283
Bernstein, Irving, 310
Black, Duncan, 292, 311
Blum, John M., 171
Borcherding, Thomas E., 292, 303
Bornet, Vaughn Davis, 309
Boudreaux, Donald J., 283, 306
Bourne, Randolph S., 309
Brennan, Geoffrey, 71, 290
Breton, Albert, 311
Brinig, Margaret F., 302
Brownlee, W. Elliot, 306, 308
Buchanan, James M., 39, 40, 57, 68, 69, 71, 91, 283, 290, 293, 297, 302, 312
Burgess, John W., 295
Bush, George H. W., 181, 244

Cain, Michael J. G., 287

and Progressivism, 170
and socialism, 26
triumph of, 245–49
and the U.S. Constitution, 1
Democratic party, 128, 129
as the conservative party, 190
formation of, 100–102
and Populism, 164
Demsetz, Harold, 281
De Witt, Benjamin Parke, 301
Diamond, Jared, 285, 287
Dietz, Gottfried, 280
Dolbeare, Kenneth M., 290
Donald, David, 295
Dougherty, Keith L., 287, 288
Downs, Anthony, 278, 292, 302, 310

Economics
comparative, 29–32
and economic man, 22–24
neoclassical, 17–18
Edelman, Murray, 278
Eidelberg, Paul, 288
Eisenhower, Dwight D., 211, 233, 234–35
Ekirch, Arthur A., Jr., 301
Electoral college, 6, 93–96, 182, 246
Emancipation Proclamation, 118, 119
Employment Act of 1946, 229–30

Fabricant, Solomon, 304
Factions. *See* Interest groups
Farrand, Max, 288
Federal Deposit Insurance Corporation, 214
Federal Reserve System, 166, 173, 213
Feer, Robert A., 281
Fenton, William N., 284, 285
Ferguson, C. E., 22, 281
Finegold, Kenneth, 308
Flack, Horace Edgar, 295
Foldvary, Fred, 312
Franchise, extension of, 8
Franklin, Benjamin, 52, 53
Free banking era, 127

Friedman, David, 279, 283, 312
Friedman, Milton, 27, 280, 307
Friedman, Rose, 280
Friedrich, Carl J., 277, 278, 280
Fugitive Slave Law, 116
Fukuyama, Francis, 19, 32, 35, 251

Galbraith, John Kenneth, 309
Galeotti, Gianluigi, 311
Glasson, William Henry, 297, 298
Gold standard, 165–66
Goldwater, Barry, 248
Goldwin, Robert A., 281
Goodman, Robert, 292
Government
corporations, 199–201
growth of, 78–80, 138–41, 158–59, 187–89, 193–203
as a necessary evil, 2, 272–75
Gould, Lewis L., 301
Grand Army of the Republic, 147–51
Graymont, Barbara, 285, 286
Great Depression, 43, 195, 208, 213
Great Society
and democracy, 239–41
legacy of, 241–45, 248, 250
motivation for, 232–37
and the Nixon administration, 242
programs, 237–39
Griffiths, David B., 300
Grinde, Donald A., 284, 286
Gwartney, James D., 312

Hafen, Le Roy R., 294, 299
Hagan, J. D., 302
Hamilton, Alexander, 98, 99, 107, 129, 169, 170, 184–85, 247, 288
Hardin, Russell, 311
Harding, Warren G., 189–90, 202
Hart, Jeffrey, 310
Harwell, Richard Barksdale, 296
Hawley, Ellis W., 190, 304, 305
Hayek, Friedrich A., 30–31, 32, 71, 280
Heimann, Fritz F., 310